# DESCRIPTIVE LINGUISTICS

## An Introduction

second edition

# DESCRIPTIVE LINGUISTICS

## An Introduction

# Winfred P. Lehmann
The University of Texas, Austin

RANDOM HOUSE
NEW YORK

Second Edition

987654321

Copyright © 1972, 1976 by Random House, Inc.

Library of Congress Cataloging in Publication Data

Lehmann, Winfred Philipp, 1916–
    Descriptive linguistics.

    1.    Linguistics.    I.    Title.
P121.L448    1976    410    75-33671
ISBN 0-394-30265-6

Composed by Westminster Graphic, Inc., Woodside, N.Y. Printed and bound by R.R. Donnelley & Sons Company, Crawsfordsville, Indiana.

Manufactured in the United States of America.
Text design: Meryl Sussman Levavi

To Elenore Lehmann

# PREFACE

The second edition of this book has been substantially modified from the first, to reflect the achievements and changes of direction in linguistic study during the past four years. Many of the modifications have been made in response to the suggestions of past users. For example, this edition incorporates more of the findings of typological study, which has improved our understanding of language at all levels. And a resurgence of interest in the history of language has led to the inclusion of a chapter on historical linguistics. Furthermore, although the book remains an introduction to linguistics, it reflects an interest in the language-oriented approach and can, therefore, be used in introduction to language courses.

Linguistics is presented in these pages as a behavioral science, on the grounds that language must be examined in its various uses if the science of language is to avoid becoming academic or even sterile. Thus, such topics as current brain research in its relation to our understanding of language and the acquisition of language by children have been dealt with. And the historical concern with language has not been ignored. Some of the most readable treatises on language were produced by the Greeks and Romans, for example, Plato's *Cratylus* and Quintilian's "Advice to an Orator." Much of our terminology was devised in the course of this earlier concern. An introduction to linguistics cannot then limit itself to one school; rather, it must present the general principles necessary to the study of language. The problems encountered by the once-dominant transformationalist school illustrate the need for familiarity with earlier studies of language, if only to avoid unproductive formalistic manipulation of data and the rediscovery of previous accomplishments.

It is impossible to present all of the concerns of linguistics in an elementary textbook. However, linguistics is an empirical science and as such demands the inclusion of much linguistic data, that is, examples of the spoken language. Faced with the terrific variety and richness of language and the need to develop a clear pedagogical perspective, one is constrained to choose one's linguistic examples carefully. Data should be taken from the native language of students; that from other languages should only be given to supplement examples in English. A wide variety of languages is presented in the workbook, which has been prepared to accompany and supplement the text. Students should use every opportunity to collect and study data from other languages. As they acquire adequate techniques for assembling and analyzing linguistic materials, they should also scrutinize data from their formal and informal styles of speech.

In order to gain control of linguistics, the data of language must first be summarized and mastered, beginning with the simplest areas. Accordingly, Chapter 1, which is new to this edition, serves as a needful introduction to the fundamental concerns of linguistics and of the book. Chapter 3 introduces students quickly to difficult concepts and defines terms and procedures that they will need to understand and use later on. The text then deals with phonology, followed by presentations of syntax, various aspects of phrase-structure grammars, and semantics. After completing these chapters students should have an understanding of linguistics proper. The major interdisciplinary topics, historical and comparative linguistics, psycholinguistics, sociolinguistics, and applied linguistics, are treated in subsequent chapters. A final chapter summarizes some of the findings of linguistics and touches on some of linguistics' future tasks.

Students are urged to complete all the exercises given here, as well as those in the workbook. Moreover, since linguistics is changing rapidly, the student of linguistics must keep up with current publications in the field.

Any author of a book on linguistics owes a great deal to his or her predecessors, colleagues, and students. The task is difficult, for the requisite theory must be formulated by extracting the central elements from the mass of observations on language. However, one stands to profit greatly from this process, for in the course of it one's own views on linguistics are clarified. To all who contributed to this clarification and to this book I express my gratitude.

*Austin, Texas*                                                    W. P. Lehmann
*September, 1975*

# CONTENTS

x    CONTENTS

# DESCRIPTIVE LINGUISTICS

## An Introduction

# WHAT IS LINGUISTICS?

## CHAPTER 1

Linguistics is still such a recent science that a linguist is often asked questions like the title of this introductory chapter: What is linguistics? Other questions he or she may be asked to answer are: Why study linguistics? What does a linguist do? In answer to the first question the linguist may reply: Linguistics is the scientific study of language. This response may simply lead to the further question: What does it mean to study language scientifically? This introductory chapter will discuss these questions, in preparation for the further answers given throughout the book.

It may seem puzzling to characterize linguistics as a recent science, because people have always concerned themselves with language. In their speculations about language, the ancient Indians saw it as the medium to knowledge of such matters as heaven and earth, gods and humans, beasts and birds, right and wrong, true and false, good and bad. The ancient Hebrews were concerned with the names of such phenomena, ascribing the origin of some names to God, of others to humans, as in the first and second chapters of Genesis: 1:8,10 "And God called the firmament Heaven. . . the dry land Earth"; 2:20 "And Adam gave names to all cattle, and to the fowl of the air, and to every beast of the field." Such concerns with language, found in other early cultures as well, may indeed be characterized as linguistic, but not scientific.

Nonliterate cultures of today also include language in their speculations. The late John Rupert Firth, an energetic and imaginative Yorkshireman who delighted in stimulating others to think about language, enjoyed confronting nonliterates in Africa and India with the statement that their language had no grammar. They would indignantly deny such an assertion, pointing out that they taught their children to follow certain rules and also to avoid certain patterns of language. They too then have linguistic concerns.

Besides having firm opinions about their own language, such nonliterates may speak several languages, as do many speakers in literate societies. For this reason the term *linguist* is often used for an individual who can speak several languages. And when linguists identify their interest, they may be asked: How many languages do you speak? In some embarrassment they may have to reply that they devote themselves to the study of one—their native language.

In an attempt to explain the scientific study of language the linguist may first define language and then give examples of general areas of concern. The definition may go as follows: Language is a system for the communication of meaning through sounds. More precisely, language, viewed as a system, consists of three subsystems or components: one semantic, one syntactic, and one phonological.

The following paragraphs illustrate some problems in semantic, syntactic, and phonological, or sound, patterns that linguists investigate in their study of a language.

For example, they may study verbs that are parallel in their uses to determine specific similarities and differences of meaning, as in the following:

1. *She persuaded Frank to sing the aria.*
2. *She urged Frank to sing the aria.*

In indicating encouragement the words *persuade* and *urge* have similar meaning. But they differ considerably in their implications. Every native speaker of English knows these, though the speaker may not be able to formulate them. Sentence 1 implies that Frank sang the aria; sentence 2, on the other hand, carries no such implication: Frank may or may not have sung it. Somewhat similarly the two following sentences also differ in their implications:

3. *Frank happened to know the aria.*
4. *Frank wanted to know the aria.*

Sentence 3, though not sentence 4, implies that Frank knew the aria. Linguists who study meaning may investigate such problems as the expression of implication in a specific language, for example, English, or even more generally in language. Such study is carried out largely with theoretical aims; it may be compared with the types of study carried out by some philosophers and logicians.

But a linguist is also concerned with varying sentence patterns. It is now clear that languages can be classified into two large sets, in accordance with the position of objects with regard to their verbs. English and most of the European languages are verb-object or VO languages; on the other hand, Japanese, Turkish, and many other languages are object-verb or OV languages. In English one says *John saw the dog,* in Japanese *John wa inu o mita,* literally 'John topic marker dog object marker saw.' As we will note in later chapters (and in Exercise 3 below), consistent VO and OV languages have specific arrangements for other constructions, such as relative clauses, adjectives, and genitives.

In studying syntactic patterns, linguists are also interested in the study and interpretation of such sentence modifications as negation. Thus the negative form of the first two examples would be:

5. *She didn't persuade Frank to sing the aria.*
6. *She didn't urge Frank to sing the aria.*

In sentence 5 the negative applies also to *sing the aria,* whereas in 6 it applies only to *urge.* The study of sentence patterns involves identifying the "simple sentences" that are the bases for complex sentences like 1 and 2. If one studies sentences in this way, one must assume that the simple sentence underlying the second part of sentence 5 is:

7. *Frank didn't sing the aria.*

Working out the simplest description of such problems may make up the major concern of a linguist, who might be further characterized as a grammarian or a syntactician.

A linguist may also be interested in the study of speech sounds and their relationship with one another. The last sound of *sing* [ŋ], for example, may be examined because of its patterning. It contrasts directly with the other two nasals (sounds pronounced with the voice going through the nose) in English, as in *sing* [siŋ] versus *sin* [sin] and *sang* [sæŋ] *versus Sam* [sæm]. But it often stands before *k* or *g,* as in Frank [fræŋk] and *longer* [lɔŋgər]. Moreover, the simple adjective *strong,* pronounced with a final [ŋ], has the alternate form with [g] in the comparative *stronger* [strɔŋgər]. Observing this pattern, some linguists propose that the basic form is found in the comparative and that the [g] is lost or deleted in the simple adjective.

There are other complexities. Many speakers of English, especially first-generation speakers with a native language like Italian, pronounce a [g] in simple forms like *long,* as in *Long Island* [lɔŋg aylənd]. This pronunciation reflects the patterning of [ŋ] in their own language, where it must always be followed by [g] or [k]. A linguist interested in the patterning of sounds might then be concerned with the patterning in Italian and other languages, as well as English.

But if a linguist specializes in problems having to do with meaning, with grammar, and with the sounds of language, she or he might be asked about the aims of such study. For what purpose can this information be used? It may be perfectly fine for a theoretician to try to understand, describe, and even explain the intricate patterning of language. But do the findings have any further significance? Are they useful in understanding humankind or society?

As linguists have come to know the intricacies of language to a greater extent, their findings have indeed contributed to the understanding of humans and social activities. The investigation of sound patterns, grammatical patterns, and patterns of meaning is of great interest in the study of language acquisition, one of the important concerns in child development. Children learn language in accordance with stages that are gradually becoming better identified. Only in the past few years has it become clear that young infants distinguish between sounds made by humans and other sounds, such as the ringing of a bell. In their first year they experiment with sounds, babbling a great variety of them. At some point, however, they note that sounds have meaning, and then they begin to discriminate—to learn to use sounds as more than an expression of sadness, happiness, or various desires. When they do, they master first a small set of contrasting sounds, such as those in *dada* and *mama*. But they add to these very quickly, so that their vowel system includes the *i* of *pipi,* the *u* of *pupu,* and so on, and the consonant system comes to include sounds such as *p b m, t d n*. This expansion proceeds very rapidly, though sounds like *r l w* may not be mastered for some time. This learning of sound agrees with observations of linguists that vowels like [i a u] are somehow more fundamental, or more simple; similarly, the consonants [p b m t d n] are more fundamental than the consonants of *church* or *judge*. Apparently, the behavior of children is in accord with the general observations of linguists concerning sound systems in language.

Sentence patterns—passive sentences rather than active sentences—are learned in similar progression. Children produce sentences like *Jenny saw the dog* earlier than their passive counterparts, such as *The dog was seen by Jenny*. The study of language acquisition then represents an extension of theoretical linguistics to an everyday situation. It interests psychologists and other students of human behavior as well as linguists.

Moreover, such study and its findings have special significance for the education of children who may have disabilities, such as deafness. It is much simpler to teach a deaf child how to speak if one has theoretical as well as practical control over the sounds of a language, their patterning, and the sentence patterns. Linguists have become increasingly involved in language disability problems and means for overcoming them, such as the sign systems that have been developed for the communication of the deaf. They have also become involved in exploring the problems of speakers who have speech difficulties, as in stuttering or the partial loss of language through the kind of brain damage that causes aphasia, the impairment or loss of control over language.

As information on aphasia has increased, it has become clear that loss of language control may involve the meaning system, or grammar, or the sounds, or combinations of these three facets of language. An aphasic may use the label *chair* to refer to a table, or may confuse sentence patterns, or may lose control of certain sounds, often those that are acquired last by children. Linguists have much to learn about such problems, in collaboration with other specialists. But even now a great deal has been learned about lateralization, that is, the functioning of the human brain in such a way that speech is controlled generally by the left hemisphere. If this hemisphere is damaged in children, control of speech may be taken over by the right hemisphere. But this is not true of adults. As linguists and other specialists come to know more about brain functions, however, means may be found to overcome some of the difficult problems of aphasia.

Concern with such problems has led to interdisciplinary activities and even to new concentrations. The new specialty **psycholinguistics,** which deals with those areas involving psychology and the study of language, had scarcely become established before concentrated study of the functioning of the brain with regard to language led to the development of **neurolinguistics.** As yet, few linguists have acquired the complex knowledge needed to work in such intricate areas. But the number is increasing. More and more linguists, especially students entering the field, will apply their findings in attempting to understand the functioning of the brain in the use of language and to solve problems that arise when such functioning is impeded.

Linguists concentrating on such problems are concerned primarily with individual speakers. Other linguists, often called **sociolinguists,** are investigating the uses of language in society. For it is clear that social groupings are held together by the use of language. In earlier days, especially when communication was restricted as in the Americas several thousands of years ago, limited communication led to the development of many languages spoken by relatively small numbers of speakers. This was also the situation in Europe in the several millennia before our era. Rome, for example, and a small area around it spoke Latin. Other sections of Italy spoke Etruscan, Greek, Oscan, or other languages. Vigorous communities like that of Rome then expanded their territorial control and extended their language to many new speakers, so that in time all of Italy and eventually most of western Europe was one social and political group, the Roman Empire, using Latin for communication. Some sociolinguists study the ways in which such social groups use language, how the language develops numerous varieties known as **dialects,** and what happens to these dialects in dynamic societies.

But social groups held together by one language or by a dialect need not be as large as the Roman Empire or our modern nations. Clusters of speakers, even in industrial societies, may constitute separate social communities, such as the foreign workers in many European cities at present or Spanish-speaking communities in American cities. Or the language used by a social group may merely be a special variety of the national language, such as soul talk, student slang, or thieves' argot. Such varieties permit groups to limit communication among themselves; in this way the special variety of language produces a feeling of independence. If the limitation becomes too severe, however, social difficulties may result. Such potential difficulties have come to the attention of modern states, for example, India, the new countries of Africa, and China.

Many linguists in these countries and elsewhere are studying the intricacies of communication resulting from the use of many languages. In making such studies they map the various forms of speech by geographical location or by social class. In India, for example, different languages often correlate with different castes.

As such differences become clear, countries may try to establish one language for general use, as the Roman Empire did Latin. India, for example, has focused on Hindi; countries in eastern Africa have focused on Swahili. China has selected a form of Mandarin Chinese for its "common language"—or in the native term, Putonghua.

Many intricacies of communication in social groups are just becoming apparent. In spite of the widespread use of mass communication by means of television, radio, and newspapers, modern industrial communities still maintain different forms of speech and may even be extending them. Besides identifying these, their functions, and their causes, linguists have come to cooperate with other specialists in attempting to solve resulting problems, such as those leading to isolated communities or isolated segments of communities. Contemporary societies attempt to solve many such problems through their school systems.

The study of language has always made up a large part of school curricula, particularly at the elementary and secondary levels. Students are to be taught to speak effectively, to read capably, and to write competently. In American schools the success of these aims can be achieved the more effectively if teachers are informed concerning the varieties of English and the attitudes toward these varieties. Lack of information on Black English or Chicano English has been cited as one of the reasons for problems that their speakers face in the school system and in society in general. To attack these problems, considerable study is now being done on the identification of dialect differences, of attitudes toward them, and of bilingualism. Together with schoolteachers, linguists are also attempting to identify the processes involved in reading, especially when these involve difficulties such as dyslexia, that is, problems in learning to read.

In Chinese schools teachers with the assistance of linguists are teaching Putonghua to children of totally different native dialects or languages. The linguists identify the characteristics of such dialects; the teachers then devise means to assist the children in shifting from their former language patterns to those of Putonghua. Linguists are also working in China to devise and teach alphabets, both for Putonghua—which generally is written in characters—and for the minority languages of the country. The language problems in China, as in most nations of the world, will require increasing linguistic information. On the basis of such information countries like India, Indonesia, and many in Africa will establish their selected national languages. Moreover, measures taken to increase literacy will absorb the energies of many linguists.

Linguistics then can scarcely be a pursuit restricted to the scientific study of language, for it has many concerns and responsibilities. Few of these have been adequately pursued in the past, partly because of the small number of linguists, partly because many of the problems are new. To be sure, many old people and many people with brain injuries have in the past suffered from aphasia. But the malady seemed so mysterious that little was done about it. When Zacharias suffered aphasia, as reported in Luke 1, because he doubted that his wife would bear him a son, there was no cure until he accepted the promise of the angel and agreed that the newly born son be called John. And when in medieval Europe certain social groups were set apart by different languages and customs, they were oppressed and often segregated in ghettos. Moreover, children who suffered from dyslexia several decades ago were regarded as stupid and passed over for further education.

Linguistics admittedly has no magical solutions for the problems cited. But since these problems involve language, there is every hope that increased understanding of language will lead to some remedies.

Linguistics therefore offers many opportunities. Societies cannot function without language, and their speakers cannot achieve full development without adequate control of language. Linguists will work increasingly with other specialists, especially in the behavioral and the biological sciences, to solve social and individual problems. For though the knowledge of language is only one key to insights into the functioning of societies and the behavior of their speakers, it is a major key.

In many respects then, linguists are the specialists primarily involved in achieving an understanding of and dealing with the activities of societies and their speakers. As insights into language increase, linguists will have increasing opportunities and responsibilities to provide speakers with improved understanding of themselves and the many problems encountered by individuals and societies. The following chapters of this book will present information gathered in the effort to comprehend, describe, and explain language. The implications of such information for the study of humanity and society will be examined. Since comprehension of language is fundamental to these efforts, it will occupy our initial discussion.

## BIBLIOGRAPHICAL NOTES

A welcome number of introductions to linguistics have been written in recent years—so many that only a few can be listed here.

*Language and Symbolic Systems* by Yuen Ren Chao (Cambridge: At the University Press, 1968) is written in the admirable humanistic tradition and gives examples from languages widely different in structure from English.

*Aspects of Language,* 2d ed., by Dwight Bolinger (New York: Harcourt Brace Jovanovich, 1975) presents many fresh insights.

*Linguistics and Language* by Julia S. Falk (Lexington, Mass.: Xerox, 1973) deals soberly with language and with applications of linguistics.

*An Introduction to Language* by Victoria Fromkin and Robert Rodman (New York: Holt, Rinehart and Winston, 1974) is a lively presentation of transformational grammar, with sections on animal languages, language and the brain, and other topics of interest.

Other introductions to the study of language will be listed in the Bibliographical Notes to Chapter 2.

## QUESTIONS FOR REVIEW

1. Give two definitions of the designation *linguist*.
2. Give a brief definition of *linguistics*.
3. Besides linguistics itself, cross-disciplinary studies of language have become prominent, notably psycholinguistics and sociolinguistics. Identify some of the topics studied by practitioners of each.
4. What are some possible applications of linguistics?

## EXERCISES

Linguists examine language for its structures of meaning, its syntactic structures, and its phonological structures. The following exercises illustrate recent studies in these three areas.

## E X E R C I S E  1

In recent studies of meaning, linguists have examined the implications of verbs, such as those listed below, and have distinguished various sets. In these studies they have been influenced by philosophers, notably John L. Austin.[1] Among Austin's sets are the following: a. Verdictives, e.g., *diagnose, estimate, grade*. b. Commissives, e.g., *agree, favor, promise*. Discuss uses of set a for rendering a "verdict" in contrast to those of set b for "committing" oneself to a definite position.

In which of the two groups would you place each of the following:

---

[1]See John L. Austin, *How to Do Things with Words* (New York: Oxford University Press, 1965).

intend                    *characterize*
*value*                   *guarantee*

## EXERCISE 2

Indicate the attitude of the mayor, as implied in the two following statements:

> *The mayor estimated the payment.*
> *The mayor favored the payment.*

What is implied about the object of the action? Was the payment completed in the situation depicted in the first sentence? Was the payment made in the situation depicted in the second?

Discuss the differing implications of the two following sentences:

> *The teacher guaranteed that there would be no final exam.*
> *The teacher intended that there would be no final exam.*

Was a final given in each situation? If so, was the teacher responsible for the final in the second?

## EXERCISE 3

In recent studies of syntax, linguists have found that languages have basic patterns that govern simple sentences as well as other constructions. Among these constructions are descriptive adjectives, genitives, and relative clauses. The following are examples in Spanish and Turkish.

a. Adjectives:              *John saw the big dog.*
   Span.                    *Juan vió el perro grande.*
                            'John saw the dog big.'
   Turk.                    *John büyük köpeği gördü.*
                            'John big dog saw.'
b. Genitives:               *John saw his neighbor's dog.*
   Span.                    *Juan vió el perro de su vecino.*
                            'John saw the dog of his neighbor.'
   Turk.                    *John komşunun köpeğini gördü.*
                            'John neighbor's dog saw.'
c. Relative constructions:  *John saw the dog that ate the meat.*
   Span.                    *Juan vió el perro que comió la carne.*
                            'John saw the dog that ate the meat.'
   Turk.                    *John eti yiyen köpeği gördü.*
                            'John meat (that) ate dog saw.'

What is the position of the descriptive adjectives, genitives, and relative constructions with regard to their nouns in Spanish? in Turkish?

What is the position of the verb with regard to its object in Spanish? in Turkish?

Can you suggest any reason for the consistent position of noun modifiers in VO languages like Spanish? In OV languages like Turkish? If modifiers, such as relative constructions, followed noun objects in Turkish, what might be the "distance" between objects and verbs? Similarly, if they preceded noun objects in Spanish, what kind of comprehension problems might be found in complicated sentences?

### E X E R C I S E  4

In Japanese the past of verbs is made with a suffix, generally *-ta* or *-da*. The following are some examples.

| | | | |
|---|---|---|---|
| Present indicative: | *mat ͨu* 'wait' | *shinu* 'die' | *nomu* 'drink' |
| Past: | *matta* 'waited' | *shinda* 'died' | *nonda* 'drank' |

What is the basis for the selection of *-ta* or *-da?*

If you were asked to make the past form of *yomu* 'read,' what would you propose? of *mot ͨu* 'hold'?

### E X E R C I S E  5

John R. Firth expressed skepticism about the ability of professors to "[define] language as 'the expression of thought.' " Instead, he proposed that "Metternich was much nearer the mark when he pointed out to the professors that one of the commonest uses of language was for the concealment of thought."[2]

Although Firth may not have been totally serious, comment on the uses of language for concealing thought, drawing on your own speech.

Henry Kissinger is said to be an admirer of Metternich. Can you cite examples of his use of language to conceal thought?

---

[2]John R. Firth, *The Tongues of Man* (London: Oxford University Press, 1964), p. 99.

# WHAT IS LANGUAGE?

## CHAPTER 2

### 2.1 Tasks of Linguistics

Like other behavioral sciences—for example, anthropology—linguistics is confronted with two major tasks. The first task is to acquire an understanding of the various languages spoken today or at any time in history. To achieve an understanding of any one language is a great task, as the inadequacy of our grammars may indicate. Providing descriptions of the 5,000 or so languages in use today, as well as languages of the past such as Old English, is a substantial goal for the future; we may illustrate the extent of the work that needs to be done by noting that the most widely translated book, the Bible, has been translated into only just over a thousand languages. Many of these languages are poorly described; others, such as the languages of New Guinea, are just beginning to be studied. But even without knowledge of many languages and with only a serious inadequate understanding of many others, linguists must set out to fulfill task number two: to comprehend language as a phenomenon. This second task of linguistics will be our main concern. We will illustrate the aims and procedures involved in carrying out this task by taking our examples primarily from one language, English.

In Chapter 1 language was defined as a device for conveying meanings through sounds. By a fuller definition, language is a system of arbitrary oral symbols by means of which a social group interacts. Sounds are said to be arbitrary because they have no inherent meaning; those in the English word *dog* happen to refer to the animal *Canis familiaris,* but German uses the sounds of *Hund* and Japanese the sounds of *inu* to refer to the same animal.

In most linguistic studies the unit of language selected for linguistic analysis is the sentence. Speakers of every language speak in sentences and interpret sentences as units. If they are literate—that is, if they display language by means of writing—they divide these units into segments; any English sentence is first marked off by punctuation marks and is then broken up into words, which are further segmented into letters. Linguists also analyze sentences into smaller segments, as we will see, but with greater rigor than the general speaker. The aim of this linguistic analysis is to understand how speakers construct and interpret any selected sentence and eventually to account for language as a phenomenon of human behavior.

Yet sentences obviously occur in contexts. For the interpretation of individual sentences, then, one must examine sentences in relation to others. Some linguists propose that longer sequences, such as paragraphs or entire texts, must be taken as basic units. The two points of view are not contradictory. When contexts or longer sequences must be examined for a proper interpretation of a sentence, a linguist does so. But linguists have found no consistent structural principle regulating either paragraphs or texts. The analysis of paragraphs or texts is left to others, such as students of rhetoric. The linguist draws on their findings, as on the findings of anthropologists and sociologists who may investigate contexts of situation, but his or her primary task is to observe, describe, and explain the structure of sentences.

Speakers of a language have the remarkable capability of constructing and interpreting sentences they have never encountered before. The sentence *A machine chose the chords* may have been produced here for the first time; yet no speaker of English has any difficulty interpreting it. Linguistics seeks to determine the basis of this capability.

In carrying out such study, a linguist is investigating human behavior. Linguistics is therefore a behavioral science. A full understanding of any sentence would involve some knowledge of human mental processes—how language is stored in the brain, how it is perceived, how it is directed by the brain. Understanding any sentence would also involve knowledge of the society in which the sentence is produced—how, for example, any speaker could assert that a nonanimate machine might select some arrangement of tones called a chord. These requirements for understanding language in detail call on so many sciences—biology, psychology, anthropology, and sociology, among others—that specialties have arisen within linguistics itself, notably phonetics, psycholinguistics, and sociolinguistics. Thorough linguistic descriptions are fundamental to all such specialties, and descriptive linguistics is the basic discipline of linguistics.

In descriptive linguistics various procedures have been devised to arrive at **grammars,** that is, to produce descriptions of a given language. (See section 2.5 for a more detailed definition.) For most purposes a linguist deals with the sounds of a sentence, using transcriptions rather than spellings. A preliminary transcription of the earlier example *A machine chose the chords* [əməšiyn čowz ðəkɔrdz] may indicate why the linguist uses transcriptions. Through various historical accidents the spelling sequence *ch* is used for three different sounds in this sentence: [š] as in *sheen;* [č] as in *chin;* [k] as in *kiss.* Unless a linguistic description identified these differing sounds, an investigator of speech perception would be misled. As the transcription indicates, a linguist may also note a vocal patterning of the words that is different from a written patterning of the words. The indefinite article *a* may be as closely linked in speech to the syllable [mə] as is the second syllable of *machine;* the plural suffix in *chords* is [z] after [d], rather than [s] as after [t] in *courts.* In studying relationships of this kind, a linguist is not simply trying to sort out sounds but also trying to determine segments that are grammatically significant. But like all scientists the linguist must limit his goals and deal with one problem at a time. As John R. Firth says:

The study of the living voice of a man in action is a very big job indeed. In order to be able to handle it at all, we must split up the whole integrated behavior pattern we call speech, and apply specialized techniques to the description and classification of these so-called elements of speech we detach by analysis.[1]

This book is an introduction to such techniques. In keeping with Firth's statement, it presents these techniques in a sequence determined by pedagogical principles. It also presents some of the findings of linguistics concerning language and human use of it. Since it is primarily concerned with the description of language, its major emphasis will be the understanding of language resulting from a linguist's observation and description of specific languages.

## 2.2 Language as Viewed by a Descriptive Linguist

Descriptive linguistics aims to provide an understanding of language by analyzing it in its various uses. Descriptive linguists generally deal with one language at a time, such as contemporary English, Chinese, or Japanese.

---

[1]John R. Firth, *Papers in Linguistics, 1934–1951* (London: Oxford University Press, 1957), p. 20.

If a speaker of Chinese said to you:

Nǐ *shì nǎguó rén?* 'Where are you from?'

you would need various kinds of information to understand the question.

One kind of information has to do with the sounds. The consonant and vowel of Chinese *shì* 'be' are pronounced somewhat like the first syllable of *Chicago;* but *shì* has an inherent falling tone, marked  . This tone resembles the fall in melody used when a single syllable is pronounced in English, as in the answer: *Sure!* By contrast, other Chinese words—for example, *rén* 'person'—have a rising tone; still other words, like *nǐ* 'you,' have a falling-rising tone. A fourth tone, marked ‾, requires a level melody, as in *sān* 'three.' To understand Chinese and to be understood, one must know the inherent tone of each syllable and word, as well as the Chinese consonants and vowels.

Besides the sounds, one must also know the words and the sentence patterns of a language. Unlike sounds, which only convey meaning, words and sentence patterns carry meaning.

Languages represent meaning in similar ways, but each also has characteristic patterns. Chinese *nǐ* is much like English *you* in its use for one or more persons. German *du,* on the other hand, is used to address one person; another form, German *ihr,* is used to address two or more. Words then may seem to carry similar meanings, but they may also differ in details.

The typical sentence pattern of Chinese is like that of English in having verbs stand between subjects and objects. Both English and Chinese are verb-object (VO) languages. Other languages have object-verb (OV) order, such as Japanese. Thus the Chinese sentence for:

*I am reading the text.*

has the same order as its English counterpart:

*Wǒ* 'I' *niàn* 'read' *kéwén* 'text.'

But unlike English, Chinese has no articles before nouns and no auxiliaries: *kéwén* = 'a/the text'; *niàn* = 'read, am reading, do read.' Japanese, on the other hand, expresses this statement:

*Watakushi* 'I' *ga tekisuto* 'text' *o yomu* 'read.'

Besides differing fundamentally in its sentence order from English and Chinese, Japanese indicates the role of nouns by means of postpositions (*ga* indicates the subject, *o* the object). In order to understand a language, then, one must know its sentence patterns as well as its words and their meanings.

Although the Chinese sentence *Nǐ shì nǎguó rén?* is a question meaning 'Where are you from?' literally the words mean: 'You *nǐ* are *shì* what-country *nǎguó* person *rén?*' To understand this question, one must know both the meaning of the individual words and the rules of sentence structure in Chinese. For example, Chinese question words are not necessarily placed at the beginning of sentences, as in English. Rather, they are placed where the requested information will be found in the answer. The arrangement of this Chinese question is accordingly determined by the arrangement of an answer like: "I am *an American* (person)."

Anyone who has mastered a language knows its system of sounds, forms, and sentences, as well as their meanings. But he or she may not be able to describe them. Such description is one of the principal tasks of linguistics. To arrive at a description of a language, one must recognize that any language is a system of symbols. In the following section we will review some of the implications of this characterization.

## 2.3  Language: A System of Symbols

To illustrate what is meant by defining language as a system of symbols we may take an English sentence and compare it with a Japanese sentence. If we analyze the pronunciation of the sentence *Could you please tell me where the station is?* we may reproduce it as follows:

$$/^2\text{kùd yùw plíyz }^3\text{tél mìy}^2 \rightarrow {}^2\text{hwèr ðə}^3 \text{ stéyšən ìz}^1 \downarrow/$$

Besides noting the consonants and vowels, we indicate stress /ˊ ˋ ˇ/ and pitch /¹ ² ³/ as well as terminals /→ ↓/. All of these are used to make up symbols, as we observe by comparing a sentence meaning *Where is the station?* in Japanese:

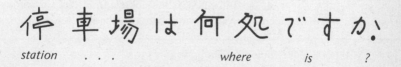

| station | . . . | where | is | ? |

For the Japanese sentence a transcription is even more essential than for English. Since conventional transliteration systems are close to usable transcriptions, we may follow one of these, the Hepburn system, in citing Japanese. Transliterated according to the principles of the Hepburn system, the sentence reads *Teishaba wa doko desu ka?*

Comparing these two sentences, we can equate segments in English with those in Japanese. Any segments that are recorded as independent entities in dictionaries we can call **words.** Of the English and Japanese segments *station* corresponds to *teishaba, where* to *doko,* and so on. The words *station* and *teishaba* are clearly oral symbols that correspond to things in the world around us. In somewhat the same way, all language consists of symbols. Japanese *doko* 'what place' is a noun, virtually as concrete as is *station*. But *where* we feel is less concrete; we interpret it not as a symbol with reference to things in the world around us but rather with reference to a set of possibilities in the linguistic system. An even less concrete symbol is the English pattern of pitch, as marked by ² ³ ¹ ↓, which corresponds to the following contour:

This intonation pattern contrasts with others, such as one with a final rise ² ³ ³ ↑, which corresponds to the following contour:

In the contrasting set of English intonations ² ³ ¹ ↓ indicates that the speaker is making a serious statement; ² ³ ³ ↑ indicates that he is expressing doubt. If someone asks the question *Where is the station?* using the ² ³ ¹ ↓ intonation pattern, he is seriously concerned with obtaining the information. If he uses the ² ³ ³ ↑ pattern, he shows incredulity; the meaning of the sentence then might be 'Did you really ask me where the station is?' or 'How could you ask me where the station is? (We're standing right in front of it.)'

The intonation pattern is then a symbol, much like a word. Other symbols are even less concrete, such as word order. The arrangement *You could tell me* contrasts with *Could you tell me?* and the contrast in order symbolizes different meanings to speakers of English.

In this way language consists of symbols, some of which may be readily related to things in the outside world, others merely to other potential patterns in the language. It is through such symbolization that we can use language to communicate. Through symbolization language has meaning.

### 2.3.1  Symbols Determined by Relationships

We have noted above that the functions of symbols are determined by their relationships to other entities in the system. The meaning of *station* is circumscribed by other words possible in the same context: *airport, school, supermarket,* and so on. The meaning of *Could you tell me?* is circumscribed by other possible arrangements, such as *You could tell me,* and so on. Throughout language the functions of symbols and the significance of linguistic entities are determined by their relationships to other entities in that language.

An example from the simplest segment of language, its sound system, may provide an illustration. In English we have a variety of *t* sounds.

Initially before stressed vowels, as in *top*, *t* is followed by a puff of air; the typical pronunciation could be transcribed [tʰap]. After *s*, as in *stop*, there is no such puff of air, and the typical pronunciation could be transcribed [st⁼ap]. In spite of this difference in sounds speakers of English consider the two entities the same; in Chinese or Hindi, on the other hand, [tʰ] and [t⁼] are considered different. Identification in each of these languages results from the interrelationships of the sounds with others in the same language. In English [tʰ] and [t⁼] never occur in the same environment. There is, on the one hand, no word *[t⁼ap]. (A preceding asterisk is used in linguistic texts to indicate entities that are not attested.) There is also no English word *[stʰap]. In contrast with some languages, such as Chinese and Hindi, the two sounds [tʰ] and [t⁼] never distinguish words in English. For this reason English speakers are not aware of any difference between the *t*'s of *top* and *stop*. The two sounds are classed together in one set; they are varying members, or **allophones,** of the same **phoneme,** or sound class. The significance of the two *t*'s for the speakers results from their relationships in the English sound system rather than from the physical differences themselves.

Japanese provides a further illustration. It too has a [t] sound in its phonological system, as we may illustrate with the brusque imperative form *mate* 'wait.' But if the *t* stands before *u*, as in the indicative *matsu*, it is followed by an [s], in much the same way that the *t* of *top* is followed by an [ʰ]. To understand the Japanese change of [t] to [tˢ], you can compare the English pronunciation [néytšər] with [néytyur] for *nature*. For the Japanese the two sounds belong in one class; a Japanese speaker is no more aware of the physical difference between the two sounds [tˢ] and [t⁼] than an English speaker is of the difference between [tʰ] and [t⁼]. Again, the important consideration is relationship. A Japanese speaker always uses [tˢ] before [u], never [t⁼]; on the other hand, he always uses [t⁼] before [e a o], never [tˢ]. What seems different in another language is classed as the same because of relationships.

In support of this statement about the patterning of languages we may note the behavior of speakers when they hear a different language. As with many terms referring to sports and recreation, Japanese borrowed *touring* from British English. Hearing the vowel as *u*, they interpreted the word as [tˢuriŋgu], for within their own phonological system the relationships between [t] and [tˢ] are such that they are exchanged automatically because of the following vowel.

These examples of the role of sounds in language may illustrate how a symbolic system has values determined by relationships rather than by physical entities. The relationships, to be sure, are linked to physical entities. But from the externals alone, or, as they are often called, the **overt,** or **surface,** phenomena, we do not determine the value or the significance of the entities. Since the value depends on interrelationships that are not obvious on the surface of language, we refer to the essence of language or of any symbolic system as its **deep** or **underlying structure.**

When we examine languages as symbolic systems, we often make comparisons with simple communication systems, such as traffic signals. In these the relationships are determined by color: red means "stop," yellow "caution," green "go." Other characteristics of a given system of traffic signals are noncentral: some systems have red above green; some have a larger lamp for red; the exact hue of red, yellow, or green may vary. Drivers take their signals from none of these nonessentials but rather from the relationships between the three colors; those of longest wavelength are interpreted to mean "stop," whether they are exactly 700 millimicrons in length or whether the number of millimicrons varies slightly. In the same way a speaker of English identifies *tin* by its difference from *pin, kin, thin, sin,* and so on.

The entities of language that convey meaning are called **morphemes,** units of form. The values of morphemes are determined by their relationships in any given language. English has a contrast between *could* and *will,* which yields a different meaning in *Could you please tell me?* as opposed to *Will you please tell me?* The meanings may be determined from the patterns in which these morphemes occur. But again, relationships are central. We do not say *\*Must you please tell me?* although the sequence *Must you tell me?* is possible. The impossibility is determined by the relationships between *please* and *must,* which simply cannot co-occur in questions. It may be difficult to specify the meaning of *must* and *please* in order to demonstrate why they cannot co-occur in such a sentence. Nevertheless, a native speaker of English does not form such a sentence. He or she knows the possible relationships of each word, and these relationships do not permit such a combined use of *must* and *please* in questions. In this way the word relationships determine their meanings.

In sum, the meaning of any entity in a symbolic system results from its relationships with other entities; the total of such entities and their values make up a symbolic system used for communication, or a language.

### 2.3.2   The Meanings of Symbols as Arbitrary

One of the longstanding problems concerning language has to do with the basis of the meanings of individual words. From the time of Plato and his *Cratylus* people have argued whether there is some inherent relationship between words and things, or whether such relationships are entirely arbitrary. The problem is reflected in reported statements like: "Pigs are called pigs because they are so dirty." Evidence is also sought in onomatopoetic words like *arf-arf* to represent the barking of dogs or *cock-a-doodle-do* to represent the crowing of a cock.

The conclusions of linguists are determined in great part by the great variation in words for the same things in different languages. Thus the word for 'pig' in German is *Schwein.* And dogs are assumed to say *wau-wau* in German, *gnaf-gnaf* in French, and other words in other languages. Moreover, the supposed word may change in time; in Chaucer's day, a cock was said to make the noise *cok cok.* Accordingly it is difficult to support any statement proposing an inherent relation between words and things.

On the other hand, speakers tend to associate the words for pleasant things or activities with pleasant feelings. Thus *friend* or *murmur* are assumed to be beautiful words, while *pig, snake,* or *disgust* are assumed to be ugly. When one compares the totally different words in foreign languages, one may find again that they have unpleasant connotations for their speakers. Accordingly it is difficult to support the view that relationships between words and the things they represent are anything but arbitrary.

### 2.3.3 The Symbols Have Meaning for One Social Group

The words and meanings of any language apply to limited social groups. Their size depends in great part on intercommunication. If travel is limited, as in rugged areas like parts of New Guinea, or if social groups impose restrictions on intercommunication, a language may be understandable to only a small number of speakers.

If, on the other hand, there is considerable intercommunication, as in a modern nation, the number of speakers using a given language may be large. English, Russian, Hindi, Portuguese, and Chinese are understood by a hundred million speakers or more, as are several other languages. Social groups may then vary in size, as may the extent of use of any given language. Whatever their extent of use, languages are systems of symbols arranged in abstract patterns, as the following section will briefly show.

### 2.4 Characteristic Patterns of Languages

Among important recent findings concerning language is the observation that basic sentences follow certain patterns and correlate with other constructions. Thus if a language places objects after verbs, it will also have prepositions and the other characteristic patterns illustrated below. Further such data will be given in subsequent chapters and their exercises. The patterns given here are designed to illustrate the necessity of regarding language as abstract underlying patterns.

Languages may be classified into two large groups in accordance with the position of objects with regard to verbs. Spanish may serve as an example of a consistent verb-object (VO) language, Japanese of a consistent object-verb (OV) language.

Simple sentences illustrate the basic patterns:

> Span. *Juan vió el perro.*
> 'John saw the dog.'
> Jap. *Tarō ga inu o mita.*
> 'Taro subject marker dog object marker saw.'

VO languages have prepositions; OV languages have postpositions, as in the following examples:

> Span.  *Juan vió el perro por la ventana.*
> 'John saw the dog through the window.'
> Jap.  *Tarō ga inu o mado kara mita.*
> 'Taro dog window from saw.'

Further, in VO languages comparisons are made with the adjective and a marker before the noun compared; in OV languages these elements stand after the noun compared:

> Span.  *El perro es mas grande que el gato.*
> 'The dog is (more big) bigger than the cat.'
> Jap.  *Inu ga neko yori ōkii.*
> 'The dog cat than big.' = 'The dog is bigger than the cat.'

The consistency of this patterning may be understood if the three constructions—government of verbs, government of particles, and relationships in comparison—are viewed as parallel. Each construction involves government, or control, by one element of another. Accordingly the arrangement in each is the same, although on the surface the constructions may seem to differ considerably.

Similar patterns can be found for the placement of relative constructions, genitives, and adjectives, as will be shown below. In consistent VO languages, such as Spanish, these follow the nouns they modify; in consistent OV languages, on the other hand, they precede the nouns they modify. Such findings demonstrate the abstractness of language patterning. One of the important tasks of descriptive linguistics is the determination of means to identify the abstract patterns of language from its surface forms.

---

## 2.5  How a Linguist Gets at Language: Discovery Procedures

In setting out to describe any language, a linguist collects a sample of data. The usable data make up a **corpus,** which the linguist then analyzes for its entities and relationships. In making the analysis, the linguist will look for entities of sound, form, and meaning. Since the phonological analysis is simplest to discuss, we deal with it first here to demonstrate linguistic method.

In our illustration we may start with the earlier example *Could you please tell me where the station is?* To determine entities in a given language, linguists select such sentence patterns, or **frames,** and explore various possible substitutions, for in determining possible substitutions, they determine the significant relationships.

In order to be certain of avoiding error, the linguist should compare entire sentences, for example, *Would you please tell me?* with *Could you please tell me?* or *Could they please tell me?* with *Would they please tell me?* and so on. But manipulating entire sentences is cumbersome, so linguists generally use single words and look for contrasts among them. Linguists are particularly concerned with pairs of words, such as *pin* versus *bin*. Any two words, or sequences, contrasting phonologically in only one item are called a **minimal pair.** In beginning an analysis of a new language, therefore, a linguist may point to objects, write down the phonological notation for them, and then proceed to describe the system of relationships found. Or if the **informant,** that is, the native speaker, is bilingual and the linguist knows one of the languages, the linguist may use a list of everyday words to elicit the words of the unknown language. A simple substitution English frame may be taken from *win*.

**Figure 1**

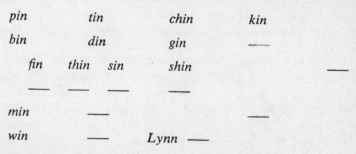

Since the initial entities contrast with one another (as they also do in other substitution frames, such as —*at*), they may be interpreted to be significant, that is, they distinguish words differing in meaning from one another.

The frame —*at* in Figure 2 would provide further significant entities.

**Figure 2**

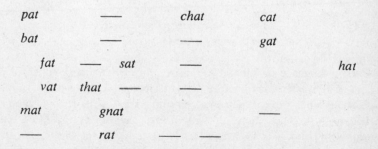

As these words and the blank spaces suggest, eventually twenty-four contrasting consonants would be found for English. To describe these, their uses, and the sounds of any language, a linguist must deal with the study of speech sounds in general. This study is known as **phonology.**

If the linguist dealt with Arabic, for *Where is the station?* he might be given the sentence [ʔilmaḥátta féːn] 'the station where?' In this sentence he notes sounds that are not significant in English: [ʔ], the glottal stop; [ħ], a pharyngeal spirant; and the underlined sounds. To be prepared to deal with the sounds encountered in any language, a linguist must have a general understanding of speech sounds. The study of speech sounds is known as **phonetics.** The study of the use of speech sounds in language is known as **phonemics.** Phonetics and phonemics make up the two subdivisions of **phonology.**

In addition to sounds and phonemes a linguist looks for contrasts of form in language. An answer to the question "Could you please tell me where the station is?" might be "Take the street over there." Another answer might be "This bus takes you directly to it." Examining such contrasts, a linguist finds sets like *take, takes, took, taken,* and *taking* and compares them with similar sets, such as *pass, passes, passed, passed,* and *passing;* or *sag, sags, sagged, sagged,* and *sagging.* Analyzing these, he finds central forms—*take, pass, sag*—and varying elements, for example, *-s, -n,* and *-ing.* There is a fundamental difference between phonemes and these elements, for the latter carry meaning. We cannot, for example, state meanings for the two elements of *win: w* and *in.* But we can for *take, pass,* or *sag,* and for the following *s,* which has the meaning "third person singular subject." Such entities that have this meaning are called **morphs;** a class of morphs is a **morpheme.** For example, {Z} is the third singular present morpheme in English. Morphemes may have varying members, or **allomorphs,** like [əz] in *passes,* [s] *in takes,* and [z] in *sags.*

In studying the morphemes of a language we must determine the entities and their arrangements. In the same way as we proceed in phonology, we find suitable frames and determine entities that may occur in them, for example:

> *A machine chose the chords.*
> *An accompanist chose the chords.*
> *A director chose the chords.*
> *A machine chooses the chords.*
> *I choose the chords.*

Clearly a language contains many more morphemes than phonemes. The study of morphemes is therefore highly complex.

Various labels have also been given to the study of morphemes and their arrangements. The study of the forms themselves is often called **morphology** but also **morphemics.** The study of the arrangements of morphemes, words, and phrases in sentences is called **syntax.** A name used by some linguists for referring to both is **grammar.** But there are problems with these labels. The term *grammar* is widely used to include phonology as well as morphology and syntax. For some linguists the two labels seem to have separated unnecessarily forms and their arrangements. Some linguists then use the name *syntax* as a label for the study of both forms and their arrangements. Because of these differences in usage, students will have to determine how individual linguists use these terms. In this book *grammar* will be used as a general term to embrace the study of sounds, or **phonology,** and forms, or **morphology,** and their arrangements, or **syntax.** Morphology, as is traditional, will refer to two types of study of forms: **inflection,** which deals with the changes in large, closely structured sets of words, such as the parts of speech; and **derivation,** which deals with smaller, less readily definable sets, for example, *retake, takeoff,* and so on.

The elements detached and described in phonology are merely markers of meaning; those detached and described in morphology are carriers of meaning. Additional procedures are necessary to deal with meaning. These procedures are traditionally applied to words, which are defined for their meaning and listed in **dictionaries** or **lexicons.** Yet dictionaries primarily list synonyms, defining one word in terms of another—for example, *horse* as *'Equus caballus'*—or where appropriate, through illustrations. *Webster's Third New International Dictionary* includes illustrations to help define *horse* and other selected items, such as *soup plate.* But the illustrations are limited; there is none, for instance, for *antelope.* And for some words—for example, *abstraction*—dictionaries would find it difficult to provide illustrations. Moreover, dictionaries do not deal with meanings conveyed through differences in intonation, for example, "Horse? Horse!" To deal with meaning in a general way, as is done with sounds, some universal criteria must be devised, such as features of meaning found in many languages. Some features of meaning are animateness or nonanimateness, human or nonhuman, male or female, and so on. If **semantic** features like these were used in definitions, users of a dictionary would not need to know the language for which it is written in order to determine meaning. The dictionary would accordingly be more general but also more abstract than are contemporary dictionaries. Semantic analysis for features parallels widely used phonological study of this kind, but it is just in its beginnings.

When such analyses, whether for sounds, forms, or meanings, are carried out, they must be done separately for each language. We have noted that [tʰ] corresponds to a phoneme in Chinese and Hindi but that in English it is only a variant of /t/ before stressed vowels. As another example we may note Italian [ŋ]. This is found in Italian before [g] as in *lungo* 'long'—compare the [ŋ] in *bank*—but not in other environments. Elsewhere [n] is found. Therefore in Italian [ŋ] is a variant of /n/. Its position in the Italian phonological system may be illustrated from the behavior of Italian speakers learning English. English words ending in [ŋ], such as *long* and *bang,* seem impossible for them, so they pronounce them with final [g], that is, /lɔŋg/, /bæŋg/. To maintain the [ŋ] they modify its phonological environment so that it is the same as in Italian.

An example from syntax to illustrate the necessity of analyzing each language for its structure may be supplied by German. In German the sentence "I see your car" is *Ich sehe Ihren Wagen.* Comparing the two, one may assume that in both languages the verb (*see* and *sehe*) follows the subject when the subject is initial in sentences. But from modified forms of the sentence, such as "I often see his car" and "If I see his car," the different syntactic principle of German becomes clear, for these sentences must read *Oft sehe ich seinen Wagen* and *Wenn ich seinen Wagen sehe.* These sentences demonstrate that the principles of word order in German are quite different from those in English; the position of the verb is not related to that of the subject but rather to other possible entities in clauses. In German independent declarative clauses the verb stands in second place, but in German subordinate clauses it stands at the end. Accordingly, the arrangement of the forms, and their significance, must be determined separately for English and German, as for every other language. Each language must be investigated independently for its patterns of syntax as well as for its phonological characteristics.

Similarly meaning relationships must be determined separately for each language. English *know* corresponds to German *kennen* when it has an animate object, to *wissen* when it has an inanimate object, and to *können* when the object is a skill, like a language. We cannot equate English *know* with these, just as we cannot equate English /ŋ/ with Italian [ŋ]. Because of this property of language, we must analyze each language in terms of its own structure.

## 2.6  How a Linguist Describes Languages: The Format of a Grammar

In the course of the study of language the formulation of descriptions has become increasingly compact and precise. Before the development of linguistics the sounds of language were often presented in alphabetical order in grammars in the Western tradition. But contemporary descriptions of language follow a linguistic format. Vowels are not listed in the sequence *a, e, i, o, u* but rather in accordance with a chart reflecting their linguistic significance. The consonants also are presented in accordance with their articulation: the labials *p* and *b,* the dentals *t* and *d,* the velars *k* and *g,* and so on, as illustrated in Figures 1 and 2 for —*in* and —*at.*

Similarly, the syntax of a language is presented systematically and compactly. Rather than discursive statements like "A sentence is made up of a subject and a predicate," a compact formula may be given, for example: S → NP VP (sentence *is rewritten as* noun phrase verb phrase). These formulas are called **rules.** For the initiated they make a description very precise; the symbolization, however, must be mastered, particularly the abbreviations and the use of signs to indicate relationships. Such grammatical formats resemble mathematical essays. Yet the information in the rules, however compact, simply corresponds to descriptions presented in more discursive grammars.

Far more fundamental than such externals is the underlying design of a grammar. Grammars of the past often presented the sound system of the language quite independently of the form system; entities of the form system in turn have been presented separately from the lexicon, or dictionary. Because of increasing understanding of language, however, grammars are being designed that relate the systems of sound and form very precisely, deriving any utterance from abstract formulas or sequences of rules. Grammars designed in this way seek to specify the entities and relationships in a language so precisely that at the same time only the possible sentences and all of the possible sentences would be produced. Using the term *generate* for "produce" or "specify," such grammars are called **generative.** A generative grammar, for example, would not permit one to produce a sentence such as *\*Must you please tell me?* Some of the precision in devising and arranging rules is achieved by means of relating structures through **transformations.** Thus the rule S → NP VP is related to formulas producing actual sentences by means of transformations. A grammar using devices of this sort is called **transformational.**

Whatever the principles by which they are produced, grammars may be regarded as theories of languages. The adequacy of grammars depends on the accuracy of observation by their author or authors and on their capabilities in applying descriptive techniques. Students of language also wish to account for phenomena of language. Some structures can be accounted for on the basis of linguistic principles, as noted in section 2.4. Others we can clarify by calling on other behavioral sciences, notably psychology and sociology.

## 2.7 **Language as Illuminated by Psycholinguistics**

As the name suggests, **psycholinguistics** combines techniques of psychology with techniques of linguistics in the study of language. The primary aim is study of the relation of language and behavior. This study may be directed at the way humans perceive one language or the problems they have in perceiving more than one. In listening to another speaker, we may capture the person's meaning through grammatical means, through phonological means, or through both simultaneously. It is fairly easy to determine that we use both; when any sentence begins "Could you . . . ," we scarcely need to hear more to predict much of what is coming. The syntactic pattern permits us to forecast a question of some kind, and we scarcely need to listen for all of its phonological characteristics. But when we are introduced to a person—for example, Mr. *Yasztremski*—we grasp the name through phonological characteristics alone. To what extent we observe the syntactic and the phonological characteristics in interpreting speech is a problem of great interest, and answers to the problem have many implications. One implication concerns language learning by children. Another involves the activity of learning a second or a third language. Others, less happily, concern the loss of language; with brain damage or increasing age, one's capability of understanding and speaking may diminish or be almost entirely lost.

A further problem is the relation between perception and cognition: Do the perceived patterns in our language determine our method of thinking and our view of the universe? All of these problems have to do with the acquisition and use of speech by an individual.

---

## 2.8  Language as Illuminated by Sociolinguistics

**Sociolinguistics** deals with the use of language and the different forms of speech found in different social groups. Social groups are set up on various patterns according to sex, age, trade or profession, geographical area, and so on. To the extent that these groupings are prominent in any society, different patterns of language may be used. In our society a men's poker club differs in speech from a women's bridge group; teen-agers do not speak like octogenarians, and the like.

Determining such linguistic groupings gives insights into the varieties of speech forms, or **dialects,** and also into the complexity of a given society. These insights may lead to attempts at modifying patterns of communication. In contemporary society the most important avenues for such modifications are schools. Schools teach a central language, possibly selecting one of the various languages used in a country, as English was selected in the United States during the last century; schools may also select one dialect of a language as a norm, such as Parisian French, Tokyo Japanese, and so on. The problems faced in establishing a norm are of great interest, especially in countries of Africa and Asia whose speakers use various languages.

Techniques to determine one variant of a language and to teach it have been largely informal, as is other study of mass communication, for example, advertising languages and international languages. Efforts to introduce international languages have been made since Latin went out of use, but the languages devised have been based primarily on modern forms of Latin, and accordingly they are not attractive to native speakers of a different language background, such as the inhabitants of Africa, Asia, and the Soviet Union. The international languages proposed are therefore poorly designed for precisely those areas with which Europeans find the greatest difficulty in communicating.

## 2.9  Language as Illuminated by Applied Linguistics

The findings of linguistics are increasingly applied in such fields as the teaching of language, the production of dictionaries, and the study of literature. Anyone teaching a foreign language must know its grammar thoroughly—particularly the contrasts between that grammar and the grammar of the learner's native language. Similarly teachers of reading or writers producing texts to teach reading must know a great deal about the phonological system and the syntactic system of that language. Frequent lack of such application in the past has permitted the production of poorly designed books. For example, a child learning to read would profit from consistent, well-selected patterns; if instead he is given words such as *Jane,* in which the symbol *a* = [ey], and *cat,* in which *A* = [æ], his understanding of the relationship between written and spoken symbols is not assisted.

Although linguistics must be applied in this way and other ways, it should be observed that linguistics is only one of the disciplines involved in practical goals such as teaching students to read, writing textbooks, and compiling dictionaries. On the other hand, such activities are hampered if the findings of linguistics are ignored. The understanding of types of communication based on aesthetic criteria is also inadequate unless specialists in these areas understand language.

Selected criteria regulate the patterns of language referred to as literature. These patterns have been intensively studied for Western tradition. They also enjoy such high esteem that they are treated separately from other social dialects. Yet often these language patterns are poorly understood, particularly by their most ardent admirers. Poetry, for example, in the Western tradition is constructed around patterns of rhythm and sound similarities, but many literary critics confuse letters and sounds and do not understand the bases of speech rhythm.

Problems involving special disciplines may bring specialists from various areas together, and the number of specialties involving the study of language will continue to increase rather than diminish. Anthropologists have interests different from those of sociologists; they have also undertaken to investigate the various uses of language in any society under the approach known as **ethnography of communication.** Similarly biologists and linguists have cooperated in investigating animal sounds. Moreover, there is interest in the relationships between language and other patterns of behavior, such as gestures. Gestures are widely used and well known to perceptive speakers of the present and the past—we have only to think of Shakespeare's Lady Macbeth—but until recently they have been poorly documented. Yet through ignorance of the use of gestures in a given society, communication has often been hampered; occasionally noninitiates, such as missionaries, have even lost their lives because they used gestures that had different meanings in another social group. The study of such accompaniments to speech is referred to as **paralinguistics.**

An understanding of language based on the control of several languages, preferably of different structure, plus observations on the use of languages by speakers is essential for understanding humankind and culture. The achievement of such understanding is one of the principal aims of linguistics.

To succeed in this aim, linguists seek to formulate a general theory of language. The extent to which such a theory can be formulated indicates in turn the understanding of language that has been achieved. Therefore much of our concern will be directed at arriving at and evaluating a theory of language.

---

## 2.10  Some Symbols Used in Linguistic Works

Brackets, [ ], are used to enclose phonetic transcriptions, for example, [tʰap], [st⁼ap].

Slant lines, / /, are used to enclose phonemic transcriptions, for example, /tap/, /stap/.

Braces, { }, are used to enclose morphemic transcriptions; for example, {Z} has the allomorphs /əz/ in *passes,* /s/ in *takes,* and /z/ in *sags.*

Angles, <>, are used to enclose semantic feature representations; for example, <+human> means that the lexical entity concerned—such as *man, girl, husband*—refers to human beings.

Illustrative examples are generally cited in italics, for example, *top, stop.*

When definitions (or translations) are given to identify citations, they are generally enclosed in single quotes, for example, Japanese *doko* 'where.'

The asterisk, *, indicates a form, or a sequence, which is not attested in a language; for example, *sgok* is not an English word; **Machine the chose chords* is not an English sentence.

BIBLIOGRAPHICAL NOTES

*An Introduction to Linguistics* by Bruce Liles (Englewood Cliffs, N.J.: Prentice-Hall, 1975) presents a transformational-generative approach to the study of language.

*Fundamentals of Linguistic Analysis* by Ronald W. Langacker (New York: Harcourt Brace Jovanovich, 1972) is another text in the transformational-generative tradition.

*An Introduction to Descriptive Linguistics,* rev. ed., by Henry A. Gleason, Jr. (New York: Holt, Rinehart and Winston, 1961) was long the standard text and still can be read with profit. The accompanying *Workbook in Descriptive Linguistics* is an important adjunct to the text.

Individual and penetrating is *A Course in Modern Linguistics* by Charles F. Hockett (New York: Macmillan, 1958), another text widely used a decade or so ago.

Because of its influence in linguistics, all students should familiarize themselves with *Language* by Leonard Bloomfield (New York: Holt, Rinehart and Winston, 1933).

Modern linguistics has been strongly influenced by Ferdinand de Saussure's *Cours de linguistique générale,* 5th ed. (Paris: Payot, 1955). The English translation by Wade Baskin, *Course in General Linguistics* (New York: Philosophical Library, 1959), is available in paperback (New York: McGraw-Hill, 1966).

John Lyon's *Introduction to Theoretical Linguistics* (Cambridge: At the University Press, 1968) presents a lucid treatment of many facets of linguistic theory.

A discussion of general principles underlying language may be found in Joseph H. Greenberg, ed., *Universals of Language,* 2d ed. (Cambridge, Mass.: M.I.T. Press, 1966).

A survey of the contributions of various linguistic groups is given in Francis P. Dinneen, *An Introduction to General Linguistics* (New York: Holt, Rinehart and Winston, 1967).

A brief outline of the history of linguistic study may be found in Robert H. Robins. *A Short History of Linguistics* (Bloomington: Indiana University Press, 1967).

## QUESTIONS FOR REVIEW

1. What are two of the tasks of linguistics?
2. Give two definitions of *language*.
3. What are some of the problems in dealing with texts in traditional spellings?
4. Discuss aims of descriptive linguistics.
5. Why is *language* defined as a system of symbols? Discuss other communication systems that are comparable to language.
6. What does it mean to say that the value of symbols is determined by relationships? Give examples.
7. Briefly characterize the term *phoneme*. What is an *allophone?*
8. What is meant by a. the term *surface structure?*
   b. the term *deep structure?*
   c. Why can the term *underlying structure* be used for *deep structure?*
9. a. Discuss some of the implications of the characterization of symbols as arbitrary.
   b. Can this adjective also be applied to words like *meow* for the noises made by cats?

     c. The word *love* is generally listed among the most beautiful words in the English language. Can you explain this evaluation of it?

     d. Why isn't the word *shove* found in such lists?

10. a. What is meant by the labeling of a language as VO?

     b. Give two characteristic syntactic patterns for VO languages.

     c. What are the contrasting patterns in OV languages?

     d. By these criteria, is English VO or OV?

11. Define: a. *phonology;*  b. *phonetics;*  c. *phonemes.*

12. Define: a. *syntax;*  b. *morphology;*  c. *inflection;*
    d. *derivation.*

13. Discuss some of the uses of the term *grammar.*

14. Define the use of the word *rule* in current grammars. Give an example of such a rule.

15. Define: a. *generative;*  b. *transformational.*

16. a. How does psycholinguistics set out to illuminate the study of language?

     b. How does sociolinguistics set out to illuminate the study of language?

17. State some applications of linguistics.

18. Give the use of the following symbols in linguistic works: a. [  ]; b. /  /;  c. *.

## EXERCISES

### EXERCISE 1

A complete grammar should permit only those sentences to be produced in a language that are accepted by its speakers. To illustrate this requirement we may propose a restricted English grammar and a small lexicon. Assuming that this grammar and lexicon generate only acceptable sentences, we would produce all possible sentences.

GRAMMAR:    1. Every sentence consists of a noun phrase followed by a verb phrase, that is, S → NP VP.

               2. The verb phrase may consist of a verb followed by a noun, that is, VP → Vb NP.

LEXICON[2]:    Nouns: *books, dogs, flowers, goats, men.*

            Verbs: *eat, like, understand, value.*

All sentences have the structure S → NP VP, for example, *Men like goats,* as the following tree in Figure 3 illustrates:

---

[2] Assume that the verbs included in the lexicon are all transitive; accordingly rule 2 given previously must be applied for every verb. All nouns are given in their plural form.

**Figure 3**

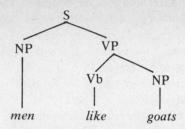

a. One hundred sentences can be produced from these rules and this lexicon. Some of these are acceptable, for example, *Goats eat flowers*. Produce ten such sentences.

b. Other possible sentences are acceptable in some cultural situations, for example, *Men eat men*. This sentence is appropriate when used of cannibalistic societies. Give examples of five such sentences.

c. Other sentences are unacceptable, for example, *Books understand dogs*. Give examples of five such sentences, using the grammar and the lexicon given previously.

d. To achieve a grammar that would generate only acceptable sentences, one must add further restrictions. For example, to rule out the sentence *Goats value books* but to permit the sentence *Men value books*, one could add the feature <+human> to the grammar and specify that <−human> nouns could not be used as subjects with *value*. Suggest features that would keep this grammar from producing sentences like the following:

> *Flowers understand men.*
> *Men eat books.*
> *Books like goats.*

e. The possibility of generating large numbers of sentences may be recognized if we expand the rules given above and the lexicon. If the second rule read: VP → Adv Vb NP, and the lexicon were expanded to include the adverbs *often* and *always*, how many sentences could you produce?

EXERCISE 2

The following are Japanese sentences with translations. (English *the* has no formal equivalent in Japanese; *otoko wa,* for example, could also be translated 'man.')

1. *Neko ga inu o mimasu.*     'The cat sees the dog.'
2. *Inu ga neko o mimasu.*     'The dog sees the cat.'
3. *Otoko ga inu o mimasu.*     'The man sees the dog.'
4. *Ane ga inu o mimasita.*     'The older sister saw the dog.'

a. Identify the lexical items in these sentences, that is, the Japanese words for 'man,' 'dog,' 'cat,' 'older sister,' 'see.'
b. Indicate briefly the functions of *ga* and *o* (cf. section 2.4). In the following sentences *wa* indicates the topic, which is equivalent in these sentences to the subject.
c. How is the present of the verb *see* formed? the past? Note the past form *kanda* in sentences 7 and 8.
d. What is the word order of Japanese in terms of subject, verb, object? Compare this order with the English word order in simple declarative sentences.

The following are additional sentences:

5. *Otoko wa ookii inu o mimasita.*      'The man saw the big dog.'
6. *Otoko wa ane no neko o*              'The man saw the cat of his
   *mimasita.*                           older sister.'
7. *Otoko wa inu ga kanda neko*          'The man saw the cat that the
   *o mimasita.*                         dog bit.'
8. *Inu ga kanda otoko wa neko o*        'The man whom the dog bit saw
   *mimasita.*                           the cat.'

e. What is the position of the relative clause, the genitive construction, and the adjective with regard to the word modified? Compare this position with the order of the comparable entities in English.

EXERCISE 3

In a visit to a school for deaf children, the students and I were asked by a young girl to say their names; she then proceeded to finger-spell them. When my turn came, I said: *Win;* she finger-spelled this as *when*. Account for this spelling, indicating whether you would distinguish between *wh* and *w*. In what part of the country is *e* confused with *i* before *n*? How would a sociolinguist account for her spelling? (Would you expect a girl from the northern part of the United States to use such a spelling?)

EXERCISE 4

In some areas of the world whistle languages have been developed. Discuss the possible origin of such a system of communication. (Note that the wolf whistle has been explained as based on the intonation pattern of expressions like: "Oh boy!" or "Some gal!") Can you propose other patterns of whistle language for particular meanings? Whistle languages are found particularly in mountainous regions. Can you account for this distribution? Cite other kinds of "auxiliary" languages.

# GRAMMARS AS THEORIES OF LANGUAGE

## CHAPTER 3

### 3.1 Theories Based on Latin Grammatical Tradition

If language is to be understood as a phenomenon, the components of language must be dealt with as parts of a whole. In the past such understanding of language was attempted indirectly, for the procedures available were inadequate to deal with the complexities of communication systems. Only recently have adequate procedures been devised by mathematicians and symbolic logicians as well as linguists. The procedures employed today in the description of language are increasingly formal, and the statements regarding language often resemble mathematical formulas.

Until the end of the nineteenth century in the Western grammatical tradition, languages were accounted for by a framework based on Latin and Greek. As the complexity of language became increasingly apparent, the advantage of describing all languages as variants of one selected language became obvious, for problems like the relationship of the phonological component to the syntactic component or of the syntactic component to the semantic component need not then be discussed. Presumably these relationships would be the same in all languages. Yet the procedure is not unlike one in which all games might be treated as variants of one game, possibly football. Baseball, tennis, and other games, such as soccer, would then be viewed as modified forms of the selected game, and no real understanding of games as such would result.

Moreover, since such comparison would deal largely with externals, an inadequate picture would be given of all games—or of all languages. By this approach, for example, nouns in Japanese were listed as having inflections, even though they are uninflected. Japanese nouns and some postpositions were equated with the Latin case forms: *hito no* 'of man' was called a genitive, as though it were an inflected form like *hominis* from *homo; hito o* was called an accusative, like *hominem,* and so on. When Japanese is compared with Latin, no adequate means is available to deal with *hito wa,* which indicates the topic of a sentence, as opposed to *hito ga,* which was interpreted as the nominative. As increasing numbers of languages were studied in the nineteenth century, more and more insoluble problems were encountered in the use of a framework based on Latin.

Steps were then taken to devise procedures for viewing languages independently of one another and for comprehending each language as a system having its own structure. Besides leading to unbiased descriptions of individual languages, ultimately such procedures yield generalizations about language in somewhat the same way as phenomena are comprehended in other sciences—economic systems in economics, political systems in political science—and universal features are disclosed.

A part of the impetus for a formal description of language was given by the grammar of Sanskrit ascribed to Panini, produced approximately 400 B.C. Made known in Europe at the beginning of the nineteenth century, Panini's grammar consists of a set of highly compact rules arranged in a definite order. It differs remarkably from grammars in the Latin tradition by providing rules for semantic, syntactic, morphological, and phonological patterns in a sequence that permits a concise description of Sanskrit. The very last rule of the grammar, a rule that in transliteration is simply *a a,* specifies that the entity referred to as *a* throughout the grammar is to be pronounced [ə]. This rule was placed last in the grammar to permit simpler statements of grammatical phenomena than would have been possible if *a* had been treated earlier for its overt, or surface, manifestation [ə]. In this way Panini was dealing with the underlying patterns of Sanskrit rather than with its surface structure alone.

Because Panini's grammar came to be known a century and a half ago, it might have been expected to influence Western grammatical approaches earlier and more extensively than it did. But nineteenth-century linguists had many gaps to fill in the study of language. For one thing, their repertoire was limited. Only gradually did linguists come to know languages like those of the Americas, the Caucasus, and Africa, which differ considerably in their structures from Latin. And since the major concern of earlier grammarians was with dead languages, especially Latin,

Greek, and Hebrew, there was little knowledge of the sounds of language, or phonetics. Besides filling these gaps—assembling information from the study of numerous languages for subdisciplines of linguistics—linguists of the nineteenth century devoted much of their energy to the historical study of languages. In the course of their activities they contributed especially to the understanding of the background of languages. An important contribution to the understanding of language as a phenomenon came in 1916 with the posthumous publication of Ferdinand de Saussure's lecture notes.

---

## 3.2 Saussure's View of Language as a Structure Based on Oppositions

One of Saussure's major concerns was the demonstration that the surface structure may not permit an unambiguous identification of a sentence. Using the eight symbols [sižlaprã] to represent a French sentence, Saussure pointed out that there is no way of determining on the basis of the sounds alone, that is, from the surface structure, whether the sentence is [si-ž-la-prã] *si je la prends* 'if I take it' or [si-ž-l-aprã] *si je l'apprends* 'if I comprehend it.' In discussing such problems, Saussure made important theoretical observations about language, as on the necessity of distinguishing between the underlying structure (in his term **form**) of language and its surface structure (in his term **substance**). The underlying structure is based on oppositions, such as French *a : ā*.

In spite of his insights Saussure did not formulate a model of language. He did not even leave behind a handbook. What we have of his observations had been compiled from the lecture notes taken down by his students and published as the *Cours de linguistique générale*. Some of the further contributions made by Saussure to general linguistic theory are discussed in Chapter 16.

During the decades after 1916 Saussure's conception of language, as an abstract system underlying the varying speech forms of its users, was applied largely to the phonological component of language. Fleshing out this application to phonology required the major energies of linguists in the thirty years after the publication of Saussure's *Cours*. Little advance was made in the comprehension of the syntactic component of language until principles were applied to it that resembled those developed for the phonological component of language. Just as linguists proposed abstract constructs, called phonemes, for phonological entities, so they now proposed abstract constructs for morphological and syntactic entities. As we have noted, the actual sounds of a language may differ considerably from the proposed phoneme; in English [ʔ] is classed in the /t/ phoneme, as in pronunciation of the word *bottle,* although in "substance" it differs markedly from the [tʰ] in *top*. Similarly in syntax abstract constructs like NP VP are proposed as underlying units, although the speech material that makes up an NP may vary even more widely than do the allophones of English /t/.

Most linguists agree today that they must assume for language an underlying or deep component and a surface component that is a reflection of the underlying component. What the deep component may be and how to relate it to the surface component have been matters of extensive discussion. We may sketch briefly some contributions to our understanding made by two great linguists, the American Leonard Bloomfield and the Dane Louis Hjelmslev.

## 3.3  Linguistic Approaches of Bloomfield and Hjelmslev

Bloomfield, and linguists following him, was concerned primarily with exploring the implications of the relationship of **substance** versus **form** in phonology and secondarily with morphology and syntax. Semantics seemed outside the capabilities of scientific study in the 1940s and 1950s, for Bloomfield considered the description of meaning a goal of all sciences, not only linguistics. Useful statements about meaning might be made only as these sciences progressed. For example, it seemed futile for linguists to define *atom* unless physicists had learned enough to do so. Accordingly linguists concentrated on examining problems in phonology, such as the position in the underlying phonological system of the English substance manifestation [tš], as in *chip, pitch*. Linguists examined such a problem to determine whether one underlying form, one phoneme, was to be assumed, /č/, or two, /tš/.

In this concern the problem was strictly delimited. An answer was to be furnished by study of the phonological system of English with no appeal to the position of the entity in the syntactic system. Phonemes were held to be markers of syntactic relationships with no more intimate relationship to syntactic patterns. This conception, which originated in a tactical decision on Bloomfield's part, had a pervasive effect on the conception of language at the time. Language was conceived of as a series of independent levels, or strata. In dealing with a language, linguists determined the phonology with no regard for the syntax. Syntax and morphology were treated independently. Relationships between the two proposed levels could then be defined, in an intermediate area called **morphophonemics.** The aim of dealing independently with such strata and then to seek relationships between them has been maintained in **stratificational grammar.**

For many linguists following Bloomfield, attempts to comprehend meaning were tentative. It is not surprising, therefore, that in the 1940s and 1950s much of the effort of linguists went into **discovery procedures,** or attempts to seek out grammatical rules on the basis of collections of data. Among the most precise of these are Kenneth Pike's efforts in **tagmemics.** By this approach the position, or slot, filled or occupied by an element and the class of that element make up a unit known as a tagmeme. In this way special attention is given to the function of linguistic components. Articles and structural sketches presenting the data acquired with these procedures provided information on increasing numbers of languages, primarily on their phonology and morphology.

If linguists following Bloomfield applied their major energies to the compilation of data, Hjelmslev was almost exclusively concerned with theory. To emphasize his departure from other current linguistic concerns, he devised a new term for his approach, **glossematics.** The term was based on the Greek word for 'tongue' *glōssa,* as the term linguistics is derived from the Latin *lingua* 'tongue.'

For Hjelmslev the essential task of linguists was to devise an abstract system for understanding language, a calculus for language. In this task a linguist would concern himself with **semiotics,** the study of sign systems in general. Hjelmslev conceived of his own role in this concern as that of a formulator of the structure of the necessary calculus. Accordingly his publications are highly theoretical and composed in philosophical terminology that may readily be misinterpreted. In an introductory text only a few examples may be included.

Throughout language Hjelmslev assumed a distinction between **content** and **expression.** For example, in systems of traffic signals a red light on the plane of expression corresponds on the plane of content to 'stop.' Such a relationship is achieved through **commutation;** as red corresponds to 'stop,' so green has a commutative relationship with 'go.' The correspondences, however, are not one to one. Words and other linguistic signs can be broken up into components, such as phonemes, that have no parallel in the content system.

Using the principle that language consists of a plane of expression and a plane of content, a linguist explores the relationships in successive text, or in the linguistic system. The textual relationships are syntagmatic, that is, in horizontal or linear sequence; the systematic relationships are paradigmatic, that is, in vertical or columnar arrays. Hjelmslev examined and provided terms for many of the possible relationships. It is clear from his work that he assumed in language a series of levels or hierarchies. The content within one hierarchy might be the expression within a higher hierarchy. But he did not define these hierarchies precisely, nor did he devise a model of language.

Others concerning themselves with semiotic systems have also proposed only general guidelines for embracing communication systems. Many have followed Charles Sanders Peirce in stating that a semiotic system consists of three components: **syntactics,** the relationships between signs, for example, the relationship among red, yellow, and green in a traffic light system; **semantics,** the relationships between signs and the outside world, for example, red's denoting 'stop'; and **pragmatics,** the relationships between signs and behavior, for example, the prudent driver's stopping on a red signal. But only very recently have theories of language been constructed that permit explicit discussion of these and other relationships with reference to a comprehensive conception of language as a system of communication. The term **model** is often used for such comprehensive theories.

## 3.4  A Sketch of American Linguistics

Like other disciplines, the study of language in the nineteenth century was based on European academic work. Some Americans had concerned themselves with linguistic problems; for example, Thomas Jefferson encouraged the study of American Indian languages. But the first important American linguist, William Dwight Whitney (1827–1894), did not appear until around the middle of the century. Whitney wrote several books on language, notably *Language and the Study of Language* (1867). He was also an eminent Sanskrit scholar, producing a *Sanskrit Grammar* (1879), which is still the standard work on the subject. In addition, he was greatly concerned with practical applications of linguistics; he was the editor of the large Century dictionary, a work still unsurpassed in many respects. Whitney was also in close contact with European students of language and might well be considered a member of the community of Western linguists, rather than a distinctively American scholar.

American linguistics proper was in many respects inaugurated by Franz Boas (1858–1942), an anthropologist trained in Germany who spent his teaching career in this country. Boas undertook a revision of John W. Powell's *Introduction to the Study of Indian Languages,* and in the process he produced a *Handbook of American Indian Languages* (1911–1922), with a number of collaborators. Boas himself wrote the introduction, outlining in it the procedures used for the grammars of the individual languages. These dealt with phonetics, with meaning categories, and with the grammatical processes used to express these meanings. Boas's *Introduction*[1] as well as the work itself set American linguistics on a course of empiricism that it maintained until very recently.

One of the linguists who came to work with Boas was probably the most gifted student of language who developed in America, Edward Sapir (1884–1939). Also an anthropologist who dealt imaginatively with a great number of disciplines, Sapir was one of the pioneers in understanding the phonological structure of language. In several brilliant articles he demonstrated the need to deal with underlying phonological elements, or phonemes. He defined the phoneme as a psychological unit and in this way expressed views that generative grammarians find highly sympathetic. His sole book, *Language* (1921),[2] is devoted in large part to typology. While remarkable for its many insights and advances over previous

---

[1]Franz Boas, *Introduction to the Handbook of American Indian Languages* (1911; reprint ed., Washington, D.C.: Georgetown University Press, 1968).
[2]Edward Sapir, *Language: An Introduction to the Study of Speech* (New York: Harcourt Brace Jovanovich, 1955).

typologies, Sapir's approach to morphology and syntax is primarily concerned with surface structure. Not until recently has typology been directed at underlying structures, as illustrated above in discussions of OV and VO patterning.

Among Sapir's major contributions was his classification of the American Indian languages into six stocks. His articles, displaying insights into languages from a descriptive as well as a historical point of view, are among the most important in linguistics. They bear reading and rereading.

Yet in spite of his brilliance, Sapir was not the dominant influence on American linguistics in his day. This role fell to Leonard Bloomfield (1887–1949), who through his teaching and publications dominated American linguistics until long after his death. His book, *Language,* was regarded as the major theoretical work on the subject and is still important.

In *Language* Bloomfield frankly adopted a mechanistic approach to the study of language. In contrast with the psychological definition of the phoneme propounded by Sapir, Bloomfield's phoneme was a behavioral unit. Defined as a "bundle of distinctive features," it, like his other linguistic units, was based on *"materialistic* (or, better, *mechanistic*) theory."[3] Assuming the reality of a mind seemed to him only to obfuscate research.

With his mechanistic approach Bloomfield is often characterized as rejecting the study of meaning. Yet he stated clearly that "the study of speech-sounds without regard to meanings is an abstraction . . . the *meaning* of a linguistic form [is] the situation in which the speaker utters it and the response which it calls forth in the hearer." But he also held that "the meaning of a linguistic form [must be defined] in terms of some other science."[4] From his point of view, then, linguistics could not deal appropriately with meaning until other sciences had compiled the necessary "scientific knowledge." Until such knowledge had been compiled, linguists would do best to deal with the sounds and forms of language, from both a descriptive and a historical point of view.

In keeping with the views of Boas, Bloomfield treated the phonemes and morphemes of language in terms of the structure in which they were found. This approach, followed by the most articulate younger linguists in the 1940s and 1950s, came to be known as **structuralism.** Used as a pejorative term by many subsequent linguists, structuralism implies for them a limitation of concern to surface structures, largely of phonology and morphology, and a lack of attention to meaning. This view of structuralism seems mistaken, inasmuch as linguistics currently deals with language as an even more tightly related structure than did Bloomfield and his followers. Moreover, the treatment of phenomena as structures is

---

[3]Leonard Bloomfield, *Language* (New York: Holt, Rinehart and Winston, 1933), p. 33.
[4]*Ibid.,* pp. 139–140.

viewed favorably in such related disciplines as anthropology, where structuralism is anything but a term of opprobrium. Nonetheless, in many linguistic writings the terms structuralist and structuralism are applied unfavorably to Bloomfield and his followers, presumably because they are considered to have disadvantageously limited the study of language, as we have noted.

The limitation of concern among Bloomfield and his younger contemporaries was as much directed by the requirements of the period as by the theoretical approach. Young linguists were encouraged to describe the many Indian languages, most of them on the point of extinction. The resulting descriptions were scarcely carried beyond phonological and morphological analyses, partly because of lack of time. And during the early forties virtually all American linguists became involved in writing grammars of languages that were important because of the war: Japanese, Chinese, Russian, various forms of Arabic, and so on. Even the available earlier grammars of the major languages of Europe were unsuitable because they had been composed to give students a reading knowledge of German, French, Italian, Spanish, and so on. The need now arose for an oral command of these languages. This need accentuated the empirical tradition, and attention was given primarily to a mastery of the sounds necessary for oral competence and a mastery of the forms necessary to speaking and understanding simple sentences. Moreover, completion of the demanding tasks involved in learning and describing new languages left most linguists little time for concern with theoretical advances.

The major exception was Zellig Harris, a student of Sapir's. Harris applied the methods of structuralism to increasingly complex segments of language. In a series of articles,[5] Harris attempted to deal with morphological, syntactic, and discourse structure with the same rigor used in phonological analysis. His procedures are discussed in his book *Methods in Structural Linguistics*.[6] They led to a device and a term that has been prominent in subsequent linguistics, **transformation.**

Before examining transformational theory we may note briefly another widely used approach in the study of language, **tagmemics.** Developed by Kenneth Pike, tagmemics accords with much of Bloomfield's thought. Pike was primarily concerned with procedures for analyzing large numbers of hitherto unwritten languages. The chief theoretician in a large group that set out to translate the Bible into all languages, Pike devised methods whereby such languages could be learned and mastered by members of this group, the Wycliffe Bible Translators. For him the tagmeme is a slot-filler class. The class of elements before transitive verbs in English and the element-slot would be tagmemes, that is, the elements that may be used as subject. The same technique can be used for the utter-

---

[5]See, for example, Zellig Harris, "From Morpheme to Utterance," *Language* 22 (1946): 161–183; and also, "Discourse Analysis," *Language* 28 (1952): 1–30.

[6]Zellig Harris, *Methods in Structural Linguistics* (Chicago: Chicago University Press, 1955).

ances of any language. Using the principles of tagmemics, members of the Wycliffe Bible Translators have recorded and described languages in all parts of the world that had been virtually unknown previously. In this way they, and their procedures, have made inestimable contributions to linguistics. But tagmemics is essentially concerned with surface structures. Since the development of transformational grammars, however, some of the proponents of tagmemics have expanded the approach to deal with underlying structure. In spite of its restrictions, tagmemics continues to be a useful approach for the initial task of recording and analyzing hitherto unrecorded languages.

## 3.5 The Transformational Approach in Contrast with Previous Grammatical Approaches

Textbooks on language and grammars have treated sentences as individual units that must be analyzed for their parts or constituents. A sentence like *Anne ate the avocado* was divided into two parts: the subject *Anne* and the predicate *ate the avocado*. The predicate was then further divided into a verb *ate* and its object *the avocado*. Phrases like *the avocado* were in turn divided into the article and the noun. Dividing sentences in this way, through successive cuts, is a well-known procedure practiced in elementary schools as well as in higher institutions. It was the procedure applied by such linguists as Bloomfield in **immediate constituent** or **IC** analysis.

Zellig Harris concerned himself with a major problem in such analysis: the differing descriptions of sentences with the same meaning. For example, sentences like *Anne ate the avocado* and its passive *The avocado was eaten by Anne* have essentially the same meaning, yet by an IC analysis they receive different analyses and their parts are labeled differently. In the passive sentence, *the avocado* is labeled as the subject rather than as the object (which it was labeled in the active sentence), and *was eaten by Anne* is labeled as the predicate. The two sentences, which seem alike in meaning, are thus treated as different structures by grammarians and linguists.

Moreover, other apparent variants are also treated separately. For example, instead of saying *Anne ate the avocado,* a speaker might use the form *What Anne ate was the avocado* or *It was the avocado that Anne ate.* Rather than treat such sentences as independent of one another, it seems economical to treat them as variants of a basic sentence type.

Harris proposed such a procedure and used the term **kernel** for the simplest form, which is illustrated by *Anne ate the avocado.* In syntactic analysis, then, kernel sentences would be treated as the central concern, and variants, such as passive sentences, would be treated as derived from kernels with which they are equivalent.

The term that Harris used to express relationships between such sentences is **transformation,** a term borrowed from mathematics, where it means precisely 'relationship.' If one uses this procedure for dealing with sentences, syntactic analysis is greatly simplified. A central portion of the grammar can deal with the basic or kernel sentences of a language; a further portion will deal with derived sentences. The kernels can be described in a few rules. The derived sentences will be related to kernel sentences, and the differences will be stated.

Because of the resultant clarification of linguistic analysis, linguistic students, specialists in other areas, administrators, and the general public became greatly enthusiastic about transformational grammar. Textbooks were rewritten, incorporating transformations. And linguistics attracted great attention in the universities and in the general community.

Unfortunately, however, language is a tremendously complicated system. Much of the initial excitement waned, as teachers in the schools and others found transformations difficult to understand and as linguists came to have varying views of transformations and of the structure of language.

---

### 3.6  Transformational Grammars as Reflecting the Psychological Competence of Speakers

Harris, as we have observed, clarified the analysis of sentences by proposing that complex sentences are variants, or transforms, of simple or kernel sentences. He achieved this simplification by relating sentences of equivalent meaning, for example, active and passive variants. But his procedure focused on surface forms, as in *Anne ate the avocado*. Shifting attention to the fact that such sentences with equivalent meaning differ primarily because they are expressed in different surface forms, Harris's student, Noam Chomsky,[7] proposed that linguists should concentrate on the abstract structures underlying sentences. He asserted that the mind when handling language must deal with such patterns, rather than with the surface words and utterances that are pronounced.

Accordingly, in Chomsky's version of transformational grammar, the patterns for kernel sentences are expressed in formulas or rules. And the formulas used for producing complicated sentences are related to such simple rules by a different kind of rule. The basic rules are known as **phrase structure rules,** or simply **P-rules.** The different kind of rules indicating relationships between these P-rules and more complex formulas is known as **transformational rules,** or **T-rules.** Transformational grammar, which is based on this view of T-rules, has been most widely followed; it will, therefore, be briefly dealt with here and then discussed in greater depth in the course of the book.

---

[7]Noam Chomsky, *Aspects of the Theory of Syntax* (Cambridge, Mass.: M.I.T. Press), 1965.

The P-rules state the processes by which the simple abstract structures underlying utterances are generated. Thus in English the structure underlying utterances like *Anne ate the avocado* begins with a symbol for sentence, generally S. (Later in this book, the Greek Σ will be used to avoid confusion with S = subject.) This initial symbol is rewritten as NP VP by a P-rule:

1. S → NP VP

The single-shafted arrow is used in P-rules. This formula may be read: S is rewritten as NP VP; or, less commonly, sentence is rewritten as noun phrase verb phrase; or S goes to NP VP. Since in this way rules rewrite earlier patterns, they are called **rewrite rules.**

By a second rule the verb phrase is rewritten:

2. VP → V NP

By a third rule the noun phrase of the predicate is rewritten as Det (for determiner) and N (for noun):

3. NP → Det N

By a fourth rule the NP in rule 1 is also rewritten as N:

4. NP → N

With these four rules an enormous number of sentences can be generated for any English noun or verb, and any determiner (*the, that, this,* et cetera) can be put into the appropriate position. Consequently, a small number of P-rules suffices to generate the basic sentences of English, or of any language. Since P-rules are highly abstract and fundamental, they are said to belong to the **underlying** or **deep structure.**

Another segment of the deep structure is the **lexicon,** composed of words like *Anne, avocado, eat,* and *buy.* Lexical elements are assumed to be stored in the mind as complexes of semantic features, such as common (noun), human, and so on. Here for simplicity we may list them as words:

N: Anne, avocado
V: eat, buy
Det: the

With the P-rules they make up the **base** of a grammar. For this reason the P-rules are also called *base rules*. The abstract structures generated in the mind from the P-rules and the lexicon are known as *deep structures*.

It should be noted that both P-rules and lexical elements have meaning. The formula S → NP V NP obviously has a different meaning from S →

NP V inasmuch as it would generate such utterances as *Anne ate the avocado,* while S→ NP V would only generate such utterances as *Anne ate* and *Anne left.* By the standard theory of transformational grammar all of the meaning of an eventual utterance is contained in the deep structure.

The remainder of the syntactic component of the grammar simply rearranges elements or introduces functional elements characteristic of derived sentences, for example, *The avocado was eaten by Anne* or *What Anne ate was the avocado.* The rearrangements are carried out by transformational rules.

We can illustrate the format of T-rules by reviewing one proposal for generating passive structures. It must be remembered that T-rules operate on P-rules, or on structures known as **P-markers.** The term P-marker is used for a representation of abstract structures, which are usually given in tree form.

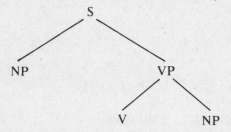

For purposes of simplicity we will omit here the output of rule 3. The P-marker above yields the formula S → NP V NP. On the basis of this formula utterances like *Anne ate meat* are generated.

If, however, the passive variant *Meat was eaten by Anne* is to be generated, a T-rule shifting the positions of the NP's and specifying functional markers like *was . . . en* and *by* would have to be used. This process is indicated by a T-rule, which specifies the change necessary in the P-marker underlying *Anne ate meat* in order to obtain the sentence's passive variant.

$$\text{SA} \quad \text{NP} \qquad\qquad \text{V} \qquad\qquad \text{NP}$$

$$1 \qquad\qquad 2 \qquad\qquad 3 \qquad \Rightarrow$$

$$\text{SC} \quad 3 \qquad 2 + \text{Aux} + \text{BE} + \text{D}_2 \quad by + 1$$

As this rule illustrates, T-rules consist of two parts. One is the **structural analysis (SA),** that is, the output of specific P-rules, also called the structural description (SD) or the structural index (SI). The operation to be performed on the SA is indicated by a segment given after a double-shafted arrow and labeled **SC** for **structural change.** The passive transformation involves shifting the position of categorial elements; numerals are used to mark the place of these in the original sequence as well as in the output.

In this way transformational rules produce the P-markers leading to such variants as those given above; they also yield surface structures in general. Transformational rules then are very complex. That given here for the passive is greatly simplified; it will be amplified later on. Moreover, linguists hold different views of both transformations as a whole and of specific structures. Even the relatively simple derivation of the passive has been contested, and no analysis is generally accepted. Yet in spite of such disputes, the general role of the transformational component in a transformational grammar is widely understood as relating P-markers to P-markers. The transformational component makes up the second part of a transformational grammar.

The outputs of T-rules are known as **surface structures.** These consist of such sequences as the third line of the T-rule given above accompanied by the lexical elements in question. Surface structures are still abstract elements and must be specified for the actual utterances. Surface syntactic structures are the final output of the syntactic component of the grammar.

The actual phonetic output is specified in the phonological component. Phonological rules indicate, for example, that the past tense form of *eat* is pronounced [eyt], or by many British speakers [et]. They also indicate that the abstract formula *eat* + Aux + BE + $D_2$ is pronounced [wəz iytən]. The phonological component, which is the third component of a transformational grammar, thus generates the actual utterance.

The material generated by these components in the standard form of generative syntactic grammar is purely linguistic. As noted above, it is meaningful. But the meaning may be regarded as descriptive, in the same way as are definitions in dictionaries and the explanations in grammars. Language, however, is used with reference to the outside world. Such specific references are indicated in the fourth component of a transformational grammar, the semantic component. By this component connections are pointed out between linguistic expressions like *avocado* and the actual fruit, between *eat* and the actual process, or between a sentence formula NP V NP and the meaning carried by a statement (as opposed, for example, to a question). The semantic rules are referred to as **projection rules.** The semantic component yields a semantic interpretation of the meaning intended by the speaker.

## 3.7  Generative Syntax: The Standard Theory

This model has been labeled the standard theory of transformational grammar. It may be represented as follows:

**Chart 1.   A Model of the Grammar of Language**
   Syntactic component

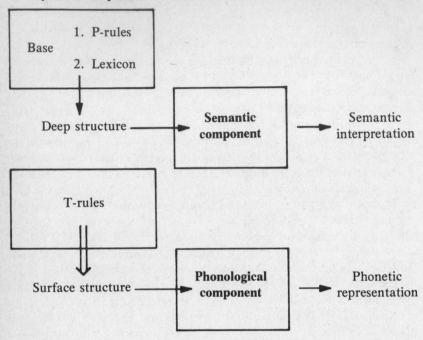

Since in this view the syntactic is the central component, in making any utterance a speaker would draw first on his or her control of it. Then a deep structure would be produced, leading to a surface structure, and finally a phonetic representation. The meaning would already be in the deep structure, and, therefore, a semantic interpretation would be made at this stage.

To illustrate, if somewhat crudely, this view of grammar, we may indicate the successive outputs in the generation of a speaker's report that the mother in the household had located the family's cat. In English the speaker might say *Mother saw the cat,* in Japanese *Haha ga neko o mita.*

|  | English | Japanese |
|---|---|---|
| Output of base: |  |  |
| Deep structure | NP    V  Past Definite | NP NP   NP  V   Past |
|  | *mother see* | *cat haha neko mi* |
| Output of T-rules: |  |  |
| Surface structure | *mother see* Past Det *cat* | *haha* subject marker |
|  |  | *neko* object marker |
|  |  | *mi* Past |
| Output of phonological rules: |  |  |
| Phonetic interpretation | [²məðər sɔ̀ ðə ³kǽt¹ #] | [haha ga neko o mita] |

The semantic interpretation will yield the same interpretation for the English and Japanese deep structures. Using the P-rules and available lexical features, the ultimate output could be produced in any language. Moreover, it could have various shapes in English, depending on the T-rules used subsequently; if the speaker applied the passive transformation, the phonetic output would be: *The cat was seen by mother*. Thus, a grammar constructed according to the generative syntax model envisages the generation of any given utterance.

## 3.8  Generative Semantics

In contrast with this generative syntactic approach, a group of linguists have pursued the view that language is a product of the mind. For them this implies that in producing a sentence the initial step is the formation of a concept or a series of concepts. The semantic component would, therefore, not be interpretive but be instead the initial component in the production of sentences. Since sentences are assumed to be in the first instance generated as semantic entities, the deep structure proposed by these linguists included the semantic component and is indeed labeled in this way. The approach is known as **generative semantics.**

The generative semantics model has an appearance of greater simplicity than the generative syntax model; but since the deep structure component combines both the base of generative syntax and its semantic component, the initial component of a generative semantic model is extremely complicated. Little has been done in applying generative semantic analysis to specific languages. Some scholars have even argued that generative semantics and generative syntax are merely notational variants of each other. Yet one approach in accordance with the generative semantic view has been fruitful, so-called **case grammar.**

Expounded largely by Charles J. Fillmore, it illustrates, on the one hand, the greater abstraction introduced in linguistic theory through the incorporation of semantics and, on the other hand, the greater generality sought in deep structures proposed for language.

In case grammar a sentence is generated from the constituents **modality** or **qualifier (Q)** and **proposition (Prop, P).** The Q constituent introduces such categorial elements as interrogation, negation, and volition. The P constituent introduces the categorial elements for the basic message conveyed in a sentence; it consists of a verb and various categories that resemble cases, such as **agentive (A,** animate actor); **instrumental (I,** inanimate mechanism involved in action); **locative (L,** place of action); **dative (D,** animate being affected by action); and **objective (O,** items affected by action).

The deep structure categories of the propositions underlying the following sentences would be as follows:

> *The chauffeur raised the car with a jack.*     A V O I
> *The jack raised the car.*     I V O
> *The car was raised by the chauffeur with a jack*     O V A I L
>     *on the parking lot.*
> *The chauffeur raised the car for the owner.*     A V O D

In case grammar, verbs fill the central role in the proposition. Lexical entries for verbs must specify the deep structure cases with which verbs may occur. For example, *raise* requires O, as in *The car was raised;* optionally, it may be accompanied by A I L D as well, as illustrated in the sentences above.

Moreover, various classes of verbs are proposed. For example, some English verbs, like *break,* may be transitive or intransitive, as in *The glass broke* and *June broke the glass.* For such verbs the transitive use is very similar to the causative of such languages as Japanese; that is, *June broke the glass* is really *June caused the glass to break.*

It may also be noted that by this approach the deep structure analysis of the two sentences given above would be the same. Whether expressed in the active as *Anne ate the avocado* or in the passive as *The avocado was eaten by Anne,* the nouns would have the same categorial marker: *Anne* in both utterances would be the agent, *avocado* the objective.

A case-grammar approach to language is useful in incorporating the insights concerning VO and OV languages. The base rules are unordered. Only in the subsequent, or transformational component, would either the VO or the OV order be specified for a given language.

In spite of these advantages, case grammar, like other transformational grammar, has been applied to the description of very few languages. The proponents of transformational grammar have been primarily concerned with developing a theory, rather than using that theory to provide deeper insights into the structure of specific languages. They have, however, carried out restricted investigations, determining, for example, constraints on elements and patterns. Fillmore, for example, has pointed out that verbs like *precede/follow, make into/make out of* are governed by similar constraints in the passives that may be formed of them, as in:

> *A Sunday follows every Saturday.*

and:

> *Every Saturday is followed by a Sunday.*
> *Every Sunday follows a Saturday.*

but not:

> *\*A Saturday is followed by every Sunday.*

Investigations of such constraints, which involve the study of quantifiers like *every, some,* and *any,* of adverbs like *personally,* and of qualifier categories are being widely pursued. But the difficulties met in producing grammars that will account for the many ways language is used by each speaker have led to pessimistic statements concerning our understanding of language and the capabilities of our grammars. Yet despite many unsolved problems, current linguistic theory has led to an understanding of many aspects of language.

## 3.9  Current Linguistic Interests

It is difficult to distinguish clearly the major interests of one's contemporaries at any time, but it may be said that linguists are currently less dogmatic about particular theories than they have been in recent years. Moreover, among many the major interest now focuses on the understanding of language rather than on any specific theory. If case grammar seems more appropriate than another approach for handling a specific problem, it may be applied. Linguists, to be sure, are still interested in attempting to determine which theory may be most illuminating, but arguments purporting to establish one theory over another arouse less fervor than they have in the past.

Transformational grammar has come under heavy attack for its focus on ideal language rather than on the varied language of society. The attack emanated in great part from sociolinguists. But sociolinguists have benefited in their researches from the advances made by the transformational approach. Moreover, they have attempted to deal with the multitude of data they have gathered with much the same rigor the transformationalists have applied to the study of linguistic theory.

Besides large-scale attention to the study of language in society, linguists are concerning themselves with all forms of communication. Among their major interests are the language of children; language disabilities; language typology, especially with reference to syntax; sign language and gestures accompanying speech; and the application of linguistics in overcoming social problems. In comparing the many activities of linguistics today with those of the past, one must note the huge increase in the number of linguists. Several decades ago there were no academic departments of linguistics. Linguists held positions in language or anthropology departments. Today linguistics is solidly established as a discipline. The wealth of publication and other linguistic activity indicates its recognition as one of the central behavioral sciences.

## BIBLIOGRAPHICAL NOTES

For an introduction to the stratificational approach to language see *Outline of Stratificational Grammar* by Sydney M. Lamb (Washington, D.C.: Georgetown University Press, 1966). For an introduction to the tagmemic approach see *Language in Relation to a Unified Theory of the Structure of Human Behavior,* 2d rev. ed., by Kenneth L. Pike (The Hague: Mouton, 1967). A sketch of the background of contemporary linguistic study may be found in *An Introduction to General Linguistics* by Francis P. Dinneen (New York: Holt, Rinehart and Winston, 1967).

Any student concerned with linguistic theory must master Ferdinand de Saussure's *Cours de linguistique générale,* first published in 1916, available in a translation by Wade Baskin, *Course in General Linguistics* (New York: Philosophical Library, 1959); and reissued as a paperback (New York: McGraw-Hill, 1966). Also important are *Language* by Leonard Bloomfield (New York: Holt, Rinehart and Winston, 1933); and *Prolegomena to a Theory of Language,* rev. ed., by Louis Hjelmslev, authorized translation by Francis J. Whitfield (Madison: University of Wisconsin Press, 1961). For an introduction to communication systems see *On Human Communication* by Colin Cherry (New York: Science Editions, 1961).

For Charles J. Fillmore's basic article on case grammar, "The Case for Case," see Emmon Bach and Robert T. Harms, eds., *Universals in Linguistic Theory* (New York: Holt, Rinehart and Winston, 1968). Further essays are to be found in journals, such as Fillmore's "Lexical Entries for Verbs," *Foundations of Language* 4 (1968): 373–393, and in reports, such as his "Subjects, Speakers and Roles," *Working Papers in Linguistics no. 4* (Columbus, Ohio: Computer and Information Science Research Center, Ohio State University, 1970), pp. 31–63.

For a highly literate treatment of problems in syntax and semantics see Dwight Bolinger's *Aspects of Language,* 2d ed. (New York: Harcourt Brace Jovanovich, 1975), especially Chapter 6, "Syntax" and Chapter 7, "Meaning."

## QUESTIONS FOR REVIEW

1. State some of the disadvantages of describing all languages by means of a framework based on Latin.
2. What are some of the differences between Panini's grammar of Sanskrit and traditional Latin grammars?
3. Define the terms *substance* and *form* as used by Saussure, providing also contemporary definitions for them.
4. How was the study of linguistics restricted in Bloomfield's day?
5. What is meant by *discovery procedures?*
6. Define *syntactics, semantics,* and *pragmatics* as they are used by some students of semiotics.
7. Describe briefly glossematics and tagmemics, noting the chief proponent of each.
8. Identify Whitney, Boas, Sapir, Bloomfield, Harris, and Pike.

9. In what respects does Chomsky's theory of language differ from that of Bloomfield and his students?
10. Distinguish between *generative syntax* and *generative semantics*.
11. What is meant by *case grammar?*


## EXERCISES

## EXERCISE 1

Provide a description of one of the following sentences, in accordance with the theory presented in this chapter, sections 4 and 5:

> 1. *The children laughed.*
> 2. *The men should walk.*
> 3. *His brother owned the book.*


## EXERCISE 2

The following are examples of three types of Sumerian sentences:

1. *lugal-e é mu-n-dú.*   'The king built the house.'
   *lugal* 'king'   *é* 'house'   *mu-* (finite verb indicator)
   *-n-* (agent indicator)
   *dú* 'built'

2. *é dingir-ak ba-dú.*   'The house of the god was built.'
   *é* 'house'   *dingir* 'god'   *ba-* (verb indicator)
   *-ak* (genitive suffix)   *-dú* 'built'

3. *dingir maḫ-am.*   'The god is illustrious.'
   *dingir* 'god'   *maḫ-* 'illustrious'
   *-am* (sentence indicator)

Distinguish between the three types and discuss the formal characteristics of each.


## EXERCISE 3

The following are Sumerian verb forms:

|  |  |
|---|---|
| *igarren* | I set |
| *igarre* | he sets |
| *igarrenden* | we set |
| *igarrene* | they set |

| | |
|---|---|
| *abgarren* | I set (caus) |
| *abgarre* | he sets (caus) |
| | |
| *immigarren* | I set thereon |
| *immigarre* | he sets thereon |
| | |
| *immibgarren* | I set thereon (caus) |
| | |
| *nugarren* | I do not set |
| *nugarre* | he does not set |
| *nugarrenden* | we do not set |
| *nugarrene* | they do not set |
| | |
| *nubgarren* | I do not set (caus) |
| *nubgarre* | he does not set (caus) |
| | |
| *nummigarren* | I do not set thereon |
| *nummigarre* | he does not set thereon |
| | |
| *nummibgarren* | I do not set thereon (caus) |

a. Determine the various morphemes and briefly describe their function.
b. Translate: *he sets thereon* (caus); *he does not set thereon* (caus).

# THE STUDY OF SPEECH SOUNDS:
## Articulatory Phonetics

CHAPTER 4

## 4.1 Three Types of Phonetics

The sounds of speech may be studied in three ways, for 1) their production by the speech organs, or their **articulation;** 2) the physical effects of this production, or their **acoustic** make-up; and 3) the results of these effects when they reach the ear, or the **auditory** interpretation.

Study of the production, or articulation, of speech sounds is known as **articulatory phonetics.** Study of the physical effects on the surrounding air is known as **acoustic phonetics.** Study of the results of these effects on the ear, the nerves leading to the brain, and the perception in the brain is known as **auditory phonetics.**

Until recently most work in phonetics dealt almost exclusively with the articulation of sounds. The reasons for this concentration on articulatory phonetics may be readily perceived. We can easily observe how most sounds are produced. For example, an [f] as in *fat* is obviously made by the lower lip being brought up against the upper teeth. Instruments for measuring the resulting sound, however, are intricate and costly, and adequate measuring devices have become available only recently. Accordingly acoustic phonetics is a relatively new discipline. If studies in acoustic phonetics have been carried out less widely than studies of articulation, auditory analyses have been virtually nonexistent. Until very recently those that were attempted depended largely on the sampling of the reactions of individuals or groups to sounds. Such reactions vary considerably. Moreover, they are related to random entities of language. In experiments one may find that speakers of English associate [i] as in *little* with smallness, [a] as in *pot* with largeness, but the associations do not apply to *big* or to *small*. Such experiments, therefore, tell us something about the reactions of English speakers rather than about the perception of sounds. Recent research on the functioning of the brain with regard to language has yielded impressive results, as on the interpretation of speech sequences. Some of these results will be presented in Chapter 13.

Since the techniques for auditory analysis and the instruments necessary to investigate sounds acoustically were developed only recently, articulatory phonetics has been by far the most prominent approach to the study of speech sounds.

The terminology describing speech sounds is also taken largely from articulatory phonetics. The [f] of *fat,* for example, articulated at the lower lip and upper teeth through a friction-producing slit, is called a **labiodental fricative.** Because articulatory phonetics has provided most of the terms for the study of sounds and also because it has been most prominent in linguistics, it is discussed first here.

## 4.2  Articulatory Phonetics

An understanding of articulatory phonetics requires at least rudimentary knowledge of the vocal organs (see Charts 1 and 2). The discussion here is highly compact, and the charts are highly stylized. A fuller understanding may be achieved from study of the works listed at the end of the chapter dealing specifically with phonetics, from study of models of the vocal organs, from motion pictures of the vocal organs in action, and from investigation of one's own articulation of the various sounds.

In discussing the sounds of languages we may treat separately the functioning of the speech organs below the larynx and those above the larynx.

The most important of the subglottal organs, the chest cavity, is controlled by the rib muscles, the diaphragm, and the abdominal muscles. It affects the timing of speech and the intensity and pitch with which individual sequences are articulated. These effects will be presented in some detail after a description of the consonants and vowels.

The speech organs, beginning with the larynx, the throat (or pharynx), the mouth, and the nose, are those primarily involved in producing the sounds that we segment into consonants and vowels. For studying the articulation of these sounds it is helpful to view the vocal organs as a tube-like passageway.

## Chart 1. The Vocal Organs

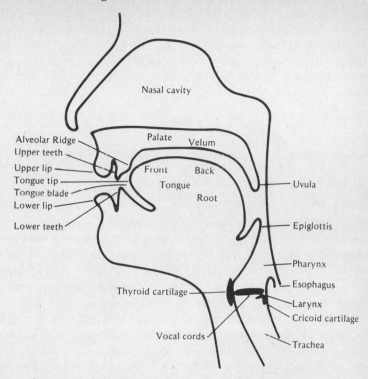

Nasal cavity

Alveolar Ridge
Upper teeth

Palate
Velum

Upper lip
Tongue tip
Tongue blade
Lower lip

Front
Back

Tongue

Root

Uvula

Lower teeth

Epiglottis

Pharynx

Esophagus

Thyroid cartilage

Larynx

Cricoid cartilage

Vocal cords

Trachea

To understand the use of the organs in speaking, it is important to note that for all of them speech is an overlaid function. Each of the vocal organs has primary functions that are fairly obvious: the lungs are used to provide oxygen to the bloodstream; the vocal cords may close the passageway to the lungs and permit strenuous action; and the teeth and tongue are used for the mastication of food. In the contemporary world, where physical activity is at a minimum and food is often ingested rapidly, the primacy of these functions may not be as apparent as they were when man flourished in a less pallid existence. But even for modern man, speech is interrupted when he undertakes a heavy exertion, like lifting, or when he reverts to unmasticated food. Both observations may be checked: to make a simple test, you may try to lift a heavy desk or a light car while speaking, or you may attempt to phonate after a bit of pizza. In the study of language, more important than these observations are the effects on language that are determined by the overlaid roles of these organs.

All human beings breathe and chew in roughly the same way. But we learn speech sounds in a given community and make them in accordance with the sounds of our associates. For example, an English speaker's [t], as in *tone,* differs slightly from a German's, as in *Ton,* or a Spaniard's, as in *ton.*

Moreover, we apparently need constant practice to maintain the accuracy required in our secondary activity of speaking; deafened speakers, for example, often lose the control over speech sounds that they acquired when they could continually test their sounds against those of their fellow speakers. In this way both our tenuous control over speech sounds and our need to learn the specific sounds used in the language that we acquire reflect the overlaid character of speech.

## 4.3   The Subglottal Organs Used in Speaking

The vocal organs below the larynx consist of the lungs with their outlets, the bronchial tubes, which merge in the trachea. The lungs serve as containers of air. They are themselves inert but are alternately filled with air or emptied as the chest cavity is expanded by the action of the diaphragm, or they are permitted to contract when the diaphragm relaxes. When the diaphragm expands the rib case, air enters the lungs because the pressure outside the chest cavity is greater than the pressure inside.

The expansion of the diaphragm, the time in which muscular effort is needed for inhalation, takes approximately half as much time as that used for exhalation. Using the stream of air that is exhaled as our chest walls push on the lungs, we have available periods of relaxation consisting of approximately 2.5 seconds for every breath. In ordinary speech stressed vowels take up .10 to .15 seconds, consonants far less time. We can therefore readily produce a sequence like *How are you this morning?* in less than 2.5 seconds.

The primary role of the lungs in producing speech, therefore, is to supply outgoing air for speaking. As we will note later, the lungs provide this supply with delicate variation in force and in timing.

### 4.3.1   The Larynx

The **larynx** is an organ at the top of the trachea, formed of cartilages and muscles. Of these, two muscular membranes make up the **vocal cords.**

The vocal cords, also called **bands, folds,** or **lips,** are one of the most important organs of speech. They are contained in a structure of cartilages: the **cricoid,** a ring-shaped cartilage at the base; the **thyroid,** two shieldlike cartilages at the sides (these have their apex at the front and may readily be felt—in some speakers they are very prominent, forming the Adam's apple); and the **arytenoid,** two pyramidal cartilages at the back of the cricoid that may be delicately manipulated. Attached to the arytenoid cartilages are the vocal cords. Because of the possibilities of delicate manipulation, the vocal cords can be brought together with great precision.

**Chart 2. The Vocal Cords from Above**

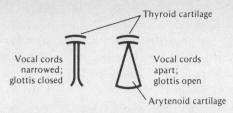

The vocal cords themselves are muscles, covered with mucous membranes, that may be brought together tightly, opened slightly, or moved relatively far apart. When brought tightly together, they produce a **glottal stop**, [ʔ], as in *mʔm* 'no' as opposed to *mhm* 'yes.'

The space between the vocal cords is called the **glottis**. In breathing and for sounds like [f θ s š p t k] the glottis is **open;** air then passes through it without friction or without producing **voice**. The sounds produced when the glottis is open are said to be **voiceless.**

When the vocal cords are brought together, so that air passing between them causes them to vibrate, the glottis is said to be closed, and the resulting sounds are voiced. Sounds like [v ð z ž b d g] are voiced, as are the resonants—for example, [m n ŋ w y l r]—and all the vowels.

To examine the difference between voiceless and voiced sounds one can produce sequences like [szszsz] or [fvfvfv]. If you feel your Adam's apple when pronouncing such sequences, you will note the vibration whenever you produce a [z] or a [v]. You can also put your hands over your ears, and when you pronounce the voiced sounds the accompanying vibration will be highly noticeable. All voiced sounds are accompanied by such vibration.

Summarizing, we may note four important positions of the vocal cords in the articulation of vowels and consonants:

1. Tightly closed for a glottal stop [ʔ].
2. Closed but permitting vibration, or voice.
3. Slightly open, so that friction is produced as air passes through, as in [h].
4. Completely open, with no effect on the airstream, as in voiceless sounds.

In a fifth widespread use, for the **whisper,** the fleshy parts of the vocal cords are closed tightly, but air is permitted to pass between the relatively harder sections, producing for normally voiced sounds the rasping effect characteristic in whispering.

Besides these important uses of the vocal cords, the cords also provide the fundamental tone of the speaker. This tone is determined by the same characteristics as any tone produced by a stringed instrument: the length, consistency, and tautness of the vocal cords. Vocal cords of males are about twenty-three millimeters long, those of females about seventeen millimeters long. Normally males produce a fundamental tone in the range of 109 to 163 cycles per second (cps), or Hz (hertz), the currently favored term; females in the range 218 to 326 Hz. But the vocal cords permit a range from 42 to 2,048 Hz.

As we will note in further detail, the fundamental tone is varied in speech, as in the intonation patterns of English sentences. A typical English sentence spoken by a male *How are you this morning?* may begin on a fundamental tone of 100 Hz, rise to 128 Hz, and then drop to 80 Hz.

Variation in the fundamental tone also gives color to speech; speech with little variation seems flat and monotonous. Such characteristics inform us about speakers in somewhat the same way as their habits of dress; in linguistic study concern with either aspect would contribute only secondary information.

In some languages tone is used as a marker to distinguish morphemes. In Japanese, for example, a variation __ ‾ used with the consonant vowel sequence *hashi* gives the meaning 'bridge,' whereas ‾ __ is used with *hashi* 'chopsticks.'

The use of the vocal cords to produce the fundamental tone of speech plus variations of tone that are significant, in addition to their use in the production of consonants and vowels, results from highly complex action. Even slow-motion films of the vocal cords in action leave many problems in our understanding of their functioning. Moreover, as careful analysis of speech will demonstrate, the vocal cords are used to produce extremely fine variations in sounds with highly delicate timing. In American English, for example, voicing is not begun immediately in initial sounds like *b* in *bad*. Similarly it is not maintained throughout such consonants when they occur finally, as in *gab*. Moreover, we may produce voiceless vowels, as often in the first syllable of *potato*. In other languages too these uses may be found: *i* and *u* are often voiceless in Japanese, especially between voiceless consonants as in the first syllables of *hitotsu* 'one' and *futatsu* 'two.' Other delicate manipulations may be employed: in Russian initial voiced stops are voiced throughout. The wide variation of use of the glottal cords leads to great differences in the details of glottal articulation from language to language.

---

## 4.4  The Supraglottal Organs Used in Speaking

The supraglottal organs of speech may be studied with reference to three cavities: the pharynx, the nose, and the mouth. Of these the mouth is by far the most important, for it can be varied considerably to produce a great number of sounds.

The **pharynx,** or throat, is a tube-shaped channel above the juncture of the trachea and the esophagus, leading to the nasal and oral cavities. At the base a cartilaginous structure, the **epiglottis,** provides a protective cover for the trachea. Some sounds may be produced by the pharynx, such as the pharyngeal consonants of Semitic languages. In addition the pharynx acts as a resonating organ.

The **nasal cavities** are passages of bone, lined with mucous membrane. They are immovable, and therefore the nose is used only as a resonating body. Access to it is governed by the **uvula,** the fleshy appendage of the roof of the mouth. When the uvula is raised, access to the nose is closed off, and we speak of a **velic closure.** When the uvula is lowered, air may pass through the nose, and nasal consonants or vowels will be produced. Examples of nasal consonants are [m n ŋ]. They correspond in articulation to [b d g] but in addition are articulated with the **velum,** or soft palate, open.

When the uvula is lowered in the production of vowels, air escapes through both the nose and the mouth. Some languages, for example, Winnebago, have a full set of nasal vowels. Others, like French, have only a few, for example [ɛ̃] as in *fin* [fɛ̃] 'end' as opposed to [ɛ] in *fait* [fɛ] 'fact'; [ã] as in *grand* [grã] 'large' as opposed to *gras* [gra] 'fat.' In still other languages, for example, English, there are no vowels distinguished by nasalization.

The **mouth** is the cavity in which most of the consonants and the vowels are characteristically formed. Consonants and vowels differ from one another essentially because of the shape of the cavity in which they are articulated. That shape is determined by various degrees of narrowing or by closure at some point. In describing consonants and vowels, therefore, we must indicate the **manner** of articulating them, and the **point,** or **place,** at which the characteristic articulation is carried out. In describing any speech sound therefore, besides noting the use of the vocal cords, we must state the **place of articulation** and the **manner of articulation** and for some the velic action.

To assist in the description of speech sounds, the mouth is labeled for **place of articulation** in accordance with its structure. These labels are complemented by those for the tongue. Bounded in the rear by the throat, on the sides by the inner walls of the cheeks, and in the front by the lips, the shape of the mouth cavity is varied by the action of the tongue.

The **tongue** is a highly flexible organ, consisting of numerous muscles, almost any part of which can be moved. Parts of the tongue are labeled by the organs opposite them. The part opposite the walls of the throat is known as the **root;** that opposite the velum as the **back,** or **dorsum;** that opposite the palate as the **front;** and that opposite the teeth as the **blade.** The tip of the tongue is also known as the **apex.** Correspondingly, we speak of **faucal, dorsal, frontal,** and **apical** sounds. The tip may also be raised and pointed toward the back of the mouth; we speak then of **retroflex** articulation.

Possibly because of the difficulty of defining the articulatory involvement of such a flexible organ, the place of articulation is generally specified by the fixed organs opposite which the tongue is used for articulation. We have already noted that the back of the roof of the mouth ends in the **uvula,** a fleshy organ that can be trilled, as in one articulation of the French uvular [ʀ]. Approximately 1.5 inches of the roof of the mouth from the uvula toward the lips do not cover an underlying bone; this section of the roof of the mouth is known as the **velum.** The 1.5 inches in front of the velum, with a bone as its base, are known as the **palate.** The part of the roof of the mouth that contains the roots of the teeth is known as the **alveolar arch,** or **alveolar ridge.** We speak then of **uvular, velar, palatal,** and **alveolar** articulation. If an intermediate position is used, we apply compound labels, as in **alveopalatal,** for example.

You may determine the extent of the alveolar ridge by putting your finger into your mouth and noting the ridge made by the roots of the front teeth. By extending your finger farther into your mouth you can locate the extent of the hard, bony roof or palate, as well as the back, fleshy part or velum. A small mirror will assist you in identifying these and other characteristic vocal organs. When the tongue is brought against the teeth, we speak of **dental** articulation; when the outgoing air is forced between the tongue and the teeth, we speak of **interdental** articulation.

The sounds articulated with the lips may be characterized by a narrowing or closure between the lips (usually the lower) and the teeth (usually the upper) or between the lips themselves. We speak then of **labiodental** and **bilabial** articulation. The lips may also be rounded, or spread, especially in the production of vowels. English [uw] as in *ooze* is accompanied by rounding; English [iy] as in *ease* is accompanied by spread lip position.

At any of the places identified, the **manner of articulation** may vary. Sounds produced with a complete closure are called **stops.** Bilabial stops are produced with closure of both lips, as in English [p b] of *pan, ban.* The closure may be made between the tip of the tongue and the alveolar ridge, as in English [t d] of *tan, Dan.* The closure may also be made between the front of the tongue and the palate, as in English [k g] of *keel, gear,* or between the back of the tongue and the velum as in English [k g] of *cool, gore.*

Stops are generally made on the outgoing stream of air. Some languages, however, have sounds involving ingressive airstream at the lips and accordingly are implosive. Such sounds are known as **clicks.** They are found in languages of southern Africa, such as Xhosa. Some clicks are used by English speakers as signals, such as the dental *tsk tsk* for expressing disapproval.

If the organs are only approximately 90 percent closed, friction is produced, and the resulting sounds are called **fricatives.** Two subclasses may

**Chart 3. Articulation of Stops**

Bilabial stop
/p/ or /b/

Alveolar stop
/t/ or /d/

Velar stop
/k/ or /g/

be distinguished by the kind of opening. If it is relatively wide we speak of a **slit fricative,** such as the labiodental [f v] in English *fear, veer;* interdental [θ ð] in *thin, then;* palatal [ç j] in German *ich* 'I,' and in dialect German *siegen* 'win'; and velar [x γ] in German *ach* 'alas,' and in dialect German *Wagen* 'wagon.' If the opening is small, permitting the onrush of air through a trough, we speak of **groove fricatives.** The opening may be made over the tip of the tongue, with onrushing air producing a hissing noise against the teeth, [s z], as in English *sip, zip.* A groove fricative may be made at the front of the tongue, with the hissing noise produced against the palate, [š ž], as in English *rush, rouge.* Groove fricatives are often called **sibilants.** The term **spirant** is variously used and accordingly must be noted with caution. For some writers spirant is equivalent to fricative; others use it only for the groove fricatives.

One further set of consonants consists of a stop with homorganic fricative, that is, stops and fricatives produced with the same articulatory organs. These are called **affricates.** Affricates may be produced at any of the points of articulation: at the lips, [p͡f], as in German *Pfad* 'path'; at the alveolar area, [ts], as in German *Zeit* 'time'; at the palatal area, [t͡š] or [č], as in English *church,* and voiced [d͡ẑ] or [j], as in English *judge;* and at the velar area, [k͡x], as in Alemannic German [kxu] 'cow.'

Because stops and fricatives are characterized by articulation involving an obstruction, they may be referred to by the general label **obstruent.** Consonants other than the obstruents are characterized by sonant qualities rather than by obstruent articulation. In producing the **resonants,** or **sonants,** the articulatory passages have relatively wide openings. We can classify the resonants into four groups: nasals, laterals, trills and flaps, and semivowels, or glides.

The **nasals** are articulated with oral obstruction at some point, but the uvula is lowered. Accordingly resonance is produced in the nasal cavity. Nasals are generally voiced, and so they correspond to oral stops accompanied by nasal resonance: bilabial [m] to [b]; dental or alveolar [n] to [d]; palatal [ɲ] to [ɟ]; and velar [ŋ] to [g]. They may however be voiceless, even in rapid English utterances like *rush 'em;* then they are transcribed with the usual diacritic for voicelessness, ̥ , for example, [rəšm̥]. Icelandic has voiceless nasals, as in *hnifur* 'knife.'

The **laterals** are produced with oral obstruction at some point, but an opening is made to the side of the obstruction. The obstruction is generally made with the tip of the tongue, and the air is permitted to pass to the right or the left of it or to both sides. Lateral resonance varies in accordance with the shape that the tongue takes. If the front of the tongue is raised, a *clear l* results, as in English *leer;* if the back is raised, a *dark l* results, as in many varieties of English *rule.* A dark, or back, [l] may be marked with a cross wavy line, as in Polish [ł]. While generally voiced, laterals may be voiceless, as in Icelandic *hlé* [ļe·] 'lee' and Welsh *ll,* as in *Llewelyn.* The French /l/ may also have a voiceless variant, as in *peuple.*

The English treatment of Welsh voiceless [ļ] illustrates how foreign sounds are often interpreted in accordance with one's native sound system. When initial, [ļ] struck English ears as beginning with a voiceless fricative. Thus the name *Llewelyn* was heard as *Fluellen*. This form of the name is used for one of the soldiers in Shakespeare's play *King Henry V*. Similarly, the name *Floyd* is based on the spoken form of *Lloyd*. (Forms of these names with initial [l] in English are, on the other hand, based on spelling pronunciations.) In this way the names of places as well as people are often modified, so that the foreign sounds are replaced by one or more native sounds.

In producing resonants, the oral passage may be closed rapidly by a vibrating organ: the uvula or the apex of the tongue. If there is a single closure, we speak of a **flap**; if repeated closures, a **trill**. For a uvular trill or flap [R] is used, as for French *ratte* [Rat] 'rat'; for an alveolar or dental trill [r]. To distinguish a flap from a trill, the diacritic [ ˇ ] is used for flaps. Often, as in some varieties of English, *r* sounds are not trilled, or even flapped, but the tongue is raised to produce slight friction. When it is desirable to specify trills, the diacritic [ - ] is used. The *r* sound may also be voiceless, as in Icelandic *hrafn* [r̥avn] 'raven.' The French *r* may have a voiceless variant, as in *quatre* 'four.'

The resonants produced by the largest degree of opening are the **semivowels,** also called **glides.** They are articulated with relatively complete closure but with an opening movement of the organs concerned. For example, [y], as in English *yet,* begins with the tongue close to the palate, in the position for [i], and continues with the tongue moved downward rapidly. The articulation of [w] is generally compound, involving the velar area and the lips, and begins with the tongue close to the velum, in the position for [u], with rounded lips, continuing with the tongue moved downward rapidly and the lips spreading. Semivowels may be voiceless, as in the pronunciation of *what* and *when* in many varieties of English.

---

## 4.5  The Consonants

The obstruents and resonants are summarized in Chart 4, which in general follows the recommendations of the International Phonetic Association (IPA). When voiceless and voiced obstruent pairs are given for a point and manner of articulation, the symbol for the voiceless consonant is always given first. Further diacritics can be added if necessary, either from those suggested by the IPA or those devised individually. This chart includes symbols not discussed above. They are used for indicating more precise analyses of English sounds and for languages with additional sounds.

**Chart 4. Consonant Symbols**

|  |  | Bilabial | Labio-dental | Dental and Alveolar | Palatal | Velar | Uvular | Pharyn-geal | Glottal |
|---|---|---|---|---|---|---|---|---|---|
| Obstruents | Stops | p  b |  | t  d | c  ɟ | k  g | q  G |  | ʔ |
|  | *Fricatives:* |  |  |  |  |  |  |  |  |
|  | Slit | ɸ  β | f  v | θ  ð | ç | x  ɣ | χ  ʁ | ħ  ʕ | h  ɦ |
|  | Groove |  |  | s  z | š  ž |  |  |  |  |
|  | Affricates |  | p̂f | t̂s | č  ǰ | k̂x |  |  |  |
|  | Nasals | m | ɱ | n | ɲ | ŋ | N |  |  |
|  | Laterals |  |  | l | ʎ | ɫ |  |  |  |
| Resonants or Sonants | Trills and flaps |  |  | r |  |  | ʀ |  |  |
|  | Semivowels, or glides | w | ʋ |  | y | (w) |  |  |  |

Diacritics: Aspirated ʰ or ˈ, for example, pʰ, pˈ. Unaspirated =, for example, p̿. Dental articulation ͟, for example, p̳. Retroflexion ˖, for example, ṭ. Palatalization ˬ, for example, t̮, d̮. Velarization ~, for example, ɫ. Ejectives ˧, for example, ṭ. Implosives ˆ, for example, pˈ. Implosives ⌣, for example, ɓd. Voiceless sounds ₒ, for example, l̥. Voiced sounds ˬ, for example, ṭ. Syllabic resonants ˌ, for example, ṇ.

The characteristic consonants of English are listed in the following chart:

**Chart 5. English Consonants**

| Obstruents | | Labial | Alveolar | Palatal | Velar |
|---|---|---|---|---|---|
| Stops and Affricates | Voiceless | p | t | č | k |
| | Voiced | b | d | ǰ | g |
| Fricatives | Voiceless | f | θ | s | š | h |
| | Voiced | v | ð | z | ž |
| Resonants | | | | | |
| Nasals | | m | n | | ŋ |
| Glides | | w | | r l y | |

## 4.6 **The Vowels**

If the articulation of the consonants is characterized by closure, that of the vowels is characterized by a relatively open position of the vocal tract. Yet despite the classification of vocal sounds into two large groups, there is no absolute distinction between consonants and vowels, as the semivowels may indicate. Semivowels begin with relatively complete closure, as consonants, and end with a larger opening, as vowels.

In the articulation of vowels the glottal tone is modified by resonating chambers formed primarily in the mouth but also in the pharynx and nose. These cavities are highly complex, and accordingly the articulation of the vowels can be presented here with only moderate precision.

### 4.6.1  Position of the Tongue

We may speak of two basic cavities, determined by the position of the tongue and the position of the lips and producing different resonance effects in the articulation of vowels.

The front cavity is before the highest part of the tongue; the back cavity is behind it. The position of the tongue, whether raised in the front, the central, or the back part of the mouth, is basic to a discussion of the vowels. From the position of the tongue's highest point, we speak of **front, central,** and **back** vowels (see Chart 6).

The shape of the vowel cavities is also determined by the degree of opening. If the tongue is as far as possible from the roof of the mouth, we speak of a **low** or **open** vowel. If it is as close as possible to the roof of the mouth, without setting up friction or producing a stop, we speak of a **high** or **close** vowel. If it is between close and open position, we speak of **mid** vowels. Other intermediate positions may be specified: **half-open** and **half-close.** We may accordingly represent the simple vowels of English by means of a

**Chart 6. English Vowels**

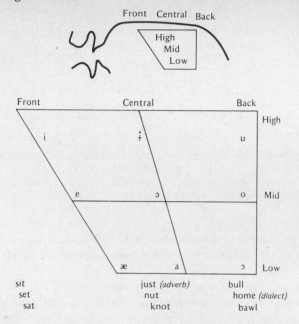

|        |  sit  |      | just *(adverb)* |     | bull          |
|--------|-------|------|-----------------|-----|---------------|
|        |  set  |      |     nut         |     | home *(dialect)* |
|        |  sat  |      |     knot        |     | bawl          |

grid (see Chart 6) with three front-back dimensions and three open-close dimensions.

### 4.6.2 Position of the Lips

The lips may be spread, pursed or rounded, or neutral. Since the rounded position has the greatest articulatory effect, we speak of **rounded** or **unrounded** vowels. Back vowels are typically rounded, for example, English [u] in *cool;* front vowels are unrounded, for example, English [i] in *keel;* and central and low vowels tend to have neutral lip position. Yet front, central, or back vowels may be either rounded or unrounded. Japanese *u,* for example, is relatively unrounded, as in *kuru* 'come.' Two dots over a vowel symbol may be used to specify front rounded vowels, as in German *München* 'Munich' and *Mönch* 'monk.' or as indicated in Chart 7, special symbols may be used.

### 4.6.3 Chart of the Vowels

In summary the vowels are listed in Chart 7, which in general follows the recommendations of the IPA. The symbols for unrounded vowels precede those for rounded vowels.

### 4.6.4 Diphthongs

For the articulation of vowels it is assumed that the vocal organs are maintained relatively steady. But vocalic segments may also be characterized by

**Chart 7. Vowel Symbols**

| | Front | | Central | | Back | |
|---|---|---|---|---|---|---|
| | u | r | u | r | u | r |
| Close | i | ü/y | ɨ | ʉ | ɯ | u |
| Half-Close | ɪ | Y | - | - | - | ʊ |
| Mid | e | ö/ø | ė | ȯ | ɣ | o |
| Half-Open | ɛ | ɔ̈/œ | ə | ɔ̇ | ʌ | ɔ |
| Open | æ | —— | a | ɐ | ɑ | ɒ |

Diacritics: Nasality ˜, for example, ẽ, Voicelessness ₒ , for example, l̩ . Length :, for example, i:. Half length ·, for example, i·.

motion from one position to another. When they are, the beginning and end points of the motion are specified, and we speak of **diphthongs** (see Chart 8).

The motion may be toward greater closure, as in English *I* [ay], and these we refer to as **falling diphthongs.** Or the motion may be toward greater opening, and we speak of **rising diphthongs,** as in French *bien* [byɛ̃] 'well.'

Although various conventions are used from language to language, in recent texts the closer portion of the diphthong has been indicated by a consonantal symbol: [y] if the diphthong moves to a front position, as in *I* [ay], *boy* [ɔy]; [w] if it moves to a back position, as in *cow* [kaw], *so* [sow]; and [h] if it moves to a central position, as in English *r*-less dialects, *dear* [dih]. Some texts indicate these three positions with [i u ə].

## 4.7 Secondary Articulation of Vowels and Consonants: Coarticulation

The position of the tongue and that of the lips are the primary articulatory characteristics in the production of vowels. Primary articulation may, however, be accompanied by involvement of other vocal organs.

Lowering of the velum adds the resonance known as **nasalization** to that of the oral cavities. French has four nasal vowels, ĩ æ̃ ã ɔ̃. In Winnebago the set of nasal vowels is as large as that of the oral vowels (see Figure 1).

**Figure 1**

## Chart 8. English Diphthongs

Diphthongs with Final Front Component

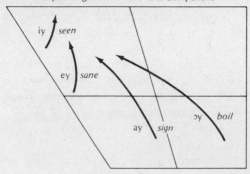

Diphthongs with Final Mid Component
(r-less dialects)

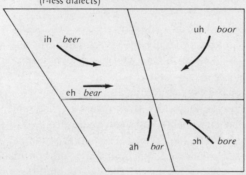

Diphthongs with Final Back Component

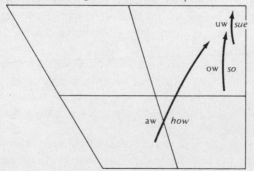

Other types of secondary articulation may be found for consonants as well as vowels. Either group may be articulated with relatively **tense** as opposed to **lax** musculature. Tenseness is often related to length; the [tt] in Japanese *katta* 'bought' is articulated tensely as opposed to [t] in *kata* 'form.' For some linguists tenseness is one of the characteristic features of the English vowel system, forming one of the distinctive criteria of *beat* as opposed to *bit; bait* as opposed to *bet;* and so on.

If, on the other hand, the dominant feature seems to be duration, a distinction may be made between long vowels, as in German *i: e: a: o: u: ü: ö:* versus *i e a o u ü ö.* In German, too, the long vowels are more tensely articulated than the short vowels. In other types of secondary articulation one articulatory position may be favored in a language to distinguish a large subclass of sounds.

In **aspiration** consonants are produced with accompanying *h*-like friction. Aspiration distinguishes the $[p^h]$ of *pa* from the $[p^=]$ of *spa,* the $[t^h]$ of *tie* from the $[t^=]$ of *sty,* and the $[k^h]$ of *cool* from the $[k^=]$ of *school.* It may also be used as a characteristic of classes of sounds, as in Indo-Aryan languages and Chinese.

In **labialization** consonants and vowels are produced by simultaneous articulation of the lips, generally by lip rounding but also by protrusion. African languages like Kpelle and Twi have such secondary articulation.

In **retroflexion** consonants and vowels are produced by a curling back of the tip of the tongue toward the palate, as in many languages of India. English [r] may be pronounced with retroflex articulation.

In **palatalization** consonants and vowels are produced by simultaneous narrowing at the front of the mouth. Russian, for example, has a virtually complete series of palatalized and nonpalatalized consonants, as in *brat̜* 'take' as opposed to *brat* 'brother.' Palatalization has been very prominent in the Indo-European languages, especially those of the East, but also in Celtic. It has also left effects in others, such as English; forms like *church* (compare Scottish *kirk*) reflect palatalization in Old English.

In **velarization** consonants and vowels are produced by simultaneous narrowing of the back of the mouth. Velarization is found in African languages, such as Kom, with sequences like [bɣ].

In **pharyngealization** consonants and vowels are produced by constriction of the throat cavity. Pharyngealization is prominent in the Semitic languages, where it is one of the components of a complex articulation labeled **emphasis.** In Arabic, for example, emphasis distinguishes *tiin* 'mud' from *tiin* 'figs.'

In **glottalization** consonants are produced by accompanying glottal closure. This type of articulation is prominent in many Amerindian languages. Winnebago, for example, has a set of glottalized consonants, or **ejectives:** *p'* besides *p, t'* besides *t,* and so on. The glottalization may be simultaneous with the primary articulation or it may be delayed. Final pronunciation of English /t/ may be compared: it is often simply [ʔ], as in [siʔ] for *sit.*

Secondary articulation may vary considerably from language to language. Even within one language there may be varying degrees of it. In Arabic, for example, four consonants have **primary emphasis,** whereas other **emphatic** consonants have less pervasive secondary articulation.

Moreover, successive sounds are affected by one another. For example, in English *twin* the *t* is labialized; in *train* it may be retroflex. Such effects are known as **coarticulation.**

Types of secondary articulation may characterize a language in general. Thus the languages of India give the impression of general retroflexion; the Slavic languages, of palatalization. And many varieties of American English have a secondary velar constriction that gives the impression of nasalization. These characteristics may have fanciful popular labels, such as the supposed nasal twang of the New Englander or the supposed "guttural" quality of German speech. Since the names are intuitive, they may match the actual articulatory feature only vaguely. German, for example, has no "throat sounds" but may have been characterized as "guttural" because of the velar [x] as in *ach*.

Moreover, the actual articulatory details of pronunciation, as of emphasis or the American nasal twang, are poorly explored. Precise methods of study should begin to clarify some of the patterns.

---

### 4.8    Articulation for Intensity, Pitch, and Timing

The phonetic entities discussed so far are made primarily by the vocal organs above the larynx. The first consonant of a rapid pronunciation of *naturally* [nǽtšərliy] is articulated by the tongue's producing a closure at the alveolar ridge, with the velum open, permitting nasality. The first vowel is made by the tongue's providing a relatively large opening in the front of the mouth; and so on, with the other sounds symbolized.

But a sequence of several sounds in English is also accompanied by differences in intensity and pitch and by variations in timing. If we pronounce *Naturally!* meaning '*Yes!*' the first vowel is louder than the other two. Furthermore, it is higher in pitch. Moreover, the timing is precisely determined. If we compare the first part of the sentence *Nat surely will come!* /²nǽt ³šə́rliy əl kə̀m¹↓/, we note a difference in the timing between the [t] and [š] of the two sequences. Such differences in timing as well as intensity and pitch are determined by the muscles controlling the outflow of air, for example, by the muscles regulating the vocal cords.

### 4.8.1    Stress

The significant use of intensity in speech is referred to as **stress.** When we compare the two utterances *Naturally* and *Nat surely will come,* we note that [nǽtšərliy] has a strong or **primary stress** on the first syllable, whereas [nǽtšə́rliy] has primary stress on the second. The difference between the otherwise similar sequence consists in the differing force with which the two syllables are pronounced.

Such differences may be noted most clearly in English nouns and verbs that differ only in the place of accent, such as *permit*. If pronounced alone, the noun is stressed [pə́rmĭt], the verb [pə̆rmít]; similarly, *refill:* noun [rí̆yfĭl], verb [rĭyfíl]; *pervert*, and so on. In contrasting such pairs, we may note the differences in articulation between the syllables marked [´] to indicate primary stress and those marked [˘] to indicate **weak stress.** While the chief difference seems to be in intensity, there are also differences in length; [pə́r] in the noun *permit*, for example, is longer than [pə̆r] in the verb *permit*. Because of such complex differences, stress is more difficult to describe and determine precisely than are consonants and vowels. Accordingly there are varying interpretations of the basis of stress, even the stress of a well-described language like English.

Moreover, stressed vowels tend to be more distinct than unstressed vowels. In pronouncing the verb *refill*, for example, the vowel of the first syllable may be [i] or even [ə]. But the noun always has the distinct vowel: [rí̆yfil]. This set of characteristics accompanying stress in English— difference in intensity, difference in length and clarity, coupled with differences in pitch—has led to varying interpretations of the role of stress, as we note further below.

A further difficulty in determining the role of stress, as well as pitch and timing, arises from their complex contrasts. When we compare *purr* and *cur*, we establish a direct contrast between the two consonants [p] and [k]. When, however, we contrast [pə́rmĭt] and [pə̆rmít], we cannot establish a direct contrast between [´] and [˘], for there is also a contrast in the second syllable between [˘] and [´]. We cannot find English utterances in which the only contrast consists in a difference of stress on only one syllable, because stress differences are determined also by contrasts in successive syllables. If there were a third word *permit* pronounced *[pə́rmít] or *[pə̆rmĭt], we would have a direct contrast. Unfortunately such direct contrasts are not found for stress, because stress is superposed on consonants and vowels. Stress, accordingly, is difficult to determine precisely, though it clearly distinguishes sequences of syllables, such as *permit*.

Pitch and timing have a similar role in language. Because this role is determined largely by their effect on a sequence of speech, they are often labeled **long components.** To illustrate further their effect on consonants and vowels, we may note the differing [p] sounds in *permit*. When the strong stress falls on the first syllable, as in the noun, the [p] is aspirated [pʰə́rmĭt]. When the strong stress falls on the second syllable, the [p] has less aspiration. Because stress, pitch, and timing have an influence over the consonantal and vocalic segments of speech, they are called **suprasegmentals,** in contrast with consonants and vowels, or **segmentals.**

The interplay of stress and other suprasegmentals has led to differing analyses of the role of stress in English. Many linguists and lexicographers assume a third stress for English in addition to the primary and the weak.

They base this analysis on the contrasts between two sequences like *a permit* [ə́ pérmǐt] and *a poor mitt* [ə̀ púr mìt] (as in answer to *What kind of a mitt caused Schroeder to drop the ball?*). In these two sequences the intensity with which [i] is produced varies considerably; we may mark the stronger [i] with a grave accent mark [`]. Such stresses, here called **middle** in contrast with weak [˘] and primary [´] stresses, fall on elements of clauses that are less prominent, as on the second elements of compounds, for example, *workbook* [wə́rkbùk] as contrasted with *worker* [wə́rkər]. They may also fall on derivational suffixes in English, for example, *stationary* [stéysənèrǐy] as contrasted with *stationing* [stéyšə̆nǐŋ].

In other languages stress may play a totally different role. In Japanese, for example, it is nonsignificant. In Latin, stress is determined by the quantity of syllables and their position with regard to the end of the word. Most monosyllables are stressed, for example, *pĕs* 'foot.' But if the second-last syllable is long, it is stressed, for example, *amā́vī* 'I loved.' If the second-last syllable is not long, the third-last syllable is stressed regardless of its quantity, for example, *amā́veram* 'I had loved.' Accordingly the position of stress in Latin is predictable in general from the quantity of vowels in the last syllables of words.

### 4.8.2 Pitch

As utterances vary in stress, they may also vary in pitch. For example, the sequence *She wrote Harriet* may have the relatively highest pitch on any of three syllables, depending on how the sequence is used in response to various questions. In answer to *Who wrote Harriet?* the pitch pattern for *She wrote Harriet* may be represented:

1. [šíy rowt heryət]

In answer to *Whom did she write to?* the pattern is:

2. [šiy rowt héryət]

In answer to *Why doesn't she do something about inviting Harriet?* the answer might be:

3. [šiy rówt heryət]

When we examine these English pitch sequences, we may note some essential contrasts in the use of pitch. The most prominent syllable is associated with the relatively highest pitch. Speech material earlier in the sentence is produced with a relatively lower pitch. At the very end of such sentences the pitch becomes quite low. To mark the contrasts, numerals may be used: [1] for the low pitch level at the end of the sentence; [2] for the normal pitch level; [3] for the pitch on the most prominent syllable.

1. [³šíy ròwt hèryət¹]
2. [²šìy ròwt ³ héryət¹]
3. [²šìy ³ rówt hèryət¹]

In English, pitch generally remains relatively constant before the most prominent vowel and trails off gradually to the end of such simple sentences. By using three numerals then, for example, ² ³ ¹ for the pitch sequence in this sentence, we can label the sequence as effectively as if we drew lines or used musical notation—and at far lower cost in printing. Accordingly numerals are generally used to mark English pitch.

Such variations in pitch are produced by our considerable virtuosity in manipulating the vocal cords. We noted previously that individual speakers speak at various pitches, depending on the length, thickness, and tautness of their vocal cords. In addition to their other manipulation the vocal cords can be made more taut so that they produce sounds higher in pitch, or the cords can be relaxed so that they produce sounds lower in pitch.

It is characteristic of English utterances pronounced with assurance that they follow a ² ³ ¹ pattern, whether they are declarative sentences, such as *He did it* /² hìy ³ díd ìt¹/ or questions introduced by *wh-* words *Who did it?* /² hùw ³ díd ìt¹/. The exact pitches will vary considerably with the fundamental tone of the speaker. A male, speaking in a bass voice, will produce his pitch³ at a far lower absolute pitch than will a female speaking in a soprano voice. But each one's pitch³ will be higher than his pitch², which in turn will be higher than his pitch¹. In one recording of a bass speaker's sentence *I'll come along,* the initial pitch was 110 Hz, the highest pitch 128 Hz, and the lowest trailed off at 80 Hz. Comparable variation would be found in the sentences of speakers having a higher speaking voice.

The primary linguistic role of pitch in English is its marking of clause patterns, as noted in the following section. In other languages the role of pitch may be quite different, as in Japanese, Classical Greek, ancient Sanskrit, and Proto-Indo-European.

In Japanese, pitch is distributed differently on various syllables of words. In standard Japanese, for example, *kaki* has a high pitch on the second syllable __‾ when it means 'persimmon' and a high pitch on the first syllable ‾__ when it means 'oyster.' This use of pitch is comparable with the English use of stress, as in English *permít* versus *pérmit*. In Classical Greek, ancient Sanskrit, and Proto-Indo-European most words have one high pitch on a given syllable of a word. Greek *patér,* for example, has this pitch accent on the last syllable, as do the ancient Sanskrit and Proto-Indo-European words for 'father.'

The use of pitch in Japanese is complicated by its double role, for in addition to distinguishing words, pitch is also used to mark sentences, as in *iimono* ‾⌐_ 'it's a good thing' versus *iimono* ‾⌐_ 'good thing' or *iimono* ⌐‾__ 'good quality.' In Japanese, therefore, clause patterns of pitch are superposed on word patterns of pitch, leading to a very complex interrelationship.

To illustrate these interrelationships, a commonly cited trio may be used (´ indicates a pitch three or four semitones higher than that of the unmarked vowels):

$$háma \text{ a girl's name}\quad haná \text{ 'flower'}\quad hana \text{ 'nose'}$$

*háma* a girl's name   *haná* 'flower'   *hana* 'nose'

If these are used in a clause—for example, *ga kírei desu* 'is beautiful'—the intonation may be:

| | |
|---|---|
| *háma ga kírei desu* | 'Hana is beautiful.' |
| *haná ga kírei desu* | 'The flower is beautiful.' |
| *hana ga kírei desu* | 'The nose is beautiful.' |

After each pitch there is a drop, and the pitch level is then steady. If the pitch remains steady, the intonation contour indicates a neutral view of the utterance.

If, however, the pitch is raised lightly, emphasis is intended. If it is raised even more, a question is intended. For example, *hana* 'nose' may be pronounced / to indicate emphasis, / to indicate question, and / to indicate an emphasis question. Intonation then manipulates pitch in a different way from the pitch on words and compounds. In this way Japanese uses only variations in pitch where English uses both stress and pitch. Presumably the same double use of pitch was present in ancient Greek, Sanskrit, and Proto-Indo-European.

Other languages use pitch in still other ways, as differing configurations on individual syllables. Such a pitch is often labeled **tone**, and the languages that use pitch this way are labeled **tone languages**. In Putonghua, for example, syllables may be pronounced with **level** tone ($^-$ or [1]), with **rising** tone (´ or [2]), with compound **falling-rising** tone (ˇ or [3]), or with **falling** tone (` or [4]). The numeral *one* for example has tone [1], $i^1$; *man* has tone[2], $jen^2$; *five* has tone[3], $wu^3$; and *two* has tone[4], $erh^4$. Some syllables with identical segmentals differ only in tone, for example, $mai^3$ 'buy' and $mai^4$ 'sell.' In addition to its use of pitch in this way Putonghua also uses pitch in sentence intonation patterns.

## 4.8.3 Timing: Juncture

**Juncture** is a term that has come to be used for the variations in timing and quality associated with the ends of clauses or lesser breaks. In *naturally* [nǽtšərliy] there is no break between any of the syllables; the [tš] is pronounced virtually as a unit and is therefore generally written with one symbol [č]. In *Nat surely will go* [²nǽt ³šə́rliyəl gòw¹↓], on the other hand, there may be a perceptible break between [t] and [š]. It is difficult to summarize the phonetic characteristics of the difference briefly. Besides an actual disjunction between [t] and [š] there are also differences in the [t] and [æ] of *Nat;* both are slightly longer than are the [t] and [æ] of *naturally,* and the [t] may be accompanied by glottal closure. Moreover, the [ə] of [šə́rliy] is more prominent than is that of [nǽtšərliy]. By means of such delicate differences ends of syllabic sequences, or clauses, may be signaled. The break between [nǽt] and [šə́rliy] is often called **plus juncture** and is indicated by a plus mark [+]. Since it is very frequent, however, it is commonly omitted in transcriptions, and a blank space is left to represent it. The contrast between **close juncture,** as between [š] and [ə], or the [t] and [š] of [nǽtšərliy], and open or plus juncture is then indicated by a space, as in [nǽt šə́rliy].

We may note that in rapid speech plus junctures are often disregarded, as are weakly stressed vowels. Many speakers frown on such speech, associating it with rebellious juveniles, labeling it "slurvian," and objecting to pronunciations like [nǽčərliy] rather than [nǽčərəlìy]. Whatever one's attitude, the process of reducing elements in rapid articulation has gone on for some time, leading to such pronunciations as British English [láybriy] in contrast with American English [láybrèriy] for *library,* or [čə́mliy] for the place name *Cholmondely,* as well as [hay] for *How do you do?* and *Good-by* for *God be with you.* As these reductions indicate, in place names and greetings, junctures may be so consistently disregarded that ultimately other parts of the sequence are affected as well.

Signals based on timing are also used to mark clauses as distinct sequences. These are known as **terminal junctures,** or **terminals.** They, too, are difficult to distinguish from other phenomena, in part because of their close association with other phonetic features.

English has three terminal junctures /#, ||, | /. **Double cross,** /#/, is characterized by a rapid drop of pitch, with fading of the speech material. It is used in crisp, businesslike pronunciation, as in assertions and questions with *wh-* words: *He's coming. Who's coming? She took the car. Hurry up.* It may also be used in greetings like *Good-by.* When it is, however, the businesslike connotation of /#/ virtually makes the greeting mean 'Good-by and good riddance' or 'It's about *time* you left.' If arrows are used, /#/ is written /↓/.

**Double bar,** /|||/, also written /↑/, has a slight upturn of the voice. It indicates politeness, a gentle, occasionally wistful mood, and is used when we do not wish to sound hard-boiled: *Why, that's Billie. Come in. Sure, honey, you can take the car.* It should be noted that in all of these utterances the pitch and stress patterns can be the same, with only the terminal differing. For example, *Come in* /² kə̀m ³in¹ #/, a blunt request, with no hint of pleasure at the arrival, may be contrasted with /² kə̀m ³ín¹ |||/, a welcome suggesting happy anticipation. Generally, greetings are pronounced with /|||/, unless relationships are ruptured and external appearances, nevertheless, require some kind of utterance.

The third English terminal, **single bar,** /|/, also written /→ /, is neither fading nor slightly rising, but level. It suggests continuation and is typically used at the ends of clauses that are followed by others in the sentence, for example, *Come in . . . and take a seat*. When such clauses are used, the pitch pattern is often /² ³ ²/, as in /²kə̀m ³ín²→ ²ǽnd . . ./. In this way terminals are often associated with specific pitch patterns.

We may illustrate these English pitch patterns by means of another example, *Who's that lady?* The following are common patterns:

/²hùwz ðǽt³ léydiy¹#/ (a factual question)
/²hùwz ðǽt³ léydiy¹‖/ (a friendly question)
/²hùwz ðǽt³ léydiy²→ / (an incomplete question, probably concluded with a clause like *you were talking about*)

---

## 4.9  Intonation Patterns

Such pitch patterns associated with terminal junctures are known as **intonation patterns,** or contours. Here are some examples for *It's a yellow-head:*

| | | |
|---|---|---|
| ² ³ ¹ # | /²ìtsə ³yéləhèd¹#/ | (indicating assurance) |
| ² ³ ³ ‖ | /²ìtsə ³yéləhèd³‖/ | (indicating doubt) |
| ² ³ ² │ | /²ìtsə ³yéləhèd²│/ | (indicating incompleteness) |

These intonation patterns are essentially unchanged when the clause is extended, for example:

*It's a genuine yellowhead.*
*Maximilian is a genuine yellowhead.*
*Maximilian certainly looks like a genuine yellowhead.*

Any sequence covered by such an intonation pattern may be called a **phonological clause.**

Phonological clauses generally correspond to syntactic clauses, but they may not. For example, in ´deliberate speech one might say ²Màxi ³miliàn² │²is a ³génuine² │³yéllowhèad¹#.

There are numerous intonation patterns in English. Their description is a portion of English grammar. We may note further here that the three-pitch patterns may be abbreviated when the first syllable of the clause is stressed. ³ ¹ # may then be used rather than ² ³ ¹, as in ³Jóe was the wìnner¹#. Although English intonation patterns typically are made up of three pitches and a terminal, they may in this way contain only two significant pitches.

When intonation patterns are accompanied by emphasis or emotion, the strongest stress may be on any prominent syllable, and it may be accompanied by a very high pitch. For example, if one saw a totally unexpected woman, one might ask /²hùwz ⁴ðǽt lèydiy¹↓/. In such an emphatic question the pitch may be considerably higher than in a normal question. To indicate it, a ⁴ may be used. Some linguists object to the assumption of a fourth pitch, associating the very high pitch in such utterances with gesturelike accompaniments to speech, such as those represented by *ahem* or *tsk tsk*.

Just as there may be vigorous use of pitch when one speaks excitedly, in routine speech one may keep the pitch sequences unvaried. In counting, for example, one may avoid variations in pitch, as in the following:

$$/^1w\acute{\delta}n^1 \rightarrow {}^1t\acute{u}w^1 \rightarrow \theta r\acute{i}y^1 \rightarrow {}^1f\acute{o}r^1 \rightarrow {}^1f\acute{a}yv^1\#/$$

or in the livelier:

$$/^2w\acute{\delta}n^2 \rightarrow {}^2t\acute{u}w^2 \rightarrow {}^2\theta r\acute{i}y^2 \rightarrow {}^2f\acute{o}r^2 \rightarrow f\acute{a}yv^1\#/$$

Contrast further rapid counting, which may be done as though the numerals make up a clause:

$$/^2w\grave{\delta}n \; t\vartheta \; \theta riy \; for \; {}^3f\acute{a}yv^1\#/$$

Whatever the specific patterns, in every language a set of consonants, vowels, and suprasegmentals make up the sequences known as utterances. These entities have been discussed from an articulatory point of view. They may also be examined from an acoustic point of view.

## BIBLIOGRAPHICAL NOTES

Students who have no previous acquaintance with articulatory phonetics will find highly useful *The Pronunciation of American English* by Arthur J. Bronstein (New York: Appleton-Century-Crofts, 1960). One of the standard general works is *General Phonetics* by Roe-Merrill S. Heffner (Madison: University of Wisconsin Press, 1949). Another is *Elements of General Phonetics* by David Abercrombie (Chicago: Aldine, 1967). See also *Preliminaries to Linguistic Phonetics* by Peter Ladefoged (Chicago: University of Chicago Press, 1972). For capable phonetic studies of languages other than English see *A Phonetic Study of West African Languages,* 2d ed., by Peter Ladefoged (Cambridge: At the University Press, 1968); *Japanese Phonology* by Mieko Shimizu Han (Tokyo: Kenkyusha, 1962); and *The Phonology of Colloquial Egyptian Arabic* by Richard S. Harrell (New York: American Council of Learned Societies, 1957). The Japanese and Egyptian Arabic examples in this chapter are based on these presentations, which may be consulted for further details. For detailed data on English intonation see *The Intonation of American English* by Kenneth L. Pike (Ann Arbor: University of Michigan Press, 1946).

QUESTIONS FOR REVIEW

1. Identify three different approaches to the study of speech sounds, characterizing each briefly.
2. Discuss the role of the following in speech: a. the lungs; b. the vocal cords; c. the nose; d. the mouth.
3. Identify briefly: a. glottis; b. voice; c. velum; d. palate; e. back, front, blade, and tip of tongue; f. alveolar ridge.
4. Define: a. manner of articulation; b. place of articulation.
5. Cite examples of: a. labial stops; b. alveolar stops; c. palato-velar stops; d. labiodental fricatives; e. interdental fricatives; f. groove fricatives; g. affricates.
6. Describe the articulation of: a. nasal consonants; b. a lateral; c. a flap; d. two semivowels.
7. State the articulatory characteristics of English: a. *a*; b. *u*; c. *æ*, d. *aw*; e. *ay*.
8. Define *coarticulation*. Illustrate your definition by analyzing the production of the initial *k* in *quick* and the final *d* in *board*.
9. What is the primary articulatory feature of: a. stress; b. pitch; c. juncture?
10. Identify three intonation patterns of English.

EXERCISES

THE TRANSCRIPTION OF ENGLISH

English spelling is based in part on morphological patterning. For example, the spelling *s*, as in *horses*, indicates nicely the marker for the plural of the noun, but in *cats, dogs*, and *horses, s* differs in pronunciation depending on the last phoneme of the noun to which it is added. In these three examples the plural suffix is spelled the same but pronounced differently [kæts, dɔgz, hɔrsəz]. Similarly, the bases of many words, for example, *concave* and *concavity*, are spelled with the same vowel <a>, but the pronunciation differs. Because of the basis of our spelling system, it is important for us to learn to transcribe phonologically. In learning to do so, you should begin by rigidly following rules, such as those given below.

There will be few, if any, difficulties with the consonants. Some instructors, however, may prefer differing transcriptions for the "compound vowels." Several practices are possible, each of which has its uses. The practice recommended here signals the diphthongal articulation of English "compound vowels" as opposed to the "long" or "tense" vowels of many other languages. If your instructor wishes to emphasize these qualities, you may substitute macrons over vowel symbols for the *y* and *w* in the following charts, or you may use colons after the vowel symbols. Whatever the practice, you must learn to transcribe consistently and continue to transcribe. The set of exercises given here is graded for progressive mastery of the various problems you will find in learning to transcribe English.

The following are symbols for writing English consonants and vowels in phonemic transcription. The conventional spelling is given after each word. The symbols / / are used to mark off materials given in phonemic transcription. When essential for accurate understanding, the symbols < > are used to indicate citations in conventional spelling.

Your own pronunciation, especially of the vowels, may differ from that indicated here. If you have the vowel written /i/, you may distinguish it from a weakly stressed pronunciation of <just>; similarly, /o/ is distinguished from a short pronunciation of the vowel in words like <home>. The system of transcription is designed in such a way that all varieties of English speech may be represented by it (see Charts 9 to 11).

### Chart 9. Consonants

| | | | |
|---|---|---|---|
| /pin/ *pin* | /tin/ *tin* | /čin/ *chin* | /kin/ *kin* |
| /bən/ *bun* | /dən/ *done* | /jin/ *gin* | /gən/ *gun* |
| /fin/ *fin* /θin/ *thin* | /sin/ *sin* /šin/ *shin* | | /hip/ *hip* |
| /væn/ *van* /ðen/ *then* | /zip/ *zip* /ruwž/ *rouge* | | |
| /rəm/ *rum* | /rən/ *run* | | /rəŋ/ *rung* |
| /wel/ *well* | /rip/ *rip* | /lip/ *lip* /yel/ *yell* | |

### Chart 10. Vowels

| | | | |
|---|---|---|---|
| Simple vowels | /sit/ *sit* | /i/ *just* (adverb) | /bul/ *bull* |
| | /set/ *set* | /nət/ *nut* | /o/ *home* (dialect) |
| | /sæt/ *sat* | /nat/ *knot* | /bɔl/ *ball* |
| Compound vowels (vocalic nuclei) +Y | /siyd/ *seed* /seyn/ *sane* | | |
| | | /sayd/ *side* | /sɔy/ *soy* |
| +W | | | /suw/ *sue* /sow/ *so* |
| | | /haw/ *how* | |
| For R-less pronunciation) +H | /hih/ *hear* /beh/ *bear* /bæh/ *bare* | /bəh/ *burr* /bah/ *bar* | /buh/ *boor* /boh/ *bore* |

If you are a native speaker of British English, you may wish to note the vowel system of English for "many speakers of RP" ("received pronunciation," the normal British pronunciation).[1]

**Chart 11. The Vowels of British RP**

| | Simple | | Complex | | | |
|---|---|---|---|---|---|---|
| | | | +i | | +u | |
| Simple | i | tin | i$^i$ | tea | | |
| | e | ten | e$^i$ | tay | | |
| | a | tan | a$^i$ | tie | a$^u$ | town |
| | ə | ton | | | ə$^u$ | toe |
| | o | toss | o$^i$ | toy | | |
| | u | took | | | u$^u$ | two |
| Complex +ə | i$^ə$ | tier | | | | |
| | e$^ə$ | tare | | | | |
| | a$^ə$ | tar | a$^{iə}$ | tire | a$^{uə}$ | tower |
| | ə$^ə$ | turn | | | | |
| | o$^ə$ | tore | | | | |
| | u$^ə$ | tour | | | | |

EXERCISE 1

a. Write the following words in transcription:

1. foot
2. half
3. but
4. make
5. feet
6. pay
7. shad
8. yet
9. rout
10. day
11. mine
12. sky
13. vein
14. thing
15. tight
16. bait
17. boot
18. thin
19. sign
20. wait

21. eight
22. law
23. whose
24. talk
25. use (verb)
26. use (noun)
27. cheap
28. cot
28. son
30. shook
31. wolf
32. rude
33. then
34. knot
35. old
36. leech
37. sight
38. who
39. shock
40. chin

41. eve
42. sit
43. owl
44. awe
45. pique
46. walk
47. boil
48. cat
49. hymn
50. go
51. joy
52. rote
53. all
54. dough
55. caught
56. put
57. fun
58. cue
58. leave
60. died

---

[1]This system is discussed in Michael A. K. Halliday, Angus McIntosh, and Peter Strevens, *The Linguistic Sciences and Language Teaching* (Bloomington: Indiana University Press, 1964), p. 239.

b. From the previous list determine the spellings by which the following vowels and vocalic nuclei are written in conventional English orthography. For example, /ə/ is spelled <u> in *fun;* /ay/ as in 11, 12, 15, 19, 60; /ow/; and /ɔ/.

c. In the words of the previous list determine the vowel phonemes that are represented by the English spelling <o> as in 28, 29, 31, 34, 35, 38, 39, 50, 52; by <u>.

EXERCISE 2

a. Write the following words in transcription:

| | | |
|---|---|---|
| 1. heard | 21. card | 41. tired |
| 2. leered | 22. poured | 42. lured |
| 3. wired | 23. cared | 43. pew |
| 4. place | 24. trimmed | 44. clapped |
| 5. cringed | 25. preyed | 45. cute |
| 6. quick | 26. sloop | 46. swift |
| 7. broad | 27. glide | 47. dues |
| 8. Dwight | 28. groaned | 48. wire |
| 9. smell | 29. sneaked | 49. string |
| 10. squint | 30. spleen | 50. scrounge |
| 11. sprained | 31. fuse | 51. shrimp |
| 12. flit | 32. three | 52. frank |
| 13. view | 33. muse | 53. news |
| 14. fir | 34. fear | 54. fare |
| 15. fire | 35. far | 55. sprout |
| 16. bore | 36. cured | 56. boor |
| 17. mare | 37. mere | 57. scream |
| 18. sure | 38. shore | 58. star |
| 19. charmed | 39. course | 59. hurled |
| 20. warmth | 40. learned | 60. worked |

b. Determine the initial consonant clusters with /r/ as second member in the words listed above; those with /r/ as third member. What generalizations can you make about the first consonant in the clusters of three? about the second in clusters of three? What generalizations can you make about the first consonant in clusters of two?

c. Determine the vowels and compound vowels that precede /r/ in your speech. Contrast these with your total set of vowels.

EXERCISE 3

Many English words consist of two syllables, one of which is strongly stressed, the other weakly stressed, for example, *sinner* /sínər/ and *pertain* /pərtéyn/. The strong stress, called *primary,* is marked /´/. The weak is often unmarked, though if one is explicit, it should be marked with / ˘ /. Accordingly any vowel unmarked for stress is assumed to have weak stress.

Write the following words in transcription, including the stress marks /´˘/. Note that by the principles followed here each English syllable must contain a vowel.

| | | |
|---|---|---|
| 1. debtor | 21. today | 41. awful |
| 2. battle | 22. lawyer | 42. heavy |
| 3. butler | 23. owlish | 43. suited |
| 4. heiress | 24. yelling | 44. sighted |
| 5. undone | 25. reset | 45. boiling |
| 6. consent | 26. prefer | 46. cement |
| 7. obtuse | 27. mention | 47. defend |
| 8. drama | 28. shoulder | 48. gallop |
| 9. people | 29. demur | 49. abstain |
| 10. suggest | 30. perverse | 50. subtract |
| 11. ginger | 31. manner | 51. stronger |
| 12. apply | 32. hanger | 52. simple |
| 13. joyful | 33. biscuit | 53. attract |
| 14. heaven | 34. across | 54. nation |
| 15. needle | 35. issue | 55. resent |
| 16. creature | 36. gentle | 56. acquire |
| 17. salmon | 37. measure | 57. column |
| 18. persuade | 38. water | 58. many |
| 19. volume | 39. anguish | 59. awake |
| 20. beauty | 40. liar | 60. suppose |

EXERCISE 4

Besides a strong /´/ and a weak stress /˘/, a third stress is found in English. This middle stress is marked with a grave / ` /. It is particularly apparent when one contrasts words having an affix with sequences of two words, for example:

*suffer* /sə́fər/          *cat fur* /kǽt fə̀r/
*unvoice* /ə̀nvóys/      *some voice* /sə̀m vóys/

Middle stress is also found in words of three syllables, when two of the syllables are roots rather than affixes. In some words it helps to distinguish nouns from verbs:

*forgotten* /fərgátə̀n/          *four-handed* /fòwr hǽndə̀d/
*envelop* (v.) /ə̀nvélə̀p/       *envelope* (n.) /énvə̀lòwp/

Between words such as *cat fur* and between elements of compounds such as *four-handed* there is often a slight pause. This may be indicated in transcription by a blank, but it may also be marked with a / + / if one wishes to be explicit. The pause, which is accompanied by other phenomena, is known as *plus juncture*. Compare contrasts like:

| | |
|---|---|
| *herring* /hérǐŋ/ | *key ring* /kíy + rǐŋ/ |
| *heighten* /háytə̌n/ | *high tone* /háy + tòwn/ |

In transcribing the examples that follow, use your own pronunciation. If you are not a native speaker of English, ask a native speaker to read the words to you. You may find that there are differences in the occurrence of middle stress and of plus juncture, depending on the location of these words in sentences and on the speed of utterance.

| | | | |
|---|---|---|---|
| 1. die-hard | diet | 11. one portion | apportion |
| 2. blackbird | blacker | 12. a tent show | attention |
| 3. dollhouse | dollar | 13. new pewter | computer |
| 4. deep end | depend | 14. insert one | insertion |
| 5. folklore | solar | 15. a rare steak | majestic |
| 6. forecast | forlorn | 16. office hour | officer |
| 7. grassland | grassless | 17. personnel | personal |
| 8. longhorn | longing | 18. reverse gear | reversion |
| 9. seven-up | several | 19. Near East | nearest |
| 10. passkey | passage | 20. substitute | substantial |

## EXERCISE 5

In this exercise we deal with special problems in English.

a. In order to distinguish between /yuw/ and /uw/, transcribe the following words. Be careful about preceding alveolars, as in pairs 7 to 12, for many speakers do not have contrasting pairs.

| | | | |
|---|---|---|---|
| 1. feud | food | 7. tutor | tooter |
| 2. beauty | booty | 8. dew | do |
| 3. pure | poor | 9. sue | Sioux |
| 4. mew | moo | 10. lute | loot |
| 5. cue | coo | 11. mature | detour |
| 6. hue | who | 12. assume | summit |

b. In order to distinguish /ž/, transcribe:

| | | | |
|---|---|---|---|
| 1. vision | fission | 4. measure | mesher |
| 2. azure | Asher | 5. leisure | legion |
| 3. rouge | rush | 6. beige | badge |

c. In order to distinguish consonantal resonants from sequences of weak vowels plus resonants, transcribe:

| | | | |
|---|---|---|---|
| 1. elm | alum | 6. calm | column |
| 2. bubble | bubbling | 7. single | England |
| 3. nation | national | 8. even | evening |
| 4. lyre | liar | 9. lair | layer |
| 5. boor | booer | 10. more | mower |

d. Here are further words that cause problems for some speakers. Transcribe:

| | | | |
|---|---|---|---|
| 1. singer | 11. white | 21. was | 31. hoof |
| 2. finger | 12. wight | 22. orange | 32. proof |
| 3. ginger | 13. one | 23. sorry | 33. roost |
| 4. long | 14. on | 24. foreign | 34. soot |
| 5. longer | 15. not | 25. tomorrow | 35. spoon |
| 6. length | 16. doll | 26. dog | 36. Cooper |
| 7. anguish | 17. from | 27. mock | 37. room |
| 8. whales | 18. wash | 28. hog | 38. roof |
| 9. Wales | 19. want | 29. haunt | 39. root |
| 10. choir | 20. watch | 30. broom | 40. bloom |

EXERCISE 6

In transcribing the following sentences, use only written forms of the symbols you have mastered. Capital letters must be avoided; they have special uses in transcriptions.

A typical English clause or simple sentence has at least one strong stress, for example, *Come closer*/kəm klówsər/. Other syllables may have almost as strong a stress, and this may also be marked /´/. Some syllables may, however, have a somewhat weaker stress, marked /ˋ/ and called *middle*. This sentence then might be pronounced with middle stress on the verb /kə̀m klówsər/.

In addition to differences in stress, English sentences are characterized by differences in pitch. A simple English sentence begins at a middle pitch level, rises somewhat higher on the strongest stress, and then may fall to a low pitch (if the sentence is pronounced with an expression of certainty). The levels of pitch are referred to by numbers. A more complete transcription, then, would be /²kəm ³klówsər¹↓/. The final arrow indicates the trailing off that is used to convey certainty.

Transcribe the following sentences, pronouncing them to indicate certainty:

1. *Rick hit his chin.*
2. *Ben sells shells.*
3. *Catch that calf!*
4. *Hud cut one.*
5. *Shocks stop clocks.*
6. *Wolf should pull.*
7. *Saul called Paul.*

## EXERCISE 7

As noted in the set of sentences in Exercise 6, certainty is indicated in English by the trailing off of the voice at the end of a clause. This method of ending a clause, or this terminal of a clause, is indicated by an arrow pointing downward /↓/, or occasionally by /./, or by /#/. The last symbol is often called the *double cross juncture*. The following sentences may be spoken with the voice trailing off at the end, thus producing the intonation pattern /² ³ ¹ #/. Transcribe:

1. *She needs three keys.*
2. *They stayed eight days.*
3. *I'll try my side.*
4. *Whose group moved?*
5. *Joe's boat won't float.*
6. *How loud now?*
7. *Lloyd's voice joined Roy's.*

## EXERCISE 8

Sentences may also be pronounced so as to indicate doubt, question, or uncertainty. In these instances the voice rises at the end of the clause. This type of intonation has the pattern /² ³ ³ ↑/. It is typical of yes-no questions, such as the first sentence in the list that follows. The final terminal may be indicated by a rising arrow or by /||/. The last symbol is often called the *double bar juncture*.

The terminal /||/ is also used to make a statement sound less abrupt, as in greetings. Instead of the businesslike *Good morning!* /²gùd ³mɔ́rniŋ¹#/, we commonly say /²gùd ³mɔ́rniŋ¹||/.

Transcribe each of the following sentences with one of the terminals discussed in the statements in Exercises 7 and 8, noting the meaning conveyed by the terminal that you choose:

1. *Was she there too?*
2. *Why don't we go?*

   3. *He'll take his car.*
   4. *Here are the tickets.*
   5. *Turn to the right.*
   6. *Help yourselves.*
   7. *Don't walk on the grass.*
   8. *Do your own homework.*

## EXERCISE 9

The allophones of phonemes differ as their environments vary. Differences in the allophones of vowels of English may be correlated with the consonants that follow them. Before /r/ the allophones of vowels differ considerably from their allophones elsewhere. The following sentences are designed to have you observe your own pronunciation and to determine the most accurate representation of your vowels before /r/. In some variations of American English this is the simple vowel; in others a vocalic nucleus consisting of the simple vowel plus /y/ and /w/; in still others, in which the /r/ is lost, the representation may be the simple vowel and /h/ or /ə/. Transcribe:

   1. *Her pearls were in the first purse.*
   2. *We're here, near the pier.*
   3. *There was very little air in the ferry.*
   4. *A special fairy cared for Marion.*
   5. *Clark's heart wasn't in his art.*
   6. *The four horses snorted hoarsely before morning.*
   7. *You're sure you're cured?*
   8. *The fire devoured our spire.*

## EXERCISE 10

Sentences may consist of two or more clauses. When they do, a nonfalling, nonrising terminal may be used to indicate the linking of the first clause with a following clause. This terminal is often marked /l/ and labeled *single bar.* It may also be marked /→/ or /, /. It is commonly associated with the pitch sequence /² ³ ²/, for example; /²s̆ìy ³stártəd²/²bət sùwn kèym ³bǽk¹#/.

   1. *The dogs snatched up the rug and dashed out.*
   2. *Five-sixths went down the drain, not five-eighths.*
   3. *While they rested, they dropped sticks off the bridge.*
   4. *She stayed calm through all the night, he reported.*
   5. *His neighbor asked how Hugh could stoop so low.*
   6. *"Let me try the beige rouge," she lisped.*
   7. *Rich dodged and hit the ditch.*

8. *Though he thought and thought, he couldn't spell cough or hic-cough.*
9. *If you used all your strength, it'd budge.*
10. *From there the slough looked like a trough.*

EXERCISE 11

In practicing transcription, you can profit from selecting passages of non-sense verse to transcribe because such passages play with sound. Another good choice is rhymed verse several centuries old, in part because changes in pronunciation may have removed the rhymes, so that your attention is directed to careful transcription.

a. Transcribe the following limerick by Edward Lear:

There was a Young Lady of Russia,
Who screamed so that no one could hush her;
   Her screams were extreme,
   No one heard such a scream,
As was screamed by that Lady of Russia.

b. Write in normal English spelling:

/²ðèr wə́zən òwld pə́rsən əv ³díyn²|
²hùw dáynd ɔ̀n wə̀n píy ənwə̀n ³bíyn¹#
  ²fòr iyséd mòr ðən ³ðǽt²|
  ²wùd méyk mìy tùw ³fǽt¹#
²ðæt kɔ́šəs òwld pə́rsən əv ³díyn¹#/

c. Transcribe the following selection from "Alexander's Feast," lines 75–83, by John Dryden:

He sung Darius great and good.
By too severe a fate
Fallen, fallen, fallen, fallen,
Fallen from his high estate,
And weltering in his blood;
Deserted at his utmost need
By those his former bounty fed;
On the bare earth exposed he lies
With not a friend to close his eyes.

EXERCISE 12

Besides literary texts it is also useful to transcribe sentences in which similar linguistic material may be pronounced differently. Transcribe:

1. *Dogs are used to hunt with.*
   *Dogs are used to hunting.*
2. *Is that all the time you have to spend?*
   *Is that the time you have to leave?*
3. *This is the course she has to take.*
   *Are these the only clothes she has to take?*
4. *He gave her dog biscuits.*
   *He gave her* (some) *dog biscuits.*
5. *Let's go by ourselves.*
   (You take the car.) *Let us go in the taxi.*
6. *Go to the forward cabin.*
   *They tried a forward play.*
7. *Without his permit they didn't permit him to enter.*
8. *The suspect seemed to think no one would suspect him.*
9. *If you contrast similar sentences, the contrast in question really becomes apparent.*

# THE STUDY OF
# SPEECH SOUNDS:
## Acoustic Phonetics and
## Phonemic Analysis

## CHAPTER 5

### 5.1 Acoustic Phonetics

In dealing with speech as sound, we must know something about acoustics, the study of sound. Sounds are produced by bodies in motion. The movements may be articulatory movements like those described in sections 2 to 6 of Chapter 4.

The vocal cords are an example of moving bodies. By opening and closing rapidly—for example, one hundred times a second—they set in vibration the air above them, producing a **glottal tone**. At a vibration rate of one hundred cycles per second, this tone is perceived by the ear as somewhat lower than the A one octave below middle C. If a male speaker spoke at this tone, we would say he had a low bass voice. To analyze his speech at this tone, we must note criteria used in the physics of sound.

**Frequency** of sounds is determined by the number of times per second the body vibrates. These are known as **cycles per second (cps)**, or **hertz (Hz)**; one Hz = one cps. They correspond fairly closely to the perception of pitch. In identifying a sound, we give as one of its dimensions the Hz or mHz (thousands of Hz) specifying its frequency.

**Intensity** of sounds is determined by the amount of energy they carry. Intensity corresponds in a complex way to loudness. We perceive loudness more readily in sounds of higher pitch around 1,000 Hz to 4,000 Hz than in sounds of lower pitch around 32 Hz to 200 Hz. Moreover, we perceive loudness on a sliding scale; a sliding unit called the **decibel** is used to measure intensity. The smallest difference in loudness that a human ear can detect is one decibel. The range of loudness perceptible to the ear extends over about 130 decibels.

The third dimension of sound is **time**. It is determined by the **period** of vibration of the moving body. Thus to define any sound acoustically, we measure its frequency, intensity, and time of vibration.

## 5.2  The Glottal Tone

Several theories have been proposed to explain the production of the glottal tone. It results from a series of "puffs" that are produced when the closing of the glottis interrupts the stream of air coming from the lungs. These puffs produce a buzzlike sound. The theories differ in accounting for the activity of the vocal cords, but we may compare this activity with that of the mouthpiece of a double-reed instrument, such as the oboe.

The frequency of sounds produced by an oboe reed is determined by the size and tension of the mouthpiece and by the air pressure behind it. The oboe player may raise the pitch by providing greater pressure. We may also note the effect of the size and tension of the mouthpiece by comparing the heavier and laxer mouthpiece of a bassoon, which produces tones lower in pitch than those of an oboe.

Observations on the relation of pitch to the properties of the vibrating mouthpiece may be applied to the vocal cords. By providing greater sub-glottal pressure, or by tensing the vocal cords, we produce a higher glottal tone. The effect of shorter vocal cords is also evident when we compare the speech of men and women. The vocal cords of men are heavier and longer than those of women, so that men generally speak at a lower pitch level than women.

The tension of the vocal cords can be changed by the action of the arytenoid cartilages to produce higher or lower glottal tones. In a language like English, in which sentence intonation depends on pitch differences, these changes in the glottal tone provide the markers for the intonation contours. Such changes were noted in Chapter 4.8.2 for one utterance of *I'll come along*. In it the glottal tone began at 110 Hz, rose to 128 Hz, and then fell down to 80 Hz.

In a tone language the glottal tone marks differences between syllables and words, as illustrated by Japanese *sumí* 'charcoal' versus *súmi* 'corner.'

## 5.3  Resonance

The production of the glottal tone is only one of the effects of the action of the vocal cords in speech. To account for others, we must briefly sketch the results of resonance in the production of sound. The role of the vocal tract above the larynx in the production of vowels and resonants is to provide resonance resulting from the cavities formed by the articulatory organs.

Sounds or modifications of sounds are not necessarily caused by direct action of the bodies themselves. All bodies have a natural frequency of vibration, and they may be set into motion by vibrations of neighboring bodies. Such secondarily induced vibration is known as **resonance**, that is, resounding. Musical instruments are designed to produce resonance and in this way give to fundamental sounds the characteristic tone color we associate with each instrument. A violin and an oboe producing the same fundamental sound, for example, differ in their effect because of the differing resonance produced by the different cavities that make up the body of the violin and the tube of the oboe.

That cavities have characteristic resonances may be demonstrated by means of a simple cavity. If one blows across the mouth of a bottle, one can produce a tone. The tone varies in frequency with the volume of the cavity and the size of the opening. By diminishing the size of the cavity— for example, by filling the bottle partially with water—one can raise the frequency of the tone.

The vocal tract above the larynx is approximately 6.5 inches long. If such a cavity were completely regular, it would have resonant frequencies at 500 Hz, 1,500 Hz, 2,500 Hz, and so on. The vocal tract is, however, irregular and is varied greatly by the actions of the tongue and other organs. Accordingly its resonance frequencies may differ considerably from those given here.

Through this varied cavity the basic glottal tone must pass. As it does, resonating frequencies are added to it, depending on the conformation of the vocal tract. These frequencies, known as **formants**, characterize the vowels and resonants of language.

---

## 5.4  Acoustic Characteristics of Vowels: Measurements of English Vowels

The resonating effect results in two primary formants for each vowel. The [i] of [kit], for example, has a first formant centered at about 350 Hz and a second formant centered at about 2,100 Hz. For the sake of simplification we will omit reference to third and additional formants. These are used in characterizing vowels but especially resonants such as [r].

In further noting the characteristics of vowels, we may compare the articulation of two additional vowels, [u] and [a], and their formants. The vowel [u], articulated with a relatively small opening between the back of the tongue and the roof of the mouth, has a low first formant, roughly at 450 Hz, and a second formant at about 1,000 Hz, much lower than the second formant of [i]. In [a] neither formant is low, centering at about 600 Hz and 1,200 Hz. As these figures indicate, the first formant of close vowels, whether front or back, is relatively low. As vowels become more open, the first formant is higher. On the other hand, the second formant is relatively higher for close vowels, though more so for front than for back vowels.

Measurements of the vowels of a selected American English speaker provide the frequencies given in Figure 1 for the first and second formants in the stressed syllables of the words cited.

**Figure 1**

| | | |
|---|---|---|
| /iy/ | teach | 350–2,050 → 400–2,200 |
| /i/ | dinner | 450–1,800 |
| /ey/ | paper | 450–1,600 → 400–1,750 |
| /e/ | set | 500–1,550 |
| /æ/ | that | 550–1,500 |
| /ay/ | five | 500–1,200 → 600–1,650 |
| /ɨ/ | just | 400–1,600 |
| /ə/ | supper | 400–1,250 |
| /a/ | sophomore | 600–1,200 |
| /aw/ | about | 500–1,200 → 650–1,350 |
| /uw/ | do | 300–1,550 → 300–1,350 |
| /u/ | book | 450–1,000 |
| /ow/ | go | 450–1,500 → 500–1,000 |
| /ɔ/ | along | 600–950 |
| /ɔy/ | joy | 400–1,700 → 600–1,100 → 500–1,650 |

All of these vowels were produced with primary stress. Under weak stress the vowels are considerably shorter, and their characteristic frequency is not maintained as long. Of the fifteen measured instances of *gonna* (*going to*), for example, formants for the vowel of the second syllable could be determined for only .04 seconds. The first formant is approximately the same as in *supper*, 450 Hz, but the second is somewhat higher, 1,350 Hz.

Formants may change as a vowel is produced, especially diphthongal vowels like those of *teach, paper, do,* and *go* in the previous list, as well as those of *five, about,* and *joy*. To illustrate such changes in formants, measurements for one instance of *five* are given in Chart 1 for every other centisecond (hundredth of a second). These figures indicate the shifting from the [a] position initially in the diphthong toward the [I] or [y] position at its conclusion.

Further examples illustrate the considerable divergence of the actual sounds produced in the articulation of vowels by one speaker. For example, three utterances of *bet* by the same speaker showed formants of

**Chart 1. Formants of the Diphthong in *Five***

| Centiseconds | Second Formant | First Formant |
|---|---|---|
| 0 | 1,250 | 500 |
| 2 | 1,300 | 600 |
| 4 | 1,350 | 700 |
| 6 | 1,350 | 700 |
| 8 | 1,400 | 700 |
| 10 | 1,400 | 700 |
| 12 | 1,400 | 700 |
| 14 | 1,450 | 700 |
| 16 | 1,500 | 700 |
| 18 | 1,600 | 700 |
| 20 | 1,650 | 700 |
| 22 | 1,650 | 650 |
| 24 | 1,750 | 650 |
| 26 | 1,750 | 600 |
| 28 | 1,750 | 600 |
| 30 | 1,700 | 550 |

600 to 1,700, 550 to 1,700, and 500 to 1,600. The measurements may in this way demonstrate the use of relative rather than absolute physical entities in language. When we class phones together, whether in phonetic units or in phonemic units, we neglect the differences and recognize classes that are in opposition to other classes.

---

## 5.5   Complexities in the Definition of Vowels: Measurements of Japanese Vowels

A further complexity in speech contributes to our need to rely on relative entities in speech. This complexity results from the different fundamental tones of speakers. A soprano speaker has a fundamental glottal tone in the range of 260 Hz to 520 Hz; an alto 185 Hz to 320 Hz; a tenor 130 Hz to 260 Hz; a bass 92 Hz to 185 Hz. Vowel formants are resonance effects associated with these differing fundamentals. Accordingly they may differ in absolute value. Yet we equate the [i] of a soprano speaker with that of an alto, a tenor, and a bass, presumably by establishing a set of relative positions for their individual vowel formants. These absolute differences lead to considerable complexities in the description of the sounds used in speech. They may also illustrate the problems facing attempted uses of speech to induce action by machines, as in voice typewriters or voice telephone dialing. The problems are not insurmountable, but neither are they simple.

To note the variation of the physical entities representing vowels in a language besides English, we may cite measurements of the five Japanese vowels as pronounced by Mieko Han[1] compared with those of a male radio announcer. They center about the frequencies represented in Figure 2.

**Figure 2**

|  | I | E | A | O | U |
|---|---|---|---|---|---|
| Han | 300–3,000 | 600–2,400 | 1,000–2,000 | 750–1,350 | 375–1,900 |
| Male Speaker | 335–2,050 | 500–1,900 | 700–1,250 | 500–1,050 | 300–1,300 |

For both speakers the first formants of [i] and [u] are lowest, those of [a] highest. Further, the second formant [i] is higher than that of [e] and [a], and the second formant of [u] is higher than that of [o]. Accordingly, the relationships among the vowels are the same for both of the Japanese speakers, even though the absolute values differ greatly.

It may be noted further that the relationships between the Japanese vowels are comparable with those of the English vowel system: [i] has a very high and a low formant; the two formants of [u] are also relatively far apart, whereas those for [a] are relatively near one another. Because of these similarities we have no difficulty distinguishing a Japanese [i] from an [a], even without understanding the language. Thus the Japanese data illustrate that the characteristics of vowels are comparable from language to language. The similarity in acoustic measurements is related to similarity in articulation. Because of these observed similarities among the languages of the world, selected characteristics called **distinctive features** have been used to specify the entities used in speech. These features have the further advantage of applying to consonants as well as to vowels.

---

## 5.6  Devices for Acoustic Analysis

Before examining the acoustic characteristics of consonants or their distinctive features, let us look briefly at the devices that have been developed for acoustic analysis. Until recently, when these devices became available, the distinction between stops like [p t k] was unclear.

The first such device to be widely available was the **sound spectrograph,** developed about 1944. It analyzes the energy in sound and makes a graphic representation of it on a **spectrogram,** indicating areas of energy by burning corresponding parts of the spectrogram. Frequency is indicated on the vertical plane and time on the horizontal plane. In one kind of spectrographic analysis intensity is indicated by the darkness of the image. Intensity is therefore the least clearly measurable characteristic of sound on these spectrograms, but other procedures can be used to determine it. These procedures will not be described here.

---

[1] Mieko Shimizu Han, *Japanese Phonology* (Tokyo: Kenkyusha, 1962), p. 12.

The spectrograph is important in indicating where speech energy is distributed. Equally important are devices for simulating sounds, among them the **pattern playback.** With this device spectrograms can be played back to simulate speech. But not only spectrograms produced from speech can be played back. Synthetic spectrograms can also be produced, and in this way minute differences in representation can be tested. The synthetic spectrograms can be played, and the reactions of listeners can be tested. Such tests have provided additional evidence on the characteristics of consonants.

Even more capable of precise control are **electronic synthesizers,** which are now directed by computer. Such synthesizers are able to produce combinations of frequencies at various intensities over various periods of time. In this way they are comparable to computers synthesizing music. The results are highly specified sequences of simulated speech.

---

### 5.7  Acoustic Characteristics of Consonants

With the help of these various devices it has been determined that the characteristic acoustic features of stops are cues at specific frequencies. The cues for labial stops are at about 700 Hz, those for dentals at about 1,800 Hz, and those for velars at about 3,000 Hz. These cues regulate the initial portion of the second formant of vowels, or their **onset.** The indications of stop consonants are therefore carried in the first part of following vowels.

Chart 2 illustrates the initial sequences in *paw, taw, caw*, assuming that [ɔ] has formants at 600 Hz and 950 Hz.

**Chart 2. Initial Sequences in *paw, taw, caw***

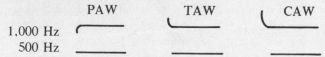

It should be noted further that the cue for dentals is higher than the second formants of some vowels and lower than those of others. Accordingly the vocalic onset interpreted as a dental sometimes rises, as toward the second formant of *tee*, and sometimes it descends, as toward the second formant of *taw*. This finding illustrates that even the phonetic markers of speech are not constant sounds but must be interpreted by their relationship to other configurations of sound.

Our identification of consonants through the modification of the initial portion of vowels may be readily determined from taped sequences that have the consonant segment removed. These are still interpreted as sequences of stop and vowel, though actually only the vowel remains. The initial section of the vowel retains enough of the characteristics of a *p b, t d, k g,* and so forth to permit identification.

Fricatives are characterized by acoustic energy at relatively high levels, though like the stops, [f] and [θ] are identified in large part by their effect on the second formant transitions. In [s] most of the friction is above 4,000 Hz; in [š] the friction is somewhat lower than for [s].

Acoustic investigation of resonants has shown that recognition of them is determined primarily by transitions in formants, notably the second and third. The transition for [w] is from a relatively low position to the second formant and that for [y] from a position somewhat above the second formant. For both [r] and [l] the third formant is important: that for [l] remains steady, whereas that for [r] begins near the second formant and rises appreciably before becoming steady.

The characteristics of the nasals and of nasalized vowels consist primarily in a weakening of the first formant. Studies by Pierre Delattre have demonstrated that this weakening is related to the velic opening, by means of which a further resonating chamber is made available. Experimental studies to determine the acoustic characteristics of the nasals in this way correlate the findings of acoustic research with well-known observations in articulatory phonetics.

## 5.8  Some Implications of Acoustic Phonetic Research

In sum, acoustic phonetic research of the past decades has considerably clarified our understanding of speech. Future studies will determine more precisely the characteristics of sounds in various environments, for example, of vowels as they differ with the consonants in their neighborhood and with various suprasegmentals. Moreover, these characteristics will be determined not only for English, in which most acoustic analysis has been done, but for other languages as well. These aims can be realized with the techniques and instruments now widely used, including procedures for synthesizing speech. Synthesized speech still lacks the qualities of natural speech. But the experiments in producing syntheses require increasingly detailed studies of speech and thus contribute to our understanding of language.

Besides this contribution to the study of language, acoustic phonetics has prompted a representation of languages by means of relationships reflecting the distinctive components of sound classes. Such representation by distinctive features rather than by phonemes or bundles of distinctive features will be discussed in the following chapter.

## 5.9  Phonemic Analysis

The sounds of a language can be studied from articulatory and acoustic points of view, but it is always necessary to note how sounds are used and patterned within the system of language. Speakers do not respond to the physical signals alone for it has long been known that these vary from speaker to speaker. Yet despite such variations we are able to accurately interpret sounds like /e a ɔ/ in any given language.

In determining the significant phonological elements of any language two criteria are taken into consideration: 1) similarity of articulation, and 2) relationships between the significant elements. As a result of the work of a Polish linguist, Baudouin de Courtenay, and his student Mikolaj Kruszewski, principles were developed to identify such elements, known subsequently as **phonemes.**

Definitions of phonemes have varied greatly, depending on the point of view from which they were proposed. Some theorists have favored regarding them as psychological entities, others as physical entities. For our purposes we will define a **phoneme** as a class of sounds, phonetically similar and distributed in complementary arrangements in a given language. The term for differing sounds in such a class is **allophone:** [c=cʰ k=kʰ] are allophones of English /k/. Each pronunciation of any sound is referred to as a **phone.**

The basis of the definitions for phonemes may be noted by reviewing the four *k* sounds in *keel, cool, car,* and *scar.* They differ from one another, yet they are more similar to each other than they are to other English sounds, such as the initials of *teal, tool, tar,* and *star.* Further, each complements the other. None of them occurs in the same environment. For example, the palatal *k* of *keel* never occurs in English before the vowel of *cool,* nor does the unaspirated *k* of *scar* occur initially in *keel, cool,* or *car.* And the midback *k* of *car* and the back *k* of *cool* do not stand before the vowel in *keel.* Accordingly we recognize that these sounds stand in **complementary distribution.** Moreover, their articulation and their distribution apply to English, not to Eskimo, Hindi, or any other language.

As a further characteristic of language, it may be noted that classes similar to one another follow similar patterning. Thus in English, *p* and *t* vary like /k/ in aspirated and unaspirated variants; compare [pʰar tʰar kʰar] with [sp=ar st=ar sk=ar]. Such patterning is taken into consideration when the classes called phonemes are determined.

In determining the /k/ phoneme for English, the linguist does not rely on the feelings of the native speaker. Rather he or she observes how the speaker talks. The linguist collects **minimal pairs** such as /tar kar/, or when these are difficult or impossible to find, **near-minimal pairs,** such as /vížən fišen/. An analysis is then made on the basis of a knowledge of articulatory phonetics and the observation of patterns of relationships in a language. This procedure for determining phonemes is known as the **commutation test,** by means of which linguists observe the patterning of sounds in a language without reference to the role of these sounds in the morphological and syntactic sets. Phonemes determined in this way are commonly referred to as **autonomous.** The next chapter will describe a varying procedure by which the grammatical system of language is taken into account when the basic phonological units are determined; such phonemes are referred to as **systematic.** German provides a widely used example that illustrates the difference between the methods used to obtain autonomous and systematic phonemes.

In German *d* and *t* are used initially and medially to distinguish words, for example, [*dank*] 'thanks' versus [*tank*] 'tank' and [*bundə*] 'alliances' versus [*buntə*] 'colorful.' When one analyzes German by the principles of autonomous phonemics, one must set up two phonemes, /t/ and /d/. Yet in comparing further forms of the words for 'alliance' and 'colorful,' one finds that both words have final [t] if no vowel follows, for example, in the singular of the noun [*bunt*] 'alliance' and in the predicate adjective form [*bunt*] 'colorful.' In autonomous phonemics these two *t*'s are assigned to the /t/ phoneme. The alternation between /bunt/ and /bundə/ is treated as a complexity in morphology and labeled a **morphophonemic variation.**

In systematic phonemics, on the other hand, a word or morpheme is assigned to an underlying form, on the basis of the patterning of morphological and syntactic sets in a language. The German word for 'alliance' would be assigned the underlying form /bund/, and the word for 'colorful' would be assigned the underlying form /bunt/. In a grammar of German positing underlying forms, the word for 'alliance' would then be listed in the lexicon as /bund/, and the nominative singular form would be derived from it by a low-level rule.

Over the past decade linguists have been intensively concerned with the validity of autonomous phonemes as opposed to systematic phonemes. Linguists who view language as a tightly related system disavow any validity for autonomous phonemes. On the other hand, linguists who are concerned with applications, such as language teaching, find great usefulness in grammars that propose autonomous phonemes. Moreover, in the estimate of such linguists, autonomous phonemes, such as German /t/ and /d/, have psychological validity for the native speaker. On the other hand, these linguists also admit the psychological validity of variations within sets and include in their grammars morphophonemes like German *D*. Proponents of systematic phonemes oppose this approach to grammar on the grounds that it produces unnecessarily complicated descriptions of language.

To resolve the conflict concerning the validity of autonomous versus systematic phonemics, further psychological experimentation and linguistic analysis will be necessary. Whatever the results of this work, students must know both approaches, for the phonological studies produced in the generation before 1960 and many subsequent studies are based on autonomous phonemic theory.

## 5.10  Behavior of Speakers Regarding Phonemes

In attempting to determine the validity of autonomous phonemes as linguistic units, let us examine the behavior of native speakers. Three types of behavior are pertinent. When adults borrow words from another language, when they learn a second language, and when any isolated word is learned in one's own language, words are interpreted as a succession of phonemes.

The Japanese /h/ phoneme may serve as an example. It has a [ɸ] before /u/ and [h] elsewhere, except that before [i] and [y] a third allophone [ç] may be used. To Japanese speakers a labiodental [f] in other languages is equivalent to their own bilabial [ɸ]. When a word like *Philippine* is taken into Japanese, the initial labial is interpreted as a form of the Japanese slit fricative, and Japanese [hiripin] results. Such behavior may be observed widely. English speakers equate the [β] of *Havana* with their own [v] and pronounce the word [həvǽnə]. They interpret German and French front rounded vowels as unrounded and pronounce *Lübeck* [líybek] and *Göttingen* [gétiŋən].

For an example of similar behavior in the learning of a second language, we may cite Germans learning English. German has no dental fricatives corresponding to English /θ ð/, as in *think* and *this*. German does, however, have dental stops [t d] and alveolar fricatives [s z]. In learning English, German speakers may classify the initial sounds of *think* and *this* with their dental stops, on the basis of the dental articulation, and pronounce [tiŋk dis], or they may give priority to the fricative articulation and pronounce [siŋk zis]. Therefore the behavior of speakers who have not yet mastered a language supports a phonological analysis positing autonomous phonemes.

Our interpretation of new names should also be noted. When introduced to a person for the first time, we have nothing to make use of but the sounds in understanding the name; as a result we may have some strange experiences. More than once in the South I have been asked my name, have dutifully said [léymən], and have at once been addressed as [mistər líymən]. My own [ey] is higher than that of the southern speakers, and without further context an erroneous phonemic replacement has resulted. Students may remember similar experiences, both in capturing unknown names and in learning a foreign language. In these processes we distinguish words by classes of sounds, not by precise identifications of sound. If a word begins with a labial stop—for example, *pan* or *Peele*—we disregard the aspiration of the stop, classing it instead for characteristics that distinguish it from other stops, as in *tan, can, Teele,* and *Kiel;* from voiced counterparts, as in *ban* and *Beal;* from fricatives, as in *fan* and *feel;* and from nasals, as in *man* and *meal*. Since aspiration is not a primary distinguishing characteristic in English, it is not one of the major criteria for recognizing /p t k/. Unless we make a detailed study of the phonetic characteristics of phonemes in our native language, we may even be unaware of these characteristics. This may cause problems in learning another language because we will interpret its classes of sounds to be like those of our native language.

Because the aspiration of stops is nonsignificant in English, native speakers of English may have problems in learning languages in which the contrast between aspirated and unaspirated stops is significant, such as Hindi. Because of such behavior regarding phonemes, anyone learning a second language is greatly assisted if he is instructed in the phonemic systems of the two languages, his own and the language he sets out to master. Moreover, an understanding of the phonemic system of any language, with its interrelationships and allophonic patterns, is of great benefit to language teachers.

BIBLIOGRAPHICAL NOTES

A brief introduction to acoustic phonetics is given in *Elements of Acoustic Phonetics* by Peter Ladefoged (Edinburgh and London: Oliver and Boyd, 1962) and in *The Speech Chain* by Peter B. Denes and Elliot N. Pinson (Murray Hill, N.J.: Bell Telephone Laboratories, 1963). For a large number of spectrographs with comments, see *Visible Speech* by Ralph K. Potter, George A. Kopp, and Harriet C. Green (New York: Van Nostrand, 1947). Some of the important studies in the field have been assembled in *Readings in Acoustic Phonetics,* edited by Ilse Lehiste (Cambridge, Mass.: M.I.T. Press, 1967). As her subtitle indicates, "an analysis [of Japanese] based upon sound spectrograms" has been made available in *Japanese Phonology* by Mieko Shimizu Han (Tokyo: Kenkyusha, 1962). The data on Japanese sounds given in this chapter are taken from her book. The data on English sounds are taken from *Selected Vowel Measurements of American English Speech* by Helen-Jo Hewitt and Winfred P. Lehmann, multilithed (Austin, Tex.: n.p., 1965).

One of the standard works dealing with phonemic analysis is *The Phoneme: Its Nature and Use,* 2d ed., by Daniel Jones (Cambridge: Heffer, 1962). Procedures for phonemic analyses were established in the thirties, and *On Defining the Phoneme,* Language Monographs 16 by W. Freeman Twaddell (Baltimore, Md.: Linguistic Society of America, 1935) is still a valuable source. Other classic treatments of phonemic analysis are two of Edward Sapir's articles, "Sound Patterns in Language" and "The Psychological Reality of Phonemes," in *Selected Writings of Edward Sapir in Language, Culture and Personality,* ed. David G. Mandelbaum (Berkeley and Los Angeles: University of California Press, 1963), pp. 33–60; and *Principles of Phonology* by Nikolaj S. Trubetzkoy, translated by Christiane A. M. Baltaxe (Berkeley and Los Angeles: University of California Press, 1969).

QUESTIONS FOR REVIEW

1. Discuss the acoustic characteristics of vowels. What is a formant?

2. Define: a. *phoneme;* b. *allophone;* c. *complementary distribution;* d. *minimal pair.*
3. Distinguish between autonomous and systematic phonemes.
4. Why do many English speakers pronounce the French word *lune* 'moon' like English *lean* rather than with a front rounded vowel? Why do many German speakers pronounce English *thin* as [tin]? Discuss possible implications of such behavior for the definition of phonemes.

## EXERCISES

### EXERCISE 1

In English the vowels differ in length in accordance with the following consonant or lack of consonant. The phonetic transcriptions below indicate this variation with · after a "half-long" vowel and : after a "long" vowel, as in:

| | | |
|---|---|---|
| *bat* | [bæt] | "short" æ |
| *bad* | [bæ·d] | "half-long" æ |
| *baa* | [bæ:] | "long" æ |

a. After examining the following words, state the condition determining the variations in vowel length:

| | | |
|---|---|---|
| | [ri·g] | [rik] |
| | [le·d] | [let] |
| [mæ:] | [kæ·b] | [kæp] |
| | [bə·g] | [bək] |
| pa:] | [pa·d] | [pat] |
| | [bu·l] | [buš] |
| [ɔ:] | [ɔ·d] | [ɔt] |
| [mi:y] | [mi·yd] | [miyt] |
| [le:y] | [le·yn] | [leyk] |
| [ra:y] | [ra·yd] | [rayt] |
| [ha:w] | [ha·wz] | [kawč] |
| [nu:w] | [nu·wz] | [nuws] |
| [to:w] | [ro·wb] | [rowp] |
| [jɔ:y] | [jɔ·yz] | [jɔys] |

b. In autonomous phonemic study phonological variants of this sort are classified into phonemes and allophones. List the vowel phonemes in these words and give the rules for the occurrence of the allophones.

EXERCISE 2[2]

The following are examples of short vowels in colloquial Egyptian Arabic. (ħ is a voiceless and e i is a voiced pharyngeal fricative.)

| | |
|---|---|
| nɪsɪ | *he forgot* |
| sɪkkɪtɪk | *your* (fem. sing.) *road* |
| weħɛs | *bad* (masc. sing.) |
| teʕɛb | *he became tired* |
| wælæd | *boy* |
| kætæb | *he wrote* |
| ħad | *boundary* |
| ʕad | *he counted* |
| kutub | *books* |
| kulluhum | *all of them* |
| ħob | *love* |
| ħokm | *regulation* |

a. Determine the three short vowel phonemes of colloquial Egyptian Arabic.
b. State the allophones exemplified here and their distribution with reference to the neighboring consonants.
c. Indicate the general patterning of low versus high allophones of the three short vowel phonemes.

EXERCISE 3

a. In his *Introduction to the Handbook of American Indian Languages* (1911), Franz Boas discusses some of the difficulties speakers of English face in the analysis of American Indian languages. As one example, he cites Pawnee, which "contains a sound which may be heard more or less distinctly sometimes as an *l,* sometimes as *r,* sometimes as *n,* and again as *d.*"[3] Boas adds that for the Pawnee speaker it is without any doubt "the same sound." In subsequent phonological study a "same sound" with different variants has been called a *phoneme.* Examine the Pawnee allophones and indicate the features they have in common. Also discuss why the four Pawnee allophones were heard by Boas and other field workers (who had English or German as their native languages) as four different sounds.
b. As another example, Boas cites Lower Chinook. It contains "a sound which is readily perceived as a *b, m,* or *w.*" What features do these three Lower Chinook allophones have in common?

---

[2] This exercise is based on Richard S. Harrell, *The Phonology of Colloquial Egyptian Arabic* (New York: American Council of Learned Societies, 1957), pp. 45–68.

[3] Franz Boas, *Introduction to the Handbook of American Indian Languages* (1911; reprint ed., Washington, D.C.: Georgetown University Press, 1968), p. 11.

c. After discussing the interpretation of such sounds by speakers of English and German, Boas goes on to say that "the Indians of the North Pacific coast have a series of *l* sounds, which may be roughly compared to our sounds *tl, cl, gl*. Consequently, a word like *close* is heard by the Indians sometimes one way, sometimes another; our *cl* is for them an intermediate sound, in the same way as some Indian sounds are intermediate sounds to our ears."[4] Account for this interpretation of English [kl].

---

[4] *Ibid.*, pp. 12–13.

# GENERATIVE PHONOLOGY

## CHAPTER 6

## 6.1 Systematic Phonemes

Phonology as discussed in the preceding chapter analyzes words and sentences into distinct segments on the basis of the patterning of the speech sounds in any given language. In recent linguistic study such a treatment of the sounds of language has been criticized as static. The flow of sounds in speech, as is clear from articulatory and acoustic analysis, is continuous. Moreover, neighboring elements affect one another. Efforts have therefore been directed at a dynamic approach to the study and analysis of the phonological component.

These efforts are based on phonological theory using **distinctive features,** which are the smallest elements constituting phonemes. Moreover, this phonological theory takes into consideration the variations that phonological elements may exhibit in grammatical classes. For example, the English past tense suffix is realized as [d] in some verbs, such as *seize, seized* [siyzd], but as [t] in others, such as *cease, ceased* [siyst]. Accordingly phonological elements have been proposed that underlie such surface forms. The proposed elements are based on syntactic and morphological as well as on phonological patterns, that is, on the entire system of language. For this reason, the resulting elements are called **systematic phonemes.**

Systematic phonemics analyzes sequences into individual segments, but the segments are more abstract than are autonomous phonemes. The treatment of English [ŋ] may be used to illustrate the differing approaches. In some words such as *strong* [strɔŋ], this nasal alternates with a sequence of [ŋg], as in the comparative form *stronger* [strɔŋgər]. Moreover, [ŋ] is generally found before [g] or [k] in English. On the basis of this patterning, an underlying form with /g/ is assumed for the simple form as well as the comparative of *strong* and also for any word ending in [ŋ], such as *sing* [siŋ]. Since, on the other hand, [n] never occurs before [g] in English, it is further assumed that the underlying nasal in words like *strong* and *sing* is /n/. The underlying forms for these words are then given as /strɔng/ and /sing/.

In the dynamic view of language discussed here, the actual pronunciations are specified by means of rules. Thus by one rule the abstract phoneme /n/ in /strɔng/ and /sing/ is identified as [ŋ]. And when *strong, sing,* and other words ending in [ŋ] are final, the underlying /g/ is deleted by a further rule. Through these procedures the list of phonemes in English is reduced by one: [ŋ] is a phonetic but not a phonemic entity.

The rules make use of representations for distinctive features rather than phonemes. Since distinctive feature analysis is relatively recent, phonologists may differ in the features they propose. Some phonologists have relied more heavily on the articulatory characteristics of sounds. Others have relied on acoustic characteristics. The resulting classifications may, however, be equivalent, with differing labels. For example, sounds produced with rounding, such as [o u], are labeled +ROUND from an articulatory point of view. Acoustically they have a flattened second formant, and therefore they have been labeled +FLAT. This chapter will not list all classifications that have been proposed. Since recent phonological studies have favored articulatory analysis, the features presented here are articulatory. After they have been identified briefly, principles and rules used in the presentation of the phonological structures of any given language will be discussed.

Through the assumption of abstract underlying forms as well as the use of distinctive features and rules, the phonological sequences of language are precisely specified. Because of these procedures, this approach to the study of the sound component of language is known as **generative phonology.**

---

## 6.2  Distinctive Features (DF)

As noted above, the distinctive features that now are most widely used are based in large part on articulatory characteristics. Distinctive features are identified for the subglottal area, the glottal area, and the nasal and oral areas. Oral articulation is further specified for manner and place of articulation.

Many phonemes are distinguished by one feature. The labial stops /p b/, for example, are distinguished by VOICE: /p/ is accordingly −VOICE and /b/ +VOICE. Because of such minimal contrasts, feature analysis generally makes use of a binary principle. The distinctive features for the phonemes in a given language are identified, and each phoneme is labeled plus (+) or minus (−) for pertinent features.

## 6.2.1 Distinctive Features Associated with Syllabic Role

The subglottal articulatory area is associated with the role of phonemes in syllables. They may occupy the central position in a syllable, as does the /i/ of *bit*. If so, they are identified as +SYLLABIC. Most such elements are vowels, and accordingly the term +VOCALIC may also be used. Since, however, elements other than vowels may occupy the central position in syllables, for example, *r* in the Czech city-name *Brno* or *s* in the English *psst*, the label SYLLABIC now has more general application.

Expiratory energy is also associated with the subglottal area. Syllables may be pronounced with stronger or weaker expiratory force, as in the noun *íncrease* versus the verb *increáse*. The feature in the more prominent syllables is labeled +STRESS in contrast with the −STRESS of the less prominent.

## 6.2.2 Distinctive Features Associated with Manner of Articulation

Phonemes are also characterized by articulatory constriction in the oral cavity. If the constriction is complete as for oral stops, or nearly complete, as for fricatives, they are labeled +CONSONANTAL. Glides and vowels are −CONSONANTAL, as are laryngeals, such as /h/ and /ʔ/.

Phonemes are also characterized for relatively open articulation, producing sonorant characteristics. Thus nasal consonants are +SO-NORANT because of nasal resonance, while they are also +CON-SONANTAL. Liquids, glides, and vowels are also +SONORANT. Obstruents, on the other hand, are −SONORANT. Since all obstruents are characterized in this way, the feature may also be labeled OBSTRUENT, with the plus and minus signs reversed; +OBSTRUENT corresponds to −SONORANT.

Phonemes are also distinguished in accordance with complete closure of the oral cavity. Thus nasals and flaps, as well as affricates and stops, have a complete oral closure; they are labeled −CONTINUANT. Fricatives, on the other hand, as well as glides, trills, and laterals, are +CON-TINUANT.

In the articulation of phonemes the release may be instantaneous or gradual. Affricates, such as /čj/, are produced with gradual release, yielding the fricative after the stop, and are labeled +GRADUAL RELEASE.

If the release is made to the sides of the oral cavity, as for /l/, the feature is +LATERAL.

Articulation may also be characterized by stridence, as for /s z/. Such phonemes are labeled +STRIDENT.

Besides differences in release, sound classes may also be distinguished by the entire characteristics of the musculature. The articulatory muscles may be relatively tense or lax. The vowels of German, for example, may be classified for tenseness; the vowel [a:] of *Staat* 'state' is +TENSE as opposed to the vowel [a] of *Stadt* 'city,' which is −TENSE. The English vocalic nuclei /iy ey æ a ɔ ow uw/ have also been classified as +TENSE in underlying forms and are written /ī ē ǣ ā ɔ̄ ō ū/.

## 6.2.3   Distinctive Features Associated with Place of Articulation

Characteristic places of articulation are associated with the position of the tongue—on the one hand the body of the tongue, on the other the blade. The body may be characteristically high, low, or retracted.

If the body of the tongue is raised above the neutral position for rest, the phonemes are labeled +HIGH. Examples are /i u y w k g ŋ č j š ž/. For such phonemes, the upper frequencies are shifted upward; accordingly they have also been labeled +SHARP.

If the body of the tongue is lowered below the neutral position, the phonemes are labeled +LOW. Examples of +LOW are /æ a ɔ/. The high vowels, such as /i u/, are also labeled −LOW, as well as +HIGH. By contrast, the mid vowels, such as /e/, are labeled −LOW and −HIGH.

If the body of the tongue is retracted, the phonemes are labeled +BACK. Velar consonants, as well as back vowels and /w/ are so labeled.

The blade of the tongue is the primary articulating agent in dentals, alveolars, and palatoalveolars, that is, in sounds in which the characteristic narrowing involves a concave or "crown" position because of the raising of the blade. The resultant phonemes, for example, /r l t d θ đ s z š ž č j/, have therefore been labeled +CORONAL.

As the distinction between articulation with the body of the tongue and its blade indicates, sounds may be distinguished for primary place of production before the characteristic narrowing and behind it, with regard to the involvement of the tongue. The /š/ may be taken as the characteristic for this distinction. Phonemes made with characteristic obstructions before /š/, that is, labials, dentals, and alveolars, are labeled +AN-

TERIOR. Palatals and velars, as well as other phonemes characterized by narrowing to the rear of that for /š/ are −ANTERIOR.

Phonemes characterized by rounding of the lips are labeled +ROUND, such as /o u/, or front rounded vowels, /ö ü/.

If the velum is relaxed, so that sounds are characterized by nasal resonance they are labeled +NASAL.

### 6.2.4 DF's Associated with Laryngeal Articulation

Sounds produced with characteristic voicing are labeled +VOICE, such as the voiced obstruents, the resonants, and the vowels.

Laryngeal articulation has also been analyzed for other characteristics, as in the production of aspirated consonants. The involvement of the laryngeal articulators in the production of such sounds is still inadequately understood. For the characterization of the elements like Sanskrit [ph bh th dh], tentative labels like +ASPIRATE may be used. As the result of further research, however, we can expect such characteristics to be more precisely determined and the creation of improved classifications.

The distinctive features presented here are adequate for the phonological analysis of English and many other languages. Until our understanding of the phonological structures of language improves, linguists will differ in the analyses and distinctive features proposed for specific languages. A knowledge of those presented here, and of the procedures applied in the description of the phonological component of languages, will permit ready interpretation of the differing classifications that may be encountered.

### 6.2.5 DF Analysis of the English Sound Classes

Before phonological rules are discussed, the sound classes posited for English will be listed with their distinctive features. The symbols / ī ū ē ō/ correspond to the compound symbols /iy uw ey ow/ used above. Moreover, like these, /ǣ ā ɔ/ are listed as tense vowels, and / ʌ/ rather than /ə/ is used for vowels such as those in *putt*.

In this chart, each of the phonemes has been labeled for each of the distinctive features. Many of the phonemes can, however, be labeled distinctively with only a few features, or even one. Thus /m n/ are the only phonemes labeled +NASAL, and this feature alone distinguishes them from all other English phonemes. And /l/ is distinguished by the single feature +LATERAL. Since the other features can be supplied by a general rule for these phonemes, they are said to be **redundant.** All resonants in English are voiced, for example, and accordingly +VOICE is said to be a redundant feature of /m n l/.

**Chart 1. English Phonemes with Their Distinctive Features**

| | ī | ū | ē | ō | æ | ā | ɔ | i | u | e | ʌ | y | w |
|---|---|---|---|---|---|---|---|---|---|---|---|---|---|
| SYLLABIC | + | + | + | + | + | + | + | + | + | + | + | − | − |
| CONSONANTAL | − | − | − | − | − | − | − | − | − | − | − | − | − |
| HIGH | + | + | − | − | − | − | − | + | + | − | − | + | + |
| BACK | − | + | − | + | − | + | + | − | + | − | + | − | + |
| LOW | − | − | − | − | + | + | + | − | − | − | − | − | − |
| ANTERIOR | − | − | − | − | − | − | − | − | − | − | − | − | − |
| CORONAL | − | − | − | − | − | − | − | − | − | − | − | − | − |
| ROUND | − | + | − | + | − | − | + | − | + | − | − | + | + |
| TENSE | + | + | + | + | + | + | + | − | − | − | − | − | − |

| | r | l | m | v | f | b | p | n | ð | θ | d | t | z | s | j | č | ž | š | (ŋ) | g | k | h |
|---|---|---|---|---|---|---|---|---|---|---|---|---|---|---|---|---|---|---|---|---|---|---|
| SYLLABIC | − | − | − | − | − | − | − | − | − | − | − | − | − | − | − | − | − | − | − | − | − | − |
| CONSONANTAL | + | + | + | + | + | + | + | + | + | + | + | + | + | + | + | + | + | + | + | + | + | − |
| HIGH | − | − | − | − | − | − | − | − | − | − | − | − | − | − | + | + | + | + | + | + | + | − |
| BACK | − | − | − | − | − | − | − | − | − | − | − | − | − | − | − | − | − | − | + | + | + | − |
| LOW | − | − | − | − | − | − | − | − | − | − | − | − | − | − | − | − | − | − | − | − | − | + |
| ANTERIOR | + | + | + | + | + | + | + | + | + | + | + | + | + | + | − | − | − | − | − | − | − | − |
| CORONAL | + | + | − | − | − | − | − | + | + | + | + | + | + | + | + | + | + | + | − | − | − | − |
| CONTINUANT | + | + | − | + | + | − | − | − | + | + | − | − | + | + | − | − | + | + | − | − | − | + |
| NASAL | − | − | + | − | − | − | − | + | − | − | − | − | − | − | − | − | − | − | + | − | − | − |
| LATERAL | − | + | − | − | − | − | − | − | − | − | − | − | − | − | − | − | − | − | − | − | − | − |
| STRIDENT | − | − | − | + | + | − | − | − | − | − | − | − | + | + | + | + | + | + | − | − | − | − |

The symbols given here are in accordance with those in Noam Chomsky and Morris Halle's influential *Sound Pattern of English* (New York: Harper & Row, 1968), pp. 163–178.

## 6.3  Phonological Rules

By generative phonological theory, underlying forms are posited with such phonemes for lexical and grammatical items. The underlying form of the numeral *eight,* for example, may be posited as /ēt/. In the ordinal *eighth,* this often has the variant /ē/, as in the pronunciation [ēθ]. Since the other ordinals also have the suffix [θ], this would be set up as the underlying form of the suffix; /ēt/ would be set up as the underlying form of the numeral *eight;* and [ēθ] would be derived from the underlying representation /ētθ/ by a rule deleting the /t/. In this way the resultant form would be related to a basic underlying representation and derived by rules indicating phonological processes.

The rules used to indicate such processes follow a standard format. The item undergoing modification is designated to the left of an arrow. The modification is indicated on the right. The conditions or environment in which the modification takes place is specified further to the right. In such rules, features are used—only those features that are sufficient to identify the phonemes involved.

For example, some speakers of English drop the /l/ before labial fricatives, saying [wəf] rather than [wəlf] for *wolf.* Since /l/ is unambiguous, labeled by the single feature +LATERAL, this feature alone is placed to the left of the arrow. Loss is indicated by the symbol ø for zero. The environment is specified after a slant line / , with the position of the phoneme in question indicated by an underline and the further elements labeled by features. The rule specifying pronunciations like [wəf] would then be written as follows:

$$[+\text{LATERAL}] \quad \rightarrow \quad \emptyset \ / \ \underline{\qquad} \quad \begin{bmatrix} +\text{CONTINUANT} \\ +\text{ANTERIOR} \\ -\text{CORONAL} \\ +\text{STRIDENT} \end{bmatrix}$$

This rule states that /l/ in underlying forms is lost before +CONTINUANT (/ r l v f ð θ z s /) and —CORONAL (/ v f h /) and +STRIDENT (/ v f /). The four features thus specify precisely the elements involved. Speakers observing this rule would then pronounce *wolf, wolves, Dolph,* and so on without /l/.

The rule was once general for English. The standard pronunciation for *half, halves, calf, calves,* and so on has no [l]. Moreover, the rule had broader scope, affecting words like *calm, palm, psalm, walk,* and *talk,* which also have no /l/. However, the /l/ was reintroduced in many words on the basis of modern spelling. Thus the name *Ralph* is commonly pronounced with /l/ in contrast with the former pronunciation indicated by the spelling *Rafe,* as in Shakespeare's *Taming of the Shrew,* Act 4, Scene 1, line 139:

There were none fine but Adam, Rafe, and Gregory; . . .

Similarly, *falcon* is now widely pronounced with [l]. In a grammar of English, then, this rule must be further limited in scope. The rule format, however, can be flexibly adapted by specifying both the phonological or morphological environment and sociolinguistic conditions. Here some of the widely found rules will be illustrated.

### 6.3.1   Feature-Changing Rules

Features of phonemes in underlying forms are often changed in specific contexts. A widely cited example is the change in voice of final German obstruents. For example, the German word for 'alliance' is *Bund* [bunt] in the singular, *Bunde* [bunde] in the plural. The adjective for 'colorful' by contrast has the forms *bunt* [bunt], *bunte* [bunte]. Similarly, the singular of *Tage* [tāge] is *Tag* [tāk] 'day'; of *Weibe* [waybə], *Weib* [wayp] 'woman.' To indicate this characteristic of German, the following rule is included in grammars:

$$[-\text{SONORANT}] \rightarrow [-\text{VOICE}] / \underline{\hspace{1cm}} \#$$

The feature $-$SONORANT distinguishes German obstruents from the resonants, such as /r l m n/. The left side of the rule thus applies to German /b d g v z/. These become voiceless at the ends of words, the environment generally specified in phonological rules by #.

Another example of a feature-changing rule is the one indicating intervocalic voicing of American English /t/ as in *butter*. If this word is identified as 'one who butts,' the underlying form must be /bʌt/. For many speakers of American English this kind of /t/ is voiced when intervocalic. Such speakers would observe the following rule:

$$\begin{bmatrix} +\text{ANTERIOR} \\ +\text{CORONAL} \\ -\text{CONTINUANT} \end{bmatrix} \rightarrow +\text{VOICE} / \text{V} \underline{\hspace{1cm}} \check{\text{V}}$$

Here V is an abbreviation for *vowel*. By this rule /t d/ would be voiced between vowels when the second vowel is weakly stressed.

This rule must be further specified for most, if not all, speakers of American English. While the /t/ of words like *data, bottom, bottle,* and *butter* is voiced by many speakers of American English, /t/ before vowel + /n/ generally is not, as in *button* [bə́tən] rather than [bə́dən].

Nevertheless, these examples illustrate rules that are widely found in languages, as will be noted further below. Since they apply in specific contexts, they are called **context-sensitive** rules, as opposed to **context-free** rules. Most rules of grammars are context-sensitive, as the study of any language will demonstrate.

### 6.3.2  Deletion and Insertion Rules

In some processes an entire element may be deleted from an underlying form, or an element may be inserted. The treatment of /l/ in some varieties of English was given above as an illustration of a deletion rule.

The adding of /t/ between consonants in English may be cited as an example of an insertion role. In many pronunciations of English *once* is produced as [wənts], not [wəns]; *lunch* as [ləntš], not [lənš]. The rule may be stated:

$$\emptyset \rightarrow \begin{bmatrix} +\text{CORONAL} \\ -\text{VOICE} \\ -\text{CONTINUANT} \end{bmatrix} / \begin{bmatrix} +\text{CORONAL} \\ +\text{NASAL} \end{bmatrix} - \begin{bmatrix} +\text{CORONAL} \\ -\text{VOICE} \\ +\text{CONTINUANT} \\ +\text{STRIDENT} \end{bmatrix}$$

By this rule /t/ would be added between /n/ and /s š/.

Examination of the features in this rule may indicate the usefulness of rule notation. All the elements concerned share the feature +CORONAL. On the other hand, by contrast with fricatives, /n/ is −CONTINUANT; furthermore, /n/ is +VOICE. In the process of articulation, the features may be modified gradually. If so, an intermediate sound may be produced that maintains the +CORONAL and all redundant features of CORONAL elements. This intermediate sound has the −VOICE feature of the second element of the original cluster, while maintaining the −CONTINUANT feature of the first element. Such a modification, by which an element becomes similar to another, is a common process in language and is known as **assimilation.**

### 6.3.3  Permutation and Coalescence Rules

Elements may also be shifted with regard to one another in a process known as **metathesis.** Thus in Old English, clusters like /sk/ and /sp/ were often permuted to /ks/ and /ps/—for example, the Old English form *ācsian* was metathesized from *āscian*, earlier *āskōjan*, yielding the variant of *ask*, generally spelled *axe*, that has been preserved in dialects.

Since in such a process the elements themselves are unchanged and only their sequence is modified, rules are written with numerals labeling each element. The Old English rule, which applied particularly to the West Saxon dialect, might then be written:

$$V \quad \begin{bmatrix} +\text{CONTINUANT} \\ +\text{CORONAL} \\ +\text{STRIDENT} \end{bmatrix} \quad \begin{bmatrix} -\text{CONTINUANT} \\ -\text{VOICE} \\ -\text{CORONAL} \end{bmatrix} \rightarrow 1\ 2\ 3$$

$$1 \qquad\qquad 2 \qquad\qquad\qquad 3$$

By this rule the original second element is shifted after the third. This rule applied for /s/ after vowels, in conjunction with labial and velar stops. Since voiced variants of /s/ did not occur in the stated environment, this feature does not need to be specified for the elements labeled 2.

If a segment coalesces with another, a similar rule format is observed. Thus in early Old English, nasals were coalesced with vowels before voiceless fricatives. By this rule the contrasts between the following English and German words (and others) were originated: English *five,* German *fünf;* English *goose,* German *Gans.* Since both Old English nasals were involved, the rule merely needs to specify that the element was +NASAL. In the process the preceding vowel was nasalized, as indicated in the rule:

$$V \quad [+\text{NASAL}] \qquad \begin{bmatrix} +\text{CONSONANT} \\ +\text{CONTINUANT} \end{bmatrix} \rightarrow \begin{bmatrix} 1 \\ +\text{NASAL} \end{bmatrix} \quad \emptyset \quad 3$$

$$1 \qquad\qquad 2 \qquad\qquad\quad 3$$

The rule indicates that the nasal, or second element was lost and also that its distinctive feature coalesced with the first element.

### 6.3.4   Additional Notational Features of Rules

If elements in a rule vary in one feature, such as voice, a rule may be written to indicate that this feature is either + or −. The device used for this purpose is the Greek letter $a,$ $\beta,$ or $\gamma,$ depending on the number of variants.

Often in languages, two successive obstruents are either voiceless or voiced. If for example a /d/ occurs before an /s/, it becomes /t/; on the other hand, if a /t/ occurs before a /z/, it becomes /d/. The feature characterizing the obstruents is −SONORANT. To indicate the equivalence in voicing, the following rule may be written:

$$[-\text{SONORANT}] \rightarrow [a\text{VOICE}]/\underline{\qquad} \begin{bmatrix} -\text{SONORANT} \\ a\text{VOICE} \end{bmatrix}$$

This rule states that all clusters of two obstruents are either voiced (for example, *dz, db*) or voiceless (for example, *ts, tp*). The Greek letters before the designation VOICE specify its value as the same in the clusters, whether + or −.

Another notational feature commonly used to indicate the number of consonants in an environment is adscript numerals. Thus $C_1$ indicates one consonant or more, $C_2$ indicates two consonants or more, and so on. $C_0$ means zero or more consonants. The following section of a rule:

$$C_0 \quad V \quad C_2$$

indicates that the vowels in question may be between zero or any number of consonants and a cluster consisting of at least two consonants.

The use of these conventions will be further illustrated in rules given below and in the exercises to this chapter.

## 6.4 Rule Ordering

In a grammar consisting of rules, these have to be arranged so that they lead to the actual forms. Differing rules may apply to the same segments; unless they are arranged accurately, erroneous forms may result. Grammars then place rules in specific orders.

An example will illustrate the need for rule order. As noted above, Old English *āscian* 'ask' underwent metathesis to the form *ācsian;* a similar change was carried out from *wascan* to *wacsan* 'wash.' But the *sk* sequence was also maintained in some forms and then changed by palatalization to [š], as in Modern English *wash*. The Modern English form for 'request, ask' then should be [æš], in accordance with words like *wush, fish,* and *ash tree*.

If now, in a grammar of English, the forms *ask* and dialectal *axe* are derived from one underlying form, and if words like *wash* are also to be accounted for, the rules for the metathesis of *sk* to *ks* and the palatalization of *sk* to [š] must be so ordered that the correct outputs are generated. The orders proposed in grammars generally reflect the historical sequence of such processes.

To specify the proper order, rules may either be so written that they require the correct output, or they may be labeled for their order of application. When so labeled, they are said to be **extrinsically ordered.** When written to provide the correct output without such extrinsic labels, they are said to be **intrinsically ordered.** We will note examples of order rules below, in syntax as well as phonology.

## 6.5 Marking

When contrasts are found in language—such as that between German *bunde* : *bunte;* or *bund* [bunt] : *bunt*—the output is often similar from language to language. As in this example, the most likely output of such a contrast is the voiceless member. The property in question, such as VOICE in these pairs, has been referred to as a **marking.** And the member of a pair like [bund] : [bunt] carrying that marking is said to be **marked;** the other member is said to be **unmarked.**

The study of **marking,** or **markedness,** has been widely pursued in recent linguistics. The notion itself was studied by the Prague Circle in the

1930s and made notable by Roman Jakobson in a brilliant and influential monograph translated as *Child Language, Aphasia and Phonological Universals*. In this monograph Jakobson pointed out that children generally master the unmarked phonological elements first. On the other hand, if speakers lose control of the phonological elements of language because of brain injury, the marked members are first affected. Since these phenomena occur in all languages, Jakobson related them to principles that presumably govern the structure of phonological systems and accordingly are said to be **universal.**

Among such universal principles are those concerning the presence of nasals in language. Nasal vowels are found only in languages with nasal consonants and often result from the loss of their specific environments, as in the Old English examples cited above. Moreover, nonnasal vowels are far more widespread than are nasal vowels.

This and other examples indicate that some phonological elements are more complex than others. Investigations to determine these have led to general conclusions about language.

## 6.6  Natural Rules

The rules that lead to the simpler or unmarked elements have been labeled **natural.** By such rules the marked elements in a phonological system tend to be eliminated, yielding to unmarked elements.

If these observations are accurate, we would expect to find change in language yielding simple elements. Evidence for such change can be cited. For example, rounding is held to be more natural accompanying back vowels like [u o] than front vowels. In early Old English, and in Old High German, front rounded vowels were produced when [u o] were assimilated to a following [i y] in the process known as **umlaut.** The front rounded vowels are still maintained in the German standard language, as in *Füsse* [flüsə] and *zwölf* [tsvölf]. But in English they came to be unrounded by the time of late Old English, leading to the Modern English forms *feet* and *twelve*. Many German dialects also have unrounded the umlaut vowels. These developments, then, are in accordance with the view that unrounded front vowels are more natural than rounded front vowels and thus will tend to develop from them.

We have also observed above that nasalized vowels are assumed to be more marked or less natural than simple, oral vowels. There is considerable evidence that nasalized vowels are also changed to oral vowels. Thus the former nasal vowels in earlier forms of English *goose, five*, and so on are now oral. And in many Chinese dialects, final nasals have coalesced with preceding vowels, giving rise to nasalized vowels. Thus the term of address *péngyoumen* 'friends' may be pronounced [pʌyoumə̃]. In many dialects, however, this has become [pʌyoumə], with the nasalization lost. This development too is in keeping with natural processes.

## 6.7  The Results of Phonological Research

The study of phonology and phonological processes has in this way led to general hypotheses about the use of sounds in language. Many further investigations are being carried out to explore such generalizations. These investigations center around language acquisition, language pathology, or the structure of phonological systems in various languages. Besides adding to our understanding of phonological elements and their interrelationships in languages, they will also lead to improved methods of dealing with such problems as those encountered by children in learning their language or by speakers with the disabilities of aphasia and deafness. Practical application of theoretical research will in turn lead to a deeper understanding of phonology.

BIBLIOGRAPHICAL NOTES

An early presentation of distinctive feature analysis may be found in *Fundamentals of Language* by Roman Jakobson and Morris Halle (The Hague: Mouton, 1956). The most influential work in generative phonology is *The Sound Pattern of English* by Noam Chomsky and Morris Halle (New York: Harper & Row, 1968). More recent treatments are *Generative Phonology* by Sanford A. Schane (Englewood Cliffs, N.J.: Prentice-Hall, 1973) and *The Organization of Phonology* by Stephen R. Anderson (New York: Academic Press, 1974). These works contain bibliographies, including generative phonological treatments of other languages. Further conventions used in generative phonological study are also given in these texts. Roman Jakobson's monograph, first published in 1941, is available in an English translation by A. R. Keiler with the title, *Child Language, Aphasia and Phonological Universals* (The Hague: Mouton, 1968).

QUESTIONS FOR REVIEW

1. Distinguish between systematic and autonomous phonemes.
2. What are the characteristics of the following distinctive features: +SYLLABIC, +CONSONANTAL, +SONORANT?
3. Distinguish between the distinctive features +CONTINUANT and +GRADUAL RELEASE, giving examples of each.
4. Why is the distinctive feature +LATERAL adequate to characterize one of the phonemes of English? What is meant by the statement that the remaining features of this phoneme are redundant?
5. Name and define some of the distinctive features associated with characteristic places of articulation.

6. Which distinctive features are associated with articulation in which the body of the tongue is most characteristically involved? the blade of the tongue?
7. What are the three segments of phonological rules?
8. What is: a. a feature-changing rule; b. a deletion rule; c. a permutation rule?
9. Explain the following elements found in rules: a. C₀; b. *a*, c. V
10. What is meant by *rule ordering?*
11. Distinguish between extrinsic and intrinsic rule ordering.
12. What is meant by *metathesis?*
13. Discuss markedness, indicating how the marked member of a pair may be determined.
14. What is meant by a *natural rule?*
15. Discuss universals, indicating a phonological universal.

EXERCISES

EXERCISE 1

Give the distinctive features of the following:

/s b n ǣ e/

EXERCISE 2

Since the possible consonants occurring initially before English [r] followed by a vowel are limited in number (see Chapter 4, Exercise 2), it is not necessary to indicate all the distinctive features for the initial consonants of *prey, train,* and *crane*. Which would have to be specified so that [p t k] would be distinguished from any other consonants in this position?

EXERCISE 3

Only one consonant is possible before *pr, tr,* and *kr,* as in *sprain, strain,* and *scrap*. What single feature would be adequate to indicate [s] in this position in English? Why could the others be omitted?

EXERCISE 4

If you were distinguishing the pronunciation of *shrimp* as [šrimp] from the [srimp] pronunciation of some speakers, what would be the varying distinctive feature?

EXERCISE 5

The underlying form of the third singular present morpheme in English verbs may be posited as /z/.
  a. When used after verb roots ending in −VOICE phonemes other than sibilants, this morpheme is realized as /s/, as in *hits, cuffs,* and so on. Write a rule specifying this form. Which of the types of rules discussed in 6.3 is your rule?
  b. After verb roots ending in sibilants, this morpheme is realized as /əz/, as in *push, buzz,* and *budge.* Write a rule specifying this form, identifying the type.

EXERCISE 6

The underlying form of the past morpheme in English verbs may be posited as /d/.
  a. When used after roots of regular verbs ending in −VOICE phonemes other than dentals, this morpheme is realized as /t/, as in *dip, kick,* and *hush.* Write a rule specifying this form, indicating the type of rule.
  b. When used after such roots ending in /t/ or /d/, this morpheme is realized as /əd/, as in *bat* and *seed.* Write a rule specifying this form, indicating the type of rule.

EXERCISE 7

Assume that the phonemes as given for English in Chart 1 are modified as follows in an obscure area of the English-speaking world. Indicate the phonemes and the modified forms.

a.
$$\begin{bmatrix} -\text{CONTINUANT} \\ +\text{ANTERIOR} \\ +\text{CORONAL} \end{bmatrix} \rightarrow \begin{bmatrix} +\text{CONTINUANT} \\ +\text{STRIDENT} \end{bmatrix} \Big/ \text{V} \underline{\quad} \text{V}$$

Indicate the type of rule. State whether this is a natural rule.

b.
$$[+\text{NASAL}] \rightarrow \emptyset \quad \text{V} \underline{\quad} \begin{bmatrix} +\text{CORONAL} \\ +\text{STRIDENT} \end{bmatrix}$$

Indicate the type of rule, stating whether it is a natural rule.

c.

$$
V \begin{bmatrix} +\text{CONTINUANT} \\ +\text{CORONAL} \\ +\text{STRIDENT} \\ -\text{VOICE} \end{bmatrix} \begin{bmatrix} +\text{CONSONANT} \\ -\text{CONTINUANT} \\ +\text{ANTERIOR} \\ -\text{VOICE} \end{bmatrix} \rightarrow 1 \quad 3 \quad 2
$$

1                2                            3

Indicate the type of rule, stating whether it is a natural rule.

EXERCISE 8

In Chapter 4 a phonological analysis was given of English in which three stresses were posited: [ ´ ] strong, [ ` ] middle, and [ ˘ ] weak. Thus a sequence of strong and weak was posited for *blacker* [blǽkə̆r] and strong and middle for *blackbird* [blǽkbə̀rd]. Note also *explain* [ekspléyn] and *explanation* [èksplə̆néyš̆ə̆n].

Recent phonetic analysis has challenged the assumption of three stresses, on the grounds that three grades of differing intensity cannot be demonstrated. Instead of these degrees of stress then, the phenomena in these forms have been represented by distinctive features. In a preliminary version of a text on phonetics Peter Ladefoged has proposed the following features: STRESS, TONIC ACCENT, and FULL VOWEL. Tonic accent indicates that the syllables in question may contain the major pitch change.

Stress on these words would then be indicated as follows:

|  | *explain* | *explanation* |
|---|---|---|
| STRESS | − + | + − + − |
| TONIC ACCENT | − + | − − + − |
| FULL VOWEL | + + | + − + − |

a. Give the accentual distinctive features for the following: *multiple, multiply; regular, regulate; observe, observation*.
b. Compare the two analyses of English stress, commenting on such matters as the phonetic characteristics of stressed syllables and the reduction of full vowels in unstressed syllables. Which analysis is more accurate?

Other phonetic characteristics are associated with stressed vowels, for example, greater length. Could a distinctive feature like LENGTH be proposed to represent stress in English? Would it substitute for any of the features proposed by Ladefoged?

# MORPHOLOGY

## CHAPTER 7

### 7.1 Morphology: The Study of Meaningful Forms

In the three preceding chapters we have dealt with the phonological elements of language, noting that these are markers of meaning rather than carriers of meaning. The unit for conveying meaning in language is the sentence, as indicated in Chapter 2.1. Thus in conveying information we use sequences like *The car blew a tire, The plane carried 325 passengers,* and our earlier example *A machine chose the chords.* To be sure, shorter sequences may be complete utterances, such as the statement: *325 passengers.* But to be completely meaningful this sequence would have to be given in some context, such as after the question: *What did the plane carry? 325 passengers* is then a shortened sentence that the speaker and hearer understand because of additional information they possess that permits them to construct the entire sentence. In dealing with the meaningful sequences of language, then, we must begin our examination with sentences.

Sentences obviously are made up of smaller elements that also have meaning. Such elements are readily determined by substitution. Thus instead of *passengers,* the second sentence above might have read: *The plane carried 325 mailbags* or *The plane carried 325 tourists.* Such smaller meaningful elements that can be sorted out of sentences are known as words. Many of them, such as *mailbags,* can be further analyzed into meaningful forms that may or may not stand alone. Such meaningful elements are known as **morphemes** or as **formatives.** Morphemes are defined as the smallest meaningful elements in a language. The study of such forms, their variation, and their combinations in words is known as **morphology.**

Morphology is often viewed as a section of syntax. In syntactic study, sentences are analyzed into smaller constituents. Since the smallest meaningful constituents are morphemes, morphology is concerned with the examination of meaningful units that make up sentences. In this way it can properly be included in the syntactic component of grammars.

Moreover, in morphological study, the same linguistic processes must be noted as in the study of sentences, notably the processes called **selection, arrangement,** and **modification.** In framing any sentence we select from a number of possible entities. If we produce sentences in an SVO language like English, we select a noun or a nounlike element for the S and O, such as *plane* or *passenger.* Similarly, in producing forms, such as *mailbag,* we select from a set of possibilities, such as *-man* to make the form *mailman* or *-box* to make *mailbox.* **Selection,** or determination of the entities to be used in any syntactic or morphological construction, is one of the basic syntactic processes. Because the possibilities are taken from sets known as **paradigms,** the process of selection is often referred to as one carried out on the **paradigmatic** plane.

Besides selecting the proper entities, we must arrange them in accordance with the specific relationships maintained in a language. In an English statement the subject precedes the verb. And in noun phrases, articles and other modifiers precede nouns. Similarly, in English compounds like *mailbag,* the modifier precedes the element modified. We refer to the sequencing in syntactic constructions as **arrangement** or **order.** The process of arrangement is often referred to as one carried out on the **syntagmatic** plane.

In arriving at sequences, we may modify the entities selected. The last item in *He saw her* is generally pronounced [ər]. We may cite the object form of *she* as [hər], but in sentences we generally modify it, dropping the [h]. Similarly, in compound words like *mailman* and *gentleman* the last item is generally pronounced [mən], even though the simple word may be given as [mæn]. The syntactic process of changing items in accordance with their surroundings is known as **modification** or **sandhi.** Between words it is referred to as **external sandhi,** within words as **internal sandhi.**

Finally, each English sentence is accompanied by a basic pattern of intonation, such as those given in Chapter 4. Intonation is the fourth syntactic process that must be specified in descriptions of the sentences of any language.

Morphology, the topic of this chapter, is generally divided into the study of the modifications of language in closely structured sets of words, or their **inflection,** and the study of structure of less readily definable sets, or **derivation.** The following four sections will deal with inflection, and then derivational classes and processes will be examined.

## 7.2  Inflection: A Means of Marking Selection

In some languages parts of words belonging to one class, such as nouns or verbs, may be modified consistently according to sets. In English, for example, verbs may be modified by the addition of a suffix in the third singular present, for example, *sees;* by a change in the stem in the past, for example, *saw;* or by the addition of a suffix in the past participle, for example, *seen,* and in the gerund, for example, *seeing.* In this way English verbs consist of sets of five forms: the base, often called the **infinitive;** the third singular present; the past; the past participle; and the gerund. A set of inflections for a word class is known as a **paradigm.**

### 7.2.1  The Scope of Inflection

Various parts of speech may be inflected. By contrast with English, in which nouns and verbs are inflected as well as a small number of adjectives and pronouns, nouns are not inflected in Japanese; only verbs are. In other languages—for example, Russian, Latin, Greek, and Sanskrit—inflection is made for many word classes and is highly complex. Latin, for example, has six case forms for nouns and as many for adjectives, in addition to inflections for gender. Latin verbs are inflected for three persons; for two numbers; in six tenses, four of these in two moods; and in two voices, active and passive. In Irish, prepositions are inflected. Since the inflections of English and Japanese are relatively simple, we will examine them for some of the processes and categories found in inflection.

We may note first that inflection is not universal in language. Chinese has none; in it syntactic relationships must be determined by the devices of arrangement, modification, and intonation.

In languages having inflection, the possibilities of selection are narrowed and made explicit. Latin *amō* 'I love' is quite explicitly a first person singular present indicative active verb form. English *love,* on the other hand, may be a noun, or it may be a verb in any form of the present but the third, and it may be used like an adjective, as in *love potion.* The Latin noun *amor,* however, is quite distinctively marked in contrast with the verb *amō.* As in the maxim of Chaucer's Nun, *"Amor vincit omnia,"* there can be no question of the role of any of these words if one knows the Latin inflections: *amor,* nominative singular masculine, can only be the subject; *vincit* 'conquers,' third singular present indicative active, must be the accompanying verb; *omnia* 'all things,' neuter plural nominative/accusative, must be the object. Yet with a plural verb *omnia* could be the subject of a sentence. Moreover, in a different context *amor* could also be a first singular present indicative passive verb form. Even with these possibilities, selection in highly inflected languages is far more specific than it is in languages with little inflection.

While inflection is explicit in this way, it may also duplicate other syntactic information. Masters of Latin find it useful that the category of singular is indicated in both the subject and its verb, though indication in one form would be adequate in most instances. And when, as in adjective-noun phrases, each item must be indicated for the Latin categories of inflection—as in line 89 of Ovid's *Metamorphoses, "Aurea prīma sata, est aetas"* 'Golden first sown was age' or 'The first age to develop was the Golden'—inflection may seem redundant.

Moreover, even in highly inflected languages some categories have homonymous inflections. In Latin the genitive singular and the dative singular of adjectives like *aurea* have the same form, *aureae*. And as the quotation from Ovid illustrates, inflectional categories are not consistently indicated by the same endings. Final *a*, as in *aurea prīma sata,* is a widespread marker of the nominative singular feminine in Latin, but *aetas* is also a nominative singular feminine, though it lacks the final *a*. Accordingly inflections are often burdensome to learn, and some scholars have labeled them unnecessary luxuries. And many speakers seem to agree, for the modern forms of Latin—French, Italian, Spanish, and the other Romance languages—have in the course of time abandoned the complex inflections of Latin. English too has far fewer inflections than did Old English, and Chinese has lost the inflections that have been proposed for the common ancestor of Chinese and Tibetan. Nevertheless, many languages maintain their inflections or have even introduced new ones, such as the *-ing* form of English. Therefore, we have had to devise procedures for comprehending inflections as simply as possible.

### 7.2.2  Analysis of Inflections

In analyzing the inflections of a language, we must determine: 1) the patterns of selection; 2) the arrangement of inflected elements; and 3) any modifications involved.

**Selection** classes are generally called **parts of speech.** These in turn are classified by word patterns of inflection. The English verb *live,* for example, is inflected by means of suffixes, with no modifications of the underlying form [liv]. Accordingly it is classified as a **regular verb.** English *give,* by contrast, undergoes inflection of the underlying form; thus it is called an **irregular verb.** Since irregular verbs—for example, *strike, sing,* and *bear*—follow a variety of patterns, we set up various subclasses. When such subclasses are large, they are called **conjugations** for verbs. In Latin, for example, there are four conjugations.

For nouns, pronouns, and adjectives, classes of inflection are called **declensions.** Latin has five noun declensions. The Latin first declension is made up of nouns like *rosa* 'rose,' which end in *a* in the nominative singular. Most first declension nouns belong to the feminine gender, though some, like *agricola* 'farmer,' do not. The Latin second declension is made up of nouns ending in *us* or *um* in the nominative singular, for example, *hortus* 'garden' and *oppidum* 'city.' The nouns ending in *us* are masculine, those in *um* neuter. The third, fourth, and fifth declensions follow other patterns.

In a highly inflected language like Latin the large selection classes, or parts of speech such as nouns and verbs, may be identified by the inflection they undergo. But in a language with little inflection, like English, parts of speech may be determined largely by their relationships to other parts of speech: *apple* is a noun because it belongs to the class of words that follow *the,* and so forth. The twofold criteria used in setting up parts of speech may lead to difficulties of classification. Because of its *-ing* ending, *awarding* may be called a verb, but it may be used as a noun, as in *the awarding of the prize.* When a grammar of a language is produced, such problems must be solved. Here we will deal primarily with the actual changes in form involved in inflection and with some of the categories indicated.

In analyzing inflected forms we determine the central element, or the **base,** and its modifications generally by means of **affixes.** The central element may also be called the **root.**

Each such minimal element of form with a specific meaning is a **morpheme;** {live}, for example, is a base verb morpheme in English. We may write morphemes either in the conventional spelling, as here, or in transcription, but to indicate that any cited element or elements are to be regarded as morphemes, we enclose them in braces { }. The affix in the third singular present *lives* is generally written {Z}. The conventional spelling is not used, because it varies, as in *hisses* versus *hides,* nor is a phonemic transcription used, because the pronunciation varies, depending on the last phoneme of the base, as in /livz/, /snifs/, and /hisəz/. Accordingly the capital {Z} has come to be used as a symbol. Moreover, since the usual suffix for forming noun plurals, as in *dogs, cats,* and *horses,* is identical with the third singular present suffix, we also label it {Z}. To distinguish these morphemes, subscripts are used. By this notation $\{Z_1\}$ is the noun plural suffix in English. The genitive morpheme is also homonymous, as in *dog's, cat's,* and *horse's.* It is labeled $\{Z_2\}$, for when the plural and the genitive are used together, the plural morpheme stands first, as in *children's.* The verb suffix is labeled $\{Z_3\}$.

Below we will deal further with problems of English inflection and with other problems involved in the labeling of morphemes, but it may be noted here that morphemes must be determined both for bases and for affixes.

### 7.2.3  Patterns of Arrangement for Inflectional Morphemes

Inflectional morphemes are classified by their position with regard to the base. If they precede the base, as does *a* in Sanskirt *a-bhavam* 'I became,' they are called **prefixes**. If they follow the base, as does *mi* in *bhavā-mi* 'I become,' they are called **suffixes**. If they are placed inside the base, as in *na* in Sanskrit *yu-na-jmi* 'I yoke,' they are called **inflexes**. The base is then said to be **discontinuous**. Affixes may also be suprasegmental; in some verbs of Proto-Indo-European, for example, the accent is on the base in the singular, on the endings in the plural. Affixes consisting of pitch or stress are called **superfixes**.

A special kind of affixation involves the repetition of all or part of the base and is known as **reduplication**. Reduplication is widespread in English derivation, for example, *ack-ack*. It often involves modification of a part of the base, as in *raggle-taggle*, but may also be total, without changes of the base, as in Austronesian languages; compare place names like *Pago Pago*. As with other forms of affixation, reduplication may not only be initial in bases but also medial or final, as in the jocular patterns of reduplication with [š], for example, *marry-shmarry;* in *Ping-Pong;* and differently still in *rat-a-tat*.

Partial reduplication is used in Sanskrit, Greek, and Latin with various forms of verbs. Most Greek perfects reduplicate the first consonant with *e,* for example, *lé-lū-k-a* 'I have loosed' and *pé-pau-k-a* 'I have stopped.' Reduplication may come to be greatly modified, so that in some actual forms no item of the root is maintained, as is illustrated by forms of the root for 'stand' in the Indo-European languages. Theoretically *st* plus vowels should be found in all forms, as in Gothic *stai-stald* 'gained,' but we also find in Latin *si-stō* 'I stand,' in Sanskrit *ti-stā-mi* 'I stand,' and in Attic Greek *hi-stē-mi* 'I stand.' In this way, through subsequent change, reduplicated elements may come to be scarcely recognizable as such.

### 7.3  Modification of Morphemes

Morphemes in general vary widely in shape, in accordance with their environment. These variants are known as **allomorphs.** We will illustrate the possible variations by examining English inflections; the same procedures apply in the analysis of bases and derivations. Few morphemes are used throughout all forms without modification, that is, without more than one allomorph. English {ing} [iŋ] is an example of a morpheme with one shape, although many speakers use a variant [in], especially after bases like *ring* that end in [ŋ]. In dealing with inflection, therefore, we must note the allomorphs and set up a base morpheme. To illustrate the procedure, we may use the suffix in the English third singular present, as in [livz snifs hisəz].

After identifying the allomorphs, we must determine their distribution. In standard English [əz] is used after groove fricatives or sibilants, as in *hiss, whiz, rush, rouge, clutch,* and *budge;* of the three variants of {Z₃} its distribution may be specified most readily, and accordingly we list it first. The [s] is used after voiceless phonemes other than /s š č/ and is the second most readily specifiable. It is used after /p t k f θ/, as in *rap, hit, hack, laugh,* and *sleuth.* After other voiced stops and fricatives and after resonants and other vowels, [z] is used. Since it is least specifiable, we use it as the label for the morpheme {Z₃}.

When allomorphs can be determined by phonological criteria, as in the cited English verbs, we say they are **phonologically conditioned.**

Consistent phonological conditioning is rare. Even for the relatively simple English third singular present morpheme, some verbs follow a different pattern from that described previously. The auxiliary *can,* for example, though phonologically identical with the verb *can,* makes its third singular present with no ending, as in *She can go* versus *She cans apples.* We call this a **zero allomorph.** Since we can determine the distribution of the zero only from the type of verb, we say it is **morphologically conditioned.**

Morphological conditioning is very prominent in the past of English verbs. We may label the past morpheme {D₁}. Having a remarkable parallelism with {Z}, the past morpheme has three principal variants. The morpheme [əd] occurs with verbs ending in the phonemes most like the suffix /t d/, for example, *butt* and *bud.* The /t/ ending occurs after voiceless phonemes other than /t/, as in *rap, hack, laugh, sleuth, hiss, rush,* and *clutch.* The /d/ occurs elsewhere, except in the irregular verbs. These follow various complex patterns that must be described, and subclassification of the bases must be proposed. One consistent subclass is made up of verbs ending in nasals or the nasal /ŋ/ plus /k/, for example, *swim, begin, spin, ring, sing, spring, drink, shrink, sink,* and *stink.* Here the allomorph consists of a replacement, with [æ] replacing [i] of the base; this replacement may be represented by the rule /i/ → /æ/ before /m n ŋ ŋk/. In some English verbs the replacement is a consonant: /d/ → /t/, as in the base /bend/, past /bent/, and also in *send, spend,* and *build.*

Morphological conditioning is equally prominent in the participle. Because the most widespread form is like that of the past, as in *butted, rapped,* and *rubbed,* we also label the participial morpheme {D}. To distinguish it from the past, we add a subscript: {D₂}. The numbering has a basis in forms like *spoken,* which has a replacive allomorph of {D₁} in the past *spoke* and adds to this the {D₂} affix in the participle *spoken.*

As this form indicates, the English participle may be made with both internal change and with a suffix, especially when the allomorph is /n/ or /ən/. Similarly many irregular verbs have a participial suffix /t/ plus internal change, for example, *bring, think, keep,* and *sleep.* A full list of the allomorphs of the English morphemes {D₁} and {D₂} would accordingly be lengthy and would require specification of bases as well as affixes.

The modifications of bases and affixes in morphological processes are known as **morphophonemic changes,** and their study is called **morphophonemics.** As we may note from the following discussion of the morphophonemics of Japanese, morphophonemic changes differ from language to language, but they also follow general processes. These help us to account for the modifications.

### 7.3.1  Accounting for Morphophonemic Modifications

As we noted in Chapter 5, neighboring phonological items influence one another. A frequent negative prefix in English, for example, is *in-,* as in *inactive.* Before labials, however, a labial nasal is used, as in *impenitent.* The nasal has been modified in accordance with the following sound. Sanskrit grammarians refer to such modifications as **sandhi** 'together + binding'—pronounced [sə́ndiy]. The term is widely used today for modification.

Sandhi differs widely from language to language. In Turkish preceding vowels influence vowels of inflections. In pre-Old English, on the other hand, vowels of endings influenced the vowels of stems; reflexes are still evident, for example, *men* versus *man* and *feet* versus *foot.* Nouns like these had a front vowel in their nominative plural ending, for example, pre-Old English *\*manniz, \*fotiz.* (The asterisk indicates a form inferred from historical examples, but not actually attested.) The stem vowel then became fronted, as in Old English *menn* and *fēt,* which developed into Modern English *men* and *feet.* As these examples may indicate, the precise type of modification cannot be predicted for any language, but general patterns can be described. The most common type of modification is substitution, in which one or more phonemes replace others.

### 7.3.2  Assimilation

The most widespread type of substitution is **assimilation.** In assimilation one or more sounds come to be articulated like another sound. The variation of {Z₃} provides a simple example: when the base ends in a voiceless element other than a sibilant, /s/ is the allomorph; when the base ends in a voiced element, /z/ is the allomorph.

Assimilation may be of various kinds, as we may illustrate with the past of Japanese verbs. The suffix is {TA} When the base ends in *n* —for example, *shinu* 'die'—the past is *shinda.* The *t* is voiced, in accordance with the preceding voiced sound [n]. Assimilation in which a preceding element modifies a following is called **progressive.**

When the base ends in *r*—for example, *toru* 'take'—the past is *totta.* The *r* is devoiced in accordance with the following voiceless stop and is modified to a stop. Assimilation in which a following element modifies a preceding is called **regressive.**

When the base ends in *m*, as in *sumu* 'live,' the place of articulation of *m* is modified to that of the *t*, and the *t* is voiced like *m*, yielding *sunda*. Assimilation in which both elements are affected is called **reciprocal**.

In these examples the assimilation involves contiguous elements. Assimilation may also be noncontiguous, as we may illustrate with Proto-Germanic, the earlier form of Old English and Old High German. Here noncontiguous assimilation was regressive. Back rounded vowels of stems were fronted, yielding front rounded vowels, as in standard German *Hüte* 'hats' versus *Hut* 'hat,' *Götter* 'gods' versus *Gott* 'god,' and *Mäuse* 'mice' versus *Maus* 'mouse.' The low back vowel was merely fronted, as in *Männer* 'men' versus *Mann* 'man.' The contrast was widely extended in German, especially to indicate noun plurals, while in English it was largely abandoned. It is often referred to by a term borrowed from German, **umlaut**.

In descriptions of assimilation, it is useful to note the characteristic features of sounds, for in the modification of one or more characteristic features, assimilation is brought about. Reviewing examples from the past tense of Japanese verbs, we may note how specific features are modified. Assimilation may be made in place of articulation, as when the base *sum* becomes *sun* in *sunda* 'lived.' Assimilation may be made in manner of articulation, as when the resonant *r* becomes a stop in *tor* > *totta* 'took.' Assimilation may be made in the articulation of the vocal cords, as when *t* becomes voiced in *shinda* 'died.' When modification takes place in the middle of words, as in the Japanese examples here, it is called **internal sandhi**. Modification may also be made between words, and it is then called **external sandhi**. We may illustrate assimilation of various kinds with English examples of external sandhi.

In the common form /gɔ́nə/ > /gunə/ of *going to* there is assimilation in place of articulation of [ŋ] > [n] before [t]. The [t] then is lost. In the negative used in questions, for example, *can't you* and *won't you* /kǽnčə wównčə/, there is assimilation in manner of articulation, as well as in the use of the vocal cords; [y] in the sequence [ty] becomes devoiced and narrowed to a fricative [š], yielding [tš] [č]. In the sequence *give me* [gímmiy] [gímiy] there is assimilation in velic articulation; the fricative becomes nasalized.

Assimilation toward specific places in the articulatory tract is characteristic of specific languages. Thus, in the Semitic languages emphasis is widespread; in the languages of India retroflexion is widespread; and in the Indo-European languages palatalization is widespread. The following are contemporary examples of palatalization in English:

| | | | |
|---|---|---|---|
| *didn't you* | [dídənčə] | *did you* | [díǰə] |
| *(we'll) miss you* | [míšə] | *(we'll) lose you* | [lúwžə] |

In addition to assimilation, a morphophonemic change that we can account for by articulatory moves toward ease of articulation, other types that have a different basis must be noted.

### 7.3.3   Other Morphophonemic Processes

**Dissimiliation** is a type of substitution in which two phonemes become less like each other. It may be accounted for through psychological rather than articulatory processes. When two complex activities must be carried out, we find it simpler if they differ slightly. In keeping with this observation, dissimilation generally affects complex phonemes, such as the aspirates or the resonants. To cite an example in word formation, English *turtle (-dove)* is a dissimilated form of *tur-tur,* the name given the bird after its call.

When dissimilation leads to loss of an entire syllable, it is called **haplology** (literally, the simplifying of a word). Examples may be found in English adverbs ending in *-ly*. From *slow* we may make an adverb *slowly*. But if the base already ends in [liy], for example, *lively* or *friendly,* we do not maintain the form *\*livelyly* [layvliyliy] but rather use [layvliy] as the adverb, as in *He stepped lively*.

**Metathesis** is change in the order of phonemes. In the West Saxon dialect of Old English, for example, *r* is metathesized before vowels in many words, such as *birnan* 'burn' (compare Gothic *brinnan,* German *brennen*), *hors* 'horse' (compare Old Saxon *hross*), and so forth. Metathesis may be understood if we note the phonological patterning in a language. In West Saxon, sequences of short vowels followed by *r* + consonant are one of the standard patterns, as in verbs like *weorpan* 'throw (warp),' *beorcan* 'bark,' and so on. It is natural then for verbs like pre-Old English *\*brestan* to become *berstan* 'burst' in agreement with the predominant pattern.

Two further morphophonemic changes are **addition** and **deletion.** Both can usually be related to articulatory processes in a given language. An example of addition is found in the Japanese past ending in *s;* for example, *mōshita* of *mōsu* 'speak.' Japanese does not permit consonant clusters other than with *y,* as in *Tōkyō* and *Kyōto*. The addition of *i* after bases ending in *s* solves the difficulty by producing a consonant-vowel sequence. Addition is widespread in inflected and derived forms when two nonfavored sequences come to stand together. For example, when the *tu* participle was formed from the verb *emō* 'buy' in Latin, a *p* was added, yielding *emptus*. Such additional phonemes are often called **epenthetic** or **anaptyptic.** When initial, they are called **prothetic.** For example, prothetic vowels developed in Late Latin before *sp, st,* and *sc,* leading to forms like *espiritum* from *spiritum* and ultimately French *esprit*.

An example of loss is found in the Japanese present *kau* 'buy,' from a base *\*kaw-u;* compare the negative *kaw-anai*. As in *kau,* in which a labiovelar resonant is lost before a back vowel, loss may often be understood as a kind of phonetic absorption. Loss may also occur when contiguous elements do not fit the patterns of a language. In Proto-Germanic, for example, the past suffix was added to preforms of English *bring, think,* and so on. The resulting sequences were *-aŋxt-.* In these sequences the nasal was lost, giving rise ultimately to the modern English forms *brought* and *thought*—modern German *brachte* and *dachte.* When ŋ was lost, the preceding vowel *a* was lengthened to *ā,* as a kind of compensation. Such a process is called **compensatory lengthening.**

When final vowels are lost, as in modern English noun and verb forms compared with Old English—for example, *I find* versus Old English *finde*—they are said to be **apocopated,** literally, cut off. The process is referred to as **apocope** or when medial as **syncope,** for example, Latin *\*ferere* 'bear' >*ferre.*

---

## 7.4 Japanese Verb Forms

Although we have already noted some Japanese verb inflections, we will survey the Japanese verb system, in part to observe some of the morphophonemic processes involved in a set of inflected forms.

There are two subclasses of *u* verbs in Japanese: those whose bases end in vowels (for example, *ne* 'sleep') and those whose bases end in consonants (for example, *tor* 'take'). From each subclass nine simple forms can be made (see Figure 1). The labels give a general indication of each verb's use. The alternative, however, may need explanation; used in pairs of verbs, it corresponds to English sequences indicating alternate actions, like *At times he sleeps, at times he dashes around.* As is clear from the forms of *neru* 'sleep,' when endings are added to the vowel subclass, there are no morphophonemic changes.

In the consonant subclass, however, both the final consonant of the base and the initial consonant of the ending may be changed. To determine the underlying form, it is useful to start from a derived form, the negative. This form has the ending *anai.* Before indicating the morphophonemic changes of individual bases, we should observe the nine simple forms having the base *tor;* several endings in the consonant subclass differ from those in the vowel subclass. Moreover, the most striking morphophonemic change, that in the past (see Figure 2), is the same as that in the three other forms with initial *t* in the ending.

After identifying the base of the consonant subclasses from analysis of the negative, we will become aware of the morphophonemic changes

**Figure 1**

| Indicative | *ne-ru* | Past | *ne-ta* |
|---|---|---|---|
| Infinitive; Adverbial | *ne* | Participle | *ne-te* |
| Hypothetical | *ne-reba* | Conditional | *ne-tara* |
| Conjectural | *ne-yō* | Alternative | *ne-tari* |
| Imperative | *ne-yo ne-ro* | | |

**Figure 2**

| Indicative | *tor-u* | Past | *tot-ta* |
|---|---|---|---|
| Infinitive | *tor-i* | Participle | *tot-te* |
| Hypothetical | *tor-eba* | Conditional | *tot-tara* |
| Conjectural | *tor-eyō* | Alternative | *tot-tari* |
| Imperative | *tor-e* | | |

in the paradigm by studying the indicative, the infinitive, and the past, for the base is the same in the other forms of the first column as it is in the indicative. For *toru* 'take' we set up two allomorphs of the base, *tor* *tot*. To illustrate the allomorphs of other verbs, we may cite four forms, as in Figure 3. In the infinitive, palatalization may be observed, as in *mat* and *mōs*. Forms of the past exemplify various kinds of assimilation, of both the affix and the base. Bases ending in a voiced consonant other than *w* assimilate the *t* of the past affix. The dental of the past affix, on the other hand, assimilates the labials of *tob, nom,* and *kaw*. Velars, as in *kik* and *kag,* on the other hand, are dissimilated to vowels. In this way even the simple verb system of Japanese illustrates several morphophonemic changes. Each of the simple forms, as well as the derived forms, may be made from these verbs with the information given here.

Japanese has many derived forms. In these the affixed endings are added to one another with little morphophonemic change and in successive orders. A language with such a structure is called **agglutinative.** By contrast, English, Sanskrit, Greek, Latin, and the Semitic languages are known as **inflectional** languages because the affixes usually merge in part with the base, as in *gives, gave,* and so on.

Among the derived, or secondary, forms of the Japanese verb are the following. The causative is formed by the addition of *saseru* to vowel verbs and *aseru* to consonant verbs, for example, *nesaseru* 'cause to sleep' and *mataseru* 'cause to wait.' The passive is formed by the addition of *rareru* and *areru,* as in *nerareru* and *matareru.* The Japanese passive has three major uses: as a true passive, for example, *kawareru* 'is bought'; as a potential, for example, *tobareru* 'can fly'; and as a form indicating suffering the result of an action, for example, *shinareru* 'suffer the death of.'

**Figure 3**

| Roots ending in | | Ind. | Inf. | Past | Neg. |
|---|---|---|---|---|---|
| *t* | 'wait' | *matsu* | *machi* | *matta* | *matanai* |
| *n* | 'die' | *shinu* | *shini* | *shinda* | *shinanai* |
| *b* | 'fly' | *tobu* | *tobi* | *tonda* | *tobanai* |
| *m* | 'drink' | *nomu* | *nomi* | *nonda* | *nomanai* |
| *k* | 'hear' | *kiku* | *kiki* | *kiita* | *kikanai* |
| *g* | 'smell' | *kagu* | *kagi* | *kaida* | *kaganai* |
| *s* | 'speak' | *mōsu* | *mōshi* | *mōshita* | *mōsanai* |
| *w* | 'buy' | *kau* | *kai* | *katta* | *kawanai* |

As these examples illustrate, the term *passive* is only partially applicable as a designation for this category. Many other grammatical designations apply similarly to only one major use of a form. The term *possessive,* for example, applies to only one of the uses of the English inflection: *John's car* may be interpreted as a true possessive but scarcely *John's eye, John's friend,* or *John's grades.* For this reason the term *genitive* is widely used, though it too is only partially applicable. Most grammatical labels, like the Japanese *passive,* must be interpreted separately for each language.

In keeping with the agglutinative characteristics of Japanese, a passive can be made from a causative, for example, *mataserareru* 'be caused to wait.' The causative, the passive, and the causative-passive are treated as simple verbs and further inflected through the simple forms given for *neru,* for example, in the past: *mataseta, matareta,* and *mataserareta.*

Before examining other secondary inflections, we may note the *i* class of Japanese verbs, for example, *takai* 'be tall,' as in *ki ga takai* 'the tree is tall.' These are also inflected in the simple forms, as in Figure 4.

In further secondary forms, the negative and the desiderative, the inflectional endings are like those of *i* verbs, for example, *matanai* 'does not wait' and *matanakatta* 'did not wait.' The negative may also be made from secondary conjugations, for example, *mataserarenai* 'is not caused to wait.' Such extended forms may be further inflected, for example, *matasenakatta* 'did not cause to wait.' The desiderative is also inflected like *i* verbs, for example, *machitai* 'I want to wait.' Added to the passive, it generally has a meaning corresponding to 'please' plus the imperative, as in *mataretai* 'I'd like you to wait.' Here as in many other languages, for example English *I'd like this done,* a passive construction is used to soften requests.

In this way the Japanese verb system contains a large number of forms. But because of the simple morphophonemics and the straightforward order in which the endings are added, the system is easy to master. In addition to the forms given here, there are various compound forms, adding richness to the Japanese verb. These will be touched on in section 7.7 below.

**Figure 4**

| Indicative | *takai* | Hypothetical | *takakereba* |
|------------|---------|--------------|--------------|
| Adverbial | *takaku* | Past | *takakatta* |

## 7.5 Selected Categories of Inflection

As the relatively simple Japanese verb system indicates, there are various categories of inflection from language to language. The Japanese categories do not differ strikingly from those of the Indo-European languages, for even the desiderative is a category of Sanskrit. Moreover, it corresponds closely to expressions like English [wánə] in *I want to see it*. In some languages, however, the categories differ considerably from those of English. In some Amerindian languages the inflected verb form must indicate whether the subject is sitting, standing, or lying. In others the inflected verb must indicate whether the object is within sight, not within sight but within hearing, or neither. The precision that such inflections afford also occasions large numbers of inflected forms; an estimate for the Oneida verb is more than a million.

Besides receptivity to a variety of inflectional categories one must note that all such categories are linguistic rather than natural. Linguistic categories can be related in general to logical or natural categories, as is gender with sex: masculine, feminine, and neuter generally correspond to male, female, and neither. But one can scarcely learn more than a few words of German before noting that all words ending in the diminutive suffixes *chen* and *lein* are of neuter gender (compare English *-kin*, as in *lambkin* and *catkin*, and *-ling*, as in *darling*). Accordingly *Mädchen* 'girl' and *Fräulein* 'young lady' are neuter. But in general there is so close a relationship between gender and sex that even highly competent linguists have been led to fanciful explanations for sets in gender classes. For example, names for trees in Latin are feminine, even those like *ulmus* 'elm' with a masculine ending. Some linguists have proposed that trees belong to the feminine gender in Latin because they bear fruit. Such simple correlations must be regarded with suspicion.

Gender is a **congruence** category. The reasons for membership in any such category are various, partly historical, partly based on patterning in classes because of form or meaning. For any inflectional category one must first determine the linguistic usage and then relate this usage to natural and logical classes. One must not be misled by the terminology of the grammars, such as *masculine* or *feminine*, or *present*, *past*, and *future* in verbs. Such terms have been introduced into the study of language in attempts to provide graphic terminology, but they apply in a concrete way to only a few uses of the forms in question. As frequent expressions indicate—such as *We go to town tomorrow*, in which the present tense indicates future time, or *If we went to town tomorrow*, in which the past tense indicates future time—labels given to categories correspond only partially to their natural and logical meaning.

### 7.5.1   Inflectional Categories Associated with Nominal Elements

Categories widely found with nouns, pronouns, and adjectives are **number, gender,** and **case.** Categories widely found with verbs are **voice, tense, aspect, mood, person,** and **number.** In the following sketch of these categories the distinction between linguistic and natural categories may be further observed.

**Number** is apparently a straightforward category, referring to quantities. Yet the use of number is often nonlogical, as examples from well-known languages may indicate. In a simple number system we might expect a category for one, **singular,** and a category for more than one, **plural.** Some number systems have a category for two, **dual,** for example, ancient Greek and Sanskrit. A few number systems have a category for three, **trial.** For a general analysis of number systems we would need to speak of categories for countable nouns, such as English *cat, compass,* and *meaning,* and for uncountables, such as English *cattle, compassion,* and *tact.* The use of these nouns in English is evident not only from their inflection—*cat, cats* but not *cattle,* *\*cattles*—but also from their relationships to other syntactic entities: *He has no cats* versus *He has no cattle* and *He has a cat* versus *He has cattle.*

Relationship, as we have variously noted, is important for determining linguistic classes. Besides the relationships pointed to in the previous paragraph, specific relationships determine which nouns can be classed together for counting. We may say *A cat and a dog are animals.* But we do not class together *a cat* and *a hair,* saying, for example, *\*A cat and a hair are on the sofa.* In this way linguistic expression determines what can be counted or associated in a given language.

In English, for example, the word *cousin* refers to males and females: we can therefore say *John and Mary are cousins.* In German there are distinct words for 'male cousin' *der Vetter* and 'female cousin' *die Base/Kusine.* Hence one must say *Hans und Marie sind Vetter und Base.* Conversely, for 'brother' and 'sister' German has a collective, *Geschwister.* Accordingly, to correspond to *John and Mary are brother and sister,* German permits *Hans und Marie sind Geschwister.* One may also compare such simple items as *scissors,* a plural in English but a singular in German, *die Schere;* or *glasses* versus *die Brille;* or conversely *hair* versus *die Haare,* a plural in German.

Such minute variations are often neglected by polyglots. For example, the word for *vacation* is plural in Latin, *feriae.* The word was borrowed into German and is used as a plural, *die Ferien;* similarly, in French the term is plural, *vacances.* Nonnative speakers of English with French or German as their native language will frequently speak of *their vacations.* Speakers of German may also seek *informations,* on the pattern of German *Auskünfte.* All of these examples illustrate the primacy of linguistic rather than "natural" categories in language.

But it is scarcely necessary to go beyond one language to illustrate the primacy of linguistic categories in linguistic patterns. If John ate several oranges for breakfast, his wholesome gustatory practice may be reported either with a plural, *He ate more oranges than one,* or with a singular, *He ate more than one orange.* Whether the linguistic report uses a plural or a singular, John ate the same number of oranges.

The nouns exemplified previously can be counted and are therefore often referred to as **count nouns.** By contrast, **mass nouns** cannot be counted, or if they are, the reference is to separate items, for example, *money, sugar,* and *experience.* Each of these may be used after *He didn't have much . . . ,* though a count noun like *book, shoe,* or *idea* may not.

If we say *There are several sugars in those jars,* it is understood that the reference is to several kinds of sugar, for example, $C_{12}H_{22}O_{11}$ or $C_{12}H_{10}O_5$. We may also use auxiliary nouns like *kinds of sugar, types of money,* or *head of cattle* with numerals, for example, *two kinds of sugar, three types of money,* or *seven head of cattle.* In some languages, for example Chinese and Japanese, all nouns must be treated in this way. Rather than speaking of two pencils, one might say *ni hon* 'of pencils' in Japanese. *Hon* is used with long round objects. For flat things like sheets of paper one must say *ni mai* 'of paper'; for people *ni jin* 'of men'; for birds *ni wa* 'of birds'; and so on. Such auxiliary nouns are known as **numeral classifiers.** Comparison with English mass nouns may provide some understanding of Chinese and Japanese nouns. The latter are neither singular nor plural, simply aggregate.

**Gender** is a congruence category. By means of gender, nouns and their modifiers are linked together. In the first line of the *Odyssey,* for example, there is no question about the nouns modified by *polútropon* 'experienced':

> *ándra moi   énnepe, moūsa,   polútropon,   hòs mála pollà*
> 'man to-me tell-of,   oh-muse, experienced, who very many (things)'

As a masculine accusative singular, it must modify *ándra* rather than *moi* or *moūsa.* Gender in this way limits the possible associations of selection classes and permits greater freedom of arrangement.

**Case** is a selection category that specifies selection of nouns in greater detail. Noun systems may have two cases, as in English, four as in German, six as in Latin, eight as in Sanskrit, or even more, as in Finnish and Hungarian. Cases may refer primarily to grammatical relations (for example, the Sanskrit nominative and accusative) or primarily to locational relations (for example, the Sanskrit ablative and locative), or they may single out entities, for example, the vocative. In general, the nominative is used in Latin and Sanskrit to indicate the subject of the action, the accusative to indicate the object.

Since in English grammatical relationships have no overt markers, the term *case* is also used to indicate semantic categories, as in "case grammar." Traditionally, however (as in this section), it is a term used for overtly inflected forms. Languages may use cases to express differences in meaning that are expressed by lexical entities in other languages. In the following Latvian examples the difference between a single present action and a general mode of behavior is indicated by a contrast between the dative and the accusative cases:

(*es* 'I'; *klausīt* 'obey'; *savs* 'own, my own'; *vecāki* 'parents')
*Es klausu saviem vecākiem.* (dative) 'I am obeying my parents (now).'
*Es klausu savus vecakus.* (accusative) 'I always obey my parents.'

Like all grammatical categories, then, case forms must be analyzed and described for their uses in specific languages.

### 7.5.2  Inflectional Categories Associated with Verbal Elements

**Voice** is a category specifying the relation of the subject to the action expressed by a verb. Latin has two voices: an **active,** indicating that the subject performs the action expressed by the verb (for example, *He reads many books*); and a **passive,** indicating that the subject undergoes the action expressed by the verb (for example, *Many books are read by him*). Classical Greek has another voice, the **middle,** which is found also in Sanskrit; the middle voice indicates that the subject performs an action for his own benefit. The notion of 'eating,' for example, can be expressed by the Classical Greek middle, as in *édomai* 'I eat (for my own benefit).'

**Tense** is a category specifying the time of the action. Latin tense categories are as rational as any that might be expected: present, past, and future. Old English has no tense for the future; instead the present tense is used, as in *We see them tomorrow*. Because of the absence of a future tense inflection in Old English and in Modern English, some linguists prefer to label the two English tense forms **past** and **nonpast.** It should be noted that these are grammatical labels and that the relationships expressed may not correspond to the natural meaning. The past tense may refer to present or future as well as past time; compare *If she did her homework regularly, If she did her homework before we left town tomorrow,* and *She did her homework last Friday*.

Instead of tense, or coexistent with tense, many languages have a category referred to as **aspect.** Aspect reflects the status of the action rather than its time relationship. An action may be completed or incompleted. If completed, the aspect is called **perfective,** if incompleted, **imperfective.**

Aspect categories are notable in the Slavic languages. The Semitic languages also have verb inflection for aspect. In ancient Hebrew, for example, *kātal* means 'killing has been completed by him,' and *yiktol* means 'killing by him is not yet completed.' The perfective frequently corresponds to a past tense, so that *kātal* is often translated 'he killed,' and the imperfective *yiktol* is often translated as the present tense 'he kills.' Yet the uses of many aspectual forms may not be compatible with the verb forms of a tense system. It is instructive and engaging to compare translations from Hebrew into languages that have tense, such as Latin. Saint Jerome's translation of the opening of Psalm 121 reads *Levāvi oculōs* 'I have lifted up my eyes'; the King James version by contrast reads 'I will lift up mine eyes.' The translators differed in their interpretation of the Hebrew aspect form.

Some verb systems have highly subtle inflectional categories. Other languages include such subtleties in the lexicon. English *look at,* for example, corresponds to a perfective form in *I looked at him,* whereas *see* corresponds to an imperfective, as in *I saw him.* When one compares additional forms—for example, *I am looking at him* and *I am seeing him*—the complexities of aspectual languages may not seem unduly forbidding.

**Mood,** or **mode,** is a verbal category that reflects the attitude of the speaker. The **indicative** indicates that the speaker presents the material with assurance; the **imperative** that he commands or requests some action. The **subjunctive** suggests uncertainty; the **optative** suggests some sort of volition. Yet the precise meaning is determined by the categories found in a language. In early Sanskrit these four moods exist side by side in the present tense of the active and the middle voices; in later Sanskrit the subjunctive is lost. In Latin the optative is lost, leaving the indicative, the imperative, and the subjunctive. In Germanic the subjunctive is lost, leaving the optative, but the use of the Germanic optative is remarkably parallel to the subjunctive of Latin, and in handbooks it is generally labeled the "subjunctive."

Besides these categories verbs may be inflected for **number,** such as singular, dual, and plural, and for **person.** Simple systems have three persons: the first corresponds to the speaker, the second to the addressee, and the third to others. Verbs may also be inflected for **gender.** In Arabic and other Semitic languages there are different forms for the second and third person masculine and feminine.

### 7.5.3  Nominal Versus Verbal Inflection

As indicated previously, some noun and verb inflections overlap, such as those for number and gender and in the pronoun *that* for person. There may be other interrelationships between nominal and verbal systems, so-called verbal nouns and adjectives. They are also called **nonfinite** to distinguish them from the **finite** forms, which are inflected for such categories as tense and person. Among nonfinite forms are **infinitives,** which often are not further inflected, and **participles,** which often are inflected throughout various case forms. Nounlike verbal forms are called **gerunds,** for example, Latin *industria in agendo* 'energy in action.' Adjectivelike verbal forms are called **gerundives,** for example, Latin *cupiditas belli gerendi* 'desire of carrying on war (of war to be carried on).' Through such forms, verbs overlap with nouns in their inflection.

Nouns, on the other hand, may be modified to verbs, often by means of auxiliaries. In Japanese, for example, many words borrowed from Chinese and English are treated like verbs through combination with the verb *suru* 'do.' Thus the Japanese noun borrowed on the basis of English 'type' *taipu* is converted into various verb forms, such as *taipu shita* 'he typed' or *taipu serareta* 'it was typed.'

### 7.5.4 Patterns of Modification and Intonation

As these illustrations indicate, inflection is a device used to demarcate classes and subclasses of selection. The classes that are marked by inflection vary widely in the languages of the world. At one extreme are the so-called **analytic languages,** such as Chinese, in which no inflection of any kind is used. In these languages syntactic relationships are indicated largely by arrangement. **Synthetic languages,** like Classical Greek and Sanskrit, have many inflections, and patterns of arrangement are freer in such languages.

Patterns of modification and intonation are also highly important as syntactic devices. The finals of words and of sentences are far more circumscribed than are initials; they indicate the bounds of syntactic sequences. In Classical Greek, for example, words end only in vowels and in *n r s*. In Sanskrit the permissible final consonants are almost as restricted in number. Modification in this way marks off syntactic sequences. Yet like inflection, specific patterns of modification cannot be expected to correlate completely with specific syntactic structures.

Intonation, on the other hand, is more definitely associated with syntactic units. In a complete grammar the patterns of modification and intonation should be described as thoroughly as those of inflection.

---

## 7.6 Derivation

**Derivation** is that section of morphology that deals with the relation of words to bases. For example, the words *purebred, purity,* and *impure* are all related to the base *pure.* Derivational sets, such as the set of nouns ending in *-ity,* usually have fewer members than do the parts of speech. For example, as we have observed in section 7.2 on inflection, most English nouns can be inflected with the suffix $\{Z_2\}$ in the possessive and with $\{Z_1\}$ in the plural. Similarly, in Japanese most verbs can be inflected for the simple forms and secondary conjugations. But only a restricted set of English bases can be affixed with *-dom, -ity,* or [ən], and other prefixes and suffixes. In Japanese only a restricted number of verbs can be affixed with *dasu* '(put) out,' *hajimaru* 'begin,' and *kaeru* 'return.' Examples are *nigedasu* 'run out,' *sakihajimaru* 'begin to bloom,' and *furikaeru* 'look back.' Such restricted sets are treated in derivation.

Derived forms are more complicated to describe than are inflected forms. English inflections have been well described, but it is difficult to find adequate descriptions of derivations such as *-ity.* We may state in general that *-ity* is suffixed to adjectives in order to make abstract nouns, for example, /pyúrĭtiy/ < /pyur/ + /itiy/ + /ʹ ˇ ˋ/. But when we continue our analysis of other /itiy/ compounds, for example *ability* and *legality,* we find that the underlying adjective is modified in derivation: /éybəl/ to /əbíl/ and /líygəl/ to /lìygǽl/. The changes that bases undergo, however, are comparable with those noted in inflection. And similar procedures are used to describe the processes involved.

As in the analysis of inflection, the form of the base or bases and of the affixes must be specified. Moreover, any modification must be described. In such description of derivations the morphophonemic phenomena discussed in the preceding chapter—substitution, deletion and addition of items, and modification of accent—will also be observed. By noting these changes, we can describe the derived elements as thoroughly as we can inflections.

In the analysis of derivations it is customary to set up two groups: 1) those containing more than one base, for example, *tapeworm, Bluebeard,* and *fourteen;* and 2) those containing one base accompanied by one or more derivative affixes, for example, *retape, bluish,* and *forty.* Members of the first group are often referred to as **compounds** proper, members of the second group as **complex** words. These two groups stand beside those entities that Otto Jespersen calls "naked words," such as *boy, bad, eat, to,* and *if,* which cannot be further analyzed.

It is often difficult to distinguish sharply between compound words and phrases. *Tape recorder,* for example, is listed as a phrase of two words in *Webster's Third International Dictionary,* but the verb *tape-record* is listed as a hyphenated compound and *tapeworm* as a compound. Other analyses of English may differ in their classification of such sequences.

In setting up classes of compounds in English, one cannot base classifications on spelling conventions. If *firecracker* is taken as a compound, *fire insurance* can scarcely be excluded from the list of compounds, nor can *fire insurance company, Western Fire Insurance Company,* or *Great Western Fire Insurance Company.* In contrast with English such lengthy expressions are written together in German, for example, *Versicherungsgesellschaft* 'insurance company,' *Feuerversicherung* 'fire insurance,' and *Feuerversicherungsgesellschaft* 'fire insurance company.' Among other languages in which lengthy compounds are found are Russian and Sanskrit.

In determining the compounds of any language and setting up classes of compounds, we follow the procedures observed in determining any linguistic classes: we observe the patterning of the items themselves and their relationships with other comparable items in the language.

Complex words present a different kind of problem. In some languages, including English, the base is not used separately, as for example in *decide* and *decision.* The base varies from /sayd/ to /siž/ and is difficult to define. Does the base mean 'cut' in a metaphorical sense, as in *incisive?* Or does it mean 'kill,' as in *parricide?* And should one relate the base to words such as *caesura* 'a metrical cut'?

Similarly difficult problems arise with other complex words, for example, *define, demand,* and *deter.* The most consistent approach requires determining the underlying forms for bound elements, that is, elements that cannot occur separately, as well as for those like *tape* and *worm,* which occur separately. Yet because the underlying form is restricted in occurrence, entire items like *define* may be treated as bases by some scholars rather than be subdivided. It is scarcely conceivable that an English treatment of derivation would analyze *fret* into a prefix *fr-*, related to *for-* as in *forlorn*, and a base *-et*, related to *eat*, although etymologists do so. In the course of time complex words may become indistinguishable from simple words, unless older texts that record the early form are available, as in Old English *fretan* and even more clearly in Gothic *fra-itan* 'eat up.' Historical linguists may be able to ferret out such earlier complex forms, but in the contemporary language itself such an analysis is difficult (if not impossible) to achieve. In derivation, therefore, a linguist does not apply strictly historical criteria. The resultant analyses may coincide with historical analyses, but some historical compound and complex forms are unrecoverable.

In derivation, then, we look for **productive** sets as opposed to **unproductive** sets. Productive sets are those to which new forms are being added, while unproductive sets are relics from the past.

## 7.7 Compounds

As noted previously, compounds may consist of two or more bases. To simplify discussion, most of the examples presented here contain only two segments, such as *pickpocket* and *lighthouse*, rather than three or more segments, such as *sister-in-law* or *snake in the grass*. The formation of larger compounds is generally based on those of two-element compounds: *lighthousekeeper* is constructed from *housekeeper* and *light-(house)* in much the same way as *housekeeper* is constructed from *house* and *keeper*, which in turn is a complex noun built up of *keep* and *-er*. Accordingly, longer compounds can be classified on the basis of the descriptions proposed for shorter compounds. We may set up four types of compounds: **coordinate, subordinate, possessive,** and **synthetic.**

### 7.7.1 Coordinate Compounds

In **coordinate compounds** the two elements are parallel. In some coordinate compounds one element is repeated with little change in meaning, as for example in *papa* and *mama*. In such Japanese compounds the effect is pluralization, collectivization, or accumulation. Thus *yama-yama* means 'a group of mountains.' Numerous Japanese adverbs indicate an intensification of the action represented, for example, *para-para* 'pit-a-pat,' *poka-poka* 'again and again.' A similar effect is observed in English compounds like *pitter-patter* and *flimflam*. Here too the effect is intensification. As exemplified by these English compounds, modification may accompany reduplication.

Some coordinate compounds are **additive,** for example, *thirteen* 'three + ten' and Japanese *eibei* 'England and America.' Sanskrit grammarians named coordinate compounds *dvandva* from a typical additive compound meaning 'two plus two.' The name *dvandva* is often used for additive compounds even in grammars of languages other than Sanskrit.

Other types of relationships may be found in coordinate compounds. For example, in Japanese some coordinate compounds are composed of opposites, such as *umu* 'being–not being, existence.' As illustrated by *umu,* or by *zehi* '(yes–no), propriety,' the literal and contrasting elements indicate the figurative meaning of the compound.

### 7.7.2  Subordinate Compounds

In **subordinate compounds** one element modifies the other. The modifying element may precede, as in *tapeworm* 'a worm shaped like a tape,' or it may follow, as in *tiptoe* '(on the) tip of one's toes.' The subordination may be of various types. Differing classes of elements may occupy either position in the compound, as we can illustrate with the first element in some English compounds: nouns, as in *clotheshorse;* adjectives, as in *greenhouse;* pronouns, as in *she-pony;* and verbs, as in *rowboat*.

Most English compounds are subordinate, with the first element modifying the second. Compounds with the second element modifying the first are largely borrowed, as in the animal name taken from Greek, *hippopotamus,* literally 'horse (of the) river.' Moreover, this pattern is apparently non-Greek. We find the same sequence in names taken over from Irish, Welsh, and other languages, for example, *Macadam* 'son (of) Adam' or *Pritchard* (Welsh *ap* 'son') 'son (of) Richard.' As Hebrew names illustrate, for example, *Ben-Gurion* 'son (of) Gurion,' this pattern is widespread in Semitic languages, as well as in many others.

### 7.7.3  Possessive Compounds

In **possessive compounds** the relationship between the elements does not provide the essential meaning of the compound; an external element must be added to interpret it. For example, a *greenback* is not a back of a given color but rather an object that possesses a green back, a bill—usually a dollar bill. *Blockhead, tenderfoot,* and *whiteface* are similar. In English such compounds often reflect lack of compassion, as do *redneck, baldhead,* and *bigmouth.* Whatever the connotation, the relationship of possession has given these compounds their name. The Sanskrit term for these compounds, *bahuvrihi,* is also widely used; it is simply an example of the class meaning 'a man who possesses a great deal of rice.' Literally it translates as 'much rice,' with a connotation similar to English *bigmouth*.

### 7.7.4  Synthetic Compounds

**Synthetic compounds** are compact expressions. They may be unabbreviated; the name of the flower *forget-me-not* is a complete imperative sentence. But commonly synthetic compounds are shortened in some way. For example, *pickpocket* reflects a sentence like 'He picks pockets.' For other varieties compare *show-off, housekeep,* and *good-for-nothing.*

Synthetic compounds are found in ancient Latin, Greek, and Sanskrit. Latin *artifex, artificem* 'artificer' is composed of a form of 'art' and a form of 'make.' In other synthetic compounds, such as Greek *Menelaos,* the verbal element precedes; the first element means 'upholds,' the second 'people.' Compound names of this sort indicated a desired attribute of the person so named.

In Japanese, synthetic compounds consist of a verbal element, for example, *rai* 'come,' and a nominal element, for example, *bei* 'America,' with the meaning 'come to America,' or *zai* 'living in,' as in *zaibei* '(living) in America.' Compounds may reflect sentence patterns. Thus the Japanese synthetic compounds illustrated here, based on a pattern borrowed from Chinese, reflect the Chinese word order: (S)VO. Japanese has compounds that are parallel in meaning and reflect both the native sentence pattern and that of Chinese. An example is *hara-kiri* 'stomach-cutting,' which reflects the Japanese (S)OV sentence pattern, as opposed to the equivalent *seppuku* 'cutting-stomach,' which reflects the Chinese sentence pattern. Both words refer to a traditional form of committing suicide.

The study of compounds therefore illuminates syntactic structures of various types: typical sentence patterns, sentence patterns with the "have" relationship, and sentence patterns with attributive relationships.

## 7.8 Complex Words

Complex words are generally analyzed by the type of affix involved. For example, the English nouns ending in the suffix *-ity* may be grouped together and described for the processes of formation, as may be the words with [for] as prefix, for example, *forbid, forecast,* and *forever.* Among the [for] words we would presumably set up at least two separate prefixes: {for₁} meaning 'away' and {for(e)₂} meaning 'in front of.' We might also propose {for₃} from the preposition *for,* as in *forsooth.* We find, then, that for this small number of complex words we must assume two, possibly three, separate homonyms, depending on whether we class {fore} and {for₃} together. Moreover, we must take into account the highly complicated changes in the nautical term *forecastle* [fówksəl]. These examples further illustrate the problems faced in the analysis of complex words.

### 7.8.1 [ən] and Related Affixes

To exemplify a set of related affixes we may examine some English complex words ending in [ən]. One group is formed from proper names:

*Elizabethan* 'pertaining to (the age of) Elizabeth,' *Lutheran* 'pertaining to Luther,' *Ohioan* 'pertaining to Ohio.' These may simply be analyzed into a base [iylízəbəθ], [lúwθər], [owháyow], and an affix [ən], having the meaning 'pertaining to.' The resulting complex forms may be either nouns or adjectives.

In many derivatives ending in (ən) the base is modified; in the example *Elizabeth/Elizabethan* it is modified in inflection only. But if the underlying form ends in [ə], for example, [ə] is deleted in the formation, as in *American* [əmérikən] from *America;* compare also *Russian* and *Californian.* In *Texan* [téksən] from *Texas,* [əs] is deleted. In some derivatives the meaning relationship to the underlying word differs somewhat from that proposed here, as in *Republican,* in which the meaning of the suffix is not simply 'pertaining to.' In other derivatives the formal modifications are considerable, for example, *Trojan* [trówjən] from *Troy* [trɔy]. In an adequate account of the [ən] affix, these relationships of meaning as well as form must be described, as well as the current status of the affix.

At one time [ən] was commonly added to stems ending in *y* or to words ending in *ia,* for example, *Asia Asian* [éyžə éyžən], some of which were in turn modified, for example, *Italy* (<*Italia*) *Italian* [itǽlyən]. A separate suffix was then produced and used with bases having no final *y: Spenser Spenserian, Shakespeare Shakespearian, Milton Miltonian.* It was also added to others with further changes of the base, for example, *Canada Canadian.* The [iyən yən] suffix is widely productive in designations of groupings, for example, *Washingtonian,* often with a change of the base, as in *Aberdonian* from *Aberdeen, physician* from *physics, logician* from *logic,* and so on. Even the form *Texian* is being propagated. The suffix [iyən yən ] illustrates how affixes are extended in languages that shorten words by dropping finals.

Even more extensive forms of the suffix have developed, as in *geometrician,* on the pattern of *mathematician* and similar forms. Instead of using the suffix *-ian,* as in the parallel underlying form *history historian,* a suffix *-ician* was taken from the supposed base and fitted onto *geometry.* This process is known as **suffix clipping.** The resultant suffix has become widespread, as in *beautician* and *mortician.* Similarly, the suffix *-arian,* as in *librarian* (based on *library*), has been extended to nouns without *-ary,* for example, *unitarian* from *unity* and *humanitarian* from *humanity.* In this way affixes may be extended in size as well as range of occurrence.

For further illustration we may compare another agent suffix, *-ist.* This suffix is now widely used to form nouns that indicate experts, for example, *economist, experimentalist, scientist,* and *physicist* versus the older *physician,* for one who studies physics.

Japanese makes many complex forms, but in the fashion of an agglutinative language the modifications are minor; *-teki,* for example, is a suffix indicating a modifying relationship. It is added to nouns, for example *kagaku* 'science,' to form phrases such as *kagakuteki shinri* 'scientific truth'; compare also *sekkyokuteki seisaku* 'positive policy.'

Various complex verbs in Japanese are made with prefixed verbs, for example, *hikkosu* 'move to' <*hiki* (the indicative *hiku* 'pull') + *kosu* 'cross.' In these *hiki* has roughly the meaning of 'perfectivization'; compare *hikidasu* 'take out,' *hiki-ireru* 'pull into,' and *hik-toru* 'take over.' Prefixed to verbs beginning with *k*, the *i* is lost, as for example in *hikkomu* 'draw back.' These examples may illustrate that the analysis of Japanese derivatives utilizes the same procedures as those employed for English.

## 7.9  Summary of Morphological Analysis

In analyzing the stock of words of a language, one must determine the simple or naked words, such as Japanese *hito* 'man,' *toru* 'take,' and *to* 'and.' Further, one may identify various compounds, such as the Japanese coordinate *jū-ichi* '(ten-one) eleven,' the subordinate *ichi-gatsu* 'first month, January,' and the synthetic *tobei* 'visit America.' In addition one must note the complex forms, such as *furusa* 'antiquity' from *furui* 'old' + *sa* '-ness.' Finally, one must account for sequences such as *nandemonai* '(what indeed it is not), trivial.' In the description of such derivatives one must deal, on the one hand, with formal characteristics and, on the other hand, with the meaning relationships. Both tasks are parallel to those used in dealing with inflection. Inflections, however, are used with compound and complex words as well as with simple words. Morphological analysis, then, consists of successive steps to first determine the simplest meaningful elements in a language and thereupon describe them and their functioning.

BIBLIOGRAPHICAL NOTES

Numerous illustrations of the varieties of inflection may be found in *Language* by Edward Sapir (New York: Harcourt Brace Jovanovich, 1921); in *The Philosophy of Grammar* by Otto Jespersen (London: Allen and Unwin, 1924); and in *Introduction to Theoretical Linguistics* by John Lyons (Cambridge: At the University Press, 1968). A recent general treatment, based primarily on Latin, is given in *Inflectional Morphology* by Peter H. Matthews (Cambridge: At the University Press, 1972).

One can find copious material, dealing with the subject of derivation, in handbooks for individual languages. *A Modern English Grammar*, vol. 6, by Otto Jespersen (Copenhagen: Munksgaard, 1942) is particularly comprehensive in its discussion of English compounds. A pioneering attempt to link compounds with larger syntactic structures may be found in *The Grammar of English Nominalizations* by Robert Lees (Bloomington: Indiana University Press, 1960), subsequently reprinted by Mouton (The Hague, 1966). A thorough treatment of English derivatives is given in *The Categories and Types of Present-Day English Word-Formation,* 2d ed., by Hans Marchand (Munich: Beck, 1969).

## QUESTIONS FOR REVIEW

1. Define *morphology.* Discuss the use in morphological analysis of: a. words; b. morphemes.
2. Identify the following processes: a. selection; b. arrangement; c. modification; d. intonation.
3. Distinguish between inflection and derivation, defining both.
4. Define: a. *paradigm;* b. *part of speech;* c. *conjugation;* d. *declension.*
5. Define, and give examples of: a. *prefix;* b. *suffix;* c. *infix;* d. *reduplication.*
6. Give examples of assimilation.
7. What is meant by *umlaut?* Give examples.
8. Define: a. *dissimilation;* b. *haplology;* c. *metathesis.*
9. What is meant by the statement that gender is a congruence category? How is it possible that a feminine noun may refer to an inanimate object?
10. Give examples that illustrate that number is a grammatical category. How can one account for the use of the plural *vacations* to refer to a single vacation?
11. Define: a. *count noun;* b. *mass noun;* c. *numeral classifier.*
12. Discuss case in language, listing several cases with statements on their use.
13. Define: a. *voice;* b. *tense;* c. *aspect.* Account for translations of the same Hebrew verb form as a past on the one hand and a future on the other.
14. Characterize the following moods: a. indicative; b. imperative; c. subjunctive; d. optative.
15. Define: a. *infinitive;* b. *participle;* c. *gerund.*
16. Distinguish between compounds and complex words, giving examples of each.
17. Identify, with examples: a. additive compounds; b. subordinate compounds; c. possessive compounds.
18. Define *productive formations,* giving examples of productive complex words.

## EXERCISES

### EXERCISE 1

English nouns are inflected in four forms, which may be labeled for *child* as follows: Nominative Singular /čáyld/, Genitive Singular /čáyldz/,

Nominative Plural /čîldr ən/, Genitive Plural /čîldr ənz/. These forms may be analyzed for base and suffix, as indicated here: Base: /čayld/ - /čild/; Plural /rən/; Genitive /z/. In preparation for analyzing the four forms of each of the following nouns, write them in transcription:

|  |  | Nom Sg | Gen Sg | Nom Pl | Gen Pl |
|---|---|---|---|---|---|
| 1. | mother | | | | |
| 2. | student | | | | |
| 3. | dog | | | | |
| 4. | chief | | | | |
| 5. | girl | | | | |
| 6. | duck | | | | |
| 7. | horse | | | | |
| 8. | judge | | | | |
| 9. | boy | | | | |
| 10. | church | | | | |
| 11. | politician | | | | |
| 12. | gentleman | | | | |
| 13. | fox | | | | |
| 14. | wife | | | | |
| 15. | house | | | | |

    a. Determine the bases of the nouns and also possible allomorphs, as in 14 and 15.

    b. Indicate the allomorphs of the affixes for the genitive singular, nominative plural, and genitive plural.

    c. State the distribution of the allomorphs of the plural affix; of the genitive affix.

    d. State the rule for the genitive plural affix, noting the genitive plural of nouns like child and woman [wúmən wúmənz wímən wímənz].

EXERCISE 2

English verbs are inflected in five forms, as follows:

*save saves saved saved saving*

These forms may be analyzed for base and suffix, as indicated here:

Base:  /séyv/
Suffixes:  /z/  /d/  /d/  /iŋ/

In preparation for analyzing the five forms of each of the following verbs, write them in transcription.

|  |  | I | II | III | IV | V |
|---|---|---|---|---|---|---|
| 1. | sun | _____ | _____ | _____ | _____ | _____ |
| 2. | live | _____ | _____ | _____ | _____ | _____ |
| 3. | slip | _____ | _____ | _____ | _____ | _____ |
| 4. | tug | _____ | _____ | _____ | _____ | _____ |
| 5. | need | _____ | _____ | _____ | _____ | _____ |
| 6. | rock | _____ | _____ | _____ | _____ | _____ |
| 7. | lay | _____ | _____ | _____ | _____ | _____ |
| 8. | bathe | _____ | _____ | _____ | _____ | _____ |
| 9. | wet | _____ | _____ | _____ | _____ | _____ |
| 10. | lull | _____ | _____ | _____ | _____ | _____ |
| 11. | mass | _____ | _____ | _____ | _____ | _____ |
| 12. | hum | _____ | _____ | _____ | _____ | _____ |
| 13. | rub | _____ | _____ | _____ | _____ | _____ |
| 14. | rouge | _____ | _____ | _____ | _____ | _____ |
| 15. | laugh | _____ | _____ | _____ | _____ | _____ |

a. After determining the base for each verb, indicate the suffixes for each of the four last forms.
b. Determine the morpheme for each of the inflections and indicate the distribution of possible allomorphs.

EXERCISE  3

The following are further English verbs. Analyze them for base and affix, as in Exercise 2.

|  | I | II | III | IV | V |
|---|---|---|---|---|---|
| 1. read | | | | | |
| 2. drink | | | | | |
| 3. take | | | | | |
| 4. tear | | | | | |
| 5. lead | | | | | |
| 6. sing | | | | | |
| 7. ride | | | | | |
| 8. shake | | | | | |
| 9. wear | | | | | |
| 10. rise | | | | | |

a. After determining the base for each verb, indicate the affixes for each of the four last forms.
b. Indicate the processes involved in the inflection of these forms.

EXERCISE  4

Figure 5 illustrates Japanese verb forms. List the bases and the affix for each of the four inflections, describing the morphophonemic patterning and stating its conditioning.

| Figure 5 | 'take' | 'wait' | 'fly' | 'hear' | 'smell' | 'buy' |
|---|---|---|---|---|---|---|
| Indicative | toru | mat$^s$u | tobu | kiku | kagu | kau |
| Infinitive | tori | mat$^š$i | tobi | kiki | kagi | kai |
| Past | totta | matta | tonda | kiita | kaida | katta |
| Negative | toranai | matanai | tobanai | kikanai | kaganai | kawanai |

EXERCISE 5

Figure 6 illustrates Turkish noun forms.

**Figure 6**

|        | 'house' | 'room'  | 'neighbor' | 'eye'   | 'friend'  |
|--------|---------|---------|------------|---------|-----------|
| Nom Sg | ev      | oda     | komşu      | göz     | dost      |
| Gen Sg | evin    | odanın  | komşunun   | gözün   | dostun    |
| Nom Pl | evler   | odalar  | komşular   | gözler  | dostlar   |
| Gen Pl | evlerin | odaların | komşularin | gözlerin | dostların |

  a. Determine the affixes for the genitive and the plural with their
     allomorphs. Describe the morphophonemic patterning and state
     the conditioning.
  b. The following are additional Turkish noun forms (with meanings
     in single quotes):

| evim | odam | babamız | köyümüz |
|------|------|---------|---------|
| 'my house' | 'my room' | 'our father' | 'our village' |
| evimin | odamın | babamızın | köyümüzün |
| 'of my house' | 'of my room' | 'of our father' | 'of our village' |
| evlerim | odalarım | babalarımız | köylerimiz |
| 'my houses' | 'my rooms' | 'our fathers' | 'our villages' |
| evlerimin | odalarımın | babalarımızın | köylerimizin |
| 'of my houses' | 'of my rooms' | 'of our fathers' | 'of our villages' |
| evimde | odalarda | babalarımızda | köyümizde |
| 'in my house' | 'in the rooms' | 'among our fathers' | 'in our villages' |

     After noting the affixes for the genitive and the plural, determine
     the affixes for the first singular and first plural pronominal suf-
     fixes. Describe the morphophonemic patterning and state its
     conditioning.
  c. Translate:

     1. *gözlerim*
     2. *odalarda*
     3. *komşularım*
     4. *villages*
     5. *in our village*
     6. *my father*

EXERCISE 6

The following are inflected Turkish verb forms:

| bilirim | gördüm | görmüş |
|---------|--------|--------|
| 'I know' | 'I saw' | 'one who has seen' |
| keşirim | geldim | gelmiş |
| 'I cut' (pres.) | 'I came' | 'one who has come' |

| görürüm | kaldım | kalmış |
|---|---|---|
| 'I see' | 'I remained' | 'one who has remained' |
| gelirim | oldum | durmuş |
| 'I come' | 'I became' | 'one who has stood' |
| kalırım | | |
| 'I remain' | | |
| dururum | | |
| 'I stand' | | |

a. Give the roots for the following: *know, cut, see, come, remain, stand, become.*

b. Give the suffixes with all allomorphs for:

1. I (first person)
2. present tense
3. past tense
4. perfect participle

c. Translate the following:

1. *bildim*
2. *bilmiş*
3. *one who has known*
4. *I stood*

EXERCISE 7

The following are English derived nouns. Analyze them for bases and the derivational affix, indicating the underlying forms and the processes involved in the derivation.

1. *actress*
2. *authoress*
3. *duchess*
4. *empress*
5. *goddess*
6. *governess*
7. *heiress*
8. *lioness*
9. *tigress*
10. *waitress*

EXERCISE 8

The following are paradigms of derivation in English:

1. *bounty : bounteous*
2. *envy : envious*
3. *grace : gracious*
4. *grief : grievous*
5. *prosperity : prosperous*
6. *religion : religious*
7. *right : righteous*
8. *superstition : superstitious*

Determine the underlying forms of the bases and the affix. Account for the allomorphs of the bases.

EXERCISE 9

The following are ordinal numerals in one dialect of English. Assuming that they are derived from the cardinals (/sévən náyn éyt/, and so forth), state the underlying form of the affix, give its variants, describe its morphophonemic changes, and indicate any changes in the underlying form of the cardinal numeral.

| | |
|---|---|
| seventh /sévənθ/ | third /θɚ́rd/ |
| ninth /náynθ/ | twelfth /twélθ/ |
| eighth /éyθ/ | fourth /fɔ́rθ/ |
| fifth /fíθ/ | hundredth /hɚ́ndrəθ/ |

EXERCISE 10

One type of compounds in Chinese may be illustrated by the following examples:

> tiān-liàng 'dawn' < 'day brightens'
> tóu-téng 'headache' < 'head aches'
> dì-zhén 'earth-quake' < 'earth quakes'

a. Identify the kinds of elements making up these compounds, and identify their order.
b. If such compounds are productive, what inferences would you draw from them about the order of elements in Chinese sentences?

# SYNTAX: PROCESSES, DEVICES, AND SYNTACTIC PATTERNS

## CHAPTER 8

### 8.1  Definition of Sentence

As noted in Chapter 7.1, four processes are involved in the production of the words and sentences of language: selection, arrangement, modification, and intonation. We may thus define a sentence as follows: A **sentence** is a sequence of selected syntactic items combined into a unit in accordance with certain patterns of arrangement, modification, and intonation in any given language.

Many other definitions of sentences have been given. Otto Jespersen referred to them as "notional kernels."[1] The term **kernel** has subsequently been applied to the smallest, most fundamental sentences of a language. But since we cannot define *notional* satisfactorily, little can be done with Jespersen's characterization. *Notebooks* might be viewed as a notional kernel, for example, but it is not necessarily a sentence. Yet when uttered with an appropriate intonation pattern, in answer to a question like *What did you want me to bring?* /³nówtbùks¹↓/ is a sentence. A sentence has also been defined, therefore, as any string of morphemes ending with a final intonation pattern.

---

[1] Otto Jespersen, *Analytic Syntax* (Copenhagen: Munksgaard, 1937), p. 15.

To provide the means for analyzing sentences or any other syntactic entities, two terms are used: **construction** and **constituent**. A **construction** is any complete group of words or morphemes. The term may be used for phrases, for example, *in the house;* clauses, for example, *if he comes;* or even sentences, for example, *She is leaving.* A **constituent** is a morpheme, a combination of morphemes, or a construction that is a component of a construction. For example, *in* is a constituent of *in the house; he comes* is a constituent of *if he comes;* and *she is leaving* is a constituent of *If he comes, she is leaving.*

In syntactic analysis, constructions are progressively analyzed into smaller and smaller entities. The phrase *in the house,* for example, is first analyzed into the preposition and its object *in + the house.* The object is then analyzed into article and noun, *the + house.* Each of these constituents is known as an **immediate constituent,** that is, one of the two (or less commonly three or more) constituents into which a construction may be analyzed.

A major aim of syntactic analysis is to determine the constructions and constituents of sentences.

---

### 8.2  Syntactic Devices

The basic patterns of a language may be extended in various ways or by various devices.

### 8.2.1  Coordination, or Conjoining

In such extensions parallel entities are arranged side by side, that is, **coordinated,** or **conjoined.** Instead of the two sentences *John takes cream* and *John takes sugar,* we may conjoin the objects and say *John takes cream and sugar.* Or we may conjoin differing subjects or differing verbs and say *John and Mary take cream and sugar* and *John takes and enjoys cream.* Coordination, or conjoining, is one of the basic syntactic devices. Although simple, it is carried out in accordance with specific patterns in any language. For example, in English conjoined noun expressions, we may use *and* with the last noun, *John, Mary, and Joe,* as well as between each noun. In Japanese, on the other hand, *to* 'and' is used between each noun and may even be used after the last, for example, *Tarō to Fujiko to Jirō (to) wa* 'Taro and Fujiko and Jiro.' The constructions produced by coordination must be determined for each language.

### 8.2.2  Subordination, or Embedding

In a further type of extension, entities are arranged in hierarchies; one entity or construction is **subordinated** to, or **embedded** in, another. Embedding may be indicated by special words, such as English relatives and subordinating conjunctions, for example, *John, who likes sugar* and *when John drinks coffee*. In Japanese, on the other hand, an embedded clause is simply placed before the entity it is subordinated to, for example, *Koohii o nomu Tarō* 'Taro who drinks coffee.' Similarly in English, adjectives may be embedded in nominal constructions without the use of a special marker, for example, *black coffee*. Formerly in Japanese, embedded adjectives had a special marker *-ki*, for example, *takaki yama* 'high mountain' versus *yama wa takashi* 'the mountain is high.' In the analysis of embedded constructions the term **head** is used to refer to the center of the construction, the term **attribute** for the modifier. A clause in which another is embedded is referred to as a **matrix** clause.

### 8.2.3  Endocentric and Exocentric

The terms **endocentric** and **exocentric** are used to classify constructions. An **endocentric construction** is one in which the primary constituent or constituents are comparable to the complete construction. For example, *Good old John* and *John and Mary* are endocentric because their central constituents, *John and Mary,* are nouns that function like the combined construction.

An **exocentric construction** is one in which the primary constituent or constituents do not function like the complete construction. For example, *in the house* is exocentric because the constituent *the house* functions differently from a prepositional phrase. Sentences are exocentric because the constituents function differently from the whole. For example, in *John takes coffee* none of the constituents is comparable to the entire sentence.

### 8.2.4  Substitution

**Substitution** is a third syntactic device. Through it replacements, or **substitutes,** often called **pro-forms,** stand for the central entities of basic patterns. Substitutes may be used in separate basic patterns or when basic patterns are added to one another. Occasionally the replacement for an entity may be zero, as in the sentence *I like this tie better than (ø) that one*. In the second part of this sentence (ø) substitutes for a second use of *I like*.

As substitutes for nouns, **pronouns** are used in many languages. Instead of *John likes cream* we may say *He likes cream* or *He likes it*. Other pro-forms in English are *this, that, one, ones, the former, the latter,* and so on. While a pro-form may introduce ambiguity in a sentence when its antecedent is not clear, pro-forms must often be used to avoid awkwardness. For example, rather than *I like this tie better than I like that tie,* we may say *I like this tie better than that one*. If we are pointing to the ties, we may prefer *I like this one better than that one* or *I like this better than that*. When the context is clear, substitutes convey a feeling of informality;

when it is not, as in the sloppy use of *this* with poorly specified antecedents, the feeling engendered may instead be annoyance.

Substitutes may also be used for verbs. A common pro-form for English verbs is *do,* for example, *He likes coffee and she does too.* Modals are also widely used as substitutes, for example, *He'll take coffee and so will she.* Modals and auxiliaries are common substitutes in tag questions, for example, *You'll go, won't you? He went, didn't he? If I went, would you?* Other languages use different devices to produce substitutes that are at once more complex and more simple than their counterparts in English. We may cite such substitutes as the French *n'est-ce pas?* which need not be modified to agree with the substituted verb or the German *nicht wahr? nicht?* as in *Du gehst mit, nicht?* 'You're going along, aren't you?' Besides substituting modals and auxiliaries, we may substitute *to* for verbs, as in *Will you go? I'd like to.* Other entities have different substitutes, for example, *so* for adjectives: *This coffee is dark and so is that* or *This coffee is dark and that is even more so.* And in some patterns no overt forms are used at all; for example, rather than *\*She's not as old as he is old,* we simply say *She's not as old as he is,* or even *. . . as he.* The substitute then is zero.

### 8.2.5  Function Words and Content Words

Entities used as substitutes generally fall into the set of items known as **function words.** These convey relationships among the **content words,** such as nouns and verbs, in a language. Examples of function words are auxiliaries, conjunctions, determiners, interjections, postpositions, prepositions, and relatives. They are the primary items in many languages for specifying the relationships between the basic constituents of constructions.

### 8.2.6  Concord and Government

Constructions may also indicate interrelationships through inflection or other patterns involving selection. These indications are the result of concord or of government phenomena.

**Concord,** or **congruence,** is the agreement in form of one word with another. For example, *this* must be modified to *these* before plurals, as in *this tie, these ties; eat* must be modified to *eats* after *he.* Highly inflected languages like Latin exhibit a great deal of concord. English exhibits less, as do Japanese and Chinese. The use of **numeral classifiers,** like *head* in *two head of cattle,* is a type of concord; Japanese and Chinese have many such classifiers.

**Government** is the determination of one form by another. Verbs and prepositions govern specific forms in English, for example, *her* rather than *she* is required in *He saw her* and *to her.* Other word classes may also govern specific forms; some adjectives in German govern specific cases, for example, in *Es ist mir lieb* 'It is dear to me,' *lieb* requires the dative case *(mir)*.

In sum sentences are bound together by means of conjoining and embedding, by the use of substitutes and function words, and by the devices of concord and government. To describe the sentences of any language we must note which of these devices are used in the patterns of selection, arrangement, modification, and intonation found in that language.

## 8.3  Favorite Sentence Types

We have already noted the favorite sentence patterns for English and Japanese. Before examining those of English in further detail, we may briefly compare the favorite sentence patterns of Arabic.

Like English and Japanese, Arabic has two favorite sentence types, one with verbs, the other without. The verb type consists of verb, followed by subject and object if they are present, as for example:

> *katab kita·b.*　　　　　　'He wrote (a)-book.'
> *katab ʔal-usta· ð kita·b.*　'He-wrote the professor (a)-book =
> 　　　　　　　　　　　　　　The professor wrote a book.'

The nonverb type may be illustrated by a construction consisting of noun and adjective, for example:

> *ʔal-be·t kibi·r.*　'The-house (is) big.'

This sentence may be contrasted with the noun phrase:

> *ʔal-be·t ʔal-kibi·r* ('the house the big') = 'the big house'

As is illustrated by these two examples, the nonverb sentence type of Arabic is distinguished from an adjective phrase by the lack of a definite article before the adjective. Besides illustrating the Arabic pattern, this example indicates the possible variety of sentence constructions to be found in language.

To illustrate syntactic patterns and syntactic devices, we may pursue the sentence types of English in somewhat greater detail. The two basic favorite sentence types of English, **verb sentences** and **BE sentences,** have the following subtypes:

| Verb Sentences: | 1. | *They came.* | $N^1$ V | | |
|---|---|---|---|---|---|
| | 2. | *They became friends.* | $N^1$ V | $N^{(1)}$ | |
| | 3. | *They saw her.* | $N^1$ V | $N^2$ | |
| | 4a. | *They gave her candy.* | $N^1$ V | $N^2$ | $N^3$ |
| | b. | *They elected her mayor.* | $N^1$ V | $N^2$ | $N^{(2)}$ |

BE Sentences:        a. *It is cold.*            N   BE Adj
                     b. *It is here.*            N   BE Adv
                     c. *It is Jack.*            N   BE N

In describing these types and noting their expansions we must observe the use in English of the syntactic processes: selection, arrangement, modification, and intonation.

Since we have already dealt with intonation in Chapter 4, we will not discuss it here. We will also omit a discussion of modification here, such as the normal use of [its] for the *It is* of the last three examples, as details on such modifications would take up considerable space.

---

### 8.4   Arrangement in English Sentences and Selection Classes

Arrangement is straightforward in English basic sentence patterns. The subject must precede the verb and BE; objects and complements follow. In expanded sentences arrangement is more complex. If, for example, adverbs are added to one of the basic patterns, such as *today, very,* and *here* to *It is cold,* they must be arranged in accordance with a small number of possible orders:

> *It is very cold here today.*
> *Today it is very cold here.*

and occasionally:

> *Here it is very cold today.*

but not:

> *Very it is cold here today* (and so on).

Although patterns of arrangement are highly limited in this way, in analyzing the basic sentence patterns of English, we find that selection is an important syntactic process. Sentences are built up of a small number of constituent classes, often known as **parts of speech.** The four large classes are nouns, verbs, adjectives, and adverbs. These constituent classes are, in turn, built up of selection classes, which have fewer members. Further, as noted previously, the members may be replaced by proforms. Moreover, in most actual sentences the selected content words are accompanied by function words.

An essential problem in English syntax is the determination of the various subclasses of constituent classes and function words. A detailed classification could only be given in a large grammar. To illustrate the problem briefly, we may note some of the subclasses of verbs.

### 8.4.1   Subclasses of English Verbs

The four classes of verb sentences proposed in section 8.3 are based on four subclasses of verbs. All grammars and dictionaries distinguish two of these, calling the verbs of subclasses 1 and 2 **intransitive,** those of 3 and 4 **transitive.** The further subclassification given here and in many recent grammars also distinguishes between intransitive verbs that do not require a following noun or adjective and those that do. Some grammars call verbs like *become* and *seem* **linking verbs.**

Similarly, transitive verbs are subdivided here into two large groups, one of which requires only an object, the other an object plus a noun or a pronoun. Verbs used in type 2 sentences may be subdivided in turn into those followed by an adjective, such as *look, seem,* and *sound,* and those followed by a noun, such as *become, remain,* and *stay.* Subclassifications of this sort may at the outset seem superficial, but they illuminate other segments of the language, as for example, compounds. We may make the compound *strange-looking,* but we cannot say *\*friend-becoming.* Through subclassification, then, we come to observe the general patterns in language, not only those under scrutiny at the moment.

Similarly the verbs in type 4 sentences can be further subclassified on the basis of patterning. We may illustrate one difference by means of substitutes. Instead of *They gave her candy,* we can say *They gave her it,* or more commonly *They gave it to her.* But we cannot say *\*They elected her it.*

Additional subclassification becomes more delicate. We may distinguish between verbs like *call* and *consider* and between verbs like *elect* and *select* on the basis of the relationship of the two objects. *Call, consider,* and so forth indicate a permanent attribute; *elect, select,* and so forth indicate a temporary one. Verbs like *call* and *consider* may, however, be used to indicate a temporary attribute if we add an adverbial expression, as in *Let's call the puppy Fido until Susie thinks of a better name,* or *Let's consider this a solution for the time being.*

In this way constituent classes may be put into even smaller subclasses. In a complete grammar all parts of speech—for example, nouns, adjectives, adverbs, and function words—would also be subclassified in this way.

### 8.4.2   Overt Versus Covert Selection Classes

Such subclassification may lead to the recognition of relationships that are not **overt** in the language. Among sentences of subclass 3 in section 8.3, we may distinguish between a set like *They saw her* and a set like *They stopped the car.* Sentences belonging to the second set may be rephrased as subclass 1, with the former object as subject: *The car stopped.* Verb constructions of this type are comparable to **ergative** constructions in many languages, for example, Caucasian or Eskimo. The subject performs an action affecting the object, whereas in *I saw her,* there is no such effect. Nor can we say \*_Her_ (or _she_) _saw_ but only _She was seen_. In English the relationship expressed by verbs like _stop_ is hidden or **covert.** In Caucasian languages, on the other hand, there is a specific case form for subjects entering into ergative relationships, and accordingly the relationship is overt.

The uncovering of covert relationships has been one of the major concerns of recent syntactic study. It gives credence to the assumption of universals in language (another topic of increased interest in recent linguistic study). For through finer and finer subclassification of English verbs and nouns, covert categories have been discovered that match the overt categories of languages widely different in their surface syntactic system.

### 8.4.3  Subclasses of Function Words

Subclasses of English function words are often specified according to gross sets: those used with verbs as **auxiliaries** and those used with nouns as **determiners** and **prepositions.** Determiners may be classified in turn into numerous subclasses, some of which may consist of only one or two members, for example, the **definite article** and the **indefinite article.** As the following list indicates, determiners may or may not be used before nouns: _all, any, some, no; both; few, many; little, much; more, most, less, least; each, every; either, neither; his, her, its, my, our, your, their; whose; this, that,_ and so on. We can say _His car broke down_ and _His broke down_. But _my_ is used only before nouns, as in _My car broke down_ versus _Mine broke down_.

### 8.4.4  Subclasses of English Nouns

The use of determiners, in turn, permits subclassification of nouns. **Proper nouns** may be distinguished from **common nouns** by the impossibility of placing determiners before proper nouns. For example, _Jack_ is a proper noun in _Jack dealt the cards_ but not in _He dealt a jack to each of the players_.

Determiners assist in the further subclassification of nouns. _Some,_ for example, before _egg_ requires the plural, _some eggs,_ whereas before _sugar,_ it requires the singular, _some sugar_. These two classes have been called **count nouns** and **mass nouns.** _An egg_ is possible, but not \*_a sugar,_ as in \*_Pass me a sugar_ (unless it is used in a different sense, as 'lump of sugar'). 

Further examination of the uses of mass nouns discloses additional patterns of English usage. When preceded by _some, any,_ and so forth and inflected in the plural, mass nouns refer to individual entities: _I'll take some cheeses_ means 'I'll take some entire ensembles of cheese.' When words fall into several classes in this way, we speak of **class cleavage.** Many examples may be given for verbs, such as _move, ask, write,_ and _count,_ as in _They moved last week,_ where _move_ belongs to the class of intransitive verbs, versus *They moved the last house on the block,* where *move* is transitive.

### 8.4.5 Function Words Used with Entire Clauses

Function words may also be used with entire clauses, for example, **conjunctions** (either **coordinators** or **subordinators**) and **relatives**. Others, such as **interjections,** may be totally independent, for example, *yes, no,* and *please.* And yet other function words may be empty signalers, for example, *there,* as in *There is a man here.*

With these function words the basic sentence patterns of English may be expanded in many complex ways. Some languages have many inflected forms that indicate syntactic relationships. These specify various patterns of selection in somewhat the same way as arrangement does in English. But in English inflections are minimal.

---

### 8.5 Selection Classes Based on Inflections

English verbs have at most five forms, for example, *give, gives, gave, given, giving.* Only the auxiliary *be* has more: *be; is, am, are; was, were; been; being.*

Nouns have at most four forms, for example, *man, man's, men, men's.*

The pro-forms known as **pronouns** have four forms, for example, *I, me, my, mine.* To this class belong the seven personal pronouns, *he, she, it, I, we, you, they,* and the interrogative and relative *who.*

Adjectives have three forms, for example, *slow, slower, slowest.* A fourth form may be made from some adjectives, for example, *slowly.* But this formation is restricted. We do not say *\*Drive fastly.* And even the ancient adverb *slow,* lacking the adverbial ending *-ly,* is used generally as in *Drive slow.* As this brief summary illustrates, inflection plays a minor role in English.

---

### 8.6 Expansion of Simple Sentences

### 8.6.1 Expansion of the Verb Phrase

When we examine verb phrases in English, we find expansion by means of three sets of auxiliaries:

> A    Modals: *can, could; may, might; will, would; (shall), should; must, had to; ought to* + infinitive
> B    Have: *has, have; had* + participle
> C    BE: + gerund (form in *-ing*)

These expansions may be used with the basic patterns or in the combinations AB, AC, BC, ABC. But they may not be used in the order CB or CA; for example, *They are maying give* is impossible. Thus in English verb phrases arrangement is highly important. Examples of possible verb phrases with type 4 sentences (given in section 8.3) are:

A    *They may give her candy.*
B    *They have given her candy.*
C    *They are giving her candy.*
AB    *They may have given her candy.*
AC    *They may be giving her candy.*
BC    *They have been giving her candy.*
ABC  *They may have been giving her candy.*

With these expansions many sentences can be formed. But other auxiliarylike elements are also being introduced into English, notably *be going to* and *used to*. These are comparable to the modals used in following the pattern of A. Similar in use are verbs like *seem, want, begin, prefer,* and *try + to.* The last three may also follow the pattern of C; they are then comparable to modals as well as to BE. Another set of verbs, for example, *avoid* and *enjoy,* follows the pattern of C, as in *He began giving her candy.*

### 8.6.2   Expansion of the Noun Phrase

The noun may be expanded by determiners and adjectives placed before it and by prepositional phrases and relative clauses placed after it. In the expansions subclasses of adjectives are observed, though often distinctions become faint. We may illustrate some of these by substituting noun phrases for *they* in the sentence *They gave her candy.* The two large classes placed before nouns are distinguished by their order: **determiners,** sometimes called **limiting adjectives,** which stand first in expanded noun phrases, and **descriptive adjectives,** which must follow them. Subclasses of the descriptive adjectives may be recognized from expansion, for example:

*their old neighbors*
*their fine old neighbors*
*their fine old retired neighbors*
*their many fine old retired neighbors*
*all their many fine old retired neighbors*

Such long expansions may become absurd, but segments of them are in general use. As may be noted from this example, participles as well as gerunds and compound adjectives stand closest to nouns. They are preceded by adjectives indicating qualities. These in turn are preceded by adjectives indicating judgments. Finally, the determiner *all* may be preposed before appropriate phrases.

Noun phrases may also be expanded by modifying nouns, for example:

*their next-door neighbors*

Complexities may be added by conjoining. Still further complexities may be added by the modifying of adjectives with adverbs, for example:

*their very fine neighbors*
*their fine, very old neighbors*

Prepositional phrases may be added to simple nouns or to expanded noun phrases, for example:

*all the fine old neighbors to the north of them*

Or relative clauses may be added, for example:

*all the fine old neighbors who attended the party*

Such relative clauses may follow expansions with adjectives and prepositions, for example:

*all the fine old neighbors to the north of them who attended the party*

Moreover, noun phrases may be extended by apposition. Many such expansions are difficult to follow and are frowned on by stylists who recommend clarity of expression. Yet that expansions of this sort are not merely constructions of grammarians may be illustrated by this almost random excerpt from a technical publication:

> *Chemically rather simple, centrally active crystalline substances, muscimol, the fly killing ibotenic acid, and the related muscazone have been discovered in the fly agaric and in other mushrooms . . . muscimol, which easily results from ibotenic acid by decarboxylation, may be considered as an essential principle of Amanita muscaria.*[2]

This citation is a relatively straightforward example of technical prose. The basic sentence patterns are simple, but elements of them, particularly the noun phrases, have been greatly expanded.

Besides these expansions noun phrases may be based on verb forms, such as:

---

[2] *Science,* March 1, 1968, p. 948.

1. gerunds and participles, for example, *Giving her candy would hardly restore you to favor.*
2. infinitives, for example, *To give her candy would be against my principles.*
3. clauses, for example, *That he gave her candy is widely known.*

The possibilities of noun expansion allow for virtually infinite variety in English prose.


### 8.6.3   Adverbial Expansions

Some adjectival expansions were illustrated in the discussion of nominal expansions. We may note briefly some adverbial expansions, as in the following sentences produced from *He drove here:*

> *He drove here in the morning.*
> *He drove here as rapidly as possible.*
> *He drove here in the morning as rapidly as possible.*
> *He drove here as rapidly as possible in the morning.*

If we classify the three adverbial phrases by **place, time,** and **manner,** we note that in English they stand in the order, PT, PTM, and PMT. In addition a small set of adverbs, such as *always, never, often,* and *sometimes,* follows another pattern. They generally stand between the noun phrase and the verb, although *sometimes* and *often* also stand initially, for example:

> *He always drove here in the morning as rapidly as possible.*
> *Sometimes he drove here in the morning as rapidly as possible.*

---

### 8.7   **Alterations of Simple Sentences**

Through such expansions of noun phrases, verb phrases, and adverbs, lengthy clauses may be produced. Yet the basic sentence patterns remain simple, for they consist only of the segments specified for the types given earlier in section 8.3. These may in turn be altered in various ways.

1. QUESTIONS: Three types of questions may be framed in English:

   A   with change of intonation, for example, *He came?*
   B   with *wh-* words, for example, *Who came?*
   C   with auxiliaries or *do,* for example, *May he come?* or *Did he come?*

Type C illustrates one of the fundamental distinctions between verb sentences and BE sentences. In questions of type C, verb sentences must introduce *do,* for example, *Did they come?* By contrast in BE sentences the arrangement is altered, for example, *Is it cold?*

Type C also provides the pattern for **tag-questions,** for example, *He came, didn't he? He didn't come, did he? That's the book, isn't it?* As the examples illustrate, tag-questions are so framed that they require a specific answer, either negative or positive. Their own pattern, whether negative or positive, is determined by the construction of the clause to which they are tags.

2. NEGATIVES: Negatives with forms of *not* are made with auxiliaries, for example, *isn't, didn't,* and *can't,* as in *It isn't cold* and *They didn't come.* They may also be made with *never* and in other ways. Since negatives may be made of questions—for example, *He never came? Who didn't come? Can't they come?*— the sentence alterations are listed in the order adopted here.

3. EMPHATICS: Emphatic clauses are made by altering intonation, generally by substituting a higher pitch, which may be labeled $^4$ for pitch $^3$, with or without the addition of *do,* for example, *They came* /²ðèy ⁴kéym¹↓ / or *They didn't come* /²ðèy ⁴dídənt kə̀m¹↓/. Both questions and negatives may be made emphatic.

4. REQUESTS: Requests are made with the simple verb or with the addition of introductory elements, for example, *Come, Give her candy, Be good,* and *Please be here promptly.* The variants may follow one or more of the three preceding clause alterations, for example, *Will you come? Won't you come?* $^4$ *Wón't you come?* Apart from requests to the addressee, requests may refer to third persons, for example, *Let him go,* or may include the speaker, for example, *Let's go* (in contrast with *Let ús go).*

5. PASSIVES: The passive alteration is made only for verb sentences of the types 3 and 4 listed in section 8.3, for example, *She was seen by him* and *She was given candy by them.* Passives may in turn be expressed in the four preceding sentence patterns, for example, *Was she seen by him? Wasn't she seen by him? (Tell me,)* $^4$ *Wásn't she seen by him? You should be seen by him.*

## 8.8  Compound Sentences

Besides these alterations, clauses introduced by function words that involve conjoining or embedding may be added to other clauses. The clauses so modified are referred to as **coordinate** and **subordinate** clauses, and the resulting sentences are **compound.**

Coordinate clauses may be introduced by a number of coordinating conjunctions. Most of these are also used to conjoin segments of clauses, for example, *They came and saw her* and *They came and are here*. As in these examples, elements of the conjoined clauses may be deleted. While *They came, and they saw her* is possible, it is less frequent than the sequence with deletion. The coordinating conjunctions follow various patterns, which can only be touched on here.

Noun phrases may be conjoined with *and;* such expressions are followed by a plural verb. If conjoined with *or* or *neither . . . nor,* however, they are followed by a singular verb. The restrictions for conjoining clauses are relatively severe. The four simple verb sentences given in section 8.3 may be conjoined with *and: They came and became friends, They came and saw her,* and *They came and gave her candy*. Restrictions on *or* are much greater, for *or* implies a parallelism between the items conjoined. Accordingly, none of the eight basic sentences given in section 8.3 may be conjoined by *or;* for example, *\*They came or saw her* is impossible. Although the general basis for the restriction is clear, the details observed for such conjoining remain to be studied. Restrictions for *but* are also severe. Adjectives and adverbs may be conjoined with *but,* as in *They came slowly but gradually* and *It is cold but pleasant*. On the other hand, noun phrases may not be conjoined with *but; \*John but Mary came* is impossible. Verb phrases may be conjoined with *but* in accordance with certain restrictions, for example, *They came but (nonetheless) became friends*.

These remarks on the uses of coordinating conjunctions may be lengthy in view of the brief sketch of English syntax presented here, but they indicate some of the complexities of an apparently simple syntactic construction. As we will note in Chapter 16, the patterns of reduction in coordinate constructions are determined in part by language types.

Subordinating conjunctions may have very simple syntactic arrangements, for example, *Because they came, they gave her candy*. Or the arrangements may be highly complex: *If they had only come, they would have given her candy*. Without pursuing these in detail, we may observe that substitutions yielding simple sentences in place of either of the clauses in this last sentence would be in the negative, for example, *They didn't come* and *They didn't give her candy*. Similar complexities may be pointed out in other subordinating patterns, for example, *However generous he was with the candy, he didn't win her over = He wasn't generous enough with the candy*. Complexities of this sort have been studied in greater detail for Latin and Greek than for English and other modern languages. A precise specification is essential, however, for an understanding of these languages and for the study of syntax in general.

A second type of sentence compounding is produced by means of the **relatives,** *who that,* and *which*. Relatives bring about embedding in accordance with various restrictions. Noun phrases must be equivalent—for example, *The man came to dinner* and *The man stayed on* may be amalgamated to *The man who came to dinner stayed on*. One pattern of relative clauses in English, the **restrictive,** is distinguished by intonation, for example:

*The man whom you met is my brother.*
/²ðə mǽn hùwm yùw mét iz mày ³brə́ðər¹↓/

contrast:

/²ðə ³mǽn² → ²hùwm yùw ³mét² → ²iz mày ³brə́ðər¹↓/

This distinction is one of the rare grammatical patterns marked by conventions of punctuation. Relatives of the second type, called **descriptive, nonrestrictive,** or **appositional,** as opposed to restrictive relative clauses, are marked off by commas.

A third type of modification is limited in standard English to BE sentences with adverbs: *There is/are . . . ;* for example, *A man is here, There is a man here, Gold is in those hills,* and *There is gold in those hills.* This pattern is more widespread in Irish English, giving rise to local color in sentences like *There is often she was under the influence.*

---

## 8.9  Minor Sentence Types

Apart from these basic sentences and their modifications, English has minor sentence types.

One of these consists of subject plus auxiliary and is called the **completive,** for example, *(Did they come?) They did. (Is it cold?) It is. (It's cold.) Isn't it?* A second consists of any single sentence component. Since it must be supplemented by the missing sections of a full sentence, it may be called the **elliptical.** Examples are *(How did he come?) Slowly. Tickets.* (= *I'd like your tickets.*)

A third consists of parallel comparison. Since it frequently occurs in aphorisms, as in *First come, first served,* it is often called the **aphoristic.** Yet it is not infrequent in other writings, as may be illustrated by the following sentence:

*Paradoxically the greater the enhancement of extraterrestrial activities or isotope anomalies by flare-particle spallation, solar-ion stopping, or secondary neutrons, the easier it may be to observe extraterrestrial material, but the harder it is to infer influx rates.*[3]

The so-called minor sentence types are so designated not because they are infrequent, but rather because they do not exhibit the possibilities of expansion and alteration that are found in the major sentence types of a language. Even the preceding lengthy example maintains the basic pattern *the . . . -er, the . . . -er.*

---

[3] *Science,* March 1, 1968, p. 942.

## 8.10   Presentation of Syntactic Patterns

Even without a discussion of the syntactic patterns of other languages, it is clear from a superficial survey of English syntactic patterns that the analysis and presentation of syntax for a given language are highly complex. Many attempts at presentation have been fragmentary. Others are little more than catalogs. Frameworks for dealing with syntax compactly and yet comprehensively have been of great interest in recent linguistic study. They involve views of a language as a totality, not simply as a listing of its sequences of words and clauses. Such a framework will be illustrated in the next chapters.

BIBLIOGRAPHICAL NOTES

One of the most useful treatments of syntax is found in Otto Jespersen's *Modern English Grammar, vols. 1–7* (Copenhagen: Munksgaard, 1909–1949). A short version of Jespersen's analysis of English is presented in his *Essentials of English Grammar* (University, Ala.: University of Alabama Press, 1964). Jespersen's syntactic theory is presented in his *Analytic Syntax* (1937; reissue, New York: Holt, Rinehart and Winston, 1968). A shorter treatment of English may be found in *A Synopsis of English Syntax,* 2d rev. ed., by Eugene A. Nida (The Hague: Mouton, 1966). The principles of transformational grammar have been presented for syntax in Noam Chomsky's *Aspects of the Theory of Syntax* (Cambridge, Mass.: M.I.T. Press, 1965). Lucien Tesnière's *Eléments de syntaxe structurale* (Paris: Klincksieck, 1959) may also be consulted for observations on syntactic problems. A recent grammar that is comprehensive but represents a "compromise position" with regard to theoretical issues is *A Grammar of Contemporary English* by Randolph Quirk, Sidney Greenbaum, Geoffrey Leech, and Jan Svartvik (London: Longman, 1972).

QUESTIONS FOR REVIEW

1. Define the term *sentence*. What is meant by the term *kernel?*
2. Define: a. *construction;* b. *constituent;* c. *immediate constituent.*
3. Distinguish between coordination and subordination. What is a matrix clause?
4. Distinguish between endocentric and exocentric constructions.
5. Discuss the device of substitution, giving some pro-forms.
6. Distinguish between context words and function words.
7. What is: a. concord? b. government?
8. Give the favorite sentence types of English. What is a contrasting sentence type in Arabic?

9. What does it mean to say that parts of speech are selection classes?
10. Give examples of: a. transitive verbs; b. intransitive verbs; c. linking verbs.
11. Distinguish between overt and covert selection classes.
12. Give examples of: a. common nouns; b. proper nouns; c. count nouns; d. mass nouns. What is class cleavage?
13. How are verb phrases expanded in English?
14. Discuss the rules governing the expansion of noun phrases in English.
15. What types of questions may be made in English? What is a tag-question?
16. Distinguish between coordinate and subordinate clauses.
17. Distinguish between restrictive and descriptive, or appositional, relative clauses in English.
18. What is a completive sentence? What is an elliptical sentence?
19. Describe the aphoristic sentence type of English.

## EXERCISES

### EXERCISE 1

Japanese has two types of sentences. The first may be illustrated by the following examples:

a. *Ano hito wa        sensei  desu.*
   that man topic particle teacher is        'He is a teacher.'
b. *Kare wa        tegami desu.*
   this   topic particle letter   is        'This is a letter.'

The second type may be illustrated as follows:

c. *Ano hito wa        hon  o        yomu.*
   that man topic particle book object particle read   'He reads books.'
d. *Kare wa        tegami o        kaku.*
   he topic particle letter object particle write   'He writes a letter.'

Identify the characteristics and basic uses of the two sentence types. How do they relate to the English sentence types noted in section 8.3?

### EXERCISE 2

The following are question forms of sentences a and c in Exercise 1:

*Ano hito wa sensei desu ka?*
'Is he a teacher?'

*Ano hito wa hon o yomu ka?*
'Does he read books?'

How are questions formed in Japanese? Make questions of sentences b and d in Exercise 1.

## EXERCISE 3

Negatives of sentences d and b are as follows:

*Kare wa tegami o kakanai.*
'He doesn't read letters.'
*Kore wa tegami de wa nai (de wa often becomes jā).*
'This isn't a letter.'

Make negatives of sentences c and a.

## EXERCISE 4

To make a negative question in Japanese, one adds *ka* after the negative form, for example:

*Kare wa tegami o kakanai ka?*
'Doesn't he read letters?'

Make questions of the other negative sentences in Exercise 3.

## EXERCISE 5

The following are Japanese sentences containing numerical expressions that consist of a numeral and a numeral classifier. The numerals are: 1 *ichi*, 2 *ni*, 3 *san*, 4 *shi/yon/yo*, 5 *go*, 6 *roku*, 7 *shichi*, 8 *hachi*, 9 *kyū/ku*, 10 *jū*. (Note that *o* indicates the object; *wa* indicates the topic, or subject. *Empitsu* = 'pencil,' *zasshi* = 'magazine,' *sara* = 'dish.')

1. *Tarō wa empitsu o ni hon kaimashita.*    'Taro bought two pencils.'
2. *Jirō wa zasshi o ni satsu kaimashita.*    'Jiro bought two magazines.'
3. *Saburō wa sara o ni mai kaimashita.*    'Saburo bought two dishes.'

   a. Identify the numeral classifier in each sentence above.
   b. Numeral classifiers are used with restricted sets of nouns, somewhat as gender classes are. If besides pencils, *hon* is also used for sticks, needles, and bottles, what is the basis of classification for nouns used with it? Besides dishes, *mai* is also used for counting paper and boards. What is the basis of the classification for these nouns?

c. The following sentences contain additional numerical expressions. Suggest the sphere of use of the four numeral classifiers in these sentences. (Note that the numerals here are linked to the classifers. *Kyaku* = 'customer,' *jidōsha* = 'car,' *inu* = 'dog,' *uchi* = 'house,' *ahiru* = 'duck.')

4. *Yonin no kyaku wa jidōsha o nidai kaimashita.* "Four customers bought two cars.'
5. *Gohiki no inu wa uchi no mae ni imasu.* 'Five dogs are in front of the house.'
6. *Shichiwa no ahiru wa uchi no mae ni imasu.* 'Seven ducks are in front of the house.'

d. Discuss the arrangements of numerical expressions in Japanese.
e. Give two ways of saying *Saburo bought eight ducks* in Japanese.
f. Some numerals, in conjunction with certain classifiers, undergo various types of modifications, so that (as in c above) the numeral and the classifier are combined into one word. For example:

| | | | |
|---|---|---|---|
| *satsu* | 1 *issatsu* | 8 *hassatsu* | 10 *jussatsu* |
| *ken* (used for 'houses' | 1 *ikken* 6 *rokken* | | 10 *jukken* |
| and 'shops') | | | |

Describe the processes of modification exemplified by these examples. If the processes are reflected most clearly in the modifications involving *ichi, roku,* and *hachi,* what underlying combining form might you propose for the number ten?

g. In conjunction with *san* 'three' the following modifications take place:

   *sambon (hon)    sammai (mai)    samba (wa)*

Describe the modifications.

## EXERCISE 6

Coordination is signaled in Japanese by conjunctions like *to* 'and' and *mo* 'and also,' as in the following examples:

*Kare wa gohon no empitsu to nisatsu no zasshi to o kaimashita.*
'He bought five pencils, and (he bought) two magazines.'
(The second *to* is not mandatory.)
*Tarō wa empitsu o Jirō wa zasshi o kaimashita.*
'Taro bought pencils, and Jiro (bought) magazines.'
*Haruyo wa zasshi o Yaeko wa hon o yonde iru.*
'Haruyo is reading a magazine and Yacko a book.'

Note the position of the deleted verbs in English as well as in Japanese. Comparing the Japanese with the English sentences, comment on the location of the deleted verbs in the Japanese examples with regard to the order of subject, object, and verb in Japanese.

EXERCISE 7

German has three patterns of word order for simple (noninterrogative) clauses, as follows:

1. *Hans liest      ein Buch.*
   'Hans is-reading a   book.'
2. *Maria schreibt   einen Brief.*
   'Mary is-writing a      letter.'
3. *Jetzt liest       Hans ein Buch.*
   now is-reading Hans  a   book =
   'Hans is reading a book now.'
4. *Heute schreibt   Maria einen Brief.*
   today is-writing Mary  a      letter =
   'Mary is writing a letter today.'
5. *Ich weiss, dass Hans ein Buch liest.*
   I   know  that Hans a   book is-reading =
   'I know that Hans is reading a book.'
6. *Ich merke, dass Maria einen Brief schreibt.*
   I   note    that Mary a      letter is-writing =
   'I note that Mary is writing a letter.'

What is the position of the verb in each of the three sentence patterns (a: 1, 2; b: 3, 4; and c: 5, 6)? What determines the position of the verb?

EXERCISE 8

The following sentences illustrate the order of adverbial expressions of time and place in German:

1. *Hans fährt  heute südwärts.*
   Hans drives today south =
   'Hans drives south today.'
2. *Maria geht    morgen  in   die Stadt.*
   Mary is-going tomorrow into-the-city =
   'Mary is going to town tomorrow.'
3. *Ilsa flog  gestern   nach Berlin.*
   Ilsa flew yesterday to-    Berlin =
   'Ilsa flew to Berlin yesterday.'

What is the standard sequence for adverbs of time and adverbs of place in German? in English?

EXERCISE   9

Following the pattern of word order used when sentences begin with an adverb of time, rewrite the three sentences of Exercise 8 beginning with *heute, morgen,* and *gestern*.

EXERCISE   10

Since German has one type of simple clause in which the verb precedes the object, as in sentences 1 and 2 of Exercise 7, and another in which it follows the object, as in sentences 5 and 6, there has been some discussion whether it is VO like English or OV like Japanese. Coordinate sentences with equivalent verbs may delete all but the first of two verbs, as in the translation of the second sentence of Exercise 6.

> *Taro kaufte   Bleistifte und Jiro Zeitschriften.*
> 'Taro bought pencils   and Jiro magazines.'

On the basis of the patterning in this construction would you classify German as VO or OV?

# PHRASE-STRUCTURE GRAMMARS

## CHAPTER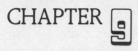

### 9.1  Analytic Grammars

Traditional grammars have been analytic. Sentences have been analyzed into successively smaller immediate constituents. Thus a sentence like

1. Parrots can talk.

is analyzed, or parsed, for the constituents subject and predicate, and the predicate is in turn analyzed into the constituents auxiliary and verb. If the intonation is taken into consideration, it is distinguished first as illustrated in Figure 1.

**Figure 1**

| | ²Parrots | can | ³talk¹# | |
|---|---|---|---|---|
| a | Parrots | can | talk | ² ³ ¹ # |
| b | Parrots | can | talk | ² ³ ¹ # |
| c | Parrots | can | talk | ² ³ ¹ # |

If desired, the analysis could be continued until all inflectional and derivational morphemes were distinguished, as in the possible step d in Figure 2.

**Figure 2**

Analysis of this type has various shortcomings. The most serious is that it fails to deal with many syntactic relationships. For example, the sentence *Everyone should sing the ballad* is closely related to the sentence *The ballad should be sung by everyone*. Yet in syntactic analysis directed at individual sentences alone, the syntactic relationships between the two sentences remain unexplored. As a result, such syntactic analysis provides only a partial understanding of the syntactic structures of a given language.

Further problems arise for sentences with modifiers, such as *Yellowhead parrots can talk*. An English speaker understands the sentence as equivalent to *Parrots that are yellowheads can talk*. Yet a simple analysis fails to specify such relationships as that between the adjectival *yellowhead* and the phrase *that are yellowheads*.

Although such analysis is used in many texts and courses dealing with linguistics and with individual languages, recent linguistic study has focused on a generative approach.

---

## 9.2  Context-Free Phrase-Structure Grammars

We have noted above that the term **generative** implies specification of the steps taken by a speaker in his or her use of language. When a speaker produces sentences, he or she presumably draws on a set of rules that have been mastered in learning his or her language. A grammar, reflecting a speaker's control of language, provides rules that operate to produce only grammatical sentences.

In such a grammar there are two types of rules. One type indicates the production of sentences by specifying the phrases of which sentences are composed, such as the noun phrase (NP) and the verb phrase (VP). Grammars of this sort are known as **phrase-structure grammars;** the rules are known as **phrase-structure rules.** Such rules, more commonly referred to as **P-rules,** are rewriting rules. A simple-shafted arrow, which corresponds to "is rewritten as," is placed between the initial element and the new elements.

The second type of rule supplies the lexical, or terminal, elements. Rules of this type are often referred to as **terminal rules.** Lexical rules commonly use a colon, :, to distinguish between the initial symbol and the terminal element.

We may illustrate such a phrase-structure grammar by noting its use for the specifications of sentences like the following:

1. *Parrots talk.*
2. *Mice bite.*
3. *Babies sleep.*

The initial string is assumed to be an S, for sentence, with initial and final boundaries indicated by #. From this string an NP and a VP are generated.

The P-rules for these sentences then would be:

$$\#S\#$$

1. S → NP VP

The terminal rules would be:

NP: *parrots, mice, babies*
VP: *talk, bite, sleep*

The P-rules given here are written so that they apply in all contexts. Grammars and rules of this type are said to be **context-free.**

The context-free phrase-structure grammar given above would then generate nine sentences. Most of these would be acceptable. Some would not, for example:

*\*Mice talk.*

To avoid the production of such sentences, further lexical classes can be set up. The word *mice* could be listed in a class with a diacritic such as x, y, or z, and an indication could be given to preclude the concurrence of all such NP's with V's like *talk*.

This kind of procedure leads to more complex rules. Since we would like to maintain the initial rule, S → NP VP, because it reflects the structure of many English sentences, NP would have to be defined as consisting of several elements. The resulting rule makes use of "curly brackets": { }. These symbols indicate that one of two or more classes may be selected. Another P-rule would then be added to this grammar of the form:

$$2.\ NP \rightarrow \quad \begin{matrix} N_x \\ N_y \end{matrix}$$

Yet even with this addition, the grammar is inadequate for generating many English sentences, such as:

4. *Mice eat corn.*

In order to have the grammar generate such sentences, the device of sub-dividing NP's could be extended to VP's, and a second subclass of VP's might be set up that would govern objects. This device would require the production of a different kind of rule, which would specify the contexts in which an entity could be used. The resulting grammar would then no longer be a context-free phrase-structure grammar.

As these examples show, context-free phrase-structure grammars are very powerful (in that they generate many structures), though through this characteristic they generate ungrammatical sentences. We will note further below that they seem to specify the procedures by which highly abstract strings of elements are generated in the production of sentences. But since they are not suitable for specifying even many simple sentences of English, we will examine a grammar with greater restrictions on the contexts in which its rules apply.

## 9.3   Context-Sensitive Phrase-Structure Grammars

Context-free grammars have rules of the form $X \rightarrow Y + Z$ or $X \rightarrow YZ$. **Context-sensitive** grammars have rules that specify the environment in which a given rule can apply. The context is indicated after a slash, /. Thus if the rule $X \rightarrow YZ$ applies only after an initial sentence boundary, the resulting rule would read: $X \rightarrow YZ/\#$ ____. The underline indicates the place at which the rewritten elements can be inserted in a string. The context itself is indicated by other symbols, such as #.

If we were to write a rule specifying the context in which the verb of sentence 4 could be used, the rule would have the form: $VP \rightarrow VP_2/$ ____ NP. This rule would indicate that a subclass of English verbs, to which *eat* belongs, would be used only in the context before an NP. Maintaining the rules proposed in section 9.2, but with modifications, we would then have to add a further rule on the pattern of rule 2. This rule would indicate that VP's in English consist of more than one subclass:

$$3.\ VP \rightarrow \begin{Bmatrix} V_1 \\ V_2 \end{Bmatrix}$$

In the terminal rules $V_1$ and $V_2$ would read:

$V_1$: *talk, sleep,* etc.
$V_2$: *eat, say,* etc.

In addition to this curly bracket notation, which indicates alternate rewritings, another device is used to produce more useful grammars. To permit the specification of phrases like *the babies* as well as *babies*, parentheses are used, ( ). These indicate that the element enclosed is optional. If we include *the* in the class commonly labeled Det for **determiner** (or in the class labeled Art for **article**), we would modify rule 2 to:

$$[\text{tentative}] \quad 2. \ NP \rightarrow \left\{ \begin{array}{cc} (\text{Det}) & N_x \\ (\text{Det}) & N_y \end{array} \right\}$$

To avoid repetition of Det, however, we would add a further rule generating $N_x$ and $N_y$ from N, giving the rules below. An alternate lexical element in these rules is the pronoun *they*. This would be added to modified rule 2, giving the form:

$$2. \ NP \rightarrow \left\{ \begin{array}{c} \text{Pronoun} \\ (\text{Det}) \ N \end{array} \right\}$$

$$3. \ N \rightarrow \left\{ \begin{array}{c} N_x \\ N_y \end{array} \right\}$$

A context-sensitive grammar, using these devices, will generate the sentences of a language like English more precisely than does a context-free grammar. We may illustrate such a grammar by writing rules for the sentence patterns given in Chapter 8.3.

---

### 9.4 A Phrase-Structure Grammar for the English Favorite Sentence Types

If the verb sentences given in Chapter 8.3 included nouns as well as pronouns in the subject position, they could be generated by the following grammars:

$$1. \ S \rightarrow \quad NP \ VP$$

$$2. \ NP \rightarrow \left\{ \begin{array}{c} \text{Pronoun} \\ (\text{Det}) \ N \end{array} \right\}$$

$$3. \ VP \rightarrow \quad V \ (NP) \ (NP)$$

$$4. \ V \rightarrow \left\{ \begin{array}{l} V_1 \\ V_2/\underline{\quad}N_{PN} = N_{Subj} \\ V_3/\underline{\quad}N \\ V_4/\underline{\quad}N \ N \end{array} \right\}$$

Pronoun : *they*
Det       : *the, his*
N         : *students, friends, parents, books*
$V_1$      : *came, left*
$V_2$      : *became, remained* (With these verbs, the PN, i.e., predicate noun, must match the subject.)
$V_3$      : *saw, met*
$V_4$      : *gave, offered*

With this grammar the following sentences could be generated. (The final symbols in the P-markers are given after each sentence.)

1.  *They came.* Pronoun $V_1$
2.  *The students became friends.* Det N $V_2$ N
3.  *His parents met the friends.* Det N $V_3$ Det N
4.  *The friends offered his parents the books.* Det N $V_4$ Det N Det N

Many further sentences could be generated, some of them unacceptable, such as:

*The books became friends.

By using further subclassification of the kinds discussed in section 9.3, such sentences would be avoided. Yet other shortcomings of this grammar will be discussed below, in section 9.6.

## 9.5  Phrase-Markers

Representations for sentences are given in two ways: through labeled tree diagrams or labeled brackets. Since these indicate the phrase-structure, they are known as phrase-markers, or **P-markers.**

A P-marker in the form of a tree would appear as follows for sentence 3 of section 9.4:

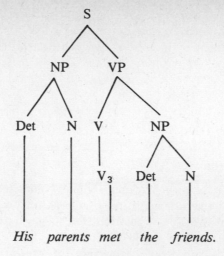

*His    parents    met    the    friends.*

A P-marker in the form of labeled brackets would appear as follows:

[   [   [His] [parents] ]      [   [ [met] ]      [      [the] [friends] ] ]
S   NP  Det   N              VP  V V₃           NP   Det   N

Such P-markers are equivalent to each other. When space is no problem, as on a blackboard, tree diagrams are generally preferred because they are easier to interpret. The labeled brackets are often preferable (as in teletype printouts), however, because of their compactness.

## 9.6  Dominance and Precedence

The P-markers serve to illustrate terminology that has come to be prominent in grammatical discussions. If an element like NP is rewritten as Det N, NP is said to **dominate** these two elements. The syntactic relationship is said to be one of **dominance.** This relationship is identical to that treated in earlier grammars as **selection** (see Chapter 8.1). The various elements generated by dominating elements are selection classes.

To indicate the sequence of elements in P-markers, the term **precedence** is commonly used. NP is said to precede VP in rules like 1 above. This relationship is that treated in earlier grammars as **arrangement** (see Chapter 8.1).

P-markers also illustrate why terms like *subject* and *predicate* are not used in many generative grammars. Such terms refer both to a dominance and to a precedence relationship. For example, the subject *His parents* in sentence 3 is, on the one hand, dominated by S and, on the other hand, followed by a VP. Since it is useful for clarity of analysis to distinguish between these two types of relationships, and since the relationships are clearly specified by the rules of a rule-ordered grammar, labels indicating the functions of syntactic elements have been avoided in many generative grammars.

## 9.7  Rule Ordering

It is clear that the rules in a grammar must be ordered, so that the proper strings may be generated. If, for example, an N were generated in the subject position before a possible Det N, any subject consisting of a determiner plus a noun would be excluded.

Rules that are ordered through internal structure are said to be **intrinsically** ordered. Such rules could be given in any sequence. The rules in section 9.4 are intrinsically ordered, since none of them would produce strings that cannot be properly rewritten.

A larger grammar may, however, require the applications of rules at successive stages in the generation of strings. If, for example, these rules included the generation of imperative sentences and intensive pronouns, it would be necessary to generate the intensive pronoun before the imperative. In a generative grammar, imperatives like:

1. *Bring the book!*

are derived from P-markers that at one point specify the subject pronoun, giving the sentence:

2. *You bring the book!*

Similarly, sentences like:

3. *Bring the book yourself!*

are also derived from such markers. If in these derivations the rule for the imperative is applied before that for the intensive, no simple procedure would be available for specifying sentences like 3, rather than unacceptable sentences like:

4. *\*Bring the book herself!*

The rules for generating these structures might then be ordered by some external notation, for example, a sequence of numbers. Such rules are said to be **extrinsically** ordered.

Many linguists prefer to devise grammars so that the rules are intrinsically ordered. Such an aim clearly requires greater complexity of the rules and of the grammar than does the admissibility of extrinsically as well as intrinsically ordered rules. Rule-ordered grammars, then, often include rules of both kinds.

## 9.8  On the Adequacy of Phrase-Structure Grammars

The sentences generated in this chapter are extremely simple. If more extensive, and more complicated, sentences were to be generated, the P-rules would have to be extended. Moreover, as indicated in section 9.3, even an extensive set of P-rules would fail to represent characteristics of the language, such as closely related structures. One could readily extend the P-rules given above so that each of the following sentence pairs could be generated:

> 1a.  *She bought the book.*
> b.  *The book was bought by her.*
> 2a.  *A cave is on their property.*
> b.  *There is a cave on their property.*

But the generation of such sentences, without reference to each other, is unsatisfactory because each sentence of the pair seems related to the other. As a result grammars have been preferred that specify not only the structure of sentences but also the relationships between pairs. The next chapter will discuss these types of grammars.

Such grammars, however, include a segment that is comparable to phrase-structure grammars (as is dealt with in Chapters 3 and 10). Linguists write grammars in an effort to understand how speakers produce the sentences of a language. As a result of various observations of language behavior, it has been concluded that speakers produce, in the first instance, simple sentences and then more complex variants of such simple sentences. In examining children learning to speak and studying the types of sentences that are used when speakers fashion their language in order to be understood by nonnative speakers, it has been found that the simple sentences readily produced by phrase-structure grammars are favored. Phrase-structure grammars, then, seem adequate for the basic sentence patterns of a language.

Moreover, phrase-structure grammars are suited for attempts to account for another human characteristic: the ability of a baby to learn any language whatsoever. A baby learns the language spoken in its environment, regardless of the structure of the language and regardless of the language spoken by its natural parents. A Japanese child brought up by an English-speaking family, for example, will learn English, even though English is VO in contrast with the OV structure of Japanese and even though the two languages are totally unrelated. To account for this capability, a grammar with simple and general rules is useful.

Accordingly, phrase-structure grammars, with even more general rules than those presented here, correspond well to findings that have been made about language and the linguistic behavior of humans. Such grammars, then, are used to account for the most basic structures of language.

## BIBLIOGRAPHICAL NOTES

Phrase-structure grammars are discussed in *Syntactic Structures* by Noam Chomsky (The Hague: Mouton, 1957). A more recent treatment, reflecting much of subsequent grammatical discussion, is given in *Syntactic Theory* by Emmon Bach (New York: Holt, Rinehart and Winston, 1974).

## QUESTIONS FOR REVIEW

1. What is a phrase-structure grammar?
2. What is a P-rule? a terminal rule?
3. Distinguish between context-free and context-sensitive rules, giving an example of each.
4. Identify the use of the following symbols: a. → ; b. { }; c. ( ); d. /; e. # (in P-rules).
5. Define *phrase-marker,* illustrating two kinds of P-markers for one sentence.
6. What is meant by *dominance?* by *precedence?* Relate these terms to the syntactic processes discussed in Chapter 8.
7. What is meant by *rule ordering?* Why is it necessary? Distinguish between extrinsically and intrinsically ordered rules.
8. Discuss the adequacy of phrase-structure grammars, indicating difficulties in using them for descriptions of entire languages. Also discuss some of their advantages and reasons for making use of them.

## EXERCISES

## EXERCISE 1

The following is a phrase-structure grammar for a portion of English:

# S #

$$S \rightarrow NP\ VP$$

$$NP \rightarrow \begin{Bmatrix} (Det)\ N \\ Pronoun \end{Bmatrix}$$

$$VP \rightarrow \begin{Bmatrix} V\ (NP) \\ is\ Adj \end{Bmatrix}$$

Det      : *the, this*
N         : *student, girl, clerk*
Pronoun : *it*
V         : *saw, remembered, wrote*
Adj     : *energetic, impossible*

a. Make ten acceptable sentences with this grammar.
b. Two categorial elements are given in parentheses, Det, and NP in the VP rule. Would the first ever be observed in this grammar? If so, under what conditions? Would the second be observed to make acceptable sentences? If so, make two such sentences.

EXERCISE 2

The following are selected English sentences.
  a. Construct a phrase-structure grammar that will generate these sentences.

> 1. *The books vanished completely.*
> 2. *His notes disappeared suddenly.*
> 3. *Their records dropped alarmingly.*
> 4. *Her glasses fell down.*

  b. Make four additional sentences that are acceptable, using your P-rules and this lexicon.
  c. Would your grammar produce any unacceptable sentences?

EXERCISE 3

The following is a phrase-structure grammar for a portion of Japanese:

$S \rightarrow$ NP VP

NP$\rightarrow$ N *ga*

N: *hito* 'man,' *sensei* 'teacher,' *gakusei* 'student'
(*Ga* indicates the subject in Japanese sentences.)
VP: *itta* 'went, left,' *kita* 'came,' *kaetta* 'returned'

Using this grammar and lexicon, make three Japanese sentences, giving their English equivalents.

# SYNTACTIC CONSTRUCTIONS AND THEIR IMPLICATIONS FOR GRAMMARS

## CHAPTER 10

### 10.1 Requirements for General Grammars

Linguists design grammars of various kinds, for various purposes. If a grammar is written to account for the grammatical structure of a specific language, such as English, it can use more specific rules than grammars designed to account for all languages. Many of the grammars produced in the past have been written as though English, and related languages like German, French, Russian, and Latin, are characteristic of all languages. These languages, however, are all SVO languages and therefore represent only one type. The phrase-structure rules of such grammars are accordingly restricted in their application. For an understanding of the general principles governing languages, the P-rules must be so designed that they apply generally.

This requirement may be clarified if we regard grammars, in agreement with recent characterizations of them, as theories about language. A theory must be framed in accordance with scientific principles, but it also reflects the knowledge of its proponents. In producing theories to comprehend the phenomena of concern to it, linguistics is far behind the physical sciences. As we noted in Chapter 1, many languages have not yet been studied. Therefore, grammars of today are based on observations concerning only a selection of human languages. It is scarcely surprising that most grammars reflect inadequate theories of language.

Most grammars (and most theoretical work on language) have been designed to fit languages that, like English, have basic sentence structures with subjects preceding verbs and verbs preceding objects. Such languages, as noted in Chapter 2.4, have many constructions expected in SVO languages, for example, postposed relative clauses and prepositions. Theoretical works reflecting such observations, and presenting P-rules of the pattern S → NP VP, will gradually have to be superseded, and works pertinent to languages in general will have to be substituted. To indicate some of the problems of general grammars, in this chapter we will examine characteristic constructions and note the implications of their analysis and description for general linguistic theory.

In examining such constructions we will use a generative grammar and assume underlying structures as well as surface structures. To account for the syntactic patterns of the underlying structures, we will use a phrase-structure grammar. This grammar will differ from the tentative grammars examined in Chapter 9. The rules will be intrinsically ordered. The categorial symbols will be unordered, so that both VO and OV languages can be accounted for. While English will be used so as to simplify presentation, some of the categories will be illustrated by other languages since they will be more abstract than those categories discussed earlier. The strings generated from the P-rules will be related to surface syntactic strings by transformational rules, though there is not sufficient space to present these in any detail. A grammar that results from this approach will be sketched in the course of this chapter.

---

## 10.2    Conjoining, or Coordination

Conjoining, as noted in Chapter 8.2.1, is a common process in language. Two or more clauses may be connected with a conjunction rather than uttered separately, for example:

1. *Jane likes peaches and Anne likes grapes.*

Moreover, such conjoined sequences may be reduced. Sentence 1 would be commonly reduced to:

2. *Jane likes peaches and Anne grapes.*

This phenomenon, known as **conjunction reduction,** is widespread, especially in SVO languages. The elements that can be deleted have been thoroughly studied. Because gaps result in such reduction, it has been referred to in recent studies as **gapping.**

Gapping differs with the type of language. In OV languages, the last of two or more equivalent verbs is maintained. If, then, in Japanese two classes with objects are conjoined, they will have the structure SO SOV, as in the following example:

3. *Tarō ga hon o katta.*
   'Taro bought books.'
4. *Jirō ga zasshi o katta.*
   'Jiro bought magazines.'
5. *Tarō ga hon o mo Jirō ga zasshi o katta.*
   'Taro bought books and Jiro bought magazines.'

Patterns of gapping may then be used to determine whether a language is VO or OV.

If, in contrast with the examples above, the conjoined sentences have the same subject, the conjoined sequence consists of a series of objects, for example:

6. *Jane likes peaches and grapes.*
   (from *Jane likes peaches, and Jane likes grapes.*)

Similarly for subjects:

7. *Jane and Anne like peaches.*
   (from *Jane likes peaches and Anne likes peaches.*)

Conjoining may in this way affect various constituents of sentences.

The constituents that are conjoined must, however, share syntactic and semantic features. We do not produce sequences like the following:

8. *\*Jane likes peaches and people like grapes.*
9. *\*Jane likes peaches and Anne bought a new car.*

The rules for conjoining are accordingly subtle, and a complete description of them for any one language would require considerable discussion, especially when the various coordinating conjunctions are considered. Languages usually include conjunctions that indicate contrast, like *but,* as well as simple coordinators, like *and.*

Since conjoining is universal in language, a rule for it must be included in the phrase-structure component. This rule is generally given as the first P-rule. It may have the form:

$$\Sigma \rightarrow \quad \text{Conjunction} \quad \Sigma^n$$

By this rule one or any number of sentence strings may be generated, with appropriate conjunctions. $\Sigma$ will henceforward be used to indicate *sentence* in order to avoid confusion with S — subject. In full form, a conjunction would be generated with each such string, for example:

10. *Jane likes peaches and Anne likes grapes and Joe likes apples.*

The final form of any conjoined sentence would be determined by transformational rules.

---

## 10.3   Embedding, or Subordination

By conjoining, two or more sentences are arranged side by side. By embedding, on the other hand, one or more sentences are introduced to qualify or in some way modify a matrix sentence or an element in it, as noted in Chapter 8.2.2.

When a sentence is embedded in a matrix sentence with reference to a noun, the resultant clause is referred to as a **relative construction,** for example:

11. *Jane likes peaches that have smooth skins.*
    (from *Jane likes peaches. The peaches have smooth skins.*)

When the sentence is embedded with reference to a dummy object or subject, this constituent is referred to as a **complement,** for example:

12a. *Jane likes it that Joe drives a Plustang.*
  b. *Jane likes Joe to drive a Plustang.*
  c. *Jane likes to drive a Plustang.*
    (from *Jane likes it. Jane drives a Plustang.*)

As these examples indicate, embedding may be accompanied by considerable modification. Such modifications vary from language to language. But as we will note below, they are in accordance with the various language types. Rules accounting for those modifications will also be illustrated in section 10.3.3.

Since embedding is universal in language, it must be accounted for in the P-rules. We can do this by adding an optional $\Sigma$ to an NP rule. If the phrase-structure grammar in Chapter 9.4 were maintained, the NP rule might be given as:

$$\text{NP} \rightarrow \begin{Bmatrix} \text{Pronoun} \\ \text{(Det) N } (\Sigma) \end{Bmatrix}$$

By this rule a $\Sigma$ could be embedded after an N like *peaches* in sentence 11 or an indefinite noun like *it* or *something* in sentence 12. The embedded sentence is then modified, in accordance with the structures of a given language.

To illustrate the structure of relative clauses in matrix sentences, a P-marker is given here for sentence 11:

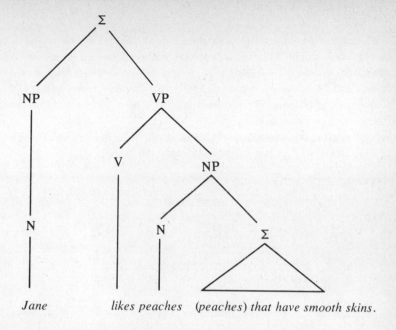

*Jane*          *likes peaches*   *(peaches) that have smooth skins.*

(A triangle Δ indicates that for the purpose under discussion the sequence so specified will not be analyzed.) The resultant modifications yielding the final sentence will be noted below.

A rule like the modified NP rule is **recursive.** That is, it reintroduces a categorial symbol that can again be rewritten. By means of such a rule, sequences similar to those in children's poems can be generated, for example:

13. *This is the maiden all forlorn, who milked the cow with the crumpled horn, that kicked . . .*

The recursive embedding rule adds greatly to the generative power of a phrase-structure grammar. We will examine its application for relative clauses and for complements.

## 10.3.1   Relative Constructions

It has long been assumed by linguists that relative constructions are derived from sentences embedded in matrix sentences having an equivalent noun phrase. Thus the following sentence is derived from two simple sentences:

14. *John is the man who saw the dog.*
    (from *John is the man. The man saw the dog.*)

In an SVO language like English, such relative clauses and the nouns to which they are attached are derived from sequences like NΣ. Accordingly, the relative clause follows its antecedent.

The processes involved in the production of relative constructions may be sketched simply. The equivalent NP in the embedded sentence is deleted and is generally replaced by a relative pronoun. This process is carried out by a transformational rule hereafter known simply as EQUI. If the noun is animate, the pronoun is *who, whom,* or *that;* if inanimate, the pronoun is *which* or *that*.

If, however, the embedded clause is attached to the object of a matrix clause, a relative pronoun is not mandatory, as in:

15. *Jane saw the dog she liked.*
    (from *Jane saw the dog. Jane liked the dog.*)

In VSO languages, relative constructions often have no relative pronoun.

Similarly, in OV languages relative constructions often have no relative pronouns or markers. Instead they precede the word modified, as in the following Japanese example:

16. *Inu    o              mita  otoko wa            Tarō desu.*

    dog   object particle   saw  man  topic particle    Taro is

'The man who saw the dog is Taro.'
(from *Otoko ga inu o mita. Otoko wa Tarō desu.*)

Relative constructions may differ in further ways from language to language. But the essential characteristics, such as the position of the modifying clause with regard to the noun modified, have been sketched above.

Languages commonly distinguish between relative clauses that simply describe the noun modified and those that delimit it. In English a distinction is made in intonation and also in punctuation. Thus, the following sentence contains a descriptive, or appositive, relative clause:

17. *McGregor, who is a good student, turned in a fine report.*

This sentence contains three intonation contours: $/^2 \ ^3 \ ^2 \ | \ ^2 \ ^3 \ ^2 \ | \ ^2 \ ^3 \ ^1 \ \#/$. The descriptive relative clause is set off by commas. By contrast, a restrictive or limiting relative clause is illustrated in the following sentence:

18. *He is the student who reported.*

Such sentences are spoken with only one intonation contour: $/^2 \ ^3 \ ^1 \ \#/$, as indicated above in Chapter 8.8. In many languages, on the other hand, less of a distinction may be made between such differing types.

To account for the differences between the two types in English, it has been proposed that descriptive relative clauses are derived from conjoined sentences; for example, sentence 17 would be understood as derived from *McGregor is a good student, and McGregor turned in a fine report*. The arguments in favor of such a derivation are inconclusive. In the phrase-structure rules proposed here, relative clauses are derived from an embedded $\Sigma$.

### 10.3.2   Modifications of Relative Clauses

We have noted above that relative pronouns are not mandatory when the deleted noun is the object in its clause, as in:

19. *The men he knew were elected.*

When relative constructions are attributive, further modifications may be made, as when the verb is the copula. Thus sentence 21 is as possible as sentence 20:

20. *The men who were most prominent in the club were elected.*
21. *The men most prominent in the club were elected.*

On the basis of the parallelism between such reduced modifiers and relative clauses, it is assumed that attributive adjectives are derived from relative clauses containing predicate adjectives.

Attributive prepositional phrases are derived in the same way, as in:

22. *The men in the club were elected.*
    (from *The men were elected. The men were in the club.*)
23. *The leaders of the club were elected.*

The relationship expressed by the prepositional phrase in sentence 23 is genitival. These examples illustrate that genitives, like adjectives, are derived from relative constructions. Thus the following sentence is also a derivation from an embedded relative clause:

24. *The club's leaders were elected.*

In many languages, such as French, Spanish, Japanese, and Turkish, relative constructions, adjectives, and genitives stand on the same side of the noun modified. This shared relationship with nouns supports the derivations proposed above.

But other languages, like English, are inconsistent in the placement of one or more of these constructions. The reasons for the inconsistency are historical, as we will note in Chapter 12. English in its early period was OV. In Old English most genitives were preposed, but this pattern has gradually been replaced, except in constructions with personal nouns, for example, *John's books*. Adjectives still observe the preposed order, except when they are further modified, as in sentence 21. By contrast with English, French and Spanish (as well as the other Romance languages) follow the VO pattern for relative constructions, adjectives, and genitives.

### 10.3.3  Transformations Used in the Derivation of Relative Clauses and Their Modifications

If we examine the P-marker for sentence 15, we may note the transformational rules that must be applied in the derivation of relative clauses and their modifications.

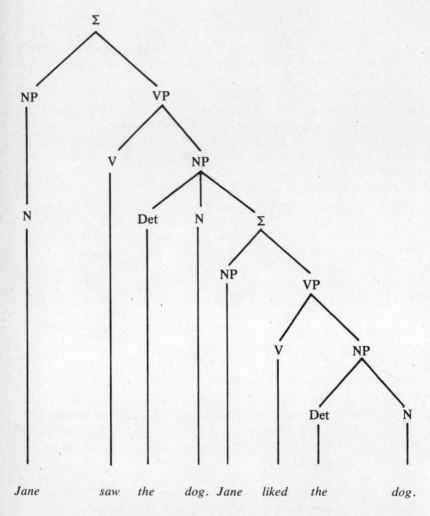

*Jane        saw    the    dog. Jane    liked    the        dog.*

In the derivation of the relative clauses, the equivalent noun phrase of the embedded sentence is moved to the position of its equivalent, yielding:

15a. *Jane saw the dog. The dog Jane liked.*

Such shifts are carried out by transformations known as **adjunction.** They belong to the group of movement transformations.

After the equivalent NP's have been adjoined in this way, a relative clause is formed. In such clauses a noun like *Jane,* with identical reference as the subject, is replaced by a pronoun, yielding:

15b. *Jane saw the dog that she liked.*

The transformation applied here is referred to as **substitution.**

Moreover, the second of the two equivalent noun phrases may be deleted, yielding:

15c. *Jane saw the dog she liked.*

This transformation is referred to as **deletion.**

These are illustrations of the three general types of transformation: adjunction, substitution, and deletion. Such transformations are represented by many particular transformational rules in individual languages. Some of the processes involved may be compared with the processes carried out in the derivation of phonological structures, as discussed in Chapter 6.3. The processes noted above, however, are more comparable to those involved in complementation.

## 10.3.4   Complementation

In contrast with relative clauses, complements function as objects or subjects of many verbs, as in:

25. *She promised that she would buy the yogurt.*

As has been suggested above, sentences like this can be derived from sequences such as:

25a. *She promised it/something. She would buy the yogurt.*

Complements are distinct from relative clauses in not having equivalent noun phrases within the matrix sentence. They have distinct markers, for example, *that* in sentence 25. These are known as **complementizers.**

In English there are three prominent types of complementizers, as illustrated by sentence 25 and the two following examples:

26. *She disliked Joe's going.*
27. *Jane intended to get up early.*

Sentence 26 can be regarded as a reduced form of sentences like:

26a. *She disliked it that Joe went.*

Since the complementizer in the sentence type exemplified by 26 consists of a possessive accompanying an *-ing* form, it is often referred to as POSS *ing*. And since at an earlier stage of the language, the complement in sentence 27 might have been introduced by *for . . . to,* this complementizer is referred to as *for . . . to* (even though today it is generally expressed simply as *to*). The designation has the virtue of distinguishing the complementizer from the many [tuw] homophones in English.

Complements behave in many ways like full sentences. Thus if they contain a transitive verb, they may be passivized, as in the passivization of sentence 25:

25b. *She promised that the yogurt would be bought by her.*

### 10.3.5   Pseudocleft Sentences and the Determination of Complements

Yet because they behave like NP's, complements must be derived from NP's. An NP can be determined by the production of **pseudocleft** sentences. Pseudocleft sentences are so named because they resemble cleft sentences like:

28a. *It is smoke that hurts my eyes.*

in which *that* "cleaves" the sentence:

28. *Smoke hurts my eyes.*

An example of a pseudocleft sentence is:

28b. *What hurts my eyes is smoke.*

This sentence is derived by the pseudocleft transformation from:

28. *Smoke hurts my eyes.*

In the pseudocleft sentence transformation, *what* is placed before the sentence, *be* after it. Stylistically ungraceful, the pseudocleft sentence is useful in grammatical analysis. NP's to be tested are taken out of the sentence and placed after *be.* If a sequence cannot stand after *be,* it is not an NP. For example, in the sentences:

29. *Robins like worms.*
30. *Robins pull worms out of the ground.*

*robins* and *worms* can be identified as NP's by means of pseudocleft sentence transformation. But, since:

30a. *What robins pull is worms out of the ground.

is impossible, *worms out of the ground* is not an NP. On the other hand, because of the sentence:

31. *What robins like is to eat worms.*

*to eat worms* must be derived from an NP. The derivation involves a deleted *it* + NP, that is, the underlying sentences:

31a. *Robins like it.*

and:

31b. *Robins eat worms.*

The examples discussed so far include complementizers that are objects. If the subject of a complement is identical with that of the matrix sentence, it is deleted. Compare the following examples:

32. *Henriette likes it (her daughter buys new clothes).*
33. *Henriette likes it (Henriette buys new clothes).*

With complementizers these yield:

32a. *Henriette likes [it for] her daughter to buy new clothes.*
32b. *Henriette likes her daughter's buying new clothes.*

but:

33a. *Henriette likes [Henriette] to buy new clothes.*
33b. *Henriette likes [Henriette's] buying new clothes.*

Thus in a transformational grammar, complements are modified by the kinds of transformations discussed in section 10.2.3 with reference to the derivation of relative clauses. Both constructions, relative clauses as well as complements, are introduced by the embedding of Σ's in P-rules. Complements can be demonstrated to be NP's by the pseudocleft transformation, for example:

32c. *What Henriette likes is her daughter's buying new clothes.*
33c. *What Henriette likes is to buy new clothes.*

In this way the interrelationships between various constructions can be used to test grammars. The surface forms found in individual languages are determined by the kinds of modification undergone by the embedded sentences.

## 10.4  Qualifier Categories

In the previous discussion we have dealt essentially with simple declarative sentences that are positive statements. Grammars must also account for modifications of these statements, as in questions, negations, and the like. These modifications affect the meanings of sentences in fundamental ways. Since it is assumed that in transformational grammar the meaning is essentially present in the deep structure, modifications like the interrogative and the negative must be introduced at this level, that is to say, these modifications must be incorporated in the P-rules.

Various devices have been proposed to account for such categories in language. In examining the problems, we may note the ways of expressing these modifications. For in English and other SVO languages, the modifications are expressed by separate words such as *not;* by intonation patterns, as in *You went too?* or by changes in word order, as in *Will you go?* From English, then, one may receive the impression that the modifications are lexical or ascribable to a section of the grammar other than the P-rules.

When, however, we examine VSO and SOV languages, it becomes clear that these modifications are treated much as verbal inflection is treated in Latin or English. Because they are universal constituents of all known languages, they must be accounted for as categories in P-rules. In Arabic, for example, interrogation is indicated by elements placed in front of the verb. In Japanese, on the other hand, the elements are placed after verbs. The patterns in these two languages are characteristic of VSO and SOV languages.

It is also noteworthy that the arrangement of markers for the categories is parallel; the markers for interrogation are placed closer to the sentence boundary than are those for negation. In VSO languages like Arabic, they are the first element from the initial boundary to precede the verb. In SOV languages like Japanese, they are the first element from the final boundary to stand after the verb, as the following examples illustrate:

34.  'Did he see the dog?'

| VSO - Arabic | SOV - Japanese | |
|---|---|---|
| *hal šāhada alkalba* | *inu o* | *mika ka* |
| Interrogative saw-he the-dog | dog object particle | saw Interrogative |

35.  'He didn't see the dog.'

| | | |
|---|---|---|
| *ma šāhada alkalba* | *inu o* | *mitanakatta* |
| not saw-he the-dog | dog object particle | saw-not |

36.  'Didn't he see the dog?'

| | | |
|---|---|---|
| *amo šāhada alkalba* | *inu o* | *mitanakatta ka* |
| Interrogative-not saw-he the-dog | dog object particle | saw-not Interrogative |

If we represented the underlying pattern of sentence 36 with categorial symbols, we might symbolize these as follows:

$$\text{Int Neg}_{\text{VSO}} \qquad \text{SOV}^{\text{Neg Int}}$$

1) Interrogative; 2) Negative; 3) Verb; 4) Subject; 5) Object; −5) (Subject); −4) Object; −3) Verb; −2) Negative; −1) Interrogative.

We might conclude that the categories for these sentence modifications should be associated in one group and derived from one node. In this book this node will be labeled Q for qualifier. Other works refer to it as Mod for modality, or T for type. To account for language, then, we modify the P-rule for rewriting sentence to:

$$\Sigma \rightarrow \quad \text{Qualifier Proposition}$$

As this rule implies, the elements dealt with above will be generated from a node P (for proposition). The initial P-rules in our grammar would now be as follows:

1. $\Sigma \rightarrow$ Conj $\Sigma^n$
2. $\Sigma \rightarrow$ Q P
3. Q $\rightarrow$ [± Interrogative] [± Negative] etc.

Tentative    4. P $\rightarrow$ NP VP

The categorial elements in P-rule 3 are treated in the same way as the phonological features discussed in Chapter 6. Every sentence must be characterized as to whether it is +Interrogative, +Negative, and so on (see, for example, sentence 36). An outline of a P-marker for sentence 36 would appear as follows:

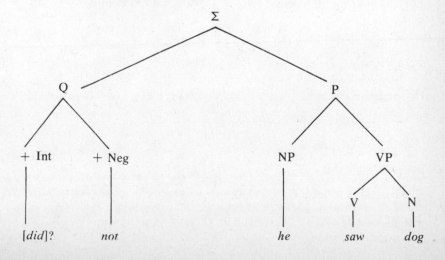

The surface form would be determined by appropriate transformational rules.

It would be essential to determine all such qualifier categories, for example, those given in P-rule 3, if one wished to write a complete grammar. However, discussion of all the qualifier categories would require undue detail for an introductory textbook. We may simply state a possible form of the rule with the categories it would introduce. These categories correspond to many of the verbal features discussed in Chapter 7.

3. Q → [± Declarative] [± Interrogative] [±Negative]
[±Middle] [±Necessitative] [±Voluntative]
[±Perfective] [±Momentary] [±Iterative] [±Causative]

Since these are universal categories, they would be included in some way for every language. It is apparent then in SVO languages, like English, the Q-categories are represented largely through function words, such as auxiliaries. By means of modal auxiliaries English represents the necessitative (*must, shall*) and the voluntative (*will, may, might, could*). The perfective is represented through the auxiliary *have* and the past participle. Study of such means of representation, in comparison with those found in other languages, is one of the most fascinating topics in linguistic research. And although the system of auxiliaries is very prominent in English, it is of fairly recent lineage, having developed only in the past few thousand years. Accordingly, the study of auxiliaries is also intriguing from a historical point of view.

Other qualifier categories are represented through function words, such as the middle, which includes reflexive patterns. These are expressed through pronominal elements in English. But these, too, are new, as comparison with closely related languages like German or with means of expression used in earlier literature that survive in colloquial usage indicates. The German reflexive in the first and second persons is simply the personal pronoun. This is the pattern in sentence 37, as opposed to the more formal *myself:*

37.  *I bought me a new typewriter.*
37a. *I bought myself a new typewriter.*

The recentness of the pattern is also reflected in the complex rules and rule orders, as noted above in Chapter 9.7, for sentences like:

38. *Drive yourself.*

An examination of the syntactic categories found generally in language, coupled with examination of this means of expression, has considerably amplified our understanding of language, while modifying our views of grammars.

## 10.5  Proposition Categories

Study of syntactic patterns in languages of various structures has led to the use of categories for verbal relationships such as those noted in the preceding section. Similarly, abstract categories have been proposed for the proposition node, particularly the nominal relationships. Rather than an NP, the proposition rule has been written to generate a series of abstract categories relating nouns with verbs. These have been called **cases.** Although this term is unfortunate, in leading to confusion with surface cases such as the nominative and accusative, it is nonetheless established and in general use.

As examples of underlying cases, agent and instrument may be cited, as in the sentences:

39. *Bill hit the ball.*
40. *The bat hit the ball.*

When these sentences are put into the passive, they read:

39a. *The ball was hit by Bill.*
40a. *The ball was hit with a bat.*

Such patterns suggest that the underlying relationships of the subjects differ in sentences 39 and 40. Moreover, they differ in systematic ways, so that the relationships between the subjects and the verb may be indicated by such labels as agent, often used for animate subjects, and instrument, used for inanimate subjects.

The relationships thus noted correspond to surface categories in many languages. Sanskrit, for example, has an instrumental case. Moreover, the great Sanskrit grammarian Panini classified the Sanskrit nominal relationships in this way, distinguishing between the surface forms and the underlying relationships, which he called *kāraka* categories. *Kāraka* is from the root *kr̥* 'do' and may be viewed as a relationship concerned with verbal action.

If the proposition P-rule given above were rewritten to yield underlying case categories it might read:

4. Proposition → V (Case, or *kāraka,* categories)

The case categories are listed as optional because some sentences have no nouns. Notable examples are sentences dealing with weather conditions in the earlier Indo-European languages, such as Latin *pluit* '(it) is raining.' If a rule is, however, accompanied by one noun or more, these may be in one of a number of cases: agent, instrument, object or target, receptor, time, place, source, manner, and possibly others.

With such a rule generating abstract nominal relationships, the grammar must have a further rule generating NP's. This rule would resemble rule 4 in the P-rules given above, and might read:

$$5. \ K \rightarrow \begin{Bmatrix} NP & K^n \\ \Sigma \end{Bmatrix}$$

By means of this rule the K-category would generate NP's with their case marker, whether it is a case ending, a preposition, or a postposition. It would also generate sentences and, accordingly, is recursive. The two rules, 4 and 5, would correspond to the former S-rule of Chapter 9.4. They would, however, be more general and would permit the generation of sentence strings in languages of all types.

---

## 10.6  Topicalization

In English and other SVO languages, subjects often stand initially in sentences. In this way they are singled out as the topic as well as the grammatical subject. But other constituents of the sentence may equally well occupy this initial position, such as adverbial expressions:

> 41. *Fish, sure we like them.*

Such processes of singling out important elements of sentences are referred to as **topicalization.**

Various devices are used to single out topics, for example, the clumsy variant of sentence 41:

> 41a. *As for fish, we like them.*

or:

> 41b. *It's fish that we like.*

or:

> 41c. *What we like is fish.*

Until recently it has been assumed that topicalization is a special device in languages and that subjects are more central grammatically. But the study of further languages has made it clear that subjects are characteristic of only some languages. In the sentence patterns of many other languages, such as Chinese, topics rather than subjects are prominent.

In Chinese, initial position indicates the topic, whether this fills the role of grammatical subject or object, as in the following examples:

42. *yú wǒ chī le*
     fish I eat aspect
'As for the fish, I ate it.'
43. *wǒ chī le        yú        le*
     I   eat aspect   fish     sentence marker
'I ate some fish.'

Moreover, if a sentence contains only one noun and an appropriate verb, it may be interpreted variously, depending on the context, as in:

44. *yú    chī    le*
     fish eat aspect
'The fish has eaten.'
'As for the fish, someone has eaten it.'

Because of the patterning of languages like Chinese, they have been referred to as **topic-prominent languages,** in contrast with languages like English, which are called **subject-prominent.** Devices for indicating topics and subjects are available in both types of language. But either topics or subjects are primary, not only subjects, as may seem natural from English.

This finding supports the grammatical analysis given in section 10.5, in which the essential nominal elements are introduced as abstract categories with specific meaning relationships. They are then subsequently arranged for grammatical function. From the point of view of such a grammar no nominal element is central to the sentence. In SVO languages, however, subjects are virtually mandatory. (S)OV languages, on the other hand, seem not to require overt subjects. In Japanese, subjects may be indicated by the postposition *ga,* but topics, indicated by *wa,* are equally prominent, as the examples in this book indicate. The Chinese favoring of topics over subjects may reflect the apparent change of Chinese toward an SOV structure.

The implications of topic prominence as opposed to subject prominence in languages have not yet been thoroughly pursued. Yet the recent recognition of topic prominence illustrates our inadequate understanding of syntax and the need to carry out syntactic studies in languages of all types of structures.

Such study has also pointed to constructions that are characteristic of subject-prominent languages. Since subjects are essential in English surface sentences, "dummy" subjects have been introduced for verbs that may not originally have required them. Thus the verbs referring to natural phenomena in Latin must have a subject in the Romance languages. These, like the *it* of *it is raining,* have no actual reference and are accordingly referred to as **dummy subjects.**

Such dummy subjects permit the possibility of a construction known as **extraposition,** that is, the placing of a constituent outside its normal position by a movement transformation. If subjects, usually lengthy subjects such as clauses, are used with certain verbs, dummy subjects may be placed initially, and the subject proper is extraposed after the verb. Thus the following sentences are natural for English:

> 45. *The tragedy happened late at night.*
> 46. *It happened late at night that he fell off the balcony.*

If the SVO pattern were followed, sentence 46 would read:

> 46a. *That he fell off the balcony happened late at night.*

By extraposition, as illustrated in sentence 47, the verb stands earlier in the sentence, where it has more prominence:

> 47. *There arose a fierce storm.*

rather than:

> 47a. *A fierce storm arose.*

Extraposed elements like that in sentence 46 place the subject in a position where it can be followed up readily in the next sentence.

Patterns like these are not central in topic-prominent languages. Topicalization, then, varies in occurrence and application according to types of language.

---

## 10.7  Passivization

The patterns discussed above, in which topicalization is common in subject-prominent languages, had to do with subjects. A pattern in which objects are topicalized is the passive. In passive constructions a direct object is generally made the object, though an indirect object may also be so modified, as in:

> 48.    *He gave his sister the money.*
> 48a. *The money was given by him to his sister.*
> 48b. *His sister was given the money by him.*

Whichever element is placed in the initial position is topicalized.

Passive constructions have attracted a great deal of attention in transformational grammar, for the passive, with its apparently straightforward relationship between active and passive sentences, seemed to be a straightforward example of a transformation. This may be written as follows, with the structural analysis (SA) stated, followed by the structural change carried out by the rule:

| SA | NP | Aux | V | by | NP |
|----|----|-----|---|-----|-----|
|    | 1  | 2   | 3 | (4) | 5 $\Rightarrow$ |
| SC | 5  | 2+BE+D | 3 | 4 | 1 |

In transformational rules the analysis of a structure (SA), also called the structural description (SD), is first given, with numerals indicating the order of the essential constituents. Then, in the part of the T-rule following the double-shafted arrow, the structural change is indicated. As noted by the rule here, the structural analysis of the active sentence undergoes a change whereby: 1) the NP in the predicate is shifted to the subject; 2) the subject is moved to the predicate, where it is preceded by the preposition *by;* and 3) the verb is modified to a phrase consisting of the auxiliary BE plus the past participle. Thus a sentence *John found the money* becomes *The money was found by John.*

While this transformation seemed transparent and simple, questions were raised concerning the situation of the passive. Among these is the derivation of agentless passives like:

49. *The money was found.*

Such sentences were assumed to be further derivations of full passives and were therefore labeled *truncated passives.* But they have come to be regarded as more central than full passives. One of the reasons for this view is the observation that they are often mastered by children before the presumably more basic forms.

Accordingly, the derivation of a passive has been accounted for by various hypotheses: 1) as a result of a transformation from an action sentence; or 2) as the result of modification by a modality feature, such as the interrogative and the negative. The latter, however, is less convincing because of the restriction of passives largely to subject-prominent languages.

The passive is, then, an example of an apparently transparent construction that is less simple than it appeared when only the English construction was examined. Other syntactic constructions are also being rigorously reviewed, with an eye to parallel constructions in other languages. But even a description of the processes generating all the English constructions discussed in Chapter 8 would be lengthy, not to mention a treatment of the syntactic constructions of the many languages that are only poorly described. Therefore the study of syntax, especially the derived syntactic constructions, presents many opportunities for further research, and many problems. These are commonly examined with reference to a transformational grammar of the type that will be sketched in the next section.

## 10.8  A Transformational Grammar

A transformational grammar of the type referred to in the preceding sections would consist of three components, a syntactic, a semantic, and a phonological component. The syntactic component includes a deep or underlying structure, with a P-structure grammar like that sketched above, and a lexicon. An example of the lexicon will be given below.

The structures generated in this part of the syntactic component have been illustrated by P-markers. But the terminal elements have been given in English spelling, rather than as lexical entries. These structures are highly abstract, including such elements as +Interrogative. The surface structures are derived from these by transformational rules. Phonological rules, as illustrated in Chapter 6, specify the actual utterances.

All of these segments of a transformational grammar have been examined above, except lexical entries. These will be discussed briefly below.

### 10.8.1  The Lexical Component of a Transformational Grammar

In the lexicon, lexical entities are specified for features that are implicit in many of the definitions found in standard dictionaries. For example, in the sentence *Esther can cook* the first lexical entity, *Esther*, belongs to the class of proper nouns and could be replaced by such words as *Johnnie, Tom,* or *Grandmother*. The features permitting this use must be specified in the detail expected in a transformational grammar.

Dictionaries provide comparable analyses of lexical items but without the necessary details. If, for example, one looks up a lexical item like *grandmother* in a dictionary, one finds two sets of descriptors. The first is *n.,* or the like; the second is "the mother of one's father or mother," and so on.

Descriptors like *n.* indicate the type of segment involved, in this instance that *grandmother* is a noun. The second descriptor indicates features of such items, for example, that an animate being is involved, with such specific features as sex and generation. These two types of descriptors are used for the lexical component of transformational grammars, but they must be specified in far greater detail. As a result the production of adequate dictionaries, or lexicons, for any language will be a colossal undertaking. Here we will note some of the procedures and problems.

### 10.8.2  Lexical Descriptors for Nouns

In the listing of lexical entities, the following conventions are often observed. First, the lexical item itself is given, usually in conventional spelling. Next, the general segment classification is given. For example, the portion of the deep structure tree arriving at *mother,* for the sentence

*Mother left* (S→NP VP, NP→N, N→*mother*), would lead to the listing in Figure 1.

**Figure 1**

Next features are provided. The major classifications are well known from some of the standard descriptions of English. They are:

1. Proper versus common nouns; for example, *Mary* is a proper noun; *mother* is a common noun. In feature classifications they are labeled <−common> and <+common>.
2. Concrete versus abstract nouns; for example, *hardtop* versus *hardship*. *Hardtop* is labeled <+concrete>; *hardship* <−concrete>.
3. Animate versus inanimate nouns; for example, *mother* versus *bother*. *Mother* is labeled <+animate>; *bother* <−animate>.
4. Human versus nonhuman nouns; for example, *mother* versus *monkey*. *Mother* is labeled <+human>; *monkey* <−human>.

While it is well to be completely explicit in one's initial lexicon, any <+human> noun is also <+animate> and <+concrete>. These designations would not, therefore, need to be specified for nouns marked <+human> but can automatically be assumed for any noun labeled <+human>. They are therefore called **redundant**. If the predictable or redundant features are omitted, a list can be reduced considerably. This principle is important in the construction of lexicons.

With these features explicitly labeled, the preceding lexical entry would be more fully specified as in Figure 2.

**Figure 2**

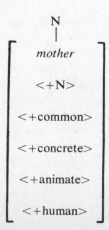

If adequate features were provided in a lexical entry, each entry would be distinguished from any other lexical term. For *mother* such an entry would require the addition of relationship features (among others). Moreover, in a complete grammar the lexical item *mother* would be indicated by means of a matrix for phonological features, in accordance with the procedures presented in Chapters 6 and 12.

### 10.8.3    Segment Structure Features for Nouns

The lexical features of many languages are parallel. For example, the Japanese word for 'mother' *haha* would have the same lexical features as those already given for *mother*. But *haha* and *mother* differ considerably in grammatical properties. Japanese *haha,* for example, cannot be labeled <+singular>, for the number category is not indicated in Japanese nouns.

Specific properties, such as number, are referred to as **segment structure items.** Like the general segment descriptors, such as <N>, these items must be indicated in lexical entries. In a grammar of English, nouns must have descriptors for number ( + or − singular) and for case ( + or − genitive). If a lexical entry in an English sentence contains the label <−singular>, a noun-suffix transformation is introduced. This will eventually produce *s.* Figure 3 shows the result of this transformation generating the form *mothers.*

**Figure 3**

$$
\begin{array}{c} N \\ | \end{array}
\left[ \begin{array}{c} \textit{mother} \\ <+N> \\ <-\text{singular}> \end{array} \right]
\text{ leading to }
\begin{array}{c} N \end{array}
\left[ \begin{array}{c} \textit{mother} \\ <+N> \\ <-\text{singular}> \end{array} \right]
\left[ \begin{array}{c} s \\ <+\text{affix}> \\ <-\text{singular}> \end{array} \right]
$$

Besides the designation for number, English nouns must be specified for case, for example, *mother's* versus *mother*. The first may be labeled <+gen> for genitive, the second <−gen>. Among further segment structure features for which English nouns must be specified is that of count versus mass noun, for example, *mother* versus *money*. *Mother* is labeled <+count>, *money* <−count>. An English noun can be tested for the classification <+count> or <−count> by its use after *many* or *much,* for example, *Many mothers joined in the march; they collected much money.* The <+count> nouns are used after *many* and take the plural after it.

On the other hand, Japanese nouns lack structure features for these classifications as well as for other features that must be specified for English, such as definiteness. For example, <+def> produces the sequence *the mother,* <−def> *a mother* or, as proposed in Figure 4, *mother.* The lexical entries for *mother* and *haha* would, accordingly, differ in the segment structure portion of the listing. Those for *mother, mother's,* and *haha* might be given as in Figure 4, though in a more complete lexicon more features would be included.

**Figure 4**

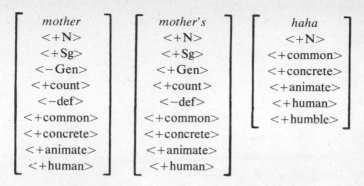

### 10.8.4  Lexical Descriptors for Verbs

The listings for lexical items labeled Vb are parallel to those for items designated N in specifying lexical and segment structure features. As with nouns, the segment structure features of verbs differ from language to language. When we examine Japanese Vb's, we find that those ending in *u,* like *yomu* 'read,' may be inflected in the forms listed in Chapter 7.4 but also in further forms like *yomitai* 'I want to read' and *yomitakatta* 'I wanted to read.' The inflection of these forms is the same as those of *katai* '(be) hard' and *katakatta* 'was hard'; that is, the inflections of entities that some grammarians classify as adjectives are found also in verbs. Consequently, we may conclude that "verbs" and "adjectives" make up one large class in Japanese.

There are grounds for making a similar analysis for English. Like verbs, some adjectives indicate action; other verbs and adjectives do not. The difference may be illustrated by the use of verbals in imperative constructions. We can say:

> *Read the story!*     but not     *\*Own the book!*
> *Be quiet!*     but not     *\*Be ignorant!*

In view of this similarity in function, both verbs and adjectives are classed as verbals and labeled <Vb>. But since verbals like *read* and *own* can be used directly after pronouns, as in *She reads many books,* while verbals like *quiet* and *ignorant* require an auxiliary verb, as in *She is remarkably quiet tonight,* verbals like *read* are further classified as <+V> and those like *quiet* are labeled <−V>.

On the other hand, members of both classes may be distinguished for "action" as <+action> or <−action>. This analysis is supported by their use with *-ing* forms. For example we can say:

> *She is reading the story*     but not     *\*She is owning the book.*
> *She is being quiet*     but not     *\*She is being ignorant.*

To account for these four verbals, the lexical entries for them are given in Figure 5 (each would also have lexical descriptors that are omitted here).

**Figure 5**

$$
\begin{bmatrix} read \\ <+Vb> \\ <+V> \\ <+action> \\ etc. \end{bmatrix}
\begin{bmatrix} own \\ <+Vb> \\ <+V> \\ <-action> \\ etc. \end{bmatrix}
\begin{bmatrix} quiet \\ <+Vb> \\ <-V> \\ <+action> \\ etc. \end{bmatrix}
\begin{bmatrix} ignorant \\ <+Vb> \\ <-V> \\ <-action> \\ etc. \end{bmatrix}
$$

Segment structure features must also be provided for the progressive and other qualifiers, as in the sentences *Esther is reading, Esther is being quiet, Esther has read, Esther has been quiet, Esther has been reading,* and so on. These features are introduced as Q. Subsequent transformations yield the surface strings, as illustrated in Figure 6 for the sentence *Mother is reading.*

Moreover, since verb forms stand in the concord relationship of number with nouns and must be related to nouns in the sentence, they must be specified for their agreement relationships to possible subjects and predicates. Appropriate features must be given for each verb. To simplify the presentation here, these features are omitted. They would be specified in each lexical entry where the feature CS (complex symbol) is given, as would the appropriate features for nouns.

A sketch of the P-marker is shown in Figure 6. (**Copula** is defined as a word or set of words, for example, the verb BE, that acts as a link between the subject and predicate complement.)

**Figure 6**

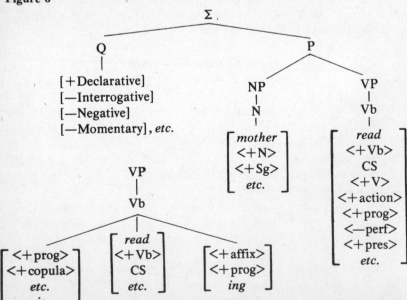

### 10.8.5   Generation of the Sentence *Mother is running*

As the following analysis indicates, a total account of any one sentence is lengthy and complex, although no more so than a total account of a natural entity like a drop of water or a DNA molecule. Assuming that a speaker wished to produce this sentence, a transformational grammar would represent the process as follows:

SYNTAX

A.  Phrase-structure rules and lexical items from the base:

    1.  Phrase-structure rules:  Σ → Qualifier (Q) Proposition (Prop; P)

                                  Q → [+ Declarative (Dec)] [ −Negative (Neg)], etc.

                                    Prop → NP VP

                                    NP → N

                                    VP → Vb

    2.  Lexicon:

$$
\begin{bmatrix}
mother \\
<+N> \\
<+Sg> \\
<-Gen> \\
<+count> \\
<+common> \\
<+concrete> \\
<+animate> \\
<+human> \\
<+kinship> \\
<-male> \\
<+older\ generation> \\
<+same\ lineality>
\end{bmatrix}
\qquad
\begin{bmatrix}
run \\
<+Vb> \\
<+V> \\
<+action> \\
<+continuous> \\
<-Perfect> \\
<+Present> \\
<+movement> \\
<+rapid> \\
<+animate\ actor> \\
<+human> \\
<+legged>
\end{bmatrix}
$$

B.  Deep structure representation:

**Figure 1**

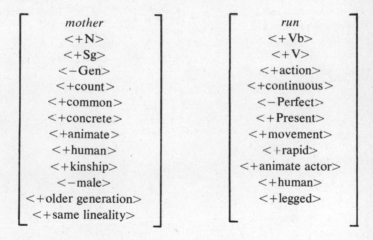

C. Transformational rules applicable to this sentence:

1. [+Continuous] transformation:

$$\begin{bmatrix} \text{Vb} \\ <+\text{Cont}> \end{bmatrix} \Rightarrow \begin{bmatrix} <+\text{Prog}> \\ <+\text{copula}> \end{bmatrix} \begin{bmatrix} \text{V} \\ \textit{run, etc.} \end{bmatrix}$$

(According to this rule the +Cont under Vb generates the segment copula before Vb, copying the grammatical features from the lexical entry *run*.)

2. Auxiliary transformation:
(<+copula> is generated)

3. Affix transformation:

$$\begin{bmatrix} \text{Vb} \\ <+\text{Cont}> \end{bmatrix} \Rightarrow \begin{bmatrix} \text{V} \\ \textit{run, etc.} \end{bmatrix} \begin{bmatrix} <+\text{affix}> \\ <+\text{Prog}> \\ \textit{ing} \end{bmatrix}$$

(According to this rule the progressive suffix is generated after the verb.)

D. Surface structure after application of the transformational rules:

**Figure 2**

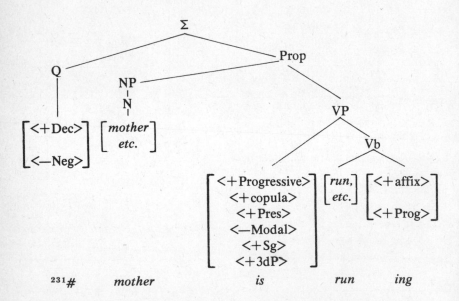

PHONOLOGICAL REPRESENTATION

From the surface structure string the actual utterance [²mə̀ ðərz ³rə́niŋ¹↓] would be derived by means of rules in the phonological component.

Instead of forms in conventional spelling, however, each entry would be listed by means of distinctive features, as presented in Chapter 4.

Moreover, in the lexicon only those distinctive features of each entry that distinguish a phoneme would be listed. For example, /m n ŋ/ would be distinguished from all other phonemes by the feature <+nasal>. The additional features of *coronal* and *anterior* distinguish the three nasals of English from one another. This set of features would make up the underlying phonological representation. To illustrate how these would be indicated, the phonemes of the sentence *Mother is running* are given in the matrix in Chart 1, with only the distinctive features of the underlying forms labeled + or −.

**Chart 1.   Distinctive Feature Analysis for *Mother is running***

|            | m | ə | ð | ə | r | i | z | r | ə | n | i | ŋ |
|------------|---|---|---|---|---|---|---|---|---|---|---|---|
| SYLLABIC   |   | − |   |   |   |   |   |   |   |   |   |   |
| CONSONANT  |   |   |   |   |   |   |   |   |   |   |   |   |
| HIGH       |   | − |   | − |   | + |   |   | − |   | + |   |
| BACK       |   | + |   | + |   | − |   |   | + |   | − |   |
| LOW        |   |   |   |   |   |   |   |   |   |   |   |   |
| ANTERIOR   | + |   | + |   | − |   | + | − |   | + |   | − |
| CORONAL    | − |   | + |   |   |   |   |   |   | + |   | − |
| ROUND      |   |   |   |   |   |   |   |   |   |   |   |   |
| TENSE      |   | − |   | − |   | − |   |   | − |   | − |   |
| VOICE      |   |   | + |   |   |   | + |   |   |   |   |   |
| CONTINUANT |   |   | + |   | + |   | + | + |   |   |   |   |
| NASAL      | + |   |   |   |   |   |   |   |   | + |   | + |
| STRIDENT   |   |   | − |   | − |   | + | − |   |   |   |   |

From these representations the actual phonetic output is derived by means of phonological rules. For example, from the combination <+nasal −coronal +anterior> we would generate all the redundant features for [m] indicated in Chart 2 in Chapter 6.2.5. Similarly, for the other phonemes the pertinent redundant features would be generated by appropriate phonological rules.

The reduced form of {iz}, however, would be derived by a rule applying specifically to this morpheme. Depending on its environment, {iz}, may be maintained or changed to [əz], as in *The horse is running;* to [s], as in *The cat's running;* or to [z], as in *Mother's running.* The phonological rules in question would determine the appropriate form of *is*.

Futher, by means of intonation rules the proper pitches and stresses would be assigned to segments in the sentence. Through rules such as those selected here, from a presumably complete grammar of English, this and other sentences are generated.

### 10.8.6    On the Phonological Component of Transformational Grammars

As noted previously, in transformational grammars morphological entities are listed by distinctive features. According to this procedure a morpheme like English third singular present $\{Z_3\}$ is not represented through autonomous phonemes but is interpreted directly as a phonetic entity in its context: after [liv] as [z], after [lift] as [s], and so on. In this way economy is sought in the description of a language, for it is not necessary to have two representations of a sentence like *Mother is running,* one syntactic and one phonemic.

In the generative phonology of transformational grammars, abstract underlying representations must also be given for families of words, such as *oblige obligation.* Other words undergo similar modification, for example, *apply application, clarify clarification.* Others differ somewhat, such as *satisfy satisfaction.* In the derivation of the noun, the final vowel of the verb in the first three examples is changed from [ay] to [i] and in the fourth from [ay] to [æ]. When such sequences are derived from underlying phonological representations, rules must be proposed for relating them. In their pioneering attempt to outline the proper procedures and to provide a generative phonology of a language, Noam Chomsky and Morris Halle proposed the following underlying forms for the roots of *oblige apply clarify satisfy:* /līg plīk fīk fīk/.

The final consonants are posited to permit formations of the nouns. To permit formation of the verbs, rules have to be provided that generate the proper surface forms. According to these rules the /g/ of /līg/ becomes −back +coronal +strident; the /k/ of /plīk/ and of /fīk/ is deleted; and the vowels are diphthongized. In the nouns, on the other hand, the vowels are shortened or laxed. To generate *satisfaction,* additional rules are necessary so that /fæk/ may be derived from /fīk/. As these examples may illustrate, the derivation of actual phonetic forms from underlying phonological representations requires ingenious and complex rules. By autonomous phonemics, on the other hand, all such words are written with phonemes much closer to the actual phonetic forms, for example,

/əpláy/ /ǽpləkéyšən/. In studying the relationship between the two forms, phonologists determine the patterns of morphemes under various conditions, such as the accent in *application* versus *apply*. Such study is called **morphophonemics.**

Generative phonologists deny the usefulness of positing autonomous phonemes on the grounds that doing so represents an unnecessary complexity in the description of language. To be sure, a rigid use of the phonemic approach has led to problems, such as the difficulty of handling the vowel in weakly stressed forms of *just* or the glottal stop in some pronunciations of *bottle*. Yet dismissing an autonomous phonemic representation leads to exceedingly complex representations of phonology, as a glance at the representations in Chomsky and Halle's *The Sound Pattern of English*[1] indicates.

Moreover, the dissatisfaction with a taxonomic phonemic representation might be compared to dissatisfaction with labels from the periodic chart of elements after the discovery of isotopes. $H_2O$ is not composed solely of atoms of hydrogen and oxygen with a molecular weight of 1 and 16, as older forms of the periodic chart indicate. Even so, the labels on the periodic chart are not without their uses. In somewhat the same way autonomous phonemic representations are useful, as in the teaching of languages. Ultimately, however, a generative phonological analysis may represent language more precisely. Often in actual practice there are relatively few differences between autonomous phonemic representations for many entities of a language and representations by means of systematic phonemes, though the theoretical bases for each are quite different.

### 10.8.7   On the Semantic Component of Transformational Grammars

In somewhat the same way as the surface syntactic structure is phonologically interpreted to produce an actual utterance, the entities of the deep structure are interpreted to provide the meaning of that utterance. The features provided here for lexical items are not complete, for no complete analysis of any language or any segment of a language has been produced. But if for the time being we assume that the feature <+kinship> would lead to a small set of English nouns with the feature <+human>, the three further features <−male + same lineality + older generation> would require the selection of *mother* from among the terms in the English kinship field. Anyone using English would make the proper semantic interpretation, both as speaker and as hearer.

Although we may assume such a procedure in the use of a language, questions remain about the relationship of the semantic component to the syntactic component. It is difficult, for example, to decide whether the

---

[1] Noam Chomsky and Morris Halle, *The Sound Pattern of English* (New York: Harper & Row, 1968).

feature <+human> is syntactic or semantic. By associating this feature with the choice of relative pronouns (*who* or *which*), we may posit a syntactic basis for it. Yet this test is not conclusive. For in fairy tales or children's stories inanimate objects may be treated like humans, for example, *the scarecrow who grew tired of standing still*. We cannot find a sharp line distinguishing between "syntactic" and "semantic" features. Accordingly some linguists propose a model of language in which the semantic component is incorporated into the deep structure.

| Deep Structure (includes semantics) |
| :--- |

| Surface Structure |
| :--- |

| Phonological Representation |
| :--- |

The linguistic approach in which semantics is included in deep structure is known as **generative semantics.**

The argumentation in favor of any one approach has been inconclusive. A model in which the deep structure includes the semantic component is more compact than the model proposed in Chapter 3.5. It results, however, in a more complex set of rules, for the "semantic" rules, such as those that select the proper meaning of *run* in conjunction with *mother,* would have to be incorporated into the deep structure with the syntactic rules presented in section 8.5. However the argumentation is resolved, linguists attempt to embrace language in its entirety and set out to provide descriptions that account for its various components.

In this attempt their goals are similar to those of many grammarians of the past who concerned themselves with language. Of these grammarians we have mentioned two groups, the Greco-Latin and the Indian. Both of these groups and the medieval Arab grammarians as well dealt to at least some extent with the system of sounds, the system of forms, and the system of meanings in language. In some respects they developed theoretical views that have not yet been surpassed.

## 10.9  Procedures for a Complete Syntactic Analysis

We have accounted for some of the segments of English declarative sentences, such as nouns with their modifiers, verbs, and adjectives. In a complete syntactic analysis of English, all entities in any of these classes would have to be completely specified. No such analysis has been produced as yet. Many observations on which such analyses can be based, however, are found in the standard grammars. These would have to be incorporated in a transformational grammar.

A complete syntactic analysis would also account for other types of sentences and other syntactic entities, such as conjunctions, prepositions, and adverbs. An account giving the procedures for handling them would be lengthy. Here only a brief statement will be included.

### 10.9.1 Types of Sentences

To account for interrogatives, for example, *Can Esther cook?* for negatives, for example, *Esther cannot cook;* and also for other sentence types, Q-categories are included in P-markers. The specification:

$$Q \rightarrow \; [+\text{Dec}] \; [+\text{Int}] \; [+\text{Neg}]$$

would yield *Can't Esther cook?* Since other categories, such as tense, may apply to the entire sentence, some analyses also introduce these categories through the Q-node, others through the P-node. The appropriate place for such categories is an unsettled syntactic question.

**Figure 7**

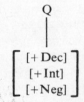

### 10.9.2 Adpositions: Prepositions and Postpositions

The use of prepositions is closely associated with nouns and verbs. Syntactically *look at* is parallel to *see,* as in *She looked at the parrot* and *She saw the parrot.* Similarly, *He stayed at home* is syntactically parallel to *He stayed in the house* and *He stayed home.* In Japanese, postpositions are similarly associated with nouns and verbs. For example, with the verb BE, *ni* is equivalent to 'in,' as in *gakkō ni imasu* 'He's in school'; with other verbs *de* is equivalent to 'in,' as in *gakkō de kikimashita* 'He heard it at school.' Further, some prepositional constructions parallel simple items, for example, *He stayed away from them* is equivalent to *He avoided them.* In view of these uses of prepositions and postpositions, these grammatical elements may best be generated from nominal or verbal nodes, depending on the relationships they express.

### 10.9.3 Adverbials

Some adverbial expressions may be introduced through the cast categories, such as place and time. Others may be analyzed as reductions of sentences. For example, *Esther can cook excellently* is derived from two sentences, the first of which is *Esther can cook;* the second is *Her cooking is excellent.* The derivation of sentences with several adverbs may be complex, as in the sentence *Esther can cook excellently when she wants to.* The second clause of this sentence is an amplification of the adverbial phrase *at times,* as in the strong *At times (when) she wants to, she can cook excellently.* The relationships of the various components of a sentence with numerous adverbs and adverbial clauses may, therefore, be specified by the incorporation of further sentences. These would be modified by transformations, including deletions, of such phrases as *at times* and of substitutions like *when.* A precise specification of the syntactic structure of such sentences would, accordingly, be lengthy but in keeping with the procedures presented here.

### 10.9.4    Ordering in Transformational Syntactic Analysis: The Cyclic Principle

In the previous discussion we dealt primarily with the deep structure of a transformational grammar, noting how a surface structure is produced from it by means of transformations. In this production the rules must be carefully ordered for maximum economy of the grammar. If, for example, the transformation obtaining *Drive!* from *You drive!* were applied before the intensive transformation, the correct *Drive yourself!* could not be produced, for the intensive *yourself* must be determined from the deleted subject pronoun *you.*

A transformational syntactic analysis is therefore carefully ordered. Moreover, when sentences are embedded in other sentences, transformational rules must first be applied to the most deeply embedded sentences. This requirement may be illustrated by the sentence:

50a. *Jane told John to help himself.*

This sentence is derived from the two underlying sentences: *Jane told John something* and *You help you.* Instead of sentence 50a, a sentence might be derived with the request in direct quotation:

50. *Jane told John: "Help yourself."*

In this sentence, as we have seen, the second pronoun with identical reference becomes a reflexive. The reflexive pronoun transformation can be applied only within a simple sentence. For example, we cannot say *\*Jane told John to help herself* even though the reference of *herself* is identical to *Jane,* for in the deep structure form of these sentences *her* would not be in the same sentence with *Jane.* Accordingly, sentence 50a can be derived only if the second sentence is properly modified before it is introduced into the first sentence. It must first be changed by the application of the indirect statement transformation to the request:

50b[1] *Jane told John (that) he should help he.

Now the reflexive pronoun transformation is applied to the embedded sentence, producing:

50b. Jane told John (that) he should help himself.

We could not have arrived at sentence 50a if instead of applying these transformations to the embedded sentence we had incorporated $S^2$ into the sentence as an NP: Jane told John: "Help yourself!" (By the pseudo-cleft sentence transformation we can demonstrate that we have an NP, for we can say "Help yourself!" was what Jane told John.) This procedure is often referred to as **cyclic.** Transformations are applied in a **cycle,** first to the most deeply embedded sentence and then successively to the others. In this way the correct forms of sentences are produced.

### 10.9.5  The Standard Transformational Theory

The transformational grammar sketched here assumes that the syntactic component is central and that the semantic and the phonological components are interpretive. This theory of transformational grammar, often referred to as the **standard theory,** is based on Noam Chomsky's *Aspects of the Theory of Syntax.* Other theories of transformational grammar have been proposed, and the standard theory has been revised by its proponents (as has been noted in Chapter 3.7 and 3.8). But it is widely observed, and it is represented in handbooks, such as Emmon Bach's *Syntactic Theory.*

A competing theory, referred to as **generative semantics,** differs from the standard theory in deriving the surface structures by transformations from a semantic base. This base, then, is not interpretive.

It must not be assumed that the standard theory does not deal centrally with meaning, for the lexicon and the various syntactic rules are concerned with meaning. For example, if one uses a rule in which a sentence is embedded in a noun phrase, this rule is obviously concerned with meaning. But by an interpretive semantics it is proposed that the semantic rules relate syntactic and lexical elements to the outside world. The term *semantic* is thus used in a special sense, one based on the usage of philosophers, notably Charles Sanders Peirce. In comparing a generative syntactic approach with a generative semantic approach, scholars have said that they are simply notational variants of each other. Discussion of the make-up of grammars has been prominent in recent linguistic publications. Many linguistic problems have been illuminated through the assumption of various types of grammars. For the understanding of such problems, and of language, it is of primary importance to indicate the type of grammar that is being used. Students must expect to encounter a variety of grammatical approaches, and also modifications of these, in the future.

BIBLIOGRAPHICAL NOTES

An explicit account of the application of the transformational approach may be found in *From Deep to Surface Structure: An Introduction to Transformational Syntax* by Marina K. Burt (New York: Harper & Row, 1971). Such application with reference to English may be noted in *The Major Syntactic Structures of English* by Robert P. Stockwell, Paul Schachter, and Barbara Hall Partee (New York: Holt, Rinehart and Winston, 1973). Among theoretical works that may be consulted are *Aspects of the Theory of Syntax* by Noam Chomsky (Cambridge, Mass.: M.I.T. Press, 1965); Charles J. Fillmore, "The Case for Case" in *Universals in Linguistics,* ed. Emmon Bach and Robert T. Harms (New York: Holt, Rinehart and Winston, 1968); and *Syntactic Theory* by Emmon Bach (New York: Holt, Rinehart and Winston, 1974).

QUESTIONS FOR REVIEW

1. State reasons for the inadequacy of current grammars.
2. How does gapping differ in OV and VO languages?
3. When is conjoining introduced in a generative grammar? State and explain the rule.
4. How are relative clauses introduced in a generative grammar? What is the relationship between relative clauses and attributive adjectives? between relative clauses and descriptive genitives?
5. Distinguish between a relative clause and a predicate complement. How are relative clauses commonly marked? How are complements commonly marked?
6. What is meant by a recursive rule?
7. Define: a. *EQUI;* b. *descriptive or appositive relative clause.*
8. Define: a. *adjunction transformation;* b. *substitution transformation;* c. *deletion transformation.* Give an example of each. What kind of transformation is EQUI? What kind of transformation is involved in the derivation of an attributive adjective form of relative clauses?
9. What are the prominent types of complementizers in English?
10. Identify a pseudocleft sentence. How are pseudocleft sentences useful in the identification of NP's?
11. Discuss the introduction of the interrogative category in a grammar. Why isn't this done through the lexical component? Discuss also the introduction of the negative category, giving examples for its marking from a VSO language and a SOV language.
12. Compare underlying case categories like *agent* with surface cases such as *nominative.* Using the first person pronoun *I* in your examples, give a sentence in which the agent is indicated in the objective form *me* rather than the nominative *I.*

13. Provide some examples illustrating surface forms in English of the underlying case *time;* of *source.*
14. Define *topicalization,* providing illustrations from English.
15. How would you distinguish between a topic-prominent and a subject-prominent language?
16. Define *extraposition,* giving examples. How do dummy subjects function in constructions leading to extraposition?
17. What is the modification known as *passivization?*
18. What is meant by the statement that passivization is a topicalization process? In German, passives may consist purely of the verb phrase with a dummy subject, as in *Es wurde getanzt,* literally 'it was danced.' Such a sentence is often translated 'Dancing was going on.' Can you also account for such sentences as examples of topicalization? How?
19. State the three principal components of a transformational grammar. Where does the transformational set of rules apply in such a grammar?
20. Describe the lexical section of such a grammar, providing illustrations of lexical entities.
21. Discuss procedures by which adpositions are introduced into sentence strings, similarly adverbials.
22. Why is ordering important in a transformational grammar? State an example. What is meant by the *cycle?*

## EXERCISES

### EXERCISE 1

a. Draw the P-markers for the following sentences, indicating the categories and the lexical items under each branch.

1. *George writes poetry.*
2. *The students cut class.*
3. *She sings the songs he chooses.*

b. Give the rewriting rules for each of these sentences.

### EXERCISE 2

a. Draw P-markers for the following sentences:

1. *The girls who drive take the team.*
2. *The class elected Henry president.*
3. *Tell the administrator.*

b. Give the rewriting rules for each of these sentences.

EXERCISE 3

Determine the NP's in the following sentences, using the passive test and the pseudocleft sentence test. (For this exercise deal only with the NP's of the basic sentence in 4 and 5 following, which are taken from the Declaration of Independence and the Constitution. You may wish to analyze further sentences of such important documents for their structure and possible ambiguities in meaning.)

1. *In winter wild birds often need additional supplies of food.*
2. *The men who cleared the streets frequently blocked the driveways of residences with the excess snow.*
3. *Quickly John snatched up the wastebasket that had caught on fire.*
4. *He has constrained our fellow citizens taken captive on the high seas to bear arms against their country.*
5. *In all criminal prosecutions, the accused shall enjoy the right to a speedy and public trial, by an impartial jury of the state and district wherein the crime shall have been committed, which district shall have been previously ascertained by law.*

EXERCISE 4

Draw P-markers for the following sentences. (In sentences 3 and 4, first produce the simple sentences from the cleft and pseudocleft examples here.)

1. *The student in the front row raised that question.*
2. *His fierce dog protects their house in the country.*
3. *It is Joe who gets the blame.*
4. *What bothers me is the constant responsibility.*
5. *For him to drive that old car annoys her.*
6. *Joe regretted leaving the party.*
7. *Mary wanted her father to buy the tickets.*

EXERCISE 5

Give at least eight lexical features for each of the following items: *fame; Bill's; the books.*

EXERCISE 6

Draw P-markers for the following sentences:

1. *Will John be ready?*
2. *Do close the door!*
3. *Wasn't that fellow ignorant!*

# SEMANTICS: THE STUDY OF MEANING

## CHAPTER 11

---

## 11.1 Approaches to the Study of Meaning

Semantics seeks to account for the relationships of words and sentences with things and events in the outside world. The lexical items of a grammar, which are often equivalent to words, have specific meanings, whether these are straightforward and concrete, such as the meaning of *bread,* or more involved, such as the meaning of *broad* or *brood.* Sentence patterns and sentence categories also have meaning. In English, for example, there is considerable difference in meaning between the syntactic patterns NP Aux V and Aux NP V, as in the utterances *I may go* and *May I go?* Moreover, all syntactic patterns and categories carry meaning, such as those indicated by intonation patterns. Thus *I may go,* spoken with the intonation pattern /² ³ ¹#/ indicates positive interest and certainty on the part of the speaker. With the intonation pattern /² ³ ³||/, on the other hand, it indicates lack of assurance. In this way, all patterns of syntax carry meaning. It is the aim of semantics to determine such meanings and to explain the interrelationships between meaningful linguistic patterns and the objects, states, and events referred to in language. In dealing with meaning a distinction is generally made between grammatical meaning, which is treated in the grammar, and referential meaning, which is treated in the lexicon.

The study of meaning is more elusive than the study of phonological or syntactic elements. For while these are relatable to entities of language like sounds or sentence patterns, the study of meaning must be concerned with concepts. The procedures for dealing with the assumed elements stored and manipulated by the mind have not received the attention given to the relatively gross elements in phonology and syntax, and consequently semantic study is in its infancy.

In the study of meaning, one of the major difficulties consists in determining what meaning is. Everyone knows meanings and makes use of meaning in language. Yet as Gilbert Ryle has pointed out, there is a considerable difference between knowing meanings and understanding what meaning is. Following his example, one might illustrate the difference by comparing the differing types of answers required for the questions: *What can I buy for this quarter?* and *What is purchasing power?* Anyone can answer the first type of question; the second requires thorough understanding of a discipline. A definition of meaning may be even more difficult to provide than one of purchasing power. Besides defining meaning, linguists must also devise procedures for determining it.

Before discussing the procedures applied in this concern, we will review briefly the attempts of some linguists to point out the problems involved in the study of meaning. These attempts have been directed in part at avoiding unduly simple approaches.

For Karl Vossler a linguistic item is a symbol or a summary of a myth shared by a linguistic community. The myth might be disclosed by noting its origin for any individual speaker in that community. For example, in our culture children probably learn to know the word *lion* through picture books and television cartoons. In this way a myth develops that the lion is a ponderous and regal beast. Thereupon lions may be associated with dramatic stories, for example, of Daniel's escape from a lions' den, or the slave who escaped because he once befriended a lion by pulling a thorn out of its paw, or the mouse in Aesop's fable who freed a lion trapped in a net. Eventually a child may see a lion in a circus or a zoo, but his myth would be directed as much by political cartoons or stone images of lions in public places as by any direct knowledge of the animal. The meaning of *lion* for a speaker of English in America or England would accordingly differ considerably from its meaning for a child in some English-speaking communities of sub-Saharan Africa.

One may readily construct similar contrasts in meaning for items like *communist, law and order,* and *flying saucer.* Vossler's approach illustrates that like other linguistic items, entities studied for their meaning must be dealt with in a framework—on the one hand, a framework within a language and, on the other hand, a framework within a culture. Yet it also represents an attempt to comprehend meaning through the concepts or the thoughts of either the speaker or the hearer. Although many students of meaning, philosophers as well as linguists, attempt to deal with meaning in this way, the approach has been criticized on the grounds that the assumed concepts or thoughts are as elusive as the meanings they are supposed to clarify.

Under another approach, meaning can best be studied by examining the use of words and sentences. Thus for Bronislaw Malinowski the meaning of linguistic items is their effect "on human minds and bodies, and through these, on the environmental reality as created or conceived in a given culture."[1] Malinowski formed his views of meaning by observing the use of language in specific contexts. One such context was a situation in which Trobriand Islanders, in a large fleet of canoes, were entering a lagoon in complete darkness. The natives' actions in avoiding the mud flats were entirely directed by the utterances of friends on the shore. For Malinowski these utterances were instruments of action, virtually as concrete as canoe paddles. According to Malinowski, meaning is also determined by concrete uses of language in our culture. "The chemist or the physicist understands the meaning of his most abstract concepts ultimately on the basis of his acquaintance with chemical and physical processes in the laboratory."[2]

Following Malinowski, then, one would determine the meanings of linguistic items by studying the behavior of their speakers in specific contexts, or as he phrased it, in a "context of situation." The meaning of *communist,* for example, like the meaning of *Fire!* (whether uttered in a crowded theater or to soldiers with loaded guns), would have to be determined by noting the accompanying activity of its users. "In order to show the meaning of words we must not merely give sound of utterance and equivalence of significance. We must above all give the pragmatic context in which they are uttered, the correlation of sound to context, to action and to technical apparatus."[3] Malinowski's views concerning the necessity of specifying the context of situation are highly important for the study of meaning. As he indicated, the meanings of linguistic entities are regulated by the locations in which they are applied, such as a scene in real life or a pattern of poetry.

Malinowski's approach is similar to that proposed by Leonard Bloomfield. For Bloomfield the meaning of any linguistic entity is a function of its occurrence. To illustrate his view, Bloomfield used a "man-from-Mars" approach. For such an unlikely visitor to earth, the meanings of language utterances would be determined by observation of the contexts in which the utterances were used. With a minimum of observation the visitor would be able to distinguish between the meanings of *chalk* and *check* or *chalk* and *talk* and so on. Bloomfield, however, did little to pursue the study of meaning. He and his followers have been severely criticized for devoting their attention primarily to the study of phonology and morphology, to the neglect of semantics.

---

[1] Bronislaw Malinowski, *Coral Gardens and Their Magic,* vol. 2, *The Language of Magic and Gardening* (London: Allen & Unwin, 1935), p. 53.

[2] *Ibid.,* p. 58.

[3] *Ibid.,* p. 60.

Even in subsequent linguistic study attention has largely been focused on other areas, such as syntax. Recently, however, the major concern of many linguists has had to do with the study of meaning. A useful approach incorporates Malinowski's views but also specifies a way of representing meaning rigorously. We may follow Paul Kecskeméti, who emphasized the "communicative and not situational" meanings of words. Objecting also to dealing with meaning through thoughts or concepts, he observed that the "thought" of an object like a cat can be evoked by many expressions other than the word *cat*. He further states that

the meaning of the word is, rather, some rule we have to observe if our communications are to be "right" within a language. The rule for "cat," and for any other English word, says something like this: If you want to make an assertion that is to be acceptable or understandable as the assertion of such and such a fact . . ., you have to use the word "cat" rather than "dog" in such and such a place in the sentence schema.[4]

The lexical rules, as noted more fully below, make use of semantic features, as Eugene Nida proposes:

But the concepts the semanticist talks about when he speaks of meaning are sets of features defined by contrasts. In fact, meaning exists only where systematic sets of contrasts exist. The meaning of *father,* in its most common sense, depends on certain contrasts with the meanings of other words within the same domain of kinship. The meaning of *father* contrasts with that of *mother* in terms of sex. It also contrasts with the meanings of *grandfather* and *son* in terms of generation, and it contrasts with the meaning of *uncle* in terms of lineality. This meaning of *father* is therefore describable as consisting of a bundle of distinctive features.[5]

## 11.2   Procedures Applied in the Study of Meaning

The basic procedures used in studying meaning are comparable to those used in the study of the system of sounds and that of syntactic patterns in a language. One must look for entities and examine their distribution, that is, their linguistic context and their situational context. In phonological study the entities are fairly concrete. In syntactic study they are more abstract, such as the categorial entities that make up sentences. In the study of meaning they are even more difficult to establish. Of the semantic studies that have been successfully carried out, most deal with relatively straightforward segments of a language, such as the system of colors or kinship terms.

[4] Paul Kecskeméti, *Meaning, Communication, and Value* (Chicago: University of Chicago Press, 1952), p. 137.

[5] Eugene A. Nida, *Exploring Semantic Structures* (Munich: Fink, 1975), pp. 14–15.

One approach to words is exploration of the entities that may be used with them. To determine the uses of *run,* for example, one examines the various entities that may be used in a pattern like *The . . . is/are running.*[6] Among classes of entities fitting into this pattern are *boy, dog,* and *centipede.* In this use *run* means 'move rapidly on legs.' The nouns that may occupy the subject position share the features of 'animateness' and 'beings with legs.' The statement may not be made, for example, of *snake* or *egg.*

If *salmon* or *smelt* occupies the subject position, *run* means 'migrate in schools,' and the subjects share the feature 'fish.' If *water* or *oil* occupies the subject position, *run* means 'flow,' and the subjects share the feature 'natural liquid.' If *motor* or *refrigerator* occupies the subject position, *run* means 'operate in place,' and the subjects share the feature 'stationary equipment with rotating parts.' If *streetcar* or *bus* fills the subject position, *run* means 'go on schedule,' and the subjects share the feature 'scheduled public vehicle.'

Further sets of subjects are *nose* or *sore,* with which *run* means 'secrete fluid'; *hose* or *slip,* with which it means 'unravel'; and *ink* and *dye,* with which it means 'spread.' In the exploration of such uses, on the one hand, the various meanings of an entity such as *run* are distinguished from one another, or disambiguated. On the other hand, features are found that occur in all members of a set and accordingly permit one to establish semantic categories. Such categories may be found in many other patterns in a language. For example, the feature 'animate versus inanimate' regulates the use of *who* and *which* in relative clauses.

The various meanings of a word may in this way be examined for the patterning of items used with it. Three distinct meanings of *plane,* for example, may be proposed if we note the items with which each is used in the following sentences: *The plane passed rapidly out of sight, The plane passed rapidly over the rough board,* and *The plane of the discussion was too complex for her to follow.* Such patternings are labeled **collocations** by Martin Joos. Like the *is/are running* pattern, they illustrate how meanings can be determined from specific linguistic contexts, in contrast to contexts of situation in Malinowski's sense.

Conclusions about meanings are sharpened when one compares words in restricted spheres, such as kinship terms or the sphere of the intellect. Such spheres are known as **fields.** By examining the words of any field in a given language, one can determine the meaning relationships in that language. For example, the two sentences *John is her cousin* and *Mary is her cousin* would permit the recognition that *cousin* is a kinship term in English applying to both males and females. In German one would find only the collocation *Hans . . . Vetter, Marie . . . Base/Kusine.* The limitations on use, such as those that restrict kinship

---

[6] Herbert Rubenstein, "Directions in Semantic Research," in *Seminar on Computational Linguistics,* eds. A. W. Pratt et al. (Washington, D.C.: Public Health Service Publication, no. 1716, 1966).

terms to collocations with animate nouns, for example, *The girl is her cousin, Doris is her cousin,* are referred to as **selection restrictions.** Accordingly, we determine the meaning of words in any language by studying their collocations and uses.

## 11.3  The Carriers of Meaning

One longstanding problem of semantic study has involved identification of the carriers of meaning and their relationship to the world around us. Plato's dialogue *Cratylus* centers about this problem. It is tempting to associate some carriers of meaning, like *pig, blackberry,* or *tintinnabulation,* with the thing referred to. Some reflection concerning other entities, such as *cranberry,* or other languages leads to the rejection of any inherent relationship between words and things (as noted in Chapter 16). To discuss meaning without confusion, most students of meaning use a set of three terms: 1) a term for the linguistic item, often a **word** but also when pertinent a morpheme; 2) the **referent,** that is, the thing referred to; and 3) the **reference,** that is, the individual's concept of the thing referred to, which according to Kecskeméti would be stated in a rule. For example, the referent of the linguistic item *lion* is *Felis leo,* but the reference may vary considerably among speakers of English, as noted earlier. For items like *pig* and *snake* or even abstract terms like *democracy* and *socialized medicine,* it is fairly simple to distinguish between referent and reference. But for others, such as *love, patriotism,* and *communication,* the distinction may not be so simple. Much of the popular discussion of meaning, or of language in general, centers around the problem of distinguishing referents from references.

Much linguistic discussion has also centered about identification of the carriers of meaning. Generally, morphemes are taken to be the minimal linguistic units having meaning. This assumption applies well to morphemes like {*pig, snake*}, even {*cran-*}, but it provides difficulties for items like the *to* of *I want to look* or the *-cis-* of *incisive*. In discussions of meaning the examples selected usually have fairly unambiguous references, like *bachelor*. But in a comprehensive treatment of meaning all linguistic items must be managed thoroughly.

Lexicographers are usually thought of as being centrally concerned with meaning. Yet the dictionaries we use are primarily repositories of synonyms. An item like *lion* may be defined through synonyms like 'cat' or 'celebrity' or even by means of an illustration. Such definitions are useful, just as it is useful to know the value of a quarter, but they do not attack the problem of meaning as a primary component of language. Further, the use of synonyms and antonyms in explicating meaning affords no universal framework for all languages. English *pig* may well be equivalent to Latin *sūs,* but a totally different Latin linguistic item would probably be necessary to translate *long pig,* which in Polynesia meant 'the human flesh eaten by cannibals.'

## 11.4  Semantic Analysis for Features

To provide a universal framework for handling meaning, the device of distinctive features has been introduced into semantic study. Semantic features, also called *semantic components,* have been used to specify small sets of the words in a language, such as relationship terms. One widely cited illustration is the word *bachelor,* for which the definitions in a small desk dictionary are fashioned as a set of features. Among the definitions given are 'unmarried person,' 'young knight,' and 'holder of a degree,' as well as 'young seal without a mate.' In defining *bachelor* by distinctive features, one important feature would be 'animate,' to contrast it, for example, with *bathtub.* To distinguish *bachelor* further from other words for animate beings, such as *husband,* additional features would be employed, such as 'unmarried.' In this way *bachelor* and all other words and morphemes might be defined.

Listing linguistic items by features has been widely practiced, for example, by the Englishman Peter Mark Roget. He classified the English vocabulary under six primary features, which he labeled according to these categories: abstract relations, space, matter, intellect, volition, and affections. If *bachelor* were listed by Roget's principles, its features would be: matter → organic matter → vitality → special → 373 man or 366 animal; 366 and 373 are two of the thousand categories in Roget's "system of classification of the ideas which are expressible by language" (Roget's preface to his *Thesaurus*). His categories may or may not be followed in further feature analyses of English. They permitted him, however, to produce a relatively comprehensive analysis of the English vocabulary. It is also clear that they can be plotted on trees, similar to those used for P-markers. The more inclusive categories would be higher in the tree, branching to more and more restricted categories. The term *bachelor* is also listed by Roget under category 904: affections → sympathetic → social → celibacy.

Whatever the eventual classification, segments of vocabularies, or semantic fields, are explored for semantic features. For the set of relationship terms in English, three features are essential: sex, generation, and lineality. Among the English relationship terms, *father : mother* are differentiated for sex, but not for generation, as are *father : son,* nor for lineality, as are *father : uncle.* Such semantic fields can be variously represented. Chart 1 represents a "paradigmatic semantic system" for selected English kinship terms and may serve to illustrate Nida's characterization of meaning as "sets of features defined by contrasts." Besides specifying the features of a semantic field, such matrices readily disclose irregular items. For example, *cousin* is aberrant in not differentiating sex. The German set of relationship terms, which has an item for 'male cousin' *Vetter* as opposed to 'female cousin' *Kusine,* would not show this irregularity. Studies of meaning consequently determine the rules stating the distinctive semantic features of words in a language.

**Chart 1.   Distinctive Features of English Kinship Terms**

|  | *Father* | *Mother* | *Brother* | *Sister* | *Son* | *Daughter* | *Uncle* | *Aunt* | *Cousin* | *Nephew* | *Niece* |
|---|---|---|---|---|---|---|---|---|---|---|---|
| Sex | 0 | 1 | 0 | 1 | 0 | 1 | 0 | 1 |  | 0 | 1 |
| Generation | 0 | 0 | 1 | 1 | 2 | 2 | 0 | 0 | 1 | 2 | 2 |
| Lineality | 0 | 0 | 0 | 0 | 0 | 0 | 1 | 1 | 1 | 1 | 1 |

From George A. Miller, "Psycholinguistic Approaches to the Study of Communication," in *Journeys in Sciences,* ed. David L. Arm (Albuquerque: The University of New Mexico Press, 1967), p. 45.

## 11.5   Types of Semantic Relationships

Besides analyzing the vocabulary of a language to determine semantic fields and the components that they share, the types of semantic relationships must also be explored. These apply for sentences as well as words.

One widely explored type is **synonymy.** It implies that equivalent items share many semantic features. Thus *lion* and *Felis leo* share all features for the primary meaning of *lion*. **Antonyms,** on the other hand, differ in one distinctive feature: for *lion : lioness* this feature is sex; for *light : dark* it is luminosity. The basis for analyzing sets in a semantic field, in order to set up charts like that for English relationship terms, and for establishing synonyms and antonyms is **inclusion.** *Light* would be labeled plus for the feature luminous; *dark* would be labeled minus. As the kinship matrix in Chart 1 suggests, the inclusion relationship is paradigmatic. Inclusion in the domain of another word is known as **hyponymy.** Thus *dog* is a hyponym of *animal*.

Relationships such as synonymity, antonymity, and hyponymity also apply to sentences. If two or more sentences are synonymous, they are referred to as **paraphrases** of one another. Thus *John is fat* is a paraphrase of *John is not thin*. Much of the recent study of semantics deals with relationships between the meanings of sentences.

Still other relationships may be cited, such as contradiction and implication. *John is slender* would be contradictory to *John is fat*. And *John is fat* might well be implied by *John couldn't possibly fit in the back seat of a Vega*.

Semantic relationships may also be syntagmatic, or in Uriel Weinreich's term, **linking.** As examples like the following show, linking relationships may be transitive or predicative:

Transitive:   *The girl laughed infectiously.*
Predicative: *The girl is infectious.*

In the first example the relationship is parallel to that in *The girl has an infectious laugh;* in the second, the relationship is quite different.

Further, attributive and predicative expressions have different semantic relationships, for if nominal expressions such as *her infectious laugh* and *the infectiousness of her laugh* are derived from *Her laugh is infectious,* their meanings differ when used as subjects of predicates like *was delightful.* The many such semantic relationships require extensive exploration.

---

## 11.6  The Treatment of Semantics in a Grammar

As we have noted above, in the standard theory of transformational grammar the semantic component of the grammar is assumed to be interpretive. By this assumption the semantic component relates the base with the outside world. The rules applied for such a purpose are projection rules. Segments of meaning carried by the lexical items of the base and by the P-rules are in this way related to objects, states, events, and so on. The lexical items, with their syntactic descriptors and semantic features, would be interpreted and related to such segments of the outside world. Thus a word like *mother* would be specified in the following way:

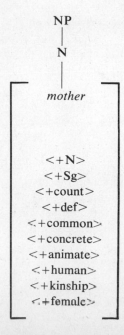

$$
\begin{array}{c}
\text{NP} \\
| \\
\text{N} \\
|
\end{array}
$$

*mother*

$$
\begin{array}{l}
<+\text{N}> \\
<+\text{Sg}> \\
<+\text{count}> \\
<+\text{def}> \\
<+\text{common}> \\
<+\text{concrete}> \\
<+\text{animate}> \\
<+\text{human}> \\
<+\text{kinship}> \\
<+\text{female}>
\end{array}
$$

In this way the semantic features would be introduced and interpreted.

If, conversely, the grammar were produced in accordance with a generative semantic theory, the base would consist of semantic structures. From these semantic structures syntactic strings would be derived by means of syntactic rules. In such a grammar the semantic component is the portion of the grammar from which the structures of sentences and words are generated. In spite of this difference between generative syntax and generative semantics, the lexical entries would be similar, such as those presented here for *mother*. Differences between the two theories have to do with the position of the semantic component, not with the inclusion of devices for the treatment of meaning or even with the consideration of meaning as a complex of semantic categories.

## 11.7  Metaphorical and Idiomatic Uses of Language

The procedures cited above deal with words and sentences for their primary references. Words also have secondary meanings, for example, those reflecting emotions. These may have wide currency, as do those for such words as *snake* or *brotherhood*. Termed by Nida 'emotive' as opposed to 'cognitive,'[7] they are important in the interpretation of specific utterances but are difficult to describe with assurance, since they vary considerably among speakers. Even a word like *snake,* which evokes negative emotions in many speakers, cannot be said to have such a secondary meaning for everyone.

Moreover, language is often used metaphorically, especially in poetry. Thus Shakespeare's line *The word is cousin to the deed* could scarcely be interpreted in accordance with the analysis of the kinship term *cousin* above. Similarly, *bread* is not used simply for one of man's principal foods. Analysis of meaning must therefore take secondary uses of words and sentences into consideration. The study of meaning then becomes highly demanding.

The secondary meanings of words vary considerably because of individual speakers' and hearers' experience and background. For example, rulers once used the term *cousin* in addressing noblemen, a use that would scarcely be understood today except by readers of Shakespeare, or other writers of the past. And the word *bread* is used to mean 'money' among some speakers. A semantic theory must account for such transferred or metaphorical meanings, as well as for the primary meanings of words. If words were listed for their semantic features, such meanings would presumably be entered with special diacritics to mark their use by literary figures or by individuals.

Michael J. Reddy has pursued the meaning of words in literary texts in this way, proposing that "the determining factor in metaphor is not

---

[7] Nida, *Exploring Semantic Structures,* p. 18.

semantic or syntactic 'deviance,' but rather the actual, contextually determined referents of the words in question."[8] In this study, and others he has carried out, Reddy illustrates the procedures that may be used in intricate literary analysis and provides models of definition that are designed to account for metaphorical uses of words.

The study of meaning must also take idioms into consideration. These are treated like extended lexical items. For example, the idiom *know which side one's bread is buttered on* would be given the interpretation 'know what is to one's advantage.' Idioms generally are characterized by lexical constraints and can be recognized in this way. For example, the idiom above must be reflexive: one cannot say *\*I know which side her bread is buttered on.* Such morphological and syntactic constraints help justify the treatment of idioms under special semantic groupings. Yet rigorous semantic study of metaphorical and idiomatic usage is still in its infancy.

## 11.8  On Performatives and Constatives

Complexities of meaning also accompany so-called **performatives,** a type of verb that is part of the action as well as of a statement. For example, the statement *I take this woman to be my lawful wedded wife* is a part of the marriage ceremony, not simply a statement with a constative verb like *I take my bath when I get up.* Such verbs have been studied in great detail since the publication of John Austin's *How to Do Things with Words.*

Performatives have syntactic characteristics as well as special meanings. They are normally in the present indicative active, and they are used with a first person singular pronoun. The performative sentence given above, or any other, would not be valid if it were in the past or in the passive, or if it had a subject other than the first person singular. For example, *This ship was named the* Peoria *by her* is not a performative sentence, in contrast with *I name this ship the* Peoria. A performative requires that the production of the utterance be a part of the performance. Performative verbs, then, contrast with **constatives,** which simply imply the content of an utterance, as in *The Joneses named their new cruiser the* Peoria.

Austin also examined utterances for another distinction, *locutionary* versus *illocutionary* force. Utterances with illocutionary force carry implications beyond those of straightforward locutions. Among illocutionary verbs identified by Austin are **verdictives,** which imply that the speaker or speakers are delivering a verdict, not simply a statement. Examples are *acquit, convict, estimate,* and *characterize.* **Exercitives,** on

---

[8] Michael J. Reddy, "Formal Referential Models of Poetic Structure," in *Papers from the Ninth Regional Meeting, Chicago Linguistic Society,* eds. Claudia Corum, T. Cedric Smith-Stark, and Ann Weiser (Chicago: Chicago Linguistic Society, 1973), pp. 493–518.

the other hand, indicate decisions, for example, *bequeath, command, name, nominate, order,* and *recommend*. **Commissives** commit the speaker to a course of action, for example, *agree, consent, intend, promise,* and *undertake*. Still other types are identified by Austin.

All such verbs with illocutionary force convey, besides their inherent meaning, the implication that the speaker wishes the hearer to understand something further. This additional, or illocutionary force, has to do with the effects described above, such as verdicts, decisions, and so on. Investigation of such meanings has been pursued by linguists as well as such philosophers as Austin. It has also broadened the sphere of linguistic investigation, leading scholars to concern themselves to a greater extent with the "context of situation" in which utterances are made. Such concerns are commonly referred to as **pragmatics**, which has to do with the origin, uses, and effects of utterances.

---

### 11.9 Semiotics

The study of meaning, and of language, may then be encompassed in a larger study: the theory of signs, or **semiotics,** also referred to as **semiotic.**

Semiotics deals with all signs, whether used by man or by other animals. Thus the signaling of bees on their return to their hive is a concern of semiotics. So are the communications of birds. Such communication may be less flexible than that of humans, but it too is used for conveying information. Bees perform dances to report on the presence of nectar, giving the direction and the distance. Birds use their calls to indicate claims over territory, to give warnings, and so on.

Linguists, notably Saussure, and philosophers, notably Charles Sanders Peirce, have dealt with human language within the broader scope of semiotics. In this way semiotic study has provided a framework for the investigation of all forms of human communication, whether of gestures, the sign language used by the deaf, or oral communication. As indicated in Chapter 2.3.1, such patterns of communication also include simple systems like those of traffic lights. This broadening of concern has put the study of meaning into broader perspective and is bringing linguistics into contact with other investigators of behavior, as will be noted in the following chapters.

### BIBLIOGRAPHICAL NOTES

Gilbert Ryle's essay, "The Theory of Meaning," has been published with other essays illustrating "the importance of language in human affairs" in *The Importance of Language,* ed. Max Black (Englewood Cliffs, N.J.: Prentice-Hall, 1962). Karl Vossler's *Geist und Kultur in der*

*Sprache* (Heidelberg: Winter, 1925) provides a sketch of his views, as Bronislaw Malinowski's *Coral Gardens and Their Magic* (London: Allen & Unwin, 1935) does of his; see especially vol. 11, pp. 52–62. This volume has been reprinted by the Indiana University Press (Bloomington, 1965) with the title, *The Language of Magic and Gardening*. For other charts of the English kinship system and additional statements on meaning see *Toward a Science of Translating* by Eugene A. Nida (Leiden: Brill, 1964). Peter Mark Roget's *Thesaurus* has been widely reprinted and re-edited and is readily available. For a comprehensive study of semantics see *Meaning and the Structure of Language* by Wallace L. Chafe (Chicago: University of Chicago Press, 1970). A reader containing many articles of interest is *Semantics,* edited by Danny D. Steinberg and Leon A. Jakobovits (Cambridge: At the University Press, 1971). John L. Austin's lectures *How to Do Things with Words* have been edited by J. O. Urmson (New York: Oxford University Press, 1962). See also *Speech Acts* by John R. Searle (Cambridge: At the University Press, 1969). For an introduction to semiotics see *Signification and Significance* by Charles Morris (Cambridge, Mass.: M.I.T. Press, 1964).

Since much of philosophical study is concerned with meaning, students will find it useful to examine its approaches in an excellent overview by John Passmore, *A Hundred Years of Philosophy,* 2d ed. (Baltimore, Md.: Penguin Books, 1968). Problems of meaning are treated clearly in *Der Wortinhalt,* 4th ed., by Ernst Leisi (Heidelberg: Quelle & Meyer, 1971). A book incorporating the important views of a wise and experienced linguist is *Exploring Semantic Structures* by Eugene A. Nida (Munich: Fink, 1975). Supporting his discussions with fascinating examples, Nida takes all of language as the domain of the linguist. Nida's breadth of interest stems at least in part from his concern with translation. A useful introduction to the study of meaning is provided in *Semantics* by Geoffrey Leech (Baltimore, Md.: Penguin Books, 1974).

## QUESTIONS FOR REVIEW

1. What is the aim of semantics?
2. In what way are syntactic patterns and patterns of intonation carriers of meaning?
3. What is meant by "context of situation"? Discuss varying meanings for utterances like *O.K., Drive!* and *That's enough* in different contexts of situation.
4. How are meanings of words disambiguated? Exemplify, using words like *dog, walk,* et cetera.
5. What is meant by *referent?* by *reference?*
6. What are semantic features? Discuss their use in the analysis of sets like kinship terms.

7. Define the semantic relationships known as *synonymy, antonymity,* and *hyponymy.* What is a paraphrase?
8. Distinguish between inclusion and linking relationships.
9. Discuss the different treatments of semantics in generative syntax and generative semantics approaches to the study of language.
10. Define *metaphor* and *idiom.*
11. What is a performative? Distinguish some of the kinds of illocutionary forces identified by Austin.
12. What is semiotics? Discuss its relation to semantics.

## EXERCISES

### EXERCISE 1

In the sentence *He received the letter, letter* may have various meanings. How do the additional sequences below help to determine specific meanings? How do they serve to disambiguate the meaning of *letter* in each of the three sentences?

1. *He received the letter after the football season.*
2. *He received the letter after he paid for the postage due.*
3. *He received the letter from his typewriter agency.*

### EXERCISE 2

Determine the various meanings of *drive* in the following sentences, indicating the entities in the context that help you determine the meaning in question:

1. *She drove the children home from school.*
2. *He drove the cattle into the barn.*
3. *He drove the nail into the wall.*
4. *They drove the enemy across the border.*
5. *He always drove a Rolls Royce.*
6. *The unfavorable publicity drove him into retirement.*

### EXERCISE 3

a. Provide sentences that permit you to disambiguate *leg* in the sense of:

1. *one of the lower limbs of a man*
2. *a support for a table*

3. *the lower segments of trousers*
4. *a portion of a course or trip*

   b. How would you disambiguate the meaning of *leg* in item 1 from its meaning in *He didn't have a leg to stand on?*

   c. Give distinctive features that permit you to indicate the meanings of *leg* in items 1 to 4 and the interrelationships of these meanings.

## EXERCISE 4

Examine the definition of any of the following in a desk dictionary, and determine its semantic features: *lion, mouse, elephant, python.*

## EXERCISE 5

After determining general classes of verbs, one may further analyze the members of such classes into subclasses based on each member's use. For example, *remember* and *decide* are alike in sentences with an object, such as:

1. *Jane remembered the issue.*
2. *Jane decided the issue.*

When, however, they are followed by clauses, they differ in possible relationships and in their meaning used in sentences.

   a. Discuss the differences in meaning of the complements in:

1. *Jane remembered to take her lunch.*
2. *Jane decided to take her lunch.*

Does each of these sentences carry the implication that Jane actually took her lunch?

   b. Discuss the implication of:

1. *Jane remembered to take his lunch.*
2. *Jane decided to take his lunch.*

1. *She happened to get her money back.*
2. *She wanted to get her money back.*

1. *Henry managed to leave.*
2. *Henry determined to leave* or *Henry was determined to leave.*

Which of the sentences carries the implication that the actor completed the action?

    c. Note your own use of *deserve*. If you use a sentence like *She deserved to win the prize*, does it imply that the subject won the prize?

    d. Discuss the implications of these sentences with the negative, for example:

        1. *Jane didn't remember to take his lunch.*
        2. *Jane didn't decide to take his lunch.*

What does the negative form of these sentences tell you about the interrelationships between the finite verb and the complement? For example, does the negated verb in sentence 2 imply that the action was not carried out? how about sentence 1?

    e. Discuss the implications of these sentences as questions, for example:

        1. *Did she happen to get her money back?*
        2. *Did she want to get her money back?*

    f. With which member of these pairs can you use adverbial expressions like *tomorrow* and *next week?* Does this possibility support your analysis in d?

    g. How would you classify the pair *authorize, permit?*[9]

---

[9] For further discussion see Lauri Karttunen, "Implicative Verbs," *Language* 47 (1971): 340–358.

# HISTORICAL AND COMPARATIVE LINGUISTICS

## CHAPTER 12

## 12.1  Irregularities in Language

When we compare the sets of forms in language, we find that some items in some sets are irregular. Thus, while the plural of *can* is *cans,* of *pan* *pans,* and so on, the plural of *man* is *men.* Such irregularities are often explained by the examination of earlier stages of a language.

The irregularities generally involve everyday words. Thus the plural of *woman* [wəmən], the modern form of an old compound *wife-man,* is *women* [wimən]. Another word in this sphere is *hussy,* originally *house-wife*. In the plural *women* and the first syllable of *hussy* a shortened form of *ī* and *ū* appears, while the modern full forms of *wife* and *house* have the diphthongs [ay] and [aw]. We will find that these and other such forms can be explained historically. During the late Middle English period, English long vowels underwent a shift known as the great English vowel shift.

Irregularities are found at all levels of the language. In the English verb system some verbs have internal vowel change, like *sing, sang, sung,* while most English verbs are regular. The past tense of BE also has a consonant change in *was : were.* To account for these changes we will need to go back further in history than the Middle English period.

We have also found irregularities in syntax. English adjectives precede nouns, while relative clauses and most genitives follow them. By contrast, in consistent SVO languages, like French and Spanish, adjectives as well as relative clauses and genitives follow nouns.

As an example of an "irregularity" in meaning relationships we can cite *teller*. In most English -*er* words the noun simply indicates what an agent of a verb does; a *singer* sings, a *writer* writes, and so on. But a *teller* doesn't "tell"; he or she counts money. By going back in history we can determine that the former meaning of *tell* was 'count' and that at this earlier period *teller* was as regular in meaning as *singer*.

Accordingly, many irregular patterns of language can be explained by an examination of earlier stages of the language. Such study is known as **historical linguistics.**

---

## 12.2  The Great English Vowel Shift and the Identification of Middle as Opposed to New English

When we examine the English of Chaucer and earlier writers, we find a vowel system quite different from that of current English. The Middle English system consisted of long vowels as well as short. The following list of words gives examples of the long vowels in Middle English (ME) and their counterparts today (NE = New English):

| ME | | NE | | ME | | NE | |
|------|---------|------|--------|------|---------|-------|---------|
| *wīf* | [wi:f] | *wife* | [wayf] | *hous* | [hu:s] | *house* | [haws] |
| *seen* | [se:n] | *seen* | [siyn] | *spon* | [spo:n] | *spoon* | [spuwn] |
| *sea* | [sɛ:] | *sea* | [siy] | *ham* | [hɔ:m] | *home* | [howm] |
| *name* | [na:mə] | *name* | [neym] | | | | |

If one plots the differences between the Middle English vowels and their current equivalents on a phonetic chart, it is obvious that the lower ME vowels were raised and the higher became diphthongs.

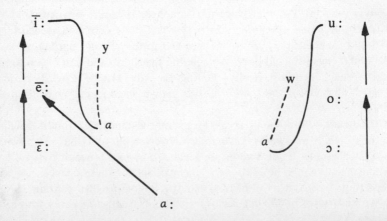

In this way the NE sound system is considerably different from the Middle English system. This change took place in the fifteenth century and is one of the features that distinguishes the two stages of the language, Middle English and New English.

If the ME vowels $\bar{u}$ and $\bar{\imath}$ were shortened, as in *hussy* and *women,* they did not undergo the shift. These words then can be accounted for, as can those that have undergone the shift.

To explain the plural form *men* we must go back further. In early Old English (OE) times, back vowels were fronted if an $\bar{\imath}$ or a *y* stood in the following syllable. Thus short and long *u* became $\ddot{u}$, $o > \ddot{o}$, and *a* $> e$. The rounding was later lost, so that short and long $\ddot{u}$ fell together with *i,* short and long $\ddot{o}$ together with *e.* In this way the plural form of *mouse* was OE $m\bar{y}s > m\bar{\imath}s$. (The great English vowel shift changed the vowel to [ay], as in *wife*.) And Old English $d\bar{o}man > d\bar{e}man$ (becoming *deem,* as in *seen,* during the great English vowel shift). Such fronting, or **umlaut,** was characteristic of early Old English as well as the other Germanic languages. The front rounded vowels are still preserved in Modern German.

These changes illustrate how language is constantly being modified. Through such modifications languages that do not maintain close contact with related languages in time manifest quite different characteristics and become distinct languages. English is a Germanic language that was brought to England in the fifth century A.D., thus losing contact with closely related languages in north Germany. These also underwent changes and developed into independent languages. In much the same way, the descendants of Latin came to be distinct when the Roman Empire no longer maintained close communication among its various parts. We will note in the next section the various dialects of Germanic and the distinct languages they have become.

## 12.3  The Germanic Languages

We assume that in the period from 1000 B.C. to 1 B.C. there was a fairly coherent group located in northern Europe that spoke a language called Proto-Germanic. The prefix **Proto-** is used to indicate that the language has been reconstructed. Reconstructed forms may be marked with an asterisk, but when the prefix *Proto-* or its abbreviation *P* is used, the asterisk may be omitted as redundant.

In the course of time the Germanic group expanded. Speakers in the various areas lost contact with each other, and various dialects developed that then became separate languages. The first division is often assumed to be one into a northeastern group and a western group. The northeastern languages in turn developed into two subgroups, one represented by Gothic, the other by the Scandinavian languages.

Gothic is the oldest of the Germanic languages for which a sizable body of materials has survived. The Bible, or parts of it, was translated into Gothic in the fourth century. The texts dating from this time are relatively archaic and are of great interest to Germanic specialists. The Goths themselves were absorbed in western Europe, except for a small group that survived in the Crimea until the seventeenth or even eighteenth century.

The Scandinavian languages are generally divided into two groups: a western, consisting of Norwegian, Faroese, and Icelandic; and an eastern, consisting of Swedish, Gotlandic, and Danish.

Our most archaic Germanic texts survived in the north. They are inscriptions written in runes. One, dated about A.D. 375, reads as follows:

> *Ek HlewagastiR*       *HoltijaR*       *horna    tawido.*
> 'I  Hlewagast           of-Holt          the horn made'

This inscription is on a horn found at Gallehus in Denmark and is accordingly known as the Gallehus inscription. As the forms indicate, Germanic at this time still had many endings. The second element of the name *HlewagastiR* illustrates these and also the pattern giving rise to umlaut. The form corresponding to *-gastiR* was umlauted in Old English, giving rise to the form *guest*.

The West Germanic languages are High German, Low German, Dutch, Frisian, and English. Texts in these are relatively late, dating from the time of the introduction of Christianity. Our earliest Old English texts are ascribed to about A.D. 700, although most are preserved in later manuscripts. The Old English period is generally dated until around 1050; and the Middle English period is dated until around 1450. High German, the standard language of Germany, Austria, and parts of Switzerland, is divided into similar stages: Old High German, 750–1100; Middle High German, 1100–1450; and New High German, 1450 to the present.

## 12.4  Germanic and the Other Indo-European Languages

To account for the vowel differences in *sing : sang : sung* and *was : were* we must go back to even earlier stages of the language. These differences are a result of vowel changes in the language from which Germanic developed, Proto-Indo-European (PIE). Much as the Germanic languages came to be distinct because of various changes, Germanic came to be distinct from the other Indo-European dialects.

One of the major differences resulted from a consonant change in Proto-Germanic referred to as the Germanic consonant shift. By this shift all the Germanic obstruents were modified. The changes are as follows:

PIE $p\ t\ k\ k^w$       >     PGmc $f\ \theta\ \chi\ \chi^w$
PIE $bh\ dh\ gh\ g^wh$     >     PGmc $b\ d\ g\ g^w$
PIE $b\ d\ g\ g^w$         >     PGmc $p\ t\ k\ k^w$

These changes clearly took place in stages. The PGmc $p\ t\ k\ k^w$, which resulted from PIE $b\ d\ g\ g^w$, did not undergo the changes of earlier PIE $p\ t\ k\ k^w$, as they might have if these had not changed earlier to PGmc $f\ \theta\ \chi\ \chi^w$.

These and other changes separated Germanic from the other Indo-European dialects, such as Latin, Greek, and Sanskrit. Words from these languages, rather than the reconstructed PIE forms, are generally used as examples to illustrate the Germanic consonant changes. (Since PIE $k^w$ $g^w\ g^wh$ developed into clusters in which the first element generally underwent the same change as PIE $k\ g\ gh$, examples will not be given here.)

The following examples illustrate the change of PIE $p\ t\ k$ to PGmc $f\ \theta\ \chi$:

| | | |
|---|---|---|
| Gk. *patér* | Lat. *pater* | NE *father* |
| Gk. *treīs* | Lat. *trēs* | NE *three* |
| Gk. *he-katón* | Lat. *centum* | NE *hundred* ($h < \chi$) |

The following examples illustrate the change of PIE *bh dh gh* to PGmc $b\ d\ g$; these subsequently became *b d g* or *y* in English:

| | | |
|---|---|---|
| Gk. *phrátēr* | Lat. *frāter* | NE *brother* |
| Gk. *eruthrós* | Skt. *rudhirás* | NE *red* |
| Gk. *khórtos* | Lat. *hortus* | NE *garden, yard* |

The following examples illustrate the change of PIE *b d g* to NE *p t k*:

| | | |
|---|---|---|
| Lith. *bala* 'swamp' | Lat. *dē-bilis* 'weak' | NE *pool* |
| Gk. *déka* | Lat. *decem* | NE *ten* |
| Gk. *génos* | Lat. *genus* | NE *kin* |

This set of changes long obscured the relationship between Germanic and the other languages. It was not, in fact, recognized until about 1820. At that time the set was described by a series of formulas, much like those presented here. These formulas, or rules, were proposed by the notable German scholar Jakob Grimm. In keeping with the terminology of the time, they were, and are still, commonly referred to as Grimm's law.

Because of these changes many English words that are inherited directly from Proto-Indo-European can be distinguished from borrowings, for example, *triad* in contrast with the native *three* and *dual* in contrast with *two*. English has borrowed many such words from Latin and Greek, and as a result many related pairs are found in Modern English. When comparable, as in *kin : genus,* they are known as **doublets.**

In addition to the change described by Grimm's law, one further change of obstruents took place in the Germanic languages. If the *f θ x* resulting from the change of *p t k* stood after an unaccented vowel but before another vowel, they became voiced *v đ g.* This change also affected *s,* yielding *z,* which later became *r.* This change is the cause of the alternations in *was : were.* It was described by a Danish linguist, Karl Verner, and is known as Verner's law.

Through the recognition of such changes, the relationship between the various IE dialects came to be clarified in the course of the nineteenth century. It became clear that the Indo-European language family extended over a large area and consisted of the following subgroups:

Indo-Iranian, of which the earliest attested form is Sanskrit; modern representations are Hindi, Bengali, and many languages of India, as well as Persian and many Iranian languages.

Armenian, spoken by a relatively small number of people.

Albanian, also spoken by a small number of people.

Slavic, with such modern representations as Russian, Polish, Czech, Serbo-Croatian, and Bulgarian.

Baltic, consisting of Lithuanian and Lettish.

Greek, once used throughout the eastern areas around the Mediterranean.

Italic, with Latin as an ancient representative and many modern descendants: Italian, French, Spanish, Portuguese, Catalan, Sardinian, Rumanian, and Rhaeto-Romance.

Celtic, with Welsh, Breton, Irish, and Scots Gaelic as modern representatives.

In addition to Germanic, several extinct IE languages may be noted: Tocharian and the Anatolian languages, especially Hittite.

The Indo-European languages are among the most widely distributed language families. They apparently have their origin about 3000 B.C. with a group of people living north of the Black Sea. From here the group spread to the east, first to Iran and then India, as well as to the west, where they eventually took over most of Europe. Since they had no writing system, the history of their spread must be determined from archeological records, and inferences must be based on the subsequent distribution of the Indo-European languages, as evolved from their Proto-Indo-European tongue. The basis of their success in taking over such a large area is unclear. But the horse, which they used for their raids into new territory, was doubtless one important factor; another was the chariot. Whatever the details, the Indo-European family became one of the most widespread language families, and much of the theoretical work in historical linguistics is based on investigation of the IE languages.

## 12.5   Methods Used in Historical Linguistics

Besides accounting for change in language, a primary aim of historical linguistics is to establish and verify relationships between languages. It does this by determining earlier forms. Thus it is clear that words like NE *guest* and NHG *Gast* have developed from the same earlier form in Proto-Germanic. A form comparable to the Proto-Germanic form is found in the Gallehus inscription *-gastiR*. Often, however, such earlier forms are not attested. They are then reconstructed by a procedure known as the **comparative method.**

By the comparative method two related forms, or cognates, are compared, and the probable earlier form is proposed. Comparing Greek *génos* and Latin *genus,* one would have little difficulty reconstructing Proto-Indo-European *\*genos*. (The asterisk indicates a form inferred from historical examples but not actually attested.) The method is often said to be one of triangulation, in which the forms compared are placed on the base of a triangle and the reconstructed form at its apex:

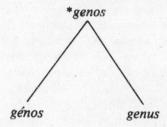

These forms are clearly easy to relate, and the earlier form is easy to reconstruct. When the relationships are not so transparent, one must draw on one's general knowledge of phonological possibilities and on the phonological structure of the languages concerned. For details, a handbook on historical linguistics can be consulted.

The problem may be illustrated however by the words cited for 'brother':

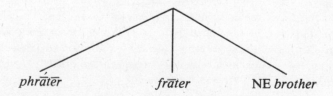

From these forms it would be difficult to decide which initial consonant to reconstruct for Proto-Indo-European. Greek has a voiceless aspirate, Latin a voiceless fricative, and Germanic a voiced stop, presumably from an earlier voiced fricative. Because the form in Sanskrit is *bhrātar,* the initial consonant is generally reconstructed as *bh.*

This reconstruction was widely accepted when the PIE obstruent system was assumed to consist of contrasting voiceless and voiced, aspirated and unaspirated stops, for example:

$$p \quad\quad b$$
$$ph \quad\quad bh$$

But recent scholarship has led to the conclusion that Proto-Indo-European had no voiceless aspirates. And accordingly, a system with voiced aspirates did not seem realistic. Therefore assumptions drawn from a general study of phonological systems have led to revisions of the system. No generally accepted conclusions have been reached, although the former voiced aspirates have been reconstructed as tense consonants by some scholars.

This example may illustrate some of the difficulties involved in the application of the comparative method. The method is impossible to use when a language is isolated or when one is dealing with a protolanguage with no known related languages. In such instances a second procedure, known as the method of **internal reconstruction,** is applied.

By internal reconstruction similar morphological items that vary phonologically are examined. For example, roots often have a specific structure in languages. In Proto-Indo-European, most roots have the structure: Consonant:Vowel:Consonant (CVC), as in NE *sit* from the PIE root *sed-, kin* from the PIE root *gen-,* and so on. There are, however, some very common roots with the structure VC, for example, *ag-* 'lead' in Latin and Greek; compare NE *agent.* Assuming that such roots also once had the structure CVC, Ferdinand de Saussure posited for them and other PIE forms some consonants that later were lost. On the basis of internal reconstruction then, he posited instead of \*ag- a root \*heg-. Advanced in 1879, this hypothesis, for which no further proof existed, was verified when Hittite was discovered around 1906 and found to include the consonants that had been lost.

Internal reconstruction can in this way amplify the conclusions based on the comparative method. Skillful use of the two methods has enabled historical linguists to determine with a high degree of accuracy the relationship of the Indo-European languages and also the interrelationships of other language families that will be discussed briefly below.

## 12.6  Borrowing

The methods discussed in the previous section are useful when one is dealing with items that have been transmitted within one linguistic tradition. Items are also adopted by speakers of one language from those of another. Thus speakers of English have adopted words like *opossum*, *squaw*, and *wigwam* from American Indian languages. Such adopted elements, most of which are in the sphere of vocabulary, are known as **borrowings.**

The oldest large group of borrowings into English was made from the Scandinavian languages of north England. These include such words as *window, skirt, sky, husband, happy, die,* and *egg.* In the English tradition *sk-* before high front vowels had become *sh-*, as in *shirt.* Borrowed words thus reintroduced the *sk-*, and in this way may be distinguished from words in the native English tradition.

A second large group of borrowings was made from French from the twelfth century onward. Additional words have been borrowed from other languages, notably Latin and Greek. Many words referring to items of higher culture were borrowed in this way. Among those borrowed from French are words for government, such as *government* itself, *country, minister, nation, people,* and *state.* Others are legal terms, such as *court, judge,* and *plaintiff.* The French influence on legal language is especially strong, in part because French was the language of the courts of justice until 1731. Besides lexical items, legal phrases were introduced and maintained, some of them with the French order of adjectives, such as *malice aforethought* and *attorney general.* The latter has been so thoroughly incorporated into English that its second element is now treated as a noun.

To what extent borrowings affect the structure of the language is still unclear. Some scholars propose that when two languages are spoken side by side, their morphology may be reduced, much like that of a pidgin, which is a simplified auxiliary language formed by a combination of two different languages. The loss of inflections in English might then be ascribed to the contact between English and Scandinavian speakers in the ninth and tenth centuries. Their languages must have been mutually intelligible, but to facilitate understanding they may well have simplified verb and noun inflections. The same process may have occurred later, when speakers of English and speakers of French were in close contact for centuries after the Norman Conquest of 1066. If these hypotheses are correct, borrowing has had a deep influence on English, as well as on other languages that have been in contact with one another. When we examine languages that have existed side by side for long periods of time, such as the Indo-European and the Dravidian languages of India, we find great similarities in syntactic and phonological patterning, as well as in vocabulary. Diffusion of linguistic structures as well as lexical items may then be one of the principal causes of change in language.

## 12.7 Other Major Language Families

As we have noted above, the procedures and theories of historical and comparative linguistics were primarily developed in the study of the Indo-European languages during the nineteenth century. Other language families, however, were also being investigated and their subgroups determined. Some of the principal groups will be listed here.

Through much of North Africa and the adjacent areas of Asia the languages belong to the **Afro-Asiatic** family, often referred to as **Hamito-Semitic.** Some of the earliest attested languages belong to this family, such as Egyptian, attested from the fourth millennium B.C., and Akkadian. Prominent modern representations are Arabic, Hebrew, and Hausa. The account in Genesis of the spread of Hebrew into Palestine is instructive in relating how languages might have been diffused thousands of years ago.

In central Africa the dominant family is the **Niger-Congo,** with Swahili as one of its widely spoken members.

In the southern part of India the principal languages, such as Telugu and Tamil, belong to the **Dravidian** family. Dravidian may have been spoken in north India when the Indo-Europeans invaded between 2000 and 1200 B.C. If so, it was gradually displaced to the south.

In eastern Asia the largest language family is the **Sino-Tibetan.** Its principal members are the Chinese or Han languages, of which there are at least eight distinct members. Efforts are now being made to generalize a common language, Putonghua, throughout the People's Republic of China. This language, based on the pronunciation of the Peking area and the syntax and vocabulary of recent scientific and technical writings, is probably the native language of more speakers than any other language, including English.

Among other large language families are the **Altaic,** which comprises the Turkic, Mongol, and Manchu-Tungus groups; and, in the northern areas of Asia, the **Finno-Ugric** languages. The most widespread language family in the world, at least until the great expansion of Indo-European speakers, was the **Malayo-Polynesian,** spoken from Hawaii to Madagascar.

Furthermore, there are languages whose relationships are difficult to determine, such as Japanese, Korean, and Basque. The numerous indigenous languages of the Americas as well as those of Africa, Australia, and New Guinea have been classified into families and stocks, though much study is still being devoted to their relationships. Historical linguistics has, however, clarified many of the genetic relationships between languages and has used its findings for their classification.

## 12.8  The Causes of Change

We have observed above that some change is ascribed to diffusion or borrowing, that is, the influence of one language on another. But this assumption is inadequate to account for all change, especially that of isolated languages. We must therefore assume other causes for change.

One of the most widely accepted is the gradual modification resulting from changes made by individuals in speech, as well as in their other social activities. This cause of change is also linked with the learning of language by children, for it is assumed that no children learn languages exactly as their parents speak them and that, accordingly, in the course of time considerable changes result. To affect a language, any such changes must be adopted by the other speakers in the social group. Each of these possible causes of change probably interacts with the others. In any event, languages are constantly changing, and over a period of centuries the cumulative changes bring about considerable differences between one stage of a language and its successors.

The change of any language is, however, regulated by the structure of that language. When the Germanic consonant shift took place, the shifted consonants came to vary only slightly from their earlier forms. They were not glottalized, prenasalized, or modified in other possible ways, but one or more distinctive features, such as continuant articulation or voice, were affected. Because over a long period of time the changes in a language will seem to be tending in a certain direction, the process of structural change has been referred to as **drift**.

As we have noted above, the preposed adjectives in English do not agree with its SVO structure, which normally has postposed adjectives, as in French and Spanish. When we look at earlier English texts, we find that genitives also were preposed, but that they have been shifting to postposed position as constructions like *the house of our neighbors* have been replacing those like *John's house*. The proportion of preposed genitives in Old English texts is about 90 percent, virtually the same proportion of postposed genitives today. Over a period of a thousand years, then, English has been "drifting" from the VO to the OV order of genitives. If we examine other characteristic constructions, we will find other OV patterns in Old English. These are understandable when we note that Proto-Indo-European was an OV language. Over the course of millennia English and its predecessors have been shifting from an OV toward a VO structure.

Through historical linguistic analysis, then, the forms and patterns of languages are accounted for. The history of a word is known as its **etymology.** The history of phonological and syntactic systems is depicted in historical grammars. Historical linguistics has provided a means for classifying languages. It is also pursued for its own sake.

Moreover, it has been useful in clarifying the earlier history of man. Languages change so consistently and completely that it is virtually impossible to reconstruct a language from more than five thousand years ago. The attempts to reconstruct the language of the speakers who first penetrated to America, or the attempts to hypothecate the origin of language cannot therefore make use of historical linguistic methodology. This methodology has, however, enabled historical linguists to clarify many of the linguistic developments and interrelationships of the past five thousand years.

BIBLIOGRAPHICAL NOTES

For an introduction to historical linguistics see *Historical Linguistics: An Introduction* by Winfred P. Lehmann (New York: Holt, Rinehart and Winston, 1973). For a survey of historical study in the last century see *The Discovery of Language: Linguistic Science in the Nineteenth Century* by Holger Pedersen, translated by John Spargo (1931; reissue, Bloomington: Indiana University Press, 1962).

QUESTIONS FOR REVIEW

1. Discuss the aims of historical linguistics.
2. What is the great English vowel shift? Give some examples. When did it take place? How can we account for the vowels in *house* and *hussy, wife* and *women?*
3. How do we account for the vowel of *men* as opposed to that of *man?* Give additional examples of umlaut.
4. Discuss the circumstances in which one language may develop into two or more distinct languages in the course of time.
5. Outline the development of Proto-Germanic to the individual Germanic languages of today.
6. Discuss the Germanic consonant shift, indicating the various changes that took place and giving examples. Why are the changes referred to as Grimm's law?
7. Name the principal branches of Indo-European.
8. What is the comparative method? the method of internal reconstruction?
9. What is meant by borrowing? Give examples.
10. If borrowing affects the structure of a language, what results are likely? What is a pidgin?
11. Name some of the large language families and indicate their location.
12. List causes of sound change.
13. What is drift?

EXERCISES

EXERCISE 1

The following are examples of translation of Matthew 14:15 from three periods of English. They have been taken from *The English Language: A Historical Reader.*[1]

---

[1] A. G. Riggs, ed., *The English Language: A Historical Reader* (New York: Appleton-Century-Crofts, 1968).

Old English (circa 1000):

Sodlīce þā hyt wæs ǣfen geworden, him tō genēalǣhton hys leorningcnihtas, and him tō cwǣdon, "Đēos stōw ys wēste, and tīma is forð āgān; forbet þas mænegeo þæt hī faron intō þas burga and him mete bicgean."

Tyndale (1534):

When even was come, his disciples came to him sayinge. This is a deserte place, and the daye is spent: let the people departe, that they maye go in to the tounes, and bye them vytaylles.

King James (1611):

And when it was evening, his disciples came to him, saying, This is a desert place, and the time is now past; send the multitude away, that they may goe into the villages, and buy themselves victuals.

a. Point out differences in vocabulary and grammar between the Old English text and Tyndale's text.
b. Discuss patterns of vocabulary and syntax in the Tyndale and the King James translations that are no longer current.
c. Determine the position of the verbs in the Old English text, indicating their order in each clause.
d. The three texts contain the following forms for 'food': OE *mete;* Tyndale *vytaylles;* King James *victuals.* Compare these with modern forms, as in *sweetmeats* and the pronunciation of *victuals,* and discuss the changes that have taken place.


EXERCISE 2

The following are Middle English forms containing long vowels and their New English counterparts in conventional spelling:

| | | |
|---|---|---|
| *rīm* | [ri:m] | 'rhyme' |
| *gēs* | [ge:s] | 'geese' |
| *deel* | [dɛ:l] | 'deal' |
| *tale* | [ta:l] | 'tale' |
| *boot* | [bɔ:t] | 'boat' |
| *mone* | [mo:n] | 'moon' |
| *mous* | [mu:s] | 'mouse' |

a. Indicate the changes that have taken place between the ME long vowels and their NE reflexes. (Be sure to write the NE forms in transcription.)
b. Using the distinctive features given in Chapter 6 for English vowels, state the rules of change.

EXERCISE 3

The following are examples of forms indicating the PIE obstruents and their Germanic reflexes:

| | | | | | |
|---|---|---|---|---|---|
| 1. | PIE *p* | | *t* | | *k* |
| Skt. | *pā́d;* Doric Gk. *pṓs* | Skt. | *tr̥nam* | Gk. | *kúōn* |
| OE | *fōt* 'foot' | OE | *đorn* | OE | *hund* 'hound, dog' |
| 2. | PIE *bh* | | *dh* | | *gh* |
| Skt. | *bhárati* | Skt. | *dhitis* | Skt. | *stighnute* |
| OE | *beran* 'bear' | OE | *dǣd* 'deed' | OE | *stīgan* 'climb' |
| 3. | PIE *b* | | *d* | | *g* |
| Lith. | *balà* 'swamp' | Skt. | *dvā* | Gk. | *géranos* |
| OE | *pōl* 'pool' | OE | *twā* 'two' | OE | *cran* 'crane' |

a. Indicate the consonant changes that have taken place between PIE and Germanic.
b. Using distinctive-feature analysis, suggest the features that have changed.
c. Give the NE counterparts of the following. (Since the Germanic counterparts of Sanskrit final syllables were lost, disregard the -*u* in the first form and the -*us* and -*as* in the last two forms.)

| | | | | |
|---|---|---|---|---|
| Skt. | *madhu* | 'sweet drink' | NE | _____ |
| Lat. | *ager* | 'field' | NE | _____ |
| Skt. | *tanús* | 'narrow' | NE | _____ |
| Skt. | *pataras* | 'flying' | NE | _____ |

EXERCISE 4

Using the comparative method, reconstruct the initial PIE consonant from the following:

Skt. *paśu;* Lat. *pecu;* Goth. *faihu* 'cattle (fee)'
Skt. *tr̥ṣyati* 'is thirsty'; Gk. *térsomai* 'become dry'; Goth. *pairsan* 'wilt'
Lith. *kerpù* 'shear'; Lat. *carpo* 'pick'; OE *hærfest* 'autumn, harvest'

EXERCISE 5

a. In the Middle English period a well-known set of terms for prepared foods was borrowed from French, such as *beef, veal, bacon, pork,* and *mutton.* On the other hand, native English words were maintained for the animals in the field, such as *cow, calf, boar, swine,* and *sheep.* Can you suggest the status of the two languages and their speakers from the borrowings?

b. Among other borrowings from French were names for trades, such as *carpenter, painter,* and *tailor,* while simple occupations maintained English names, such as *baker, miller,* and *blacksmith.* Does the contrast between these two sets support your suggestion based on the words listed above?

# PSYCHOLINGUISTICS

## CHAPTER 13

### 13.1 The Concerns of Psycholinguistics

In our discussion of language we have been proceeding as though speakers always produce accurate versions of sentences and as though all speakers of a language maintain the same grammar. But when we listen carefully to speakers, we find that their utterances may differ from our ideal representations and from the grammars we produce. For example, even a simple sentence like *Mother saw the cat* might be uttered with the kind of additional noises that are often represented by *uh* or *er*. The actual utterance might be [²mə̀ ðər ³sɔ́² | ə ə ²ðə̀ ³kǽt¹#].

The interruptions indicated here by [ə ə] are referred to as **hesitation pauses.** They may differ from speaker to speaker both in phonetic make-up and in positioning.

In other sentences we may observe grammatical lapses that are quickly modified, for example, *The Club have—I mean—has decided*. Almost any completely accurate representation of speech—usually best gained by listening to a nearby conversation and concentrating on the speech material rather than the content—illustrates that we have been discussing an ideal rather than an actual type of language.

But though the representation of sentences without hesitation pauses and other interruptions may be idealized, it reflects fairly accurately the way in which we perceive language. Unless a speaker's hesitation pauses are painfully obtrusive, we pay no attention to them. We may not even notice the lapses and extraneous noises used by our closest associates; for example, if we study with a teacher for some time, we may come to ignore completely his hesitation pauses. Because of our ways of perceiving language, linguists feel justified in excluding aberrant utterances from their basic analysis. But we still need to account for the difference between the language that we somehow consider ideal and actual speech, with its frequent extraneous entities and lapses. When we do so, we call on disciplines other than linguistics, notably psychology. The joint concern of various disciplines with the perception, interpretation, and production of speech has developed into a separate discipline known as **psycholinguistics.**

In its concerns with the procedures involved in perceiving and in directing the production of speech, psycholinguistics asks various questions: What are the processes involved in converting acoustic impulses into neurological impulses for interpretation by the brain? Are these processes roughly the reverse of those involved in directing the articulatory activities that produce speech? What are the units of perception and production: semantic entities; syntactic entities; or phonological entities such as words, syllables, or phonemes—or combinations of these?

The investigation of these questions requires carefully planned experiments. Since dedication to scientific advance does not extend far enough to prompt investigators to provide direct access, by means of instruments, to their inner ear or to their auditory nerve, many of the results in psycholinguistics must be obtained indirectly: through study of children's acquisition of language; through observation of an individual's use of different languages or the shifting from one form of language to another, as from oral to written language and the like; and from language pathologies, such as loss of speech.

Attempts are also being made to draw conclusions about human language from methods of communication found among other organisms, such as apes, porpoises, and bees. Somewhat more remote is the study of how information is stored and transmitted by cellular matter, such as DNA. When we understand all such varieties of communication better than we now do, we may derive insights into the procedures used by human beings in speaking.

Each of these topics is a large study of its own, so that only a few introductory statements about each may be made here. And though they are extensive, each of the topics requires consideration of the contrast between language as we describe it in our grammars and its often pale reflection in speech.

## 13.2 The Perception and Interpretation of Speech

It is well known that the physical events associated with the same vowels of different speakers differ. Careful measurements have shown that there is considerable overlap between such vowels as [i] and [ɪ], [ɛ] and [ɪ], [u] and [ʊ], and so on. A fundamental question then for psycholinguistic investigation is: How does the hearer interpret different physical events as the same entities? In an experiment designed to provide an answer to this question, Peter Ladefoged and Donald F. Broadbent investigated the interpretation of synthetic (that is, machine-produced) words. They made up four synthetic words, which in isolation hearers interpreted as *bit, bet, bat* or *bet,* and *but.* They also made up a synthetic sentence: *Please say what this word is.* This sentence was available in six versions, in which the first and second formants were shifted but all the other features stayed alike. When these six versions were presented to listeners (without the addition of the synthetic words), the varying versions were interpreted as the same sentence spoken by different speakers.

When, however, the four words were produced after different versions of the sentence, as in:

> *Please say what this word is: bit.*
> *Please say what this word is: bet, etc.*

they were variously interpreted. After one version the word heard in isolation as *bit* would be interpreted as *bet,* and so on. The varying interpretations could be correlated with the differences in formants of the introductory sentence.

This experiment suggests that speakers have a kind of map in their brain of the phonological system of a language they have mastered. The characteristic features of the system are not determined by fixed physical entities but rather by physical entities in relation to one another. When someone hears a sentence like *Please say what this word is,* he or she apparently charts the physical entities of the speaker in question and refers subsequent utterances of that speaker to the tentative map. Speakers then identify different physical events as the same in much the way they recognize a map of New York State whether it is depicted on a globe or on a flat surface. If, however, the map gave inadequate information—if, for example, the outlines of Long Island and Madagascar were presented in isolation—the proper identification might not be made.

Experiments like that of Ladefoged and Broadbent also demonstrate the use of relationships in the sets of a language. A given vowel cannot be identified as an entity made up of certain physical characteristics; for example, one cannot say that the [e] of *bet* is characterized by formants consisting of 550 Hz and 1,850 Hz. Rather, [e] is identified by the relationship of its formants to those of the formants of other vowels of a given speaker. The first formant for [e] of a speaker of English will be somewhat higher than will be that speaker's first formant for [i]; and any vowel may differ considerably from speaker to speaker. It is for this reason that voice typewriters and telephone dialing by voice signals have not yet been successful. Machines are designed to respond to events that are approximately the same. In order to produce a successful voice typewriter or successful dialing by voice, some means would have to be found for plotting the map of any user. At present no such means have been arranged, and therefore mechanical control by voice is possible only if the selection mechanism is set for a specific individual.

Besides noting the differing interpretations of the same physical event in different contexts, experimenters have also observed that lists of recorded words are not recognized correctly when played to a number of listeners. Gordon E. Peterson and Harold L. Barney, for example, played 1,520 isolated English words to seventy listeners; only half of the words were correctly identified by all the listeners. Such experiments have raised further questions about the interpretation of speech. Do listeners, for example, identify speech segments as phonological events, or do they interpret them through syntactic analysis as well?

### 13.2.1   The Interpretation of Syntactic Sequences

In experiments to determine whether listeners interpret sentences by analyzing them into syntactic units, experimenters have played sentences to one ear and clicks to the other ear. Jerry A. Fodor and Thomas G. Bever used the sentence *That he was happy was evident from the way he smiled*. The major syntactic break in the sentence occurs between *happy* and *was*. The experimenters varied the click so that it occurred not only at this break but also elsewhere in the sentence. Listeners were asked to write down the entire sentence and then to mark the position of the click. On examination of the results it was found that listeners tended to locate the click closer than it actually occurred to the major syntactic break. The result may be taken as an indication that listeners interpret sentences as consisting of constituents. If an extraneous feature accompanies one such constituent, it tends to be interpreted as occurring outside the constituent.

Such experiments may also indicate that listeners seek to identify not individual sounds but linguistic entities. In the course of learning a given language, listeners come to know how to analyze a sentence. Accordingly, syntactic entities as well as phonological entities are recognized in the perception of speech.

### 13.2.2   The Interpretation of Semantic Sequences

Determining whether listeners interpret semantic sequences of utterances requires even more delicate experiments than does the investigation of syntactic sequences. In some of the experiments dealing with interpretation of syntactic sequences, listeners were asked to change positive declarative sentences to negatives and passives; the time required was measured. For negatives about a second was required; for passives, about a second and a half. It may be assumed that the differences reflect different degrees of syntactic difficulty.

In attempting to determine whether similar evidence might be found for semantic patterns, Peter Wason designed an experiment to test whether listeners required a longer time to complete negative sentences about unexceptional facts than about exceptional facts. (Apparently we tend to use negative utterances in reporting exceptions.) Given a pattern of one blue and seven red dots, the speakers found it simpler to say *One dot is not red* than *Seven dots are not blue*. Yet syntactically one of these sentences is as simple as the other. The difference in difficulty disclosed by the experiment is most likely accounted for through semantic interpretation. Since sentences such as *Seven dots are not blue* afford no syntactic problems, they must be semantically difficult.

Experiments of this type have provided information about elements of language other than phonetic sequences. The experiments concerned deal with the psychological processes involved in language and are accordingly carried out in psycholinguistic study. Such study indicates once again that language may be separated into phonological, syntactic, and semantic components only for the purpose of simplifying investigation.

## 13.3  The Interpretation of Language by the Brain

For some time neurologists have known that for most speakers language is controlled by the left hemisphere of the brain. That is, humans have a specific speech center. This conclusion is supported by the observation of individuals who have lost part of their capacity for speech. For example, it has been reported by Norman Geschwind that "out of 100 adult aphasics, at least 96 percent have damage to the left side of the brain."[1] On the basis of this information, investigations are being carried out to determine how speech is processed by the brain.

Among such investigations are dichotic tests. Selected speech sequences are played separately into the right and left ears. The input to the right ear is interpreted by the left hemisphere. The investigations demonstrate that that portion of speech consisting of segmental phonemes is indeed primarily interpreted in the left hemisphere. The right hemisphere, however, is equally capable of interpreting segments distinguished by pitch, stress, and quantity, that is, those segments that make up the communication systems of nonhumans. These in-

---

[1] Norman Geschwind, "The Organization of Language and the Brain," *Science* 170 (1970): 943.

vestigations, accordingly, support the hypothesis that humans have a specific capacity for language. Moreover, since this added capacity handles segmental phonemes, it differs markedly from the capacities of other animals.

Geschwind has also determined that the left hemisphere is anatomically different from the right. Specifically, the region of the speech center is one-third larger than the corresponding section of the right hemisphere. Moreover, this difference exists from birth. Accordingly, study of the brain has demonstrated that human beings have a special capability for language and that this capability is determined by the development of the speech center in the left hemisphere. This demonstration has opened the way for some of the most remarkable investigations to be conducted with reference to language.

Particularly remarkable are the investigations on the interpretation of speech by humans with a bisected brain. The operation of bisecting the brain by cutting the corpus callosum, which connects the two hemispheres of the brain, is carried out on patients with uncontrollable seizures. After it has been carried out, the patients are not only relieved from their agonizing seizures, they also learn to function normally for the most part, as do animals on whom the same operation has been performed. But it has become clear that the two hemispheres function, in part, like separate brains. This finding has prompted numerous fascinating questions, for example, that of the relation between the mind and the brain. It has also yielded some startling experimental results.

In contrast with the functioning of the ears, each eye transmits information to only one hemisphere. Signals may thus be provided to the left eye alone and be transmitted only to the right hemisphere. As noted above, the right hemisphere is assumed to have a subordinate role in interpreting speech. Experiments with patients who have undergone the operation resulting in a bisected brain show that the right hemisphere may still interpret visual inputs, but that these inputs do not necessarily result in language comprehension.

One of the most remarkable results indicates differences between the treatment of nouns and verbs by the brain. If nouns like *knife* or *orange* are presented through the left eye to the right hemisphere, patients point out the correct object. If a picture of a house is shown to the left eye, however, without an accompanying verbal cue, patients say that they have seen nothing. But if asked to use their left hand to pick up a card with a picture of a house, they do so. We may conclude that the right hemisphere "understands" the signals provided by nouns and that it can thereupon direct appropriate actions, but that it cannot produce the verbal signals on its own.

Nouns related to verbs, however, are not even "understood" by the right hemisphere. Thus, nouns like *jump* or *locker* are not processed by the right hemisphere, though phonologically similar nouns like *butter* are.

Moreover, when verbs are presented to the right hemisphere, no understanding results. While patients point to a knife or an orange and pick up the picture of a house when directed to do so, they do not respond to instructions via visual representations of the words to *smile* or *nod* or when requested to *tap, point,* or *knock.* When, however, the directions are provided by pictures rather than verbally, the patients perform the actions of smiling, tapping, and so on. The investigators conclude that verbs are "represented poorly if at all in the right hemisphere."[2]

The findings of Michael Gazzaniga and other investigators have important implications for linguistic theory. These findings suggest that verbs are characteristic categories of the communication system developed by man, that is, of human language. Apparently the right hemisphere, which is similar to the brain of other animals, can process nouns and concepts represented by "pure" nouns. But verbs and their derivatives are processed only in the specially developed speech center of the left hemisphere in humans. Consequently, in grammars and theoretical discussions of language, verbs must be accorded the primary role in sentences. Therefore grammars that require the inclusion of verbs (though not necessarily nouns) in sentences represent the capacities for speech that exist in the human brain.

This conclusion receives support from the nounless sentences of the early Indo-European languages, such as Latin *pluit* and Greek *húei,* which we must translate with a subject: 'it is raining.' On the other hand, the conclusion requires further analysis of the nominal sentences we find in many languages, such as Plato's Greek statement *hē psúchē douleúein etoímē* 'the soul [is] ready to serve.' As we observed in Chapter 11, it has been suggested that many adjectives should be classed with verbs. This suggestion and others—for example, that nominal sentences are derived from verbal sentences—are supported by the recent investigations of neurologists.

Research of the processes involved in auditory perception is still in its beginnings, but it promises to increase greatly our understanding of language. Linguists must be grateful to the scholars carrying out such research and realize the need, for anyone interested in an understanding of language, to keep abreast of all future developments.

## 13.4 Language and Speech: A Theory of Competence and a Theory of Performance

In Chapters 3 and 16 we discuss Saussure's method of accounting for differences between an ideal language and the actual facts of speech. He

---

[2] Michael S. Gazzaniga, *The Bisected Brain* (New York: Appleton-Century-Crofts, 1970), p. 121.

assumes that speakers control language in two ways: in an ideal form he calls **langue,** which is common to all speakers of a language, though actualized only in various degrees of completeness from speaker to speaker; and in the actual, often imperfect, reflection he calls **parole.**

Saussure's terminology causes awkward problems, particularly in English. Writing in French, Saussure had three terms available: **langage** for the total language, **langue** and **parole** for its varying facets. English interpreters of Saussure's system generally use *language* for *langue* as well as *langage,* and *speech* for *parole.* Apart from the need to specify the technical implications of language and speech, this terminology seems to imply that speech somehow differs from language, that speech is one system, language another. Actually, however, both speech or *parole* and language or *langue* are linguistic constructs, produced so that the linguist can account for the phenomena observed as people communicate.

Something of this awkwardness has been removed by changing the mode of reference to the two differing approaches to the study of language: the ideal form of language, *langue,* is treated under a **theory of competence;** the activity observed, *parole,* is treated as **performance phenomena.**

When linguists observe speakers, they do so in order to describe the speakers' performance. Methods are therefore devised to account for the procedures of individual speakers as they produce utterances. Among these procedures are the neural directions for the muscular activities of the vocal organs. Clearly the brain must store some kind of directions for producing speech. We know which cranial nerves signal the muscles of the lips, the tongue, and the larynx. But we do not know as yet the activities by which these nerves and muscles direct units of speech, or even what those units are. Determining the answer to any one such question will occupy investigators for some time. Eventually their investigations will lead to a better understanding of performance, which will in turn lead to an improved theory of competence. In the meantime our views on performance and competence are based in great part on conclusions drawn from simpler forms of language, such as that of children learning to speak.

---

### 13.5   Linguistic Ontogeny: Acquisition of Language by Children

The dual view of language, through the study of competence and the study of performance, has various implications for the learning of language by children, for a child may learn with equal facility any one of the thousands of natural languages. He learns the one, or occasionally several, that is heard in infancy. It seems as though every child is equipped with the capability of learning any of the world's 5,000 languages, whatever its structure. This capability, however, seems to be lost after he has thoroughly mastered his first language or languages—roughly at the age of ten to twelve. Before this time mastery may be partial, somewhat as if he had not gained full competence in his language. Subsequently, however, he has firm control over his first language's basic structure, and he modifies primarily his vocabulary, not his syntax or phonology.

The age at which these two components of language are mastered may differ considerably in individuals, but a child has the phonological system of his language under general control roughly by the time he is three or four and the grammatical system by the time he is six years old.

Since a child learning his first language can master any natural language, it has been assumed that all languages share basic common features and that the differences between languages belong to their surface structures. The common features of the base are referred to as **universals.** Recently there have been numerous efforts to determine such universals, in part by observations taken from language learning.

Probably the most comprehensive effort was Roman Jakobson's monograph linking the entities mastered first by infants with those lost in aphasia (discussed in section 13.6). He hypothesized that the common features in these two situations are universal in language. For example, Jakobson pointed out that when infants begin to speak, they first master a small number of phonological contrasts—those well known from nursery words, such as *papa, mama, pipi, pupu,* and the like. Therefore, an infant's phonological system will initially consist of one stop, one resonant, and one or more vowels. This initial system does not include entities like [r l w]. Moreover, the sounds [r l w] are often not mastered until a child is four or five years old. These relatively late sounds are among those missing from the inventory of sounds in language; Japanese, for example, has no /l/. Further, aphasics may lose control of these sounds while maintaining control over the early set. These observations on general phenomena in language learning, language universals, and aphasia support the suggestion that some features of language are more central than others—in the syntactic and semantic as well as the phonological sphere—and also that we gain control over a basic structure of language yet may have inadequate mastery of surface elements. Since in a grammar composed of rules, those referring to surface elements are listed after the rules of the base, they are often called **low-level rules.**

The difference in time it takes to master the base rules and low-level rules may be observed in children. They often make unacceptable surface forms, such as *seed* or *buyed* rather than *saw* or *bought,* but the very production of these forms demonstrates the mastery of the base rules—for example, that the past of English verbs is made by the addition of $\{D_1\}$ to the root.

The acquisition of language has important implications for the assumption of an underlying versus a surface component in language.

Some of the low-level rules, as in irregular verbal and nominal forms, may not be mastered until a child approaches his teens. Furthermore, lower-level rules may vary among the speakers of a language. Some English speakers prefer *dived* to *dove,* some the pronunciation [áy ðər] to [íy ðər] for *either.* And individuals often require a long time to overcome surface-structure problems. We may be uncertain of the pronunciation of infrequent words, such as *paradigm* or *Oconomowoc,* or we may be unsure of the past tense of irregular verbs, such as *strive* or *lie,* although we have no problems with the more general patterns. Whatever pronunciation we may use for infrequent words, we use the phonemes that we have mastered for a language. We would not, for example, pronounce the past tense of *lie* with the front rounded vowel found in French. And whatever our particular verb form for *strive,* we make a past tense, not a perfect as in Latin or an aorist as in Greek. It may be concluded that by the time children enter their teens, they have thoroughly mastered the basic patterns of one language and achieved competence in that language.

## 13.6  Language, Perception, and Thought

What effect the mastery of a given language has on one's way of thinking has been one of the longstanding questions posed about language. Some recent linguists, notably Edward Sapir and Benjamin Lee Whorf, have maintained that language regulates thought and directs one's interpretation of the world around us. In a celebrated essay, "The Status of Linguistics as a Science," Sapir asserted that

even comparatively simple acts of perception are much more at the mercy of the social patterns called words than we might suppose. If one draws some dozen lines, for instance, of different shapes, one perceives them as divisible into such categories as 'straight,' 'crooked,' 'curved,' 'zigzag,' because of the classificatory suggestiveness of the linguistic terms themselves. We see and hear and otherwise experience very largely as we do because the language habits of our community predispose certain choices of interpretation.[3]

The most striking argument for this point of view was produced by Whorf, who enlarged the boundaries of Sapir's thesis. Whorf sought support in American Indian languages, notably Hopi and Navaho, for his hypothesis that linguistic patterns are related to cultural norms. It seemed to him that Hopi does not objectify time. Unlike a speaker of European languages, called by Whorf SAE (Standard Average

[3] Edward Sapir, "The Status of Linguistics as a Science," in *Selected Writings of Edward Sapir in Language, Culture and Personality,* ed. David G. Mandelbaum (Berkeley and Los Angeles: University of California Press, 1963), p. 162.

European), a Hopi cannot count temporal units, like days, weeks, and years, and an expression like "four days elapsed" would have to be represented by a Hopi speaker by expressions like "after the fourth day." From his analysis of Hopi (which he learned largely from one Hopi informant in New York City), Whorf concluded that speakers of Hopi had a concept of time different from that of SAE speakers. He even suggested that their concept of time, in regarding time as a fourth dimension, is comparable to that of physicists after Einstein.

Speakers of Navaho, on the other hand, seemed to Whorf to have a concern with action, a universe in motion, for Navaho speakers must indicate for each verb whether an action is in progress, whether it occurs from time to time, whether it is about to happen at some time in the future, and other stages of action much more subtle than the present, past, and future of Latin. As the Hopi language determines the Hopi speakers' concept of time, so the Navaho language predisposes the Navaho speakers toward a concern with action. The proposed effect of language on one's perception and view of the surrounding world is often referred to as **linguistic relativity,** or the **Sapir-Whorf hypothesis.**

Experiments to determine the validity of this hypothesis have been largely inconclusive. Tests designed to determine whether children of one linguistic background react differently to certain phenomena than do children of another linguistic background have not been convincing, possibly because the design and the execution of the tests have been faulty. Investigations are being continued. Yet if we assume that children have a predisposition for language and that there is a universal base for all languages, the patterns that influence speakers cannot be very deep. We have already noted that the overt patterns in one language are often represented by covert patterns in another. Some investigators have asserted that proponents of linguistic relativity have only concerned themselves with the surface structure, not with the underlying structure, and that their conclusions are therefore trivial. The often-repeated reference to names for varieties of snow among the Eskimos is an example. Such vocabulary is produced when it is necessary; skiers who use SAE languages have also produced a rich set of labels for the basis of their favorite sport. And to match the fabled variety of nouns for the camel in Arabic, one may note the variety of nouns for car or airplane in English. One does not buy a car but rather a hardtop, a Mustang, or the like.

Accordingly, linguistic relativity, if it can be demonstrated at all, may not deeply affect one's perception or the structure of one's culture. Yet what of the relation of language and thought? Among the more powerful investigators of this problem was the Russian psychologist Lev Semenovich Vygotsky. In a brilliant monograph that draws on the understanding of language found in writers like Tolstoy, Vygotsky[4] studied

---

[4] Lev Semenovich Vygotsky, *Thought and Language,* trans. Eugenia Hanfmann and Gertrude Vakar (Cambridge, Mass.: M.I.T. Press, 1962), pp. 152–153.

the "inner workings of thought and speech," concluding that the relations between them are "delicate, changeable relations between processes." "Thought is born through words. A word devoid of thought is a dead thing, and a thought unembodied in words remains a shadow." For him thought and language "are the key to the nature of human consciousness." But he also stated that he had reached only the threshold of the problem. Other investigators are now pursuing the problem further by investigation of language learning among children, by experiments such as those reported earlier in this chapter, and by observation of the various uses of language by adults.

## 13.7  Second-Language Learning

Most adults or college students learning their first foreign language have first-hand evidence that childhood is an advantageous time for acquiring languages, for acquisition of a second language after the age of thirteen or fourteen is very difficult. Perversions of borrowed words readily support this statement. While no English speaker has difficulty with the sequence /ts/ as in *cats* or /ŋ/ as in *rang,* he or she may find them impossible initially, as in *tsetse* and *Ngaio,* which may be pronounced [sétsiy] and [náyow].

Similarly, differing grammatical patterns are difficult to master. German speakers use a plural *Auskünfte* for 'information' and may be observed speaking in English of "informations." The plural French *vacances* and German *Ferien* betray speakers of these languages into referring to their "vacations" when speaking English. Though adults have such problems, children in a foreign language environment learn the second language without an accent and without grammatical problems. There may be various reasons for the difference in skill of acquisition. Children use a less complex language than do adults. They also have fewer obligations and distracting responsibilities than do their elders. Still, the difference in ability to learn a foreign language after the age of thirteen or so is striking enough to justify the assumption that children have a facility for language learning that is lost after a certain age.

Loss of the facility seems to be related to the fixing of the patterns of one language. While students in a foreign language class may assume that their primary difficulty is an inability to pronounce the new sounds, every foreign language teacher knows that they do not even perceive them. German and French front rounded vowels are heard by English speakers as unrounded. English interdental fricatives /θ ð/ are heard by Germans either as dental stops or as groove fricatives, so that Germans say [tin sin dis zis] for *thin, this.* Apparently, in learning one language thoroughly we fix our perception for all other languages. The implications of this are varied and are coming to be appreciated more generally by language teachers. We do not have the space to pursue these implications here, but we may note briefly that the shifts from one language to another are somewhat comparable to the shifts from one representation of language to another, as from speech to writing.

Until recently little attention had been given to the process of learning to read. But the far-reaching problem of illiteracy in the world has led to the study of this process. Equating the visual symbols of writing with the oral symbols of speaking is no simple problem. Skillful teachers of illiterates attempt to overcome it by relating specific shapes to sounds in words selected for their meaning. For example, to teach the relationship between the symbol *v* and the sound [v], the word *vat* might be selected as a pattern and its *v* shaped like a "vat." While such pedagogical ingenuities are useful for teaching adults to read, the process for children is not as clear. Only recently has the difficulty of a small percentage of children in learning to read become widely known. Referred to as **dyslexia,** this inability seems to involve lack of maturing in certain forms of muscular control. Dyslexia has been little investigated as yet. Its study may lead to improved understanding of the processes involved in the control of various forms of communication, as study of disabilities has led to an understanding of other human characteristics.

## 13.8  Problems of Loss of Language: Aphasia

Among the most unfortunate of language disabilities is **aphasia,** the loss of control of some segment of language. It is brought about by some form of brain injury. Many opportunities to study aphasia have been provided by the wars of 1914 and 1939, as well as by accidents in automobiles and less shielded vehicles. But the phenomenon has long been known. One Hittite king, Mursilis, ascribed his aphasia to a thunderclap; the aphasia of Zacharias, described in Luke 1:20, was interpreted as retribution for unbelief. There are many varieties of aphasia, but only recently have investigators attempted to understand the phenomenon in accordance with a theory of language.

Their investigations suggest that language is hierarchically structured. When a patient's phonological system is disturbed, the complex patterns are impaired. Similarly, when a person's grammatical system is disturbed, mastery of the grammatical rules, especially the low-level rules, is impaired. Unfortunately, the phenomena of aphasia are still little understood, particularly for effective therapy.

## 13.9  Study of Animal Languages

If the investigation of human language pathologies is complex, that of animal languages is far more so. And in spite of incautious claims, such investigation has led to one certain conclusion: that the communication systems of animals differ qualitatively from human language. Animals indeed use oral signals for communication. But the signals are stereotypic and refer to general situations, such as danger or availability of food or mating phenomena. Even the most patient attempts to teach apes or other animals how to use language as a flexible system of oral communication have failed.

In view of these failures attempts have been made recently to teach animals the forms of communication, notably sign language. Although some scholars dispute the conclusions, scientists working with chimpanzees report that they can recognize signs and symbols and communicate by means of them. Thus Ann and David Premack have taught a chimpanzee named Sarah to communicate by means of plastic symbols that can be arranged to convey messages. And R. Alan and Beatrice Gardner taught sign language to a chimpanzee named Washoe. Since Washoe was about eleven months old when the teaching began, she may have faced the difficulties that adolescents and adults would have in learning a language. Accordingly, the Gardners have now undertaken to teach sign language to chimpanzees under their control from birth. The young chimpanzees Moja and Pili started to make signs when they were about three months old. These and other experiments with animals may illuminate some of the capabilities of primates, including human beings, for communication. However, in evaluating the findings and reports, one must be cautious about making overly optimistic statements.

## BIBLIOGRAPHICAL NOTES

For a general introduction to psycholinguistics see *Psycholinguistics* by Dan I. Slobin (Glenview: Scott, Foresman, 1971). Children's language learning is treated in *Language Development: Structure and Function* by Philip S. Dale (Hinsdale: Dryden, 1972). The experiment by Peter Ladefoged and Donald E. Broadbent is published under the title "Information Conveyed by Vowels," in *Journal of the Acoustic Society of America* 29 (1957): 98–104; that of Gordon E. Peterson and Harold L. Barney as "Control Methods Used in the Study of Vowels," *Journal of the Acoustic Society of America* 24 (1952): 175–184; that of Jerry A. Fodor and Thomas Bever as "The Psychological Reality of Linguistic Segments," *Journal of Verbal Learning and Verbal Behavior* 4 (1965): 414–420; and that of Peter C. Wason as "Response to Affirmative and Negative Binary Statements," *British Journal of Psychology* 52 (1961): 133–142. For a report of other experiments concerning the perception of syntactic and semantic entities, see George A. Miller, "Language and Psychology," in *New Directions in the Study of Language,* ed. Eric H. Lenneberg (Cambridge, Mass.: M.I.T. Press, 1964), pp. 89–107. An excellent report of the remarkable results of recent work in the study of the brain and its processing of language is given by Michael S. Gazzaniga, *The Bisected Brain* (New York: Appleton-Century-Crofts, 1970). Lev Semenovich Vygotsky's *Thought and Language* is available in a translation by Eugenia Hanfmann and Gertrude Vakar (Cambridge, Mass.: M.I.T. Press, 1962). For access to the publications on animal communication, see Thomas A. Sebeok's "A Selected and Annotated Guide to the Literature of Zoosemiotics and Its Background," *Studies in Semiotics, Social Science Information* 7 (5): 103–117.

For a general article on the teaching of language to apes, see "Teaching Language to an Ape," by Ann N. and David Premack, *Scientific American* 227 (1972): 92–99. A recent statement is given in "Early Signs of Language in Child and Chimpanzee" by R. Alan and Beatrice T. Gardner, *Science* 187 (1975): 752–753.

For views on the control of language by the brain, see Norman Geschwind, "The Organization of Language and the Brain," *Science* 170 (1970): 940–944. Roman Jakobson's monograph, "Kindersprache, Aphasie und Allgemeine Lautgesetze," appears in *Selected Writings,* vol. 1 (The Hague: Mouton, 1962), pp. 328–401.

Sapir's essay "The Status of Linguistics as a Science" was first published in *Language* in 1929; it has been reprinted in *Selected Writings of Edward Sapir in Language, Culture and Personality,* ed. David G. Mandelbaum (Berkeley and Los Angeles: University of California Press, 1963).

QUESTIONS FOR REVIEW

1. What are hesitation pauses? Why do we fail to notice them in the speech of acquaintances?
2. Define *psycholinguistics,* stating some of its principal areas of concern.
3. Account for the perception of the same word as *bit* in one context, *bet* in another. What conclusions may be drawn from such experiments about the perception of speech? Why has it not been possible to design a telephone that permits one to dial by speaking the number?
4. Why do speakers tend to hear clicks between constituents of sentences rather than where they occur? What support do such findings provide for syntactic analysis?
5. Describe experiments that give evidence that speakers view some semantic structures as more difficult than others.
6. What do dichotic experiments tell us about the interpretation of speech? Which hemisphere of the brain is dominant for the interpretation of speech? What support is given to this conclusion by experiments with speakers having bisected brains?

7. Discuss the findings resulting from the study of language learning, of the presence of sounds in many languages, and of aphasia that support the notion of universals in language. Give some examples of such findings.

8. It has been proposed that the production of "regular" forms, like *seed* for *saw,* supports the hypothesis that a child constructs a grammar of the language he learns. How can such observations be used to support this view?

9. When can it be said that a child has mastered a language? Does the time of his mastery of the phonological system differ from that of the syntactic system?

10. What is meant by linguistic relativity? State some evidence in favor of the hypothesis; against it. It has been said that the word *inflammable* was replaced by *flammable* on gasoline trucks because speakers interpreted the *in-* as 'not' rather than as an intensive; would such interpretation support the Sapir-Whorf hypothesis? To what extent?

11. Why do adults have different problems from those of children in learning a second language?

12. What are some of the methods you might use in teaching illiterates to read?

13. What is meant by aphasia? Cite some instances reported in the past. Discuss possible conclusions for our understanding of the brain's control of language that can be drawn from observations of aphasia.

14. What results have been obtained in the attempts to teach animals to speak? to communicate in sign language?

## EXERCISES

### EXERCISE 1

In an essay, "On Hearing Sentences," James P. Thorne makes the following statement:

In every natural language there are an infinite number of sentences which under normal circumstances cannot be heard. The sentence *The mat adores fish on Fridays* is an example in English. Spoken normally it will always be heard as *The matadors fish on Fridays*. (Notice that, on the other hand, I do not under normal circumstances hear the word *matadors* in *The cat on the mat adores fish on Fridays*.) If I can hear that an utterance is a well-formed sentence I simply cannot also hear it as another badly formed sentence. I cannot, for example, hear *Snow fell* as an imperative or *Bring water* as a declarative.[5]

---

[5] James P. Thorne, "On Hearing Sentences," in *Psycholinguistic Papers,* eds. J. Lyons and R. J. Wales (Edinburgh: Edinburgh University Press, 1966), p. 6.

a. Account for the hearers' inability to interpret the sentence as the linguist intended. State phonological, syntactic, or semantic reasons for the hearers' interpretation of the four sentences cited by Thorne.

b. What implications of such experiments can be derived concerning perception of language? For example, do speakers base their interpretations on phonological criteria alone? To what extent are phonological criteria crucial in the perception of language? syntactic criteria, as in *Snow fell?* semantic criteria?

## EXERCISE 2

a. Teachers of foreign languages encounter many problems that result from the way we perceive language. For example, in teaching French or German to native speakers of English, teachers may pronounce a word with a front rounded vowel, as in French *lune* [lyn] 'moon,' ask students to imitate it, and receive in response a chorus of front unrounded vowels, that is, a word resembling *lean*. How do you account for this phenomenon? What would you do to teach the proper pronunciation of front rounded vowels?

b. Another problem faced by language teachers is the production of incorrect grammatical expressions such as *\*I am knowing it*. For example, native speakers of German (and many other languages) are taught that English has a "progressive present," *I am going,* an emphatic present, *I do go,* as well as a simple present, *I go,* corresponding to the one simple present form in their own language. Account for the production of incorrect sentences, like *\*I am understanding that,* by such language learners. How would you attempt to circumvent the production of such sentences?

## EXERCISE 3

Stuart Chase states that Whorf proposed the hypothesis that "the structure of language one habitually uses influences the manner in which one understands his environment."[6] This view is often called the "principle of linguistic relativity" or the Sapir-Whorf hypothesis.

One problem Whorf investigated was the question whether "our own concepts of 'time,' 'space,' and 'matter' [are] given in substantially the same form by experience to all men, or are they in part conditioned by the structure of particular languages?"[7] In pursuing the question, Whorf dealt with Hopi, noting that in it "plurals and cardinals are used

---

[6] Benjamin Lee Whorf, *Language, Thought, and Reality: Selected Writings of Benjamin Lee Whorf,* ed. John B. Carroll (New York: Wiley, 1956), p. vi.

[7] *Ibid.,* p. 138.

only for entities that form or can form an objective group. There are no imaginary plurals. . . . Such an expression as 'ten days' is not used. . . . 'They stayed ten days' becomes 'they stayed until the eleventh day. . . .' "

Whorf finds various correlations between each language and its culture. I cite only one. He says that

Our objectified view of time is . . . favorable to historicity and to everything connected with the keeping of records, while the Hopi view is unfavorable thereto. . . . Through this give-and-take between language and the whole culture we get, for instance:
   1. Records, diaries, bookkeeping, accounting, mathematics stimulated by accounting.
   2. Interest in exact sequence, dating, calendars, chronology, clocks, time wages, time graphs, time as used in physics.
   3. Annals, histories, the historical attitude, interest in the past, archaeology, attitudes of introjection toward past periods, e.g., classicism, romanticism.[8]

   a. Discuss this conclusion. It is an example of what is sometimes called the "strong form" of the hypothesis of linguistic relativity. Do you know of cultures that put less emphasis than ours on calendars, chronology, and clocks? Can you relate this cultural difference to the language? It is sometimes said that the nineteenth century was more interested in history than our century is. Can you relate a shift in interest to a change in language?
   b. As an example of the "weak form" of the hypothesis one might cite the treatment of such words as *inflammable*. Formerly used on containers for gasoline, the word has generally been replaced by *flammable*. It is assumed that the *in-* prefix was confused with *in-* 'not' as in *inept* and *inexpert,* rather than classed with the *in-* of *inaugurate* and *incite*. The confusion presumably led to incautious behavior near flammable gas drums, resulting in fires.
   Discuss this instance as an example of the weak form of the hypothesis. Do you believe it is valid? Can you produce other examples? It is sometimes said, for example, that expressions like *It's in his blood* produce erroneous notions of heredity. Would you agree? Can you provide any evidence for effects of external linguistic form on behavior?[9]

---

[8] *Ibid.*, p. 153.
[9] You may wish to examine the examples given by Whorf in *Ibid.*, pp. 135–137.

# SOCIOLINGUISTICS

## CHAPTER 14

### 14.1  Social Groups and Institutions in Relation to Language

The social groups in which we use language vary considerably, and we vary our speech in accordance with them. At work we may speak differently from the way we speak at home. Men often speak differently when with other men than when they are with women and vice versa. Young speakers have their own special speech patterns, and in many societies there are considerable differences among the speech patterns of various social classes. Furthermore, in some societies many speakers are multilingual. Finally, languages differ from area to area. When groups of speakers are isolated from other groups of speakers of a language, they tend to develop variants of that language. In time so many such variants may be introduced that separate forms of the original language may develop. All of these differences in language are related to differences in social groups. Their study is the aim of **sociolinguistics.**

In general sociolinguists set out to determine how social institutions affect language and how the varied uses of language affect social groups. Close-knit social groups favor their own special language patterns. One aim of special languages is accuracy. If, for example, a linguist refers to a sound by a special term, such as *phone* or *allophone*, other linguists will have a more accurate notion of his or her interpretation of the sound. All groups of specialists—workers, scientists, criminals—seem to develop *jargons*. While such jargons may increase the efficiency of communication within a group, they tend to exclude or even to irritate outsiders. Besides the study of special forms of languages, the effects of special language patterns are an important concern of sociolinguists.

## 14.2  Dialects

Variation in languages from area to area is the facet of sociolinguistics that has been most widely studied by linguists. Much of the terminology of sociolinguistics has accordingly been taken from the study of geographical variations. The varieties of a language are known as **dialects.** While the term *dialect* has various applications it is used by linguists to refer to a variety of a language that may be understood by other speakers of that language, although they do not necessarily share the same dialect. Speakers of American English do not understand Dutch, but they view Australian English as a slightly different form of their own language; Dutch and English are therefore spoken of as languages, American English and Australian English as dialects.

Patterned on the term *dialect,* the term **idiolect** has been introduced to refer to the language of an individual. A highly limited study may therefore be restricted to the description of one idiolect.

When the term *dialect* is applied historically, the meaning is extended to related languages that are no longer mutually intelligible; for example, German, Swedish, Dutch, and English are all said to be Germanic dialects. From this designation it may be inferred that at one time the earlier forms of these languages could be understood by people speaking any of them; in the fifth century speakers of Old English dialects could have understood the dialects spoken in north Germany.

In discussing dialects, linguists have applied the techniques and terminology of geographers. Differences in the dialects of different regions are plotted on maps, which are assembled in atlases. A **dialect atlas** may be produced to chart the variations in speech among the members of a particular country, such as France. Differences on maps are indicated by conventions used to indicate differences on weather maps, on which isotherms indicate the boundaries of given temperatures. To represent linguistic units the term **gloss** is used (based on Greek *glōssa* 'word'), and **isoglosses,** which depict the boundaries within which items are attested, are determined. Any linguistic characteristic may be mapped with isoglosses. For example, settlement movements in the United States brought about the use of the pronunciation [gríysiy] for *greasy* roughly north of the fortieth parallel, [gríyziy] south of it. Therefore, an important isogloss of American English runs east and west across northern Indiana and Illinois. When a bundle of isoglosses is found, it indicates a dialect boundary.

## 14.3  Dialects as Reflections of Social Groups

Areal dialects reflect dialect groupings. Long-settled countries, such as England, Germany, Italy, and France, especially those in which communication over large areas was once restricted, may have many dialects. Scotsmen or Yorkshiremen speak quite different types of English from those spoken in Cornwall or Kent.

In areas with many mutually unintelligible languages, such as Melanesia, a common means of communication may be found in a simplified form of one language. In Melanesia this language is English. Such simplified languages, not spoken natively by anyone, are called **pidgins.** When a pidgin is adopted so widely that it becomes the native language of many speakers, as in Haiti, it is called a **Creole.** Haitian Creole is based on French, Jamaican Creole on English.

Other distinct social groups develop various specialized forms of languages. University students have developed their own varieties of language, especially for situations of direct concern to them. An easy course may be called a *snap;* to do well in an examination may be to *ace* it. These varieties of language are as restricted as geographic dialects, though they are limited by other parameters, such as vocation and age. The term **register** is occasionally applied to varieties of language determined by use, in contrast with dialect, which is related to the user.

Rapidly changing varieties of language are often referred to as **slang.** In contemporary civilization slang is especially favored by young people. Teen-agers select terms and appropriate them for their own generation. What may be *good* on one occasion is *hot* on another, *cool* on still another, or *tough,* and so on. Much of slang is rapidly replaced, as a perusal of a dictionary of slang or literary works of the past that drew heavily on slang will prove. Besides introducing novelty, slang provides its users with a feeling of exclusiveness. If teen-agers can communicate by means hidden to others, they seem to gain assurance. Other social groups may seek assurance for their own ends. Thieves, gamblers, and others of the demimonde cherish dialects partly unintelligible to outsiders. These are often known as **cant** or **argot.**

Social groups who wish to be set apart for still other reasons may also cultivate a dialect of their own. In societies having class distinctions, one dialect may be favored by the nobility, in contrast with the dialects used more generally. In England, for example, the nobility and its imitators favor "U" (from *upper class*), others "non-U." Such distinctions may be very great in classes that seek a separate status. Religious groups, for example, often preserve an ancient form of speech, such as Latin in the Western church, Old Church Slavic in the Eastern church, and Sanskrit used by the Brahmans in India. When an elevated form of language exists side by side with the spoken language and is reserved for special uses, the situation is referred to as a **diglossia.**

The variations of language to be found among different groups or in differing situations may be highly complex and differ considerably from culture to culture and from time to time. Advertising language is obviously a recent development, but it is a dialect of its own in much the same way that thieves' language was during the Elizabethan period. And special conventions may be observed in other new activities of modern times, such as telephoning. New social situations seem to encourage new dialects. Speakers seeking versatility in language attempt to master these varieties of language and to use them as appropriately as possible.

## 14.4  Dialect Switching

Moving from one variety of language to another is known as **dialect switching.** Facility in dialect switching may be a matter of talent or choice. Anyone who uses his speech to make a living usually becomes highly adept at switching. A successful insurance broker, for example, would not use the same language when speaking to a laborer that he uses when speaking to an industrialist. Politicians are especially careful of the varieties of language they use.

All speakers of a language develop some control over its varieties. Such varieties, selected in accordance with social or intellectual contexts, are often referred to as **styles.**

Martin Joos proposed five stylistic varieties of American English: intimate, casual, consultative, formal, and frozen. Casual style is characterized by ellipses and the use of slang. Its designation suggests its sphere of use. *Think you blew it?* for example, is elliptical for 'Do you think that' and uses student slang for 'fail an examination.' Obviously it would be used by members of one social group speaking casually to others of that group. The ellipses would not occur in the consultative style, so named by Joos because the addressee is expected to participate constantly with expressions like *I see, Yes,* and so on. In this style, as possibly used by an adviser to a student, the previous statement might be phrased *Do you think that you failed the examination?* The intimate style, on the other hand, is used by members of a very small social group, such as a family, in which much of the normal component of language may be missing. Its purest form may be displayed at breakfast in many families.

The formal style is characterized by deliberateness. Speakers using it select *may,* as in *May I see that slide again?* rather than [kən]. Their pronunciation is careful, as are their syntax and use of words. Moreover, their text is often well planned and presented, and hesitation pauses are avoided. Frozen style, even more stereotyped, is so carefully composed that it may be understood from its written form alone. While intonation is for Joos an essential component of the formal style, the frozen style need rely only on a written text in conventional orthography.

Other students of style have proposed different classifications. Joos's has the advantage of presenting readily observable criteria for each style proposed.

In other cultures and in other languages the varieties of style are deter-mined by different criteria. In Japanese, for example, styles are chosen according to the status of the person addressed and the status of the ob-ject referred to. The copula provides one marker. In deferential speech *de gozaimasu* 'is' is used; *de arimasu* is polite and *de aru* factual. If one speaks respectfully of an object, *de irassharu* is used, as opposed to the neutral *desu* or *da*. Moreover, different lexical items are used, such as the humble *haha* versus the polite *okāsan* 'mother.' The use of styles in Japanese is intimately connected with the use of pronouns, so that the system is exceedingly complex.

Any stylistic framework may be used ironically as well as straight-forwardly. Whether the system is as complex as the Japanese or as relatively simple as the English, the result is a fine challenge to the skills of a sociolinguist. If an understanding of the various styles in language is difficult to achieve, the interpretation of their uses by various speakers of a language may be even more difficult to determine. Because of such in-tricacies, many second-language learners often use styles inap-propriately.

## 14.5  Social Dialects

Recent study has been greatly concerned with social dialects. In the modern world communication has not been hampered by geographical isolation, as it was several centuries and more ago when many speech communities were broken up and isolated by difficulties in com-munication. This is essentially the process by which major dialects, and subsequently their independent languages known as the Romance languages, developed in the Roman Empire. When the administrative structure broke down so that there was no longer ready communication between Paris and Rome, French came to be distinct from Italian. In the same way Spanish, Portuguese, Rumanian, and the other Romance languages developed.

Recently difficulties in communication have been determined much more by social groupings. The impoverished residents of cities have tended to form their own social groups, and as a result they have devel-oped special forms of language. Among these are Black English, Chicano English, and similar variants of other languages. Attempts have been made to describe these languages, to account for their impact on society and for their origin, and also to reduce some of the problems in com-munication caused by their existence. Such efforts have often been related to attempts to deal with bilingualism, to which our school system is devoting a great deal of attention.

In studying social dialects linguists have adopted procedures used by sociolinguists and other investigators in the behavioral sciences. When they carry out investigations of the speech used by individuals or by social groups, they concentrate on variables identified in previous linguistic study. A **linguistic variable** is any feature of a language that is represented in differing forms in the speech of one person or a social group. In English, for example, the pronunciation of *r* is a linguistic variable. It may be represented as a slight fricative, for example, *curl* [kərl]; as an elongation of the preceding vowel, [kə:l]; as a palatal glide, [kəⁱl]; and so on. A given speaker of English may use one of these variant pronunciations, or more than one.

The incidence of a particular linguistic variable may correlate with the context in which it is used. Another phonological variable in English is the pronunciation of final dental stops, as in *child, waste,* and so on. These may vary in pronunciation by including the stop, [čayld] [weyst], or omitting it, [čayl] [weys]. In their study of the occurrence of these variables, investigators have found that the dental stop is most commonly omitted after resonants and before obstruents, as in *childbirth;* and next most commonly after obstruents and before obstruents, as in *wastebasket.* Before vowels the proportion of omissions is considerably lower, as in *child author,* and lowest after obstruents, as in *waste of time.* The condition or conditions regulating such occurrences are known as **constraints.**

Investigators of the use of linguistic variables have also found that their incidence correlates with social variables. Examples of social variables are age, ethnic grouping, regional grouping, sex, social caste or status, and style. The use of various forms of *r,* for example, correlates with regional groups in English: in standard British English "*r*-less" forms are used; in much of American English a slight fricative and, in some areas, a palatal offglide are used instead. These variables may come to be associated not only with social variables but are also evaluated for prestige. Thus the *r*-less forms of English carry high prestige; many speakers ascribe superior status to users of the Queen's English. On the other hand, the palatal offglide variable has the lowest prestige. It is commonly associated with the lower-class speech of New York City, in the popular view with Brooklynese. When negative evaluations are associated with specific social variables, such as ethnic groupings, they may give rise to severe social problems.

Sociolinguists are now carrying on detailed studies to determine such linguistic variables and the constraints on them, as well as the evaluations made by the speakers of a language. These studies, especially the investigations of William Labov, have already yielded findings important to our understanding of language. They indicate that the speakers of a language have remarkable control and understanding of such variables.

Speakers not only identify variable rules, but they also know the bases for the operation of a given rule, such as the phonological context of dental stops in English. Moreover, they also know the hierarchy in application of the rules, such as the greater use of dental stops before vowels in contrast with the position before consonants. Speakers thus know intuitively that the pronunciation [weys] occurs much more frequently in *wastebasket* than in *waste of time.* In accordance with these conclusions, the control by speakers of their language, that is, their competence, applies not only to the basic grammatical, lexical, and phonological rules of the language but also to variants of such rules. As a result, an accurate and adequate grammar will be far more extensive than the relatively simple grammars produced in accordance with descriptive techniques, whether produced in accordance with transformational linguistic theory or some other theory.

Besides contributing a deeper understanding of a speaker's knowledge of his or her language, sociolinguistic investigators have shown that social and linguistic variables are intricately interrelated. For example, in studying the speech of blacks in Detroit, Walt Wolfram found that social class correlated with the frequency of application of stigmatized forms: the lower classes tended to use the less prestigious forms more often (see Chart 1).

**Chart 1. Interaction of Social Class with Three Stigmatized Rules in Detroit Black Speech**

| Social classes | [f] from [θ] | omission of [r] | omission of final stop |
| --- | --- | --- | --- |
| Upper middle | .06 | .21 | .51 |
| Lower middle | .11 | .39 | .66 |
| Upper working | .38 | .61 | .79 |
| Lower working | .45 | .71 | .84 |

From Walt Wolfram and Ralph W. Fasold, *The Study of Social Dialects in American English* (Englewood Cliffs, N.J.: Prentice-Hall, 1974), p. 114. Reprinted by permission.

The results of such findings are referred to as **implicational arrays** or as **implicational patterning** because the identification of one variable, such as [f] from [θ], implies much about the frequencies of use of the other variables. The finding that a particular speaker substituted [f] for [θ] in words like *both* in 11 percent of all occurrences permits one to infer that he will also omit [r] 39 percent of the time and the final stop in words like *child* 66 percent of the time. Such arrays illustrate the intricate mastery of a language by its speakers.

It is noteworthy that when the evaluations attached to certain uses such as 'chile' [čayl] for *child* and [weys] for *waste* are used to stigmatize certain speech as sloppy, the evaluation must be based on percentages, not on the consistent application of such a rule or the complete lack of such a rule. All speakers of English omit the stop in words like *child* in certain circumstances. But upper-class speakers use such pronunciations less frequently than do stigmatized lower-class speakers.

Such findings are of use both in devising ways to overcome stigmatization based on language and in bringing about modification of stigmatized forms. Detailed sociolinguistic study is still so new that practical applications are experimental. It is hoped, however, that improved understanding of the variation in the language of all speakers will help teachers and social workers in their evaluation of stigmatized speech patterns and lead to greater flexibility in the treatment of them.

Attitudes toward variant forms of language still vary greatly, as do the consequences of the use of such variables. It is held by some that children who use Black English or Chicano English are hampered in their educational careers and even become discouraged from pursuing their studies. Others believe that the discouragement results because of harsh criticism by teachers of students who use stigmatized speech patterns, which then leads to discouragement and dropping out. This second position seems more realistic than the first. Yet much study is still needed before the problem can be solved.

Another conclusion that formerly had some support equated the use of such forms of language with deficits. Their speakers were supposed to have inadequate forms of communication and possibly even an inability to overcome such deficits. This view has now been generally abandoned. Linguists hope instead that teachers, students, and the general public will recognize that social dialects exist in all languages.

The esteem in which such dialects are held has little to do with their usefulness as means of communication. Lower-class speakers communicate as effectively among themselves as do upper-class speakers. However, in view of social prejudices, speakers of stigmatized dialects may wish to reserve them for situations in which they are not met with disapproval and master the standard language of their social group or nation for general communication.

## 14.6  The Ethnography of Communication

A topic of increasing interest deals with the social and cultural situations in which language is used. When, for example, do people tell riddles or listen to oral epics? When and under what circumstances do children repeat poems, as in skipping or playing various games? What kinds of games do adults play with language, and what is their attitude toward such games—for example, puns? These and numerous other topics are being studied in the context of ethnographical study, giving rise to an approach known as the **ethnography of communication.**

Such studies are not merely limited to eras of the past or to exotic cultures. Our own culture provides fascinating opportunities for study. An example is an interview situation. What is the framework of a request for a job or an attempt to have a grievance resolved? If, for example, a person believes that her bill for electricity is too high or her tax bill unjust, what kind of language does she use in making her appeal? And what is the language of the response? Little specific study has been made and published about such everyday uses of language.

Another situation that bears exploring is the manner of communication on the telephone. Whether by self-examination or by overhearing someone else speaking on the phone, we can easily recognize differences between telephone language and face-to-face conversation. But the precise conventions have not been described. When someone picks up a phone in the midst of a heated conversation, the emotions are "turned off" and the answer is friendly or at least placid. Such "switches" in manner of communication are curious. It is equally curious to note their representation in literary works.

The situations in which language is used are manifold and generally taken for granted. Everyone has used some form of pig Latin as a child but probably has forgotten the rules or the situation in which pig Latin seemed appropriate. All such situations, however, provide interesting topics for investigation. Similarly, what are the patterns of politeness in our society? Or in another society, even related societies like those of Europe? When we observe the Chinese, we may be surprised at their apparent lack of patterns of politeness, their avoidance of greetings even when meeting or leaving friends. Many such situations remain to be described. The field of the ethnography of communication has scarcely been opened.

## 14.7   Differences of Attitudes Toward Varieties of Language

In attempting to determine the attitudes of speakers toward the dialects or styles of their language, a linguist must attempt to be objective. This objectivity may cause problems, because any statement about language arouses the interest of some users. Reactions vary with cultures and at different times. Few Westerners will bridle if Latin is called a "dead language," implying that it is an acquired language and not the first language of any speakers, but if this term is applied to Classical Arabic in a Muslim country, it may not be received with equanimity. Almost any statement about varieties of language is perilous. Because of their very objectivity, linguists are often accused of permissiveness about variations in language. Yet the accusation is unjust, for some linguists cultivate the formal and frozen styles as assiduously as do specialists in other areas. Professionalism in linguistics requires a neutral attitude toward all forms of language.

Attitudes toward language vary with the social views of individuals and of a society. New nations often wish to oust all nonnative elements from their language, as Turkey attempted to do in the 1920s and Germany in the nineteenth century. The same attitude may be found among ancient nations, such as Iceland, the oldest continuous democracy in the world, which attempts to use only native elements, even for all contemporary terms of civilization.

At some periods literary figures may insist on a frozen style, as did many English and American writers in the Victorian period. At other times different styles are preferred. Currently, for example, some publications even use the intimate style.

Rising social classes foster conservatism in language. The middle and lower classes who attempted to penetrate the upper classes of England in the late eighteenth century and those of England and America in the nineteenth century were largely responsible for the notion of correctness in these two cultures. Before they could achieve equality with the members of the upper classes, it was necessary to speak like upper-class people. George Bernard Shaw dealt brilliantly with the problem in *Pygmalion;* the success of the musical comedy version, *My Fair Lady,* provides ample evidence that the situation is not foreign to contemporary audiences.

While the pressure of social groups is informal, some governments or official groups attempt to regulate languages formally. The French Academy was founded to guard the French language. Similar organizations exist in many other countries, such as Canada, Belgium, the People's Republic of China, Indonesia, India, Pakistan, Turkey, and Israel. In Norway the language problems of the country are among its most important political questions. Toward the end of the nineteenth century the linguistic situation in Norway was complicated through parliamentary edicts, when the language of the west and other country areas, Landsmaal or Nynorsk, was adopted as the national language on a plane with the earlier norm, Riksmaal. As a result, a small country of approximately 4 million inhabitants is faced with the problem of teaching each child two languages, neither of which is a world language that would assist Norwegians in contacts with other countries. Today the Norwegian Parliament is passing successive edicts to merge the two languages.

The Norwegian Parliament has had some success in its aims to modify language, but in general the effects of regulatory agencies, such as academies, have been minor. The development of "Franglais," French peppered with English importations, hardly speaks for the total success of the French Academy. Apparently the attitudes of speakers are as difficult to control by linguistic regulations as their drinking habits or their customs of dress or other social behavior. Until sociolinguists acquire more information about these attitudes and their effects, it will be difficult to make precise statements about the results of varying attitudes toward language.

Attitudes toward language are not constant among all members of a society. Some speakers prefer a solemn form of speech, especially from public figures; others object to solemn, professorial language or what is called a "pulpit tone." Formerly editors of journals of opinion in this country insisted on the use of certain words, such as the editorial *we,* and on the avoidance of others, such as the well-known four-letter Anglo-Saxon component of the language. Now these journals seem to have reversed their views on both scores, permitting words to be printed that were formerly avoided in most conversation and are still forbidden in print in many contemporary publications.

Rigid avoidance of particular terms in certain circumstances is known as **taboo.** In our culture taboos exist for bathroom terms, for terms referring to the divinity, and for terms referring to death and unpleasant diseases. Although attitudes have changed, most obituaries still use circumlocutions rather than state that the deceased died of cancer. Other societies permit the use of normal words for natural events, but they may maintain other taboos; children, for example, may not be given the name of a parent if that parent is still alive.

Just as some portions of language are taboo, so others may be considered amusing—such are the London cockney dialect and Brooklynese. Yet the [əi] for [ər], as in *girl,* which is considered one of the amusing features of Brooklynese, is also found in New Orleans and other parts of the South, where such speech is not ridiculed. There are also stock attitudes toward specific languages. German is commonly referred to as guttural, possibly because of the palato-velar fricatives in *ich* and *ach* and the uvular [ʀ]; actually there are no throat sounds in the language. British English, especially the Queen's English, formerly held the highest prestige wherever attention was paid to English, but the position of honor seems to have shifted to some popular singers from among the non-U speakers of Liverpool or to similarly uncultivated forms of American English. The prestige of these types of language has resulted purely from nonlinguistic social situations.

## 14.8 Language Engineering

Specific attempts to modify languages are often referred to as **language engineering.** An excellent example is Modern Hebrew. Primarily a written language for about two thousand years, Hebrew was introduced as a spoken language around the turn of the century. In this process many innovations had to be made, especially in Hebrew vocabulary. The entire stock of words for items of contemporary civilization had to be produced. Since the procedures are well documented, Hebrew provides a convenient illustration of language engineering. It may also set something of a pattern for emerging nations that wish to engineer a national tongue. Many of these nations are multilingual, for example, India, Indonesia, and the countries of Africa. They may select a widely spoken language—Hindi, Malay, Swahili—as their national language. When they do, besides the steps necessary to assure adequate expansion of these languages to cope with contemporary civilization, the attitude of many citizens toward them is of great social interest. Many citizens of these new nations prefer a language spoken by their local group or even one of the "languages of civilization," such as English or French. As a result of these differing language preferences, bitter disputes may arise.

Another notable example of language engineering is to be found in the People's Republic of China. To permit communication among its citizens the government is promoting a "common language," **Putonghua.** Based on the phonology of Peking speech and the syntax and vocabulary of recent literary and technical materials, Putonghua is taught throughout the country. In this way the eight or more Chinese languages are being replaced as major vehicles of communication, and the 50 million non-Chinese speakers are being taught the national language. Preliminary indications suggest that the effort has been highly successful.

In addition, efforts are being made to introduce a writing system based on the Latin alphabet, **pinyin.** The exclusive use of such an alphabetic system, with the phasing out of the character system, will be possible only when Putonghua is generally used. For if each of the eight Chinese languages were written in a form of romanization, such materials would be interpretable only by speakers of that language. The Chinese character system can be interpreted variously, in much the way our numerals are interpreted by speakers of English, German, Russian, and many other languages. If, then, the Chinese character system were abruptly abandoned, major difficulties with communication would arise in China. Accordingly, the efforts in language engineering are being carefully planned and are to be carried out in long, slow stages.

To meet some of the problems of communication across nations, artificial languages have been devised, such as Esperanto and Interlingua. These languages are supposed to facilitate communication across language boundaries because many surface difficulties of natural languages have been eliminated from them. But their vocabulary, grammar, and phonology are largely based on European languages, particularly the Romance group. Little effort has been made to remove difficulties for other speakers, such as the problems caused by maintaining r and l. Since the presence of r and l causes problems for native speakers of Chinese, who substitute l for initial r, and for the Japanese, who substitute r for l—that is, problems are caused for virtually one out of every three people alive today—international languages have been successful primarily among idealists more concerned than informed about ways of removing international barriers to mass communication. In time international languages may be more adequately designed to provide easier acquisition by a variety of speakers. If such designs can be achieved, they will aid considerably in assuring broad, or mass, communication.

But even imperfect forms of mass communication have been highly successful. One example is the bending of public attitudes through the clever selection of language characteristics, such as George Eastman's ingenious coinage *Kodak.* Noting that *k* is not used before *a o u* in English orthography, Eastman devised an unusual term for his camera and achieved an unusual fortune. He also achieved for *k* a magical value in mass communication, even when placed before letters other than *a o u,* as the developers of Kleenex and Kix may testify. Today, however, the letter *x* may have surpassed *k* in producing corporate revenues, as a glance at the price of Xerox stocks indicates. On the other hand, many speakers resist slick mass communication devices. When sociolinguists understand better which devices are effective and which are not, they may share the acclaim given a George Gallup and others who supposedly measure the pulse of the masses.

Besides language itself, accompaniments of speech are important to success in communication. Among these accompaniments are gestures and the distances observed between speakers. Latin Americans communicate most comfortably at distances closer than those favored in the United States. If United States businessmen attempt to sell their wares to Latin Americans by promoting them at the distance normally preferred in the United States, their success is often limited. Study of these and other peripheral processes in communication is being pursued by many scholars and has already given rise to special branches of investigation. The study of attention to space paid by speakers is referred to as **proxemics;** the study of the use of body position and movements in speaking is referred to as **kinesics;** and the study of the use of extralinguistic sounds, like hesitation pauses, is known as **paralinguistics.**

Often highly amusing, such studies provide excellent insights into the favored means of communication in a culture. To note the American preference for maintaining a suitable distance, you need only observe a couple of students blocking a hallway in an attempt to maintain the proper decorum toward each other. For a fascinating study in kinesics you may spend a few minutes watching an Italian gesticulate to an unseen conversationalist on a telephone. Paralinguistic observations may be made on many occasions, as for example, when one listens to a speech by a hesitant or not very competent speaker or, in a more positive vein, to the gentle cooing used to a baby.

When sociolinguistic study may be carried on with no practical ends in view, the findings of sociolinguists have considerable significance for the welfare of social groups. Societies cooperate best when they have a common language. If, for example, a set of speakers in a culture is handicapped by using an inadequate form of language, as may happen in ghettos, the society may pay a heavy price for the group's unfortunate isolation. Sociolinguists can determine the linguistic inadequacies of a social group and possibly even suggest correctives. But the applications of their discoveries, as of other linguistic investigations, are generally left to specialists who have come to be known as **applied linguists.**

## BIBLIOGRAPHICAL NOTES

The number of publications in sociolinguistics is overwhelming. Among the most informative, partly because of the realistic views of its author and his capabilities in presenting them, is *Mankind, Nation and the Individual* by Otto Jespersen, first published in Great Britain in 1946 (Bloomington: Indiana University Press, 1964). *Dialects of American English* by Carroll E. Reed (Cleveland and New York: World Publishing, 1967) is an informative and clear book on geographical dialects. *The Five Clocks* by Martin Joos (Bloomington: Indiana University Press, 1962) presents the terms for English styles included here. *The Silent Language* by Edward T. Hall (Garden City, N.Y.: Doubleday, 1959) is an excellent and amusing introduction to paralinguistics. *English in Advertising: A Linguistic Study of Advertising in Great Britain* by Geoffrey N. Leech (London: Longmans, Green, 1966) gives a fine perspective on advertising language. As in any new area, readers provide useful introductions to sociolinguistics as a field. Among these are Alfred G. Smith, ed., *Communication and Culture* (New York: Holt, Rinehart and Winston, 1966); Dell Hymes, ed., *Language in Culture and Society* (New York: Harper & Row, 1964); and Joshua A. Fishman, ed., *Readings in the Sociology of Language* (The Hague: Mouton, 1968). Many of the topics discussed in these readers are now being treated individually. See, for example, Joshua A. Fishman, Charles A. Ferguson, and Jyotirindra Dasgupta, eds., *Language Problems of Developing Nations* (New York: Wiley, 1968). Major works in sociolinguistics have been produced by William Labov, notably his book *The Social Stratification of English in New York City* (Washington, D.C.: Center for Applied Linguistics, 1966); *Language in the Inner City: Studies in the Black English Vernacular* (Philadelphia: University of Pennsylvania Press, 1972); and *Sociolinguistic Patterns* (Philadelphia: University of Pennsylvania Press, 1972). For a recent general work see *The Study of Social Dialects in American English* by Walt Wolfram and Ralph W. Fasold (Englewood Cliffs, N.J.: Prentice-Hall, 1974).

## QUESTIONS FOR REVIEW

1. Discuss the aims of sociolinguistic study.
2. What is meant by *dialects? by idiolects?* How are they presented in linguistic works? Define *isogloss*.
3. Discuss the reasons for dialects in language. What is a pidgin? a Creole? Discuss the differences between dialects and registers.
4. Define *slang*. Distinguish between slang and dialects; between slang and argot.
5. What is *diglossia?* Give some examples.
6. Discuss dialect switching. Distinguish between styles in language and dialects. How can differences in style be used in ways corresponding to different pronouns, for example, in Japanese?

7. Some societies favor certain patterns of language at certain periods, such as the preference for native elements rather than borrowed words in Iceland. What is the reason for such preferences? Is there any relation between such an attitude and the objections to English elements in French, as indicated by the derogatory term *Franglais* applied by some speakers to some forms of modern French?

8. What kinds of social situations foster conservatism in language? Can you suggest reasons for the preference for the absence of a contrasted negative in the first person of BE (*isn't* and *aren't* are regularly used but *ain't* is frowned upon)?

9. For some time certain groups in this country tried to simplify English by substituting spellings like *thru* for *through* and *tho* for *though*. These efforts have been abandoned. Suggest reasons for the attempt and for its failure.

10. What is meant by *taboo?* Where do many speakers of English apply taboo? Why has the attitude toward some of these tabooed words changed?

11. State some aims of language engineering. Is it ever successful?

12. Why is *k* commonly used in English advertising terms?

13. What is meant by *proxemics?* by *kinesics?* by *paralinguistics?* Where would you expect to find greater use of gestures, in Italy or the United States?

## EXERCISES

### EXERCISE 1

Though it is useful to collect and study dialect material, it is also difficult, partly because the distinctive traits of dialects must first be known before one can secure adequate data. For this reason a well-prepared collection is very important. One such collection is the record "Americans Speaking," a recording of speakers from six dialect areas in the United States produced by John T. Muri and Raven I. McDavid. If you can obtain the recording, study some of the differences found in American dialects. The record is available from the National Council of Teachers of English, 508 South Sixth Street, Champaign, Illinois 61820. A pamphlet has been prepared to accompany the record.

### EXERCISE 2

A good exercise in sociolinguistics is determining your own language expressions. There have been several studies of university slang, such as that by Alan Dundes and Manuel R. Schonhorn.[1] In assembling their

---

[1] Alan Dundes and Manuel R. Schonhorn, "Kansas University Slang: A New Generation," *American Speech* 38 (1963): 163–177.

data, Dundes and Schonhorn gathered slang expressions for the following items. Note your own terms for these items and compare them with those of your friends, other English speakers, or those of the students at Kansas University.

1. to study extremely diligently for an examination
2. an easy college course
3. a difficult college course
4. to miss class
5. an unexpected examination
6. to cheat during an examination
7. to fail to pass an examination
8. a student who achieves a high grade on a low-scored examination, thus upsetting the class average
9. to acquit oneself creditably in an examination
10. an extremely poor and dull lecturer
11. to go alone to a dance or social function
12. to take one's partner from him or her in the middle of a dance
13. one who puts a damper on a party
14. a particularly rough and noisy party
15. a poor social evening, a wasted night
16. to get away from an unpleasant or undesirable person
17. what a person who has special influences is said to have
18. an unpleasant male date
19. a very pretty female date
20. drunk

## EXERCISE 3

Newspapers occasionally comment on language and provide information about it. In a widely syndicated column the following answer was given to the question "Is there a real word, spelled Ugh?": "Yes, it is a real Indian word. In fact, 'Ugh'—meaning to grunt—is one of the few sounds that is common to all languages. A change of inflection when saying 'Ugh' can give it any number of meanings—depending upon the speaker, and the occasion."

Discuss the information provided in this answer. For example, what "sound" can the writer have had in mind? If you were asked the same question, what would you answer?

## EXERCISE 4

In George Eliot's novel *Middlemarch,* Fred Vincy, back from the university, and his sister Rosamund have the following discussion concerning language:

[F.] Oh, there are so many superior teas and sugars now. Superior is getting to be shopkeepers' slang.

[R.] Are you beginning to dislike slang, then? . . .

[F.] Only the wrong sort. All choice of words is slang. It marks a class.

[R.] There is correct English: that is not slang.

[F.] I beg your pardon: correct English is the slang of prigs who write history and essays. And the strongest slang of all is the slang of poets.

[R.] You will say anything, Fred, to gain your point.

[F.] Well, tell me whether it is slang or poetry to call an ox a *legplaiter*.

[R.] Of course you can call it poetry if you like.

[F.] Aha, Miss Rosy, you don't know Homer from slang. I shall invent a new game; I shall write bits of slang and poetry on slips, and give them to you to separate.[2]

Discuss Fred's comments on slang, correct English, and the language of poetry. If you had to counter his statements, what would you say to his identification of these three forms of language as slang? What criteria would you propose for distinguishing various kinds of language?

EXERCISE 5

It is often said that nonnative speakers of English would be assisted greatly in their attempts to learn the language if English spelling were more "phonetic." Discuss some of the problems involved in the devising of a "phonetic spelling." Whose pronunciation would you accept as standard: that of the Queen of England or the President of the United States? If you select the latter, which President's pronunciation would you choose?

What consequences would a revision of English spelling entail? What effect would it have on extant books? Would Shakespeare still be read?[3]

How long could a revised phonetic spelling be maintained? What would you suggest for American speakers who change *t* to *d* in such words as *butter, bottle,* and *bottom?* How about the Southern speakers who make no distinction between the pronunciation of [i] and [e] before [n] as in *pen, pin?* What device would you employ so that British English speakers who "drop their *r*'s" would still be able to use the same spelling as Americans for words like *fare, far, for, fur, fire?*

---

[2] George Eliot, *Middlemarch* (New York: James Clarke, 1871–1872), pp. 102–103.

[3] In answering this question, you may wish to consult texts printed in Shakespeare's time. A convenient and elegant source is the *Norton Facsimile of the First Folio Shakespeare* prepared by Charles Hinman (New York: Norton, 1968).

# APPLIED LINGUISTICS:
## The Study of Language and Literature

CHAPTER 15

## 15.1 Applications of Linguistics

If linguists have not been widely involved in language engineering, they are concerning themselves increasingly with other applications of linguistics. Possibly the most widespread application concerns the teaching of languages, foreign as well as native. Another involves attempts to manipulate language by means of computers. A third is the production of dictionaries. Lexicography involves the close study of texts. Such study is also directed to literary texts, particularly the special manipulation of language in literature. These concerns, with the exception of the last, are commonly referred to as **applied linguistics.** As in any application, various disciplines are involved. We will deal briefly with the contributions of linguistics to each of the aforementioned, noting that linguistics merely makes a partial contribution to these applications, for they draw heavily from other specialties as well.

## 15.2 Linguistics and the Teaching of Native Languages

One of the problems in native language teaching is selection of the style to be taught and the dialect. After a selection has been made, the linguist should provide as complete a description as possible of its characteristics. These problems had not received much attention until recently because certain dialects had been selected as standard: for English the "King's English" or the "Queen's English," with adjustments in pronunciation in the United States and other areas outside England; for French Parisian French; for Japanese Tokyo Japanese; for German the stage pronunciation; and so on. But as societies have become more complex and more concerned with the education of every member, the selection of restricted dialects has brought about problems.

Possibly the greatest problems result from the difficulties caused when the selected dialect is taught to classes made up both of children who already know the dialect and of others who speak a different dialect, as in teaching classes of children to read. These problems have existed for some time in European countries; they have recently begun to receive attention in the United States. In the United States language texts had been based on the dialect of the upper middle class. The *Dick and Jane* stories were supposed to provide a simple means of teaching children to read, starting from the children's own experience and leading them to more complex patterns of language and thought. This aim may succeed with children from upper-middle-class homes. But when children from "disadvantaged" groups are given the same textbooks, they face totally different problems. The speech of many of them is different in surface grammar. For example, they often omit the copula in conversational everyday utterances, saying *He (is) good*. They may also have differences in vocabulary. Whatever the details, problems of this sort require learning and teaching techniques different from those used for many less disadvantaged children. In effect the disadvantaged are faced with two problems: learning a new dialect and learning to read. The double requirements can scarcely fail to make them drop behind their classmates, who only face the problem of learning to read.

These problems may be amplified by poorly trained teachers who repress children when they use their own dialects in informal conversations. If, for example, such children in their excitement discuss their schoolwork in their nonstandard language and their teacher upbraids them, the children may begin to feel that they cannot speak adequately in school. They may then refuse to participate in such activities as reading and ultimately lose total interest in schoolwork. Many problems, then, are caused by attitudes toward language as well as by differences between dialects.

The answers to these problems are complex and far beyond the scope of linguistics. Some visionaries suggest, for example, that computer-aided instruction may solve the problem by providing means of instructing each individual separately in accordance with his or her special difficulties. Whatever the solution, linguists can determine the language differences at the bottom of the difficulties.

The theoretical bases for such linguistic undertakings have long been provided. We know that each separate social group tends to develop individual characteristics, whether the group is as small as the family—which may maintain a few favorite expressions—or is a compact rural community or a ghetto. Linguists can determine the characteristics of any such groups. They can then contrast the restricted dialects with the dialect chosen as standard and point out where difficulties in learning may arise. Other specialists can apply this information to actual learning and teaching techniques.

Although language teaching requires many types of knowledge, applications of sound linguistic practice are among the latest to be incorporated. It was pointed out long ago that learning to read involves relating written symbols to oral symbols. Most children, with a few possible exceptions, have already mastered the oral symbols when they enter school; they may, for example, have difficulty with a few sounds like [l r]. In learning to read, their problem is to relate certain standard graphic shapes to oral symbols.

Such relationships can be conveyed most effectively if the graphic shapes are strictly limited. The initial readings can be so designed that each shape corresponds to only one oral symbol. If, for example, one of these selections uses the word *cat,* each of the three shapes making up *cat* will be used with the values [k æ t] in other portions of the text. Accordingly, words like *Dick* (with its silent *c*) and *Jane* (with [ey] for *a*) would be postponed until further configurations were introduced. Among these further configurations would be the effect of final *e.* After children have mastered the reading of selected English patterns, the modifications caused by final *e,* as in *mile, Eve, Jane, note,* and *rule,* can be presented. But initially only highly selected patterns are used. The resultant texts are restricted and carefully graded.

An alternate possibility for simplifying the teaching of reading is the introduction of separate symbols for each phoneme. This procedure, often highly acclaimed today, may readily be followed, but it leads to difficulties. Among these is the need to learn special symbols that must later be abandoned. Moreover, the "phonemic system" of English may differ from speaker to speaker; consequently, some children will be forced to learn in part a new dialect when they are taught to read.

The basic problem in learning to read is caused by the structure of language. Phonological patterns may differ from those in morphology or syntax, as a simple example like English $\{Z_1\}$ illustrates with its three principal variants [əz s z], as in *horses, cats,* and *dogs.* The spelling *s* in these three words corresponds nicely with the single plural suffix, though not with its three representatives in the phonological system. To the extent that phonological and morphological patterns differ in any language, awkward orthographic problems arise, complicating the problems in teaching speakers to read.

Some spelling systems agree relatively well with phonological patterns, such as those of Spanish and Lithuanian. Others agree with the morphological and syntactic patterns. English has such a system. Chinese is an extreme example, for each symbol corresponds to a morpheme.

The consequences of the lack of close relationship between spelling and pronunciation do not require lengthy discussion. When we learn a new language, we prefer to have the spelling system correspond to the phonological system; Spanish is generally cited as an "easy" language for this reason. If, however, a spelling system is to serve for speakers of various dialects, such as American, Australian, British, and other varieties of English, a morphologically based system is preferable. The Chinese system, used for eight distinct Chinese languages, each with various dialects, as well as for Japanese, provides an excellent example of the advantages of a morphologically based writing system. In Chinese culture the writing system, not the spoken language, is the unifying force.

As long as society finds a writing system useful, problems in learning to read or in mass communication will result. Linguistic study can disclose the source of the problems. Application of its findings depends, however, on the decisions made by many different people, printers, educators, and those concerned with mass communication, such as government officials. The extent of the problem may be understood when we recall that although George Bernard Shaw left the principal part of his estate for "reforming" the English spelling system, no such solution has ever been found.

---

## 15.3  Linguistics and the Teaching of Foreign Languages

With the increase in world communication, the teaching of foreign languages has become increasingly important and is widely discussed. Special attention is given in this country to "TESL," the teaching of English as a second language. The introduction of the acronym for this pursuit indicates the intense concern with it.

This concern has led to a specialization known as **contrastive grammar.** In contrastive grammar the descriptions of two languages are compared—the so-called **source** language and the **target** language. Difficulties arising from differences in the two systems are pointed out, and methods of overcoming these difficulties are suggested.

Most of the difficulties treated at any length in contrastive grammars are major. A contrastive grammar for German, for example, may only mention the difference between English alveolar [t d] and German post-dental [t d]. But the German affricate [ts], as in *Zeit* 'time,' and the English interdentals [θð], as in *thin* and *these,* would be dealt with at length, for as we have noted previously, adult language learners interpret other languages through their own linguistic systems. Native German speakers accordingly "hear" *thin* and *these* either as *tin* and *Ds* or as *sin* and *Zs,* and they carry their own patterns into English. This is also true of syntactic patterns. Since the verb of independent clauses stands in second place in German, native speakers may transfer this pattern to English, saying *Tonight go we to the cinema.* Vocabulary causes similar problems. German speakers may use *cinema* rather than *movies* because their word is *Kino.*

Capable, well-trained teachers have long been aware of such problems. But often the problems have not been explicitly stated, and many pedagogical grammars have not been structured to overcome them systematically. The situation becomes really acute when one wishes to undertake study of an exotic language. Available grammars are often sketchy. Designed for a large public suspicious of phonetic symbols, they may describe the foreign sounds by impressionistic methods that are difficult to interpret. Or they may equate a sound with some corresponding sound in southern British English or western Scottish English, with little benefit to the user who does not have a speaker of these dialects on hand to provide samples. Contrastive grammars, constructed in accordance with an adequate format, will help solve some of the difficulties. But much work remains to be done in the production of practical grammars. One project has yielded contrastive grammars for English and Spanish, English and German, and English and Italian. But even for the major languages of the world, to say nothing of the different forms of Spanish used in the New World, an adequate set of contrastive grammars will not be produced for some time.

## 15.4  Computational Applications and Translation

The manipulation of languages by computers is useful for many purposes, such as the production of concordances, the compilation of glossaries and lists of selected forms. But other hopes have been expressed for computational linguistics, among them translation by computer. Twenty years ago machine translation was proposed as one of the possible achievements of the fledgling computer. The aim is difficult, as is any practical application of the computer to, for example, the teaching of languages. If machine translation is to be achieved, an interlingual grammar must be prepared in addition to detailed grammars of the source and target languages. Further, complex computer-programming systems must be on hand to store these grammars, direct their use, process input text, and so on. When one reflects on the extent of analysis necessary to account for a simple sentence like *Mother is running,* the magnitude of the machine translation problem is clear. On the other hand, the technical materials for which machine translation is designed present fewer problems than does everyday language, partly because technical language is highly stylized and because all technical languages share similar vocabulary and patterns. Moreover, the continued interest in machine translation reflects a largely unfulfilled need, the rapid translation of technical materials.

Translation is important in a variety of areas. Some organizations foster the translation of important fundamental works like the Bible. Others attempt to encourage the translation of literary works. Still others, among them scientific societies, support the translation of technical material. The goals of such groups are quite different; a translator of Shakespeare's sonnets or Mishima's novels proceeds differently from translators of technical materials, which diminish in usefulness with each day that elapses after publication. When individuals confuse these goals, they contribute little to solving the problem of communication.

**Translation** can be defined as the transfer of materials in one language to another language, with the linguistic patterns maintained as closely as possible—phonologically, syntactically, and semantically, as well as stylistically. Since no two languages agree in all of these areas, a completely satisfactory translation is obviously impossible. Further, language is constantly changing. No translation will therefore be satisfactory for a long period. Translation, then, is one linguistic application with inexhaustible possibilities.

The varying procedures and aims of translation involve problems other than the linguistic questions, which are complex enough. One such problem is cultural interpretation. Most sacred texts deal with situations that are difficult to understand in the original. Hebrew and Greek are languages with long philosophical and religious traditions, in which individual terms developed highly complex meanings. Goethe's concern with the translation of the complex Greek philosophical term *lógos* illustrates the problems that a scholar faces in translating texts into languages used primarily for everyday communication. Obviously, such problems are minor in the translation of technical works, in which many of the key terms belong to the international scientific vocabulary. The chief requirement of technical translation is the transferal of these terms to the syntax of the target language.

In discussions about the need for computerized translation, the amount of technical materials published daily is often disregarded. Several million words of technical materials have been cited as the daily quota of translation from Russian alone. With the addition of German, French, Japanese, and Chinese materials, to say nothing of those in lesser-known languages such as Uzbek, it is difficult to escape the conclusion that technical materials face slow and inadequate translation until computer technology has advanced to a further degree. Moreover, when technical materials are translated by computer, automatic abstracting and data retrieval will also be possible. As in the application of linguistics to the teaching of languages, the required procedures are known. Application of these procedures, however, depends on external situations and on the attitudes of potential users.

## 15.5  Lexicography

The attitudes of potential users are important to another venerable application of linguistics, the production of dictionaries or lexicons. Dictionaries are among the oldest transmitted materials. Sumerian, the oldest documented language, whose texts date from before 3000 B.C., can be interpreted because of the existence of Sumerian-Akkadian dictionaries. In our own recent tradition glossaries were produced from the words written in Latin documents for Old English, Old High German, Old Irish, and other European languages. Known as **glosses,** these insertions differ little from the aids to memory that language teachers enjoin their students not to write in foreign language texts. In the seventh and eighth centuries in Europe such glosses were compiled into **glossaries,** either alphabetically or in accordance with classifications for meanings. In time such glossaries developed into dictionaries as we know them.

Our dictionaries, too, may be arranged by classification for meaning or for the spelling of words. A dictionary arranged by classification for meanings is often called a **thesaurus;** that produced by Roget in the nineteenth century is a good example. A thesaurus is highly useful when one wishes to note the various possible meanings in a set. But by far the most commonly used dictionaries are arranged alphabetically.

The principles guiding the production of dictionaries and the procedures followed in their compilation have been often stated. Samuel Johnson, in the preface to his eminent dictionary, spoke articulately and succinctly of the guiding principle behind lexicography: "[T]hey [lexicographers] assemble their materials from the language and put them in appropriate order." The more complete citation that follows will indicate this manner of working and serve to associate Johnson with more recent lexicographers.

Every other author may aspire to praise; the lexicographer can only hope to escape reproach, and even this negative recompense has been yet granted to very few.

I have, notwithstanding this discouragement, attempted a dictionary of the English language. . . .

Having therefore no assistance but from general grammar, I applied myself to the perusal of our writers; and noting whatever might be of use to ascertain or illustrate any word or phrase, accumulated in time the materials of a dictionary, which, by degrees, I reduced to method, establishing to myself, in the progress of the work, such rules as experience and analogy suggested to me; experience, which practice and observation were continually increasing; and analogy, which though in some words obscure, was evident in others.[1]

---

[1] Samuel Johnson quoted in Edward L. McAdam, Jr. and George Milne, eds., *Johnson's Dictionary: A Modern Selection* (New York: Pantheon, 1963), pp. 3–4.

We can thus see that producing a dictionary is a risky business and does not guarantee the lexicographer a sympathetic audience. Besides being subject to the general obloquy that Johnson describes, lexicographers are ill treated primarily because of the "status labels" they adopt. We may cite, for example, the controversy caused by the publication of *Webster's Third New International Dictionary*. It provides status labels of three kinds: temporal, stylistic, and regional (page 18a, paragraph 8.0) and also provides "usage notes" with selected entries (page 20a, paragraph 15). However, in lieu of some usage notes, citations are supplied so that intelligent users may determine for themselves the "status" of a given word. When the dictionary appeared in 1961 it was generally accused of encouraging permissiveness in the use of English. Ironically, criticism was loudest from those upon whom the dictionary's editors counted most. The editors made this statement: "A dictionary demands of its user much understanding (page 62)." Evidently, the public was not yet ready for such responsibility, and the editors were disappointed in their hope. Yet so probably were the compilers of the first Sumerian-Akkadian dictionary.

---

### 15.6  The Study of Literature and Linguistics

If attitudes toward dictionaries are firm and at times uninformed, those toward literature are often immovable. In our culture literature is venerated, though the reasons for this high esteem seem to be incomprehensible to many students.

Definitions of literature vary. From a linguistic point of view literary materials are texts composed in accordance with certain restrictions that are imposed on selected segments of the language. The restrictions most widely observed for poetry in the Western tradition apply to a portion of the phonological structure of language: materials are selected in accordance with certain principles of rhythm. Sequences of alternating prominent and nonprominent materials are set in either trochaic (-x-x) or iambic (x-x-) meter, as in the last lines of Milton's "Lycidas":

> At last he rose, and twitch'd his mantle blue:
> Tomorrow to fresh woods, and pastures new.

If two nonprominent syllables accompany a prominent, the rhythm is either dactylic, -xx -xx, or anapestic, xx- xx-. Such sequences, known as **feet,** are sometimes restricted to repeated lines of two to six syllables, as occurs in the Homeric poems. We may cite, for example, the first line of the *Odyssey:*

*ándra   moi énnepe moūsa polútropon hòs mála pollà*
   -  x    x - x x   - x    x - x x    -   x x  - x

Prominence in Greek verse is based on quantity of syllables; each prominent syllable either has a long vowel or ends in two consonants. In English verse, on the other hand, prominence is based on stress. Sets of lines may also recur in stanzas of similar construction. And as in the lines from "Lycidas," some syllables may rhyme—often end syllables, such as *blue* and *new,* but also interior syllables, such as *last* and *pasture.* Whatever the rhythmic principles are, in the Western tradition they are based on phonological criteria.

Yet other linguistic restrictions may also determine poetic rhythm. In the Hebrew verse of the Psalms the criteria are syntactic and semantic; two comparable sentence sequences are paired, as in:

The Lord is my shepherd; I shall not want.
He maketh me to lie down in green pastures; He leadeth me
beside the still waters.

Students of literature have not yet developed a general theory to include all varieties of literature produced in all known cultures, but the statements made here may suggest the possible outlines of such a theory.

Some of the characteristics of literature may be illustrated by means of one of the most famous and universally esteemed Japanese haiku.

Furu-ike ya        *Furu-ike* 'ancient pond'
kawazu tobi-komu   *kawazu* 'frog' *tobi-komu* 'jump/dive in'
mizu no oto        *mizu* 'water' *oto* 'sound'

The poem might be translated:

The ancient pond here
Taking a jump a frog strikes
Sound of the water

The Japanese transcription given here provides access to the phonological structure of the poem. (Generally speaking, all verse that is to be analyzed should be given in phonemic transcription.) A haiku is built up of seventeen syllables in sets of five, seven, five. It has no other phonological requirements. But the pairings of vowels in this haiku—such as the two initial *u*'s, the three *a*'s linking the first and second lines, and the three final *o*'s—make up a part of the additional ornamental patterning (as do the consonants) that is responsible for the poem's acclaim.

Through the use of a vowel triangle (see Figure 1) the vocalic flow of the first line of the haiku may be sketched. The flow of the last line (Figure 2) moves in the reverse direction. This analysis of the vowel sequences further indicates the masterful phonological structure of this haiku.

Morphological and syntactic patterns also contribute to the excellence of the poem. The native Japanese nominal compound *furu-ike* in the first

Figure 1

Figure 2

line is matched by the verbal compound in line two *tobi-komu*. Literature is designed to appeal to the imagination, and this poem abounds in purposeful ambiguity. The verb *tobi-komu,* for example, may be taken syntactically as a final verb; thus the first two lines would make up a sentence. But *tobi-komu* may also be taken as an attributive verb modifying *mizu,* allowing an interpretation of the first two lines as a description of the noun *mizu* 'water into which a frog jumps' or even *oto* 'sound of water produced by a frog jumping.' By his capable use of Japanese syntactic patterns the poet enriches the image conveyed by *furu-ike*.

Literature is also based heavily on semantic restriction. *Furu-ike* recalls favored Japanese scenes: an old beautifully designed pond, possibly in a temple garden. In any poetic tradition words are associated with meanings because of their continual use in a long succession of literary contexts. These poetic words accordingly may be fully interpreted only if one is familiar with the poetic tradition. In Japanese and Chinese verse the word associations are seconded by their written forms; that of *mizu* is acclaimed as one of the most beautiful—and most intriguing—and it is one that every calligrapher hopes to capture:

These brief remarks on phonology, syntax, and semantics exemplify some of the contributions linguistics can make to an interpretation of literature. The determination of still other patterns of selection is also within the province of linguistics. This haiku, for example, is not explicit; it does not report a completed action. In this way it reflects the fondness of the Japanese for the preperfect stage of affairs, as in their preference for half-opened cherry blossoms to those in full bloom. The term used for this half-open stage is *shibui* 'bitter, sober, refined.'

---

## 15.7  Style

The individual characterists of any text are the basis of its style. Concern with style is directed largely toward literary texts. But any sequence of language may include stylistic features in much the same way that any human behavior, such as dancing or skating, may exhibit style. Usually positive characteristics are singled out, such as grace in body movements in dancing. But style includes the sum total of individual features, whether ungainly or capable. Some writers, such as government bureaucrats, are excoriated for their miserable style.

While style is identified in such ways, its definition has been greatly disputed. One of the problems in the definition of style results from the wide use of the term. It is applied to individuals. Politicians may be commended for their style, as was Winston Churchill. Or they may be identified by stylistic criteria, when a series of articles on linguistic theory appeared in *Pravda* in the early fifties, scholars who had read Stalin's writings ascribed them to him because of their style. The term is also applied to literary genres or to periods. One style is identified for the period of the Renaissance, another for the Enlightenment. The term may also be used of languages. French is said to convey clarity in style, while German is often judged to be characterized by obscurity. Used of individuals, of genres, of periods, of languages, the term *style* then has a wide array of applications.

But all these applications share a characteristic: selection. Languages exhibit selection from the sum total of linguistic possibilities. From a simple feature like syllable structure, one can characterize Japanese as a language of simple and open syllables, while English has relatively many final consonants (think of the three in *consonants*), and Russian has relatively many initial consonants, as in the city-name *Pskov*. Languages in this way select from the possible phonological, morphological, syntactic, and semantic patterns. In much the same way a literary period may favor selected patterns. Renaissance authors liked richness of style to the point of euphuism, and Enlightenment authors liked clarity to the point of plainness. Similarly, individuals display preference for features in their language that permit variation. One poet may prefer front vowels, another may use consonantal clusters, and so on. The choice may be deliberate, but many such characteristics of individuals are chosen subconsciously. Because of such individual stylistic features, the writings of individuals can often be identified from the choice of certain patterns.

All of us recognize our friends by characteristics of voice, as over the telephone; we generally know who is calling us without specific iden tification. Our recognition is based on noncentral features of the voice, for example, basic pitch, variation in pitch, and duration of specific syllables; these variations are imposed on the central phonological characteristics that all speakers of the language must use.

The most spectacular identification of individual characteristics is made when specialists in style identify forgeries or anonymous writings. Such efforts have been made to identify the individual authors of the Federalist Papers. Another effort involved the *Junius* letters, a series of political pamphlets written in Britain from 1769 to 1772 and published under the pseudonym of Junius. In identifying their author as Sir Philip Francis, Alvar Ellegård examined specific characteristics—individual preferences for specific words or specific syntactic patterns. Among the words the unknown author used were *nature* and *reason;* everyone uses such words but not with the same frequency. And one of his characteristic syntactic patterns was the use of "relative clauses 'governed' by a preposition."[2] These examples may illustrate what is meant by stylistic characteristics. Individuals vary in their preference for elements at all levels of language: phonology, morphology, syntax, and patterns of meaning. If an adequate set of texts is available and if the preferences are emphatically characteristic, one may identify individual authors and their style.

If a style is pleasing to us, we hold the author in esteem. But it must not be forgotten that varying principles appeal to readers at different periods and that consequently tastes in writing and evaluations of authors vary from time to time. Style then is the configuration of individual characteristics found in a specific author, a specific type of writing, and at specific periods of time.

## 15.8  On the Translation of Literature

A brief examination of the problems involved in the translation of the haiku discussed above may reinforce some of our remarks on characteristics underlying literary works and may supplement the brief statement given earlier in this chapter on technical translation. If the purpose of translation is to transfer the patterns of a text from one language to another, a capable literary translation should match the phonological, morphological, syntactic, and semantic structuring of the original. Obviously such an aim is impossible for this haiku and for most literary texts, as we may illustrate briefly.

Phonologically, it is impossible to produce in English a set of seventeen syllables with the structure consonant-vowel. Moreover, the quality of the Japanese syllables can scarcely be matched, though a match may be attempted. The translation above attempts to reflect the three high

---

[2] Alvar Ellegård, *A Statistical Method for Determining Authorship* (Göteborg: Elander, 1962), p. 24.

vowels of *furu-i* by using three syllables ending in a nasal, *ancient pond*.

Morphologically, it is impossible to match in English the native Japanese compounds, especially verbs like *tobi-komu*. And the syntactic patterns are quite foreign to English; the ambiguous *strikes* at the end of the second line was selected by the translator to reflect the twofold possibility of *tobi-komu* as a final verb and as a verb attributive to the nouns of the last line.

A semantic reproduction is perhaps the most difficult of all. The English word *frog*, for example, does not have the connotations nor the phonological structure of *kawazu*. Similarly troublesome, in the English tradition the connotations of 'an old pond' differ considerably from those of *furu-ike*. Yet the concepts conveyed by *kawazu* and *furu-ike* are central to the poem.

The difficulties sketched here in the transferal of the phonological, morphological, syntactic, and semantic features of the Japanese poem should indicate the reasons for the despair of critics and translators. They also indicate why translation after translation is made of eminent literary works. You may find it instructive to try your hand at translating this haiku. The problems discussed also point up the contrasts between two different literary traditions and, in addition, underscore the essential characteristics of literature. Authors must observe various principles of form. Some of these are essential, like the seventeen syllables of the haiku. Others are ornamental, like the vowel patternings indicated. To illustrate the contrast, the seventeen syllables of the first line of the *Odyssey* may be compared. Its essential and its ornamental principles are quite different from those of the haiku. Yet Homer, Milton, and Bashō, the author of the haiku, followed certain requirements; the features their works share permit us to identify some characteristics of those linguistic materials known as literature.

Generally we add requirements concerning subject matter. Literary texts often deal with ideal situations, such as peaceful contemplation in a quiet setting interrupted by the splash of a frog. Literary texts may also deal with ideal periods, when, as in the Homeric poems, men readily communed with gods. In this way literary principles are often exemplified in religious texts. Yet religious texts and many other texts in elevated style are often less severely structured than the three examples given in section 15.6; they may be "prose" rather than "poetry."

Used in cultural contexts that we approve of, literary texts hold the highest prestige of any linguistic materials. They are carefully transmitted from generation to generation, whether in writing or orally, as were the Sanskrit Vedas and the Hebrew Scriptures. Such great care was devoted to their transmission that they maintained their original patterns for thousands of years. Phonological patterns, for example, were preserved in the *Rigveda* for at least 3,000 years; we can now explain them linguistically but only after detailed study that was carried on throughout the nineteenth century; this was assisted by the discovery of Hittite texts in 1906, which provided more information on Proto-Indo-European phonology. And the recently discovered Dead Sea Scrolls have provided us with texts of the Hebrew Old Testament a thousand years older than any known before; yet the differences from the previously known texts are not extensive.

People in this way choose linguistic materials with great care and preserve them with intense devotion. The application of even more rigorous principles of selection than those used in everyday language reflects the eminence human beings may achieve through communication.

---

## 15.9    On the Linguistic Interpretation of Literature

Since literary materials are constructed out of language, it is one of the obligations of linguists to concern themselves with literary texts. Examples of such concern are given in the exercises and in the suggested readings at the end of this chapter. Linguists have been criticized on two counts for their essays on literature. It is asserted that:

1. they deal only with relatively obvious facets of literature and hence produce superficial literary criticism; and
2. the linguistic models that they use, such as transformational grammar, fail to comprehend the patterns of language that are most significant in literature, such as metaphors.

These criticisms will be briefly discussed here.

It would be somewhat presumptuous of linguists to claim that linguistic analysis alone could uncover the primal characteristics of outstanding literary works. On the other hand, if a literary work reflects in its language the deeper aims of its author, such a work cannot be properly understood unless its linguistic patterns are analyzed and described for their role in the work concerned. From the point of view of linguistics, a literary critic who is uninformed about the pronunciation of the material he or she is examining, or of its syntactic patterning, will also produce uninformed literary criticism. In the difficult art of literary criticism all available tools must be used. Linguistic analysis may be the simplest of these, but it is also the most basic.

But when the analytic procedures developed under a given linguistic theory are applied to literature, it must be remembered that linguistic models are produced with various aims in mind and on the basis of various types of data. We have noted above that the standard theory of transformational grammar required modification for various reasons, among them the need to account for languages of differing structures, such as the OV languages. This theory also needs modification if it is to account for literary materials. Their eminence depends in great part on the originality and imagination of their authors, qualities leading to manipulations of language that surpass those dealt with in theories of grammar. Yet the history of linguistics reflects a broadening of the areas of concern and a broadening of theoretical concepts. If capable literary critics and linguists apply their skills to the interpretation of literature, linguistic theory may also be expanded so that it can account for the most eminent uses of language.

Applications of linguistics thus lead to improvement in linguistic theory and to an improved understanding of language. This in turn contributes to a greater understanding of the applications of linguistics, whether these be relatively simple, as in the teaching of reading, or highly complex, as in the interpretation of literature.

## BIBLIOGRAPHICAL NOTES

A booklet dealing with the teaching of English to speakers of nonstandard dialects is *The Study of Nonstandard English* by William Labov (Champaign, Ill.: National Council of Teachers of English, 1970). *The Linguistic Sciences and Language Teaching* by Michael A. K. Halliday, Angus McIntosh, and Peter Strevens (Bloomington: Indiana University Press, 1964) is a thorough statement on language teaching and includes a bibliography. For a genial, if somewhat outmoded, text on language teaching, it is difficult to surpass *The Practical Study of Languages* by Henry Sweet, the man after whom George Bernard Shaw patterned Higgins in *Pygmalion;* fortunately the book is available again (New York: Oxford University Press, 1964). Contrastive grammars have been published for a few languages by the University of Chicago Press. Among them are *The Sounds of English and German* by William G. Moulton, 1962; *The Grammatical Structures of English and German* by Herbert L. Kufner, 1962; *The Sounds of English and Spanish* by Robert P. Stockwell and J. Donald Bowen, 1965; and *The Grammatical Structures of English and Spanish* by Robert P. Stockwell, J. Donald Bowen, and John W. Martin. *Linguistics and Reading* by Charles C. Fries (New York: Holt, Rinehart and Winston, 1964) discusses in excellent detail the contributions of linguistics to the teaching of reading. *Introduction to Computational Linguistics* by David G. Hays (New York: Elsevier, 1967) deals with various applications of computers to linguistic problems.

For discussions of the procedures of lexicographers, you may examine the introduction of any large dictionary, such as the *Oxford English Dictionary, Webster's Third New International Dictionary,* or *The Random House Dictionary of the English Language.* For an excellent "casebook on the aims of lexicographers and the targets of reviewers," see *Dictionaries and that Dictionary* by James Sledd and Wilma R. Ebbitt (Chicago: Scott, Foresman, 1962). Interesting excerpts from Johnson's dictionary are given in *Johnson's Dictionary: A Modern Selection* by Edward L. McAdam, Jr. and George Milne, eds. (New York: Pantheon, 1963).

For a selection of recent essays on linguistic studies of literature see Seymour Chatman and Samuel K. Levin, eds., *Essays on the Language of Literature* (Boston: Houghton Mifflin, 1967). An attempt to characterize the formal principles in one literary tradition may be found in *The Development of Germanic Verse Form,* reprint, by Winfred P. Lehmann (Staten Island, N.Y.: Gordian Press, 1971). For a recent statement on style, see *Linguistic Stylistics* by Nils Erik Enkvist (The Hague: Mouton, 1973).

QUESTIONS FOR REVIEW

1. List some applications of linguistics.
2. In the People's Republic of China a standard form of Chinese called Putonghua is now taught in all schools. The phonological system of Putonghua is based on the language of the Peking area, which has four tones. Other forms of Chinese have eight tones. What kinds of problems would teachers face in teaching students a smaller set of tones? What kinds of problems would teachers face in teaching Putonghua to native speakers of languages, like Uighur, that have no tones? Suggest reasons for the policy decision to teach one form of language throughout the People's Republic.
3. Discuss the problems faced by schoolchildren who speak a nonstandard form of English. What linguistic measures are necessary to most effectively teach them standard English? What kinds of attitudes might complicate their learning problems?
4. What linguistic findings would you apply in devising an optimum introduction to reading for primary school children? Discuss the requirements of such an approach in relation to other matters you would have to take into consideration.
5. Various efforts have been expended to reform the spelling of English, such as the introduction of a phonetically based alphabet. If such an orthographic system were adopted in England, could it be used in the United States? Why not? What would be the effect of such a system on communication between English speakers in England, South Africa, India, and Australia?
6. What is a contrastive grammar? How would it be useful to teachers of foreign languages? Could the same contrastive grammar be used by teachers of languages as different as Japanese and Spanish? Why not?
7. Machine translation is used by some organizations, but only for technical materials. Why aren't literary materials translated by machine? The people primarily interested in machine translation are government officials, such as those in the offices of

the European Common Market, which must deal with texts in French, German, Italian, Dutch, English, and so on. What advantages might machine translation have for such organizations?

8. Sketch briefly the development of dictionaries from glossaries to modern desk dictionaries. How does a thesaurus differ from a dictionary?

9. Where does a lexicographer find his data about language? How can he indicate the "status" of individual words? What pitfalls does he face in using status labels?

10. How can linguistics be of value to students of literature? What is the basis of rhyme? of alliteration? of meter?

11. Is all poetry based, like that of Western culture, on patterning of phonological elements, with bases in meter frequently accompanied by rhyme? What other structural bases are used in poetry?

12. State the requirements for an ideal translation of literary works. To what extent can these be fulfilled?

## EXERCISES

### EXERCISE 1

One of the most widely acclaimed translations is the King James version of the Bible. Among the reasons for this translation's acclaim is the quality of its language. Taking passages at random, such as the first verse of Luke 2, we might attempt to examine the basis for this reputation. Luke 2:1 goes as follows: "And it came to pass in those days, that there went out a decree from Caesar Augustus, that all the world should be taxed."

a. Examining this passage, point out noteworthy features, for example, the selection of phonological items, items of form, patterns of syntax, and stylistic patterns. For perspective you may wish to compare other translations of the Greek original. A recent translation, entitled *Good News for Modern Man*,[3] reproduces Luke 2:1 as follows: "At the time Emperor Augustus sent out an order for all citizens of the Empire to register themselves for the census."

b. Another admired section of the King James version is 1 Corinthians 13, for example, verses 12 and 13: "For now we see through a glass, darkly; but then face to face: now I know in part; but then shall I know even as also I am known. And now abideth faith, hope, charity, these three; but the greatest of these is charity."

---

[3] *Good News for Modern Man* (New York: American Bible Society, 1966).

This passage is translated in *Good News for Modern Man* as follows: "What we see now is like the dim image in a mirror; then we shall see face to face. What I know now is only partial; then it will be complete, as complete as God's knowledge of me. Meanwhile these three remain: faith, hope, and love; and the greatest of these is love." Compare the two translations for their eminent linguistic characteristics.

c. In choosing a translation of literary materials, what would be your criteria?

EXERCISE 2

a. A passage that has long been admired for its literary qualities is Shakespeare's description of Cleopatra's first meeting with Antony, *Antony and Cleopatra,* Act 2, Scene 2, lines 196–202:

The barge she sat in, like a burnish'd throne,
Burn'd on the water: the poop was beaten gold;
Purple the sails, and so perfumed that
The winds were love-sick with them; the oars were silver,
Which to the tune of flutes kept stroke and made
The water which they beat to follow faster,
As amorous of their strokes.

Examine these lines for their melody, for example, the use of labials, the progression of vowels, and the use of *r*. Discuss other linguistic features that lead readers to admire the passage. You can consult one of the standard editions for further lines of this section.

b. T. S. Eliot based the opening of the second section of "The Waste Land" on this passage, the lines beginning:

The Chair she sat in, like a burnished throne,
Glowed on the marble, . . .

Analyze Eliot's lines for their musical qualities. Do his lines have the music of Shakespeare's? Does Eliot intend them to? If he does not, why does he depart from the elegance of Shakespeare? What is the intent of the second section of "The Waste Land"?

EXERCISE 3

In a recent essay Roman Jakobson states that in the following poem "not a letter is insignificant."[4] The poem in Blake's spelling is as follows:

---

[4] Roman Jakobson, "On the Verbal Art of William Blake and Other Poet-Painters," *Linguistic Inquiry* 1 (1970): 3–23.

My mother groand! my father wept.
Into the dangerous world I leapt:
Helpless, naked, piping loud:
Like a fiend hid in a cloud.

Struggling in my fathers hands:
Striving against my swadling bands:
Bound and weary I thought best
To sulk upon my mothers breast.

    a. In his interpretation of the poem Jakobson says:

Both riming words of any odd couplet belong to the same morphological category, end with the identical consonantal inflectional suffix, and are devoid of agreement in their prevocalic phonemes: $_1$wep-t: $_2$leap-t, $_5$hand-s: $_6$band-s. The similar formal makeup of the two odd rimes underscores the divergent semantic orientation of the two quatrains.[5]

        After determining this orientation, comment on the proposed relation between the choice of rhymes and the contrasting meanings. Do you find any pattern in the rhymes of the even couplets?
    b. Jakobson also finds patterning in the ten nouns of the poem, of which five are animates and five inanimates. Among the patterning "the five animates are confined to the four marginal lines of the two quatrains. . . . The inanimates are constantly bound with locative prepositions, whereas, of the five animates, four are used without any preposition, and one with an equational preposition (*Like a fiend*)."[6] In this patterning Jakobson sees a "spatial treatment" that "opposes inanimates to animates." How does this patterning agree with your interpretation of the poem? Do you find any patterning in the ten verbs of the poem?

## EXERCISE 4

The following two passages indicate the reaction of two Englishmen of letters to criticism: John Milton (1608–1674) and Jonathan Swift (1667–1745).

    The Milton passage is from his "Apology for Smectymnuus" of 1642; the Swift passage is from his "Tale of a Tub," written in approximately 1696.

    John Milton:

Thus having spent his first onset, not in confuting, but in a reasonless defaming of the book, the method of his malice hurries him to attempt the like against the author; not by proofs and testimonies, but "having no certain notice of me," as

---

[5] *Ibid.*, p. 3.
[6] *Ibid.*, p. 6.

he professes, "further than what he gathers from the Animadversions," blunders at me for the rest, and flings out stray crimes at a venture, which he could never, though he be a serpent, suck from anything that I have written, but from his own stuffed magazine and hoard of slanderous inventions, over and above that which he converted to venom in the drawing. To me, readers, it happens as a singular contentment, and let it be to good men no slight satisfaction, that the slanderer here confesses he has "no further notice of me than his own conjecture." Although it had been honest to have inquired, before he uttered such infamous words, and I am credibly informed he did inquire; but finding small comfort from the intelligence which he received, whereon to ground the falsities which he had provided, thought it his likeliest course, under a pretended ignorance, to let drive at random, lest he should lose his odd ends, which from some penurious book of characters he had been culling out and would fain apply. Not caring to burden me with those vices, whereof, among whom my conversation hath been, I have been ever least suspected; perhaps not without some subtlety to cast me into envy, by bringing on me a necessity to enter into mine own praises. In which argument I know every wise man is more unwillingly drawn to speak, than the most repining ear can be averse to hear.

Jonathan Swift:

However, I shall conclude with three maxims, which may serve both as characteristics to distinguish a true modern critic from a pretender, and will be also of admirable use to those worthy spirits, who engage in so useful and honourable an art.

The first is, that criticism, contrary to all other faculties of the intellect, is ever held the truest and best, when it is the very first result of the critic's mind; as fowlers reckon the first aim for the surest, and seldom fail of missing the mark, if they stay not for a second.

Secondly, the true critics are known by their talent of swarming about the noblest writers, to which they are carried merely by instinct, as a rat to the best cheese, or a wasp to the fairest fruit. So when the king is on horseback, he is sure to be the dirtiest person of the company; and they that make their court best, are such as bespatter him most.

Lastly, a true critic, in the perusal of a book, is like a dog at a feast, whose thoughts and stomach are wholly set upon what the guests fling away, and consequently is apt to snarl most when there are the fewest bones.

a. Analyze each selection for characteristic features of the author's style, such as syntactic patterns as well as choice and arrangement of words.
b. Indicate any characteristics that might be characteristic of the period rather than the author.
c. Find some other denunciation of a critic, such as President Truman's of a music critic who commented adversely on his daughter's singing, and note its characteristic stylistic features in contrast with those in the Milton and Swift passages.

EXERCISE 5

One of the well-known poems of the German poet Johann Wolfgang Goethe is called *Wanderers Nachtlied* 'Traveler's Evening-song.' It is given here with a word-for-word translation.

| | |
|---|---|
| *Über allen Gipfeln* | Above all housetops |
| *Ist Ruh,* | is rest, |
| *In allen Wipfeln,* | In all treetops |
| *Spürest du* | noticest thou |
| *Kaum einen Hauch;* | Hardly a breath; |
| *Die Vögelein schweigen im Walde.* | The little-birds are-silent in-the forest. |
| *Warte nur, balde,* | Wait only, soon |
| *Ruhest du auch.* | Restest thou too. |

a. If you set out to provide a literary translation of this poem, what aims would you establish for yourself? Would you attempt to maintain the rhymes, such as *Ruh/du, Gipfeln/Wipfeln,* and so on? If you did, what rearrangements might this aim require in syntax, or in the choice of words? You might find it interesting to prepare a translation.

# CONCLUSION:
## The Understanding of Language

CHAPTER 16

### 16.1 The Study of Language as an Independent Discipline

Applications of linguistics, as discussed in the last three chapters, contribute to the central goal of linguistics, the understanding of language. Yet this goal must be sought primarily by study of language itself. People have attempted to achieve such understanding ever since the beginnings of serious concern with language. Our first detailed knowledge of such concern dates from the classical period of Greece. The study of language was included by the Greeks in the study of human knowledge, *philosophia*, a term that might better be translated as science than philosophy. This tendency to tie the study of language to other intellectual concerns inhibited the establishment of linguistics as a separate branch of study. Like the other social and behavioral sciences, linguistics became an independent discipline more recently than the physical and the biological sciences.

Until the end of the eighteenth century concern with an understanding of language was still closely linked with disciplines that had not achieved their independence from *philosophia*. For more than another century, until the influence of Saussure came to be widely felt, much of the concern with language was dominated by historical aims. Thus intensive study of language as a phenomenon, that is, modern linguistics, is scarcely half a century old.

Although earlier concern for language was subordinated to larger aims, some of the central linguistic problems were raised and much of the terminology was produced by scholars of the past. As we survey the earlier concern with language, we will note primarily the work of scholars in the Western tradition. For although it was capable, the study of language in other traditions (notably the Indian and the Arabic traditions) has, until very recently, had little influence on Western linguistics. For this reason this brief sketch of the human concern with the understanding of language is limited to a discussion of the contributions of Western scholars.

## 16.2  Whether Names Are Given by Nature or Convention

The primary linguistic interest of the Greeks had to do with the relationship of language to the world and society. This concern was expressed in the question of whether names are given by nature or by convention. A highly influential treatment of the problem may be found in Plato's dialogue *Cratylus*. As in his other dialogues, Plato presented both points of view, with proponents of each view discussing the pros and cons. We do not know Plato's own position. But the man after whom the dialogue is named, Cratylus, and his fellows propound the view that there is indeed a natural relationship between words and things; in their opinion language is to be understood by the determination of such relationships. A philosopher, for example, is so named because he loves knowledge. On the other hand, when relationships between words and things are cloudy, the etymology—for Cratylus the "true meaning"—is to be sought in less obvious parallels. One of these, devised by a Latin successor to Cratylus, has become a common saying reflecting absurdity: *lucus a non lucendo* 'woods are so called because they do not produce light.' Such absurd etymologies are among those most commonly cited in discussions of classical concern with language. This selection of an absurdity rather than some of the accurate insights of Greek and Latin scholars reflects our own views about the nature-versus-convention controversy, for today no one maintains the position of Cratylus.

Instead, the assumption that language is the result of convention, that there is no inherent relationship between things and the words for them, is one of the central tenets of contemporary linguistics. According to Saussure, linguistic entities are arbitrary. It may seem that "nature" is involved in the source for some words, such as onomatopoetic words for the sound of a dog's bark, for example, English *bow-wow,* German *wau-wau,* or French *gnaf-gnaf* and Japanese *wan-wan*. But even these are conventional, as may be illustrated by the English *meow* for the noise of a cat versus Japanese *nyā-nyā* or by such modified words as English *cock-a-doodle-do* for the crow of a contemporary cock versus the Middle English crow of his ancestor, *cok-cok*.

Not all Greeks or Romans held that there is a natural relationship between words and things. Aristotle did not. His followers, however, concerned themselves less with linguistic theory than with applications, such as the production of grammars and the study of literature. In these applications the Greeks and the Latins made lasting contributions. The contemporary study of rhetoric has not yet surpassed that of the eminent men of antiquity, such as Longinus. And into the nineteenth century grammars were based on classical patterns. These grammars, however, deal primarily with morphology and, therefore, are storehouses of parts of a language rather than statements that might explain language as it is used for communication. Classical grammar, then, made lasting contributions to the description of language, though the understanding of the phenomenon of language among the Greeks and the Romans was hampered because their conclusions were based solely on concern with their own languages.

## 16.3 The Contributions of History to an Understanding of Language

For many scholars in the nineteenth century the key to an understanding of language and other cultural patterns lay in determining the oldest possible forms. One of the leading nineteenth-century linguists, Jacob Grimm, sought in this way to understand other cultural conventions, such as law and literature, as well as language. For example, the popular collection of folk tales compiled by him and his brother Wilhelm was undertaken because they assumed that older, and in their eyes more revealing, literary materials had been maintained by the common people. Collections of folk tales, as well as earlier literary materials, might then illuminate contemporary literature. Viewing cultural phenomena in this way, Grimm and his successors expended great energy on determining the oldest forms and the history of the languages that interested them, chiefly those in the Indo-European group.

Their work led to important contributions to human history, clarifying (among other historical events) the settlement of Indo-European speakers in northern Europe, Italy, and Greece, as well as India. But the reconstruction of earlier forms of languages did not lead to an understanding of language itself. The remarkable reconstruction of Proto-Indo-European (even though partial) demonstrated that Proto-Indo-European is no more illuminating than are contemporary languages in yielding an understanding of language. Nor are Proto-Indo-European and other ascertainable languages of the past in any sense primitive. Actually, the broad concern with all possible languages in the nineteenth and twentieth centuries has led to the conviction that no languages are known to us that might be called "primitive" and that, accordingly, we cannot arrive at an understanding of language by locating a less highly developed form of it.

All known languages have a grammatical structure capable of meeting the basic requirements for communication. They may not, however, have an adequate vocabulary for referring to all segments of culture. English, for example, is deficient in its terms for various kinds of camels or various kinds of snow or various elegant and imaginative desserts. But English has the potentiality of adding such terms and a sufficient grammar to permit their use in any required social situation. Therefore, we cannot term English more primitive than Arabic, Eskimo, or Turkish. And to the extent that we have been able to reconstruct Proto-Indo-European or determine the grammar of the oldest attested languages, such as Archaic Chinese, Sumerian, and Egyptian, we know that these languages too have adequate grammatical structures to meet the needs of any society, whether of the present or the past. Having made this discovery through careful, often brilliant work in the nineteenth century, linguists—notably Saussure—turned their attention to the study of language itself in the early part of this century.

## 16.4   Language as a Structure and Its Components

Most of Saussure's views are now so completely accepted that he is regarded as the father of contemporary linguistics. Central is his insistence on language as a system or a structure. It is now considered pointless to study an individual sound—for example *a* or *t* in any selected language or languages—or an individual form, such as the possessive or the future, without first determining the form's relationship to other comparable entities in the same language. Japanese /a/, for example, occupies a different position from English /a/ because of its relationship in the Japanese syllabic structure. We have noted how the position of /t/ in the Japanese phonological system differs from that of English /t/. The view that every language is a self-contained system leads to the conclusion that the essence of language is relationship. The meaning of the English possessive or of any grammatical category, for example, can be determined only by thorough study of its functions in the English grammatical system. Accordingly language must be viewed as a system of arbitrary signs and their signification. Moreover, as Saussure pointed out, the study of language may be assisted by the findings of **semiotics,** the study of sign systems.

The view of language as a system of signs has determined much of the course of linguistic study over the past decades, for if entities of language are signs, it is profitable to determine how human beings use signs, whether in speaking or in other forms of communication. Further, if the meaning of signs is determined by relationships, it is essential to determine the various kinds of relationships possible in language. The pursuit of these aims has led to a productive concern with language in all its variety.

One fortunate result is the increase in grammars for hitherto-unknown languages. Devoted students have been learning and describing languages in the most inadequately known parts of the Americas, Africa, and the Pacific area. Their large-scale activities have required specification of "discovery procedures," that is, methods for both determining and describing the entities of language. The study of poorly known languages has also amplified our perspective on language.

When data concerning such languages first came to be analyzed, major concern was devoted to the simplest component of language, phonology. During the first part of this century much attention was given to the study of sound systems. As one result of this concern, phonological theory was sharpened, as is reflected in Chapter 5. But theoretical contributions regarding the principles underlying phonological systems were also made by such linguists as Nikolaj S. Trubetzkoy and Roman Jakobson. Trubetzkoy, after analyzing several hundred phonological systems, proposed general laws concerning phonology, raising questions that are still central to linguistic study today.

## 16.5  On the Relationship Between the Components of Language

One of these questions has to do with the relationship of the phonological component of a language to its syntactic component. In German and Russian, for example, voiced sounds become voiceless at the ends of words. German *Rad* 'wheel,' for example, is homophonous with *Rat* 'advice,' although the genitive *Rades* has a /d/ in contrast with the /t/ of *Rates*. In this way /d/ and /t/ interchange in some German words, but others have /t/ throughout. Trubetzkoy labeled the combined entity /t͡d/, an **archiphoneme.** This conclusion implies syntactic as well as phonological analysis in the setting up of phonological entities, for it is impossible to determine archiphonemes without knowing the morphological and syntactic as well as the phonological structure of a language. There is also the implication that phonology is in a sense dependent on the syntactic structure of a language, whereas by a contrasting view phonology is largely independent of syntax.

Subsequently, as we have noted, different labels were given to the two approaches to phonology. Since autonomous phonemes were posited by linguists when structuralism was a dominant concern, linguists proposing autonomous phonemes are often referred to as **structuralists.** Proponents of systematic phonemes, by contrast, are referred to as **transformationalists,** or **generative grammarians.** As linguists and many laymen know, labels are completely arbitrary, and so if the labels distinguish the two approaches, concern with their appropriateness is secondary. But it is also clear that linguists positing systematic phonemes view language as a far tighter structure than did any of their predecessors, and, accordingly, these linguists are rigorous structuralists in a very literal sense. Yet students of linguistics should be prepared to hear the term *structuralist* applied to linguists who posited autonomous phonemes and were largely concerned with phonological systems.

The difference in the views concerning autonomous versus systematic phonemes reflects different conceptions of control of language in the brain. Proponents of systematic phonemes seem to posit one central controlling agency for all language. Proponents of autonomous phonemes, on the other hand, seem to assume that the brain has the capability of perceiving, storing, and energizing phonological structures independently of syntactic structures. Attempts to resolve the question will be instrumental in leading to an understanding of how the brain functions, a topic that has become one of the dominant concerns in linguistics.

In this concern linguists are investigating the usefulness of **markedness** and **distinctive feature analysis,** two principles that were also introduced by phonologists. The concept of markedness was introduced in the study of archiphonemes, for in archiphonemes one of the members may be viewed as more specifically characterized than the other. For example, in German /p b/, /t d/, or /k g/ may stand initially but only /p t k/ finally; /b d g/ have an additional phonetic characteristic or mark, voicing. For this reason, Trubetzkoy called them the "marked members of the pair." The unmarked elements may then be viewed as more natural. The relationships between marked and unmarked members of such sets is a matter of great interest, for not all archiphonemes are equally central in a language. On the basis of the lack of contrast between /p b/, /t d/, and /k g/ in English after initial /s/, one could set up an archiphoneme in English as well as in German and Russian. But unlike German and Russian, English makes no grammatical use of this opposition; there are no contrasts *Rat : Rades* that have one member of the archiphoneme in one category, another in a second category. Nonetheless, the presence of such marked and unmarked members of pairs seems to provide a kind of tension in the language.

Contrasting classes of grammatical elements, such as those to which *read* and *understand* belong, may affect the dynamism of the English verb. Since *read* is used in patterns such as *She is reading the Spanish text* as well as *She reads Spanish,* whereas *understand* has only the possible *She understands Spanish,* we may assume a kind of imbalance between the categories "progressive" and "simple present" and between the two classes of verbs. Similar patterns of imbalance exist throughout the grammatical systems of languages. A great deal of study will be necessary to determine the effect of such imbalance on the use of language and its development.

---

## 16.6  On the Feature Analysis of Language

Distinctive feature analysis, first applied in phonological study, is also productive for an understanding of the other components of language.

Grammatical categories, for example, may be more accurately understood if examined for their distinctive features. A Latin noun like *hortus* 'garden' has the ending *-us* marking the categories case, number, and gender. But in the homophonous dative and ablative singular, *hortō*, the distinction for cases is blurred. Similarly, in adjectives like *fortis* 'brave' as opposed to *bonus* 'good,' the gender feature is blurred, for *fortis* does not distinguish between masculine and feminine, whereas *bonus* does. Similarly, verbal categories like aspect have been analyzed for distinctive features. Continuative aspect, for example, may have a feature for iterative meaning and also for emphatic meaning. Study of the use of distinctions for categories in a language, of unbalanced oppositions, their uses and effects, may then be applied to grammatical and also to semantic sets.

As illustrated in Chapter 11, only highly structured semantic sets, such as kinship systems and color names, have been studied for their features. But on the pattern of such studies other semantic areas can be explored. We may expect that the notions of feature analysis, markedness, and observation of the structural relations in all components of language will contribute to a better understanding of the meaning component of language and of how people acquire, store, and use the huge lexicon available in any language.

Yet features are not proposed simply to assist analysis. Rather, there is evidence that our sensory organs perceive and interpret stimuli through features. Unfortunately the action of the inner ear is poorly known, and no demonstration has been made of aural perception by means of features. But feature analysis is being used to explain visual perception, and it may therefore eventually be applied to aural perception as well.

## 16.7 On the Principles Underlying the Structure of Language

While we still know little about the perception of language, the acquisition of language can be more readily determined. Of particular interest are the findings that infants learn languages rapidly and in accordance with stages of maturation. Thus it has been inferred that infants have an innate language capacity, which is not dependent on individual intelligence. All other animals, by contrast, fail to acquire a communication system comparable to human language. The conclusion seems inescapable that humans have a species-related capability for learning language.

If this is so, it is highly important to know what the extent of this capability is. Since infants learn the language or languages spoken around them, the capability may be used to acquire any or all languages, rather than just the language spoken by their genetic parents. It is difficult to avoid the conclusion that each infant is born with a capability for language and that it can be developed in accordance with the particular characteristics of any possible form of speech. Determination of this capacity has become a major research interest in linguistics. Linguists have also been concerned with the "projection problem," that is, how children can develop control over language on the basis of the snatches of utterances they hear. Ethology and psychology will help in providing answers to these questions. Various types of innate capacity identified by ethologists, such as the innate capacity of angleworms for crawling, seem comparable to the innate capacity of human beings for language. And psychology has always concerned itself with perception and cognition through language.

### 16.7.1   Constraints on Possible Linguistic Patterns

Transformational grammar has been particularly productive in disclosing constraints on patterns. An example we have referred to earlier is the use of *wh-* in words in English, which is governed by two rules: *wh-* placement and *wh-* inversion. A *wh-* word may replace either or both nouns in a sentence. For example, *John saw Bill first* can yield:

> *Who saw Bill first?*
> *Whom did John see first?*
> *Who saw whom first?*

These sentences can be used as objects, as in:

> *Do you know who saw Bill first?*
> *Do you know whom John saw first?*
> *Do you know who saw whom first?*

Examples like these demonstrate that there are no constraints on *wh-* placement and that it can even be applied several times in one sentence. But there are constraints on *wh-* inversion. The sentence *\*Do you know who whom saw first?* is impossible. Although the *wh-* placement rule may be applied twice in a clause, the *wh-* inversion rule may be applied only once. Apparently such constraints on the use of rules are determined by the manipulation of language in the brain, but the reason for this remains to be determined.

It is curious that the Slavic languages do not impose such constraints on interrogatives. It also seems strange that we readily ask:

> *He saw the car that bumped into what?*
> *He saw the car bump into what?*
> *What did he see the car bump into?*

but not:

> *\*What did he see the car that bumped into?*

Presumably such constraints are regulated by the capacity that humans have for language and by universal principles governing the possible structures of language.

But how are these underlying principles to be visualized? However it is done, they must be conceived of as a system that will permit the production of an infinite number of sentences. Explorations are being carried out on such problems as nominalization, pronominalization, and imperatives and on the relation between syntax and semantics. Such questions have also brought about a close working relationship between logic and linguistics, for, as Colin Cherry has pointed out, "logicians are concerned especially with the syntactic and semantic levels of semiotics."[1] Another type of exploration of the principles of linguistic systems is being carried out in the newly developed discipline of **mathematical linguistics.** In linguistics itself there has been a renewed concern with investigating features widely characteristic of languages.

## 16.8  Universals

Features that are assumed to be common to all languages have been called **universals.** What these are is still not well defined. But we do accept them as very abstract patterns, not the surface observations often made about languages, such as the frequency of labials as opposed to pharyngeals or of the front unrounded as opposed to front rounded vowels. Rather, universals must be potential patterns that we see fulfilled in many languages. For example, languages like Japanese, with final verbs in simple declarative sentences, have postpositions in contrast with languages like English, which have verbs standing before the objects and prepositions rather than postpositions. Apparently some underlying principle links the location of both verb and preposition with regard to an object.

Detailed syntactic analysis, such as that presented in Chapter 10, has provided insights into the basis of some abstract patterns. If we assume that the sentences of any language are produced by expansion of simple underlying patterns, the method of expansion should follow definite principles.

When the languages of the world are syntactically analyzed, the declarative sentences of some languages are found to have verbs preceding the subject and the object; other languages have the order subject, verb, object; a third group of languages has the order subject, object, verb. Joseph H. Greenberg has labeled these VSO, SVO, and SOV languages. Among the VSO languages are Arabic and Celtic; among the SVO are the Romance and Bantu languages; and among the SOV are Japanese and Turkish.

We may illustrate each type by means of two simple sentences:

---

[1] Colin Cherry, *On Human Communication* (Cambridge, Mass.: M.I.T. Press, 1957), p. 222.

|  | 'John saw the dog.' | 'Mary saw the cat.' |
|---|---|---|
| Arab. (VSO): | raʔā John ʔalkalba. | raʔat Mary ʔalgiṭṭa. |
| Span. (SVO): | Juan vió el perro. | María vió el gato. |
| Turk. (SOV): | John köpeği gördü. | Mary kediyi gördü. |

We account for the sentences in each of these languages by deriving them from a universal underlying base in which the components of the sentence have no necessary order. A child might therefore learn a language of any type.

When, however, an order is established in a given language, it is maintained in patterns other than basic sentences. A child learning an SOV language, for example, would acquire with it other definite rules of order. As we noted in presenting English syntax, a relative clause in an SVO language is embedded in NP's, whether subject or object, by means of the pattern NPΣ. Expansion of NP's in a language with verb preceding object accordingly is carried out to the right of the NP. In a language with object preceding verb, however, it is carried out to the left, by means of the pattern ΣNP. We find this arrangement in the three languages used here for illustration.

The sentence above, with the addition of a relative clause, has the following arrangement:

|  | 'John saw the dog that ate the meat.' |
|---|---|
| Arab.: | raʔā John ʔalkalba allaðii ʔakala ʔallaḥmạ. |
| Span.: | Juan vió el perro que comió la carne. |
| Turk.: | John eti yiyen köpeği gördü. |

The words corresponding to 'the meat' are allaḥmạ, la carne, and eti.

We account for this major difference in arrangement between VSO/SVO and SOV languages by regarding the V and the O as fundamental in determining the arrangement of other modifiers. If in declarative sentences objects stand to the left of verbs, nominal modifiers such as relative constructions must also stand to the left of NP's. The basic patterning of languages, then, is either VO or OV. In each type an S constituent may be used (typically according to a regular pattern).

The same patterns of arrangement are observed in adjectival modifiers of nouns—since adjectival modifiers are reduced forms of relative constructions, adjectives would be expected to observe the same arrangement as relative constructions. Compare our basic sentence with the addition of the adjective 'large':

|  | 'John saw the large dog.' |
|---|---|
| Arab.: | raʔā John ʔalkalba ʔalkabira. |
| Span.: | Juan vió el perro grande. |
| Turk.: | John büyük köpeği gördü. |

Genitives observe the same arrangement, as in:

'John saw the dog of his neighbor.'

Arab.:    *raʔā John kalba ǰārihi.*
Span.:    *Juan vió el perro de su vecino.*
Turk.:    *John komşunun köpeğini gördü.*

The arrangement observed in the relationship between verb and object is also found in constructions involving government. We note government relationships particularly in verbs and prepositions. We would then expect them to occupy similar positions in the VSO/SVO languages, as opposed to the pattern in the SOV languages. We have noted that they do, as in:

'John saw the dog through the window.'

Arab.:    *raʔā John ʔalkalba min ʔaššubbāki.*
Span.:    *Juan vió el perro por la ventana.*
Turk.:    *John pencereden köpeği gördü.*

Moreover, since as these sentences illustrate, the position of the verb is fundamental in disclosing the relationship of modifiers to the entities modified and also in disclosing the arrangements found in government, the VP seems to be the central entity in the $\Sigma$. Such an observation itself has many implications. For example, it supports a view of the sentence as consisting essentially of a verb with optional NP's, that is, $\Sigma \rightarrow$ VP (NP) (NP). And the relationship of NP's to the central VP may be limited to a small number of semantic possibilities. Panini recognized six of these, which he called *kāraka* 'action' relationships. They do not include the vocative, which may be viewed as a sentence in its own right. Somewhat similar is the set of "cases" for underlying relationships in English sentences, which has been discussed above.

Investigation of languages with regard to universals promises to have interesting results. For example, English cannot be classified as a language of a consistent type. Nor can many other languages. English is basically SVO, but it has the adjective order of SOV languages. This structural characteristic illustrates the dynamism of language, for Proto-Indo-European—the reconstructed language of approximately 3000 B.C. from which English developed—was an SOV language. Most of its descendants developed into SVO languages. Spanish, as we have seen, is a consistent SVO language, as are the other Romance languages, Greek, and Albanian. But the north European languages of the Indo-European family, Slavic, Baltic, and Germanic, are not consistently SVO. The reasons for their inconsistencies remain to be explored and may never be completely clear; among the possibilities are influences of other languages from different language families. Similar problems have been identified in other language families, such as Sino-Tibetan and Niger-Congo. These are problems for historical linguistics rather than descriptive linguistics. Their investigation will lead to further explorations and insights into the history of our language, while exhibiting the human flexibility in developing a characteristic means of communication.

## 16.9  On the Human Capability for Language

The assumption of an innate facility for learning languages leads to further intriguing questions. What is it in the brain that gives the human being a facility that all other animals lack? How does the mind work? Until recently, linguists have considered these questions outside their sphere, leaving them to psychologists to answer. Today, however, linguists propose that an understanding of language will provide the best access for determining the workings of the brain, and they consider such investigations among their most important concerns.

This view suggests a far more important role for linguistics than it has occupied in the past. Since one of the central aims of education is to understand oneself, an understanding of language should be one of the primary goals of education.

Moreover, this view puts a high premium on the study of language and of its varieties, past and present. Further, an increased knowledge of any one language aids the understanding of language in general, and increased knowledge of any variety of language—whether used by children, whether a dialect or a highly cultivated literary form—contributes to such understanding. The central importance of language to civilization gives to linguistics a significant position in the humanities and social sciences. As we now have the techniques and facilities for learning ever more about language and the use of language, linguistics can be expected to have an increasingly important role in the studies leading to an understanding of humankind.

## BIBLIOGRAPHICAL NOTES

Collections of essays important in the study of universals are Joseph H. Greenberg, ed., *Universals of Language,* 2d ed. (Cambridge, Mass.: M.I.T. Press, 1966); Emmon Bach and Robert T. Harms, eds., *Universals in Linguistic Theory* (New York: Holt, Rinehart and Winston, 1968); and Charles Li, ed., *Word Order and Word Order Change* (Austin: University of Texas Press, 1975). Greenberg's own essay in the first collection provides the basis for many of the observations made here; Charles J. Fillmore's essay on "case" is included in the second collection. *Language and Mind* by Noam Chomsky (New York: Harcourt Brace Jovanovich, 1972) contains essays on "linguistic contributions to the study of mind." For a convenient source of statements dealing with the philosophy of language see Peter H. Salus, ed., *On Language: Plato to Von Humboldt* (New York: Holt, Rinehart and Winston, 1969). Nikolaj S. Trubetzkoy's major work has recently appeared in an English translation by Christiane A. M. Baltaxe under the title *Principles of Phonology* (Berkeley and Los Angeles: University of California Press, 1969).

## QUESTIONS FOR REVIEW

1. Discuss briefly the background of linguistic study before this century.
2. What is the controversy on whether names are given by nature or by convention? What is the origin of the phrase *lucas a non lucendo?*
3. State reasons for the interest of nineteenth-century scholars in historical linguistics. Have primitive languages been found in the earlier history of mankind?
4. What is meant by "viewing language as structure"?
5. Why is linguistics included in semiotics by some scholars?
6. How is the term *structuralist* often used in linguistics? Compare this description with that of *transformationalist.*
7. What is meant by *marking?* Which member of a pair is the unmarked one?
8. Give illustrations of the use of feature analysis.
9. State evidence for the view that infants have an innate capacity for language.
10. What constraints are found in English concerning *wh-* inversion? Do these apply universally?
11. How is the term *universal* used in linguistic study?
12. What is meant by *SVO, SOV,* and *VSO languages?* Discuss some of the further syntactic patterns characteristic of such language types. Why is the basic pattern that of the verb with regard to its object?
13. Why is English not a consistent SVO language? How can the inconsistency be accounted for?

## EXERCISES

### EXERCISE 1

In his grammar of Sanskrit, Panini distinguished between *kāraka* categories for nominal forms and *vibhakti* categories. *Vibhakti* forms correspond to the actual cases of nouns, such as the nominative, the accusative, and the instrumental.

Most of the *kāraka* categories are named with derivatives of *kṛ* 'do'—for example, *kartā* 'doer' and *karma* 'what is done.' Using these terms, Panini identified the subject of a sentence like *The boy saw the cow* as a *kartā,* the object as a *karma.* In a passive sentence like *The cow was seen by the boy,* the subject is labeled *karma* even though it is in the *vibhakti* nominative case, as is the subject of the active sentence; the object is labeled *kartā* even though it is in the *vibhakti* instrumental. Accordingly, regardless of the *vibhakti* case, the word for *boy* is put into the same *kāraka* category, *kartā;* similarly, the word for *cow* is in the *kāraka* category *karma,* regardless of the *vibhakti* case.

a. Panini's *kāraka* categories have been compared with deep structure categories. Would you agree with this identification?
b. If you do, what is the basis of Panini's "deep structure"? Is it semantic or syntactic?
c. Some linguists reject a deep syntactic structure, preferring instead to assume a deep semantic structure, or the approach known as *generative semantics*. Would you consider Panini to be more like a generative semanticist or a generative syntactician? State your reasons.

## EXERCISE 2

One of the procedures used in syntactic analysis is generating sentences that seem to parallel acceptable grammatical sentences and then checking their acceptability. At times such sentences are not grammatical, for example, sentence 5 following:

1. *Their teacher gave them a comprehensive exam.*
2. *How comprehensive an exam did their teacher give them?*
3. *For the exam on that lesson he wrote comprehensively.*
4. *How comprehensively did he write for the exam on that lesson?*
5. *\*How comprehensively did the teacher give them an exam?*

Since questions 2 and 4 are possible, it would also seem possible to produce question 5. Yet English speakers do not consider this question grammatical. Why not? What conclusions can you draw from question 5 about moving elements out of NP's and converting them into adverbs?

## EXERCISE 3

A pattern that may be explored for its pertinence in typology is comparison. In an SVO language like English, for example, one finds sequences like the following:

*The dog is bigger than the cat.*

In analyzing such sentences one may refer to *cat* as the "standard" and indicate the structure of the comparison: compared noun:adjective: pivot:standard.
In SOV languages, like Turkish, the comparable sentence is:

*köpek kediden daha büyük.*
'dog cat-from more big'

that is, standard:pivot:(comparative particle) and adjective.

a. Account for the two patterns in terms of the two structures, SVO and SOV. Can you relate the comparative construction to the position of the V with regard to the O? If you can, how does this relationship support the classification of adjectives as Vb's?

b. In Spanish this sentence is:

> *El perro es más grande que el gato.*
> 'The dog is more big than the cat.'

On the basis of this comparative construction, would you label Spanish as SVO or SOV?

c. In Rigvedic Sanskrit, comparatives are found in expressions like *svādoḥ svādíyo* 'sweet-from sweeter,' in which *svād* is the standard, *oḥ* is the pivot, and *svādíyo* is the adjective in comparative form. Judging by this example, would you consider Rigvedic Sanskrit to be VSO, SVO, or SOV?

# SELECTED
# BIBLIOGRAPHY

Increasing numbers of books on linguistics are being published. In an introductory text only a selection can be included. The following items are listed in the hope that students will become acquainted with them and use them as a basis for further reading. Additional books have been listed after each chapter.

Allen, J. P. B., and Corder, S. Pit, eds. *Techniques in Applied Linguistics.* Vol. 3. The Edinburgh Course in Applied Linguistics. London: Oxford University Press, 1974.

Austin, John L. *How to Do Things with Words.* Edited by J. O. Urmson. Cambridge, Mass: Harvard University Press.

Bach, Emmon. *Syntactic Theory.* New York: Holt, Rinehart and Winston, 1974.

Bailey, Charles-James N. *Variation and Linguistic Theory.* Washington, D.C.: Center for Applied Linguistics, 1973.

Bar-Adon, Aaron, and Leopold, Werner F. *Child Language: A Book of Readings.* Englewood Cliffs, N.J.: Prentice-Hall, 1971.

Bauman, Richard, and Sherzer, Joel, eds. *Explorations in the Ethnography of Speaking.* London: Cambridge University Press, 1974.

Benveniste, Emile. *Problems in General Linguistics.* Translated by May Elizabeth Meek. Coral Gables, Fla.: University of Miami Press, 1971.

Birdwhistell, Ray L. *Kinesics and Context: Essays on Body Motion Com-*

*munication*. Philadelphia: University of Pennsylvania Press, 1970.

Bloomfield, Leonard. *Language*. New York: Holt, Rinehart and Winston, 1933.

Bolinger, Dwight. *Aspects of Language*. 2d ed. New York: Harcourt Brace Jovanovich, 1975.

Chafe, Wallace L. *Meaning and the Structure of Language*. Chicago: University of Chicago Press, 1970.

Chapman, Raymond. *Linguistics and Literature: An Introduction to Literary Stylistics*. London: Edward Arnold, 1973.

Chatman, Seymour, and Levin, Samuel R. *Essays on the Language of Literature*. Boston: Houghton Mifflin, 1967.

Chomsky, Noam. *Aspects of the Theory of Syntax*. Cambridge, Mass.: M.I.T. Press, 1965.

Dale, Philip S. *Language Development: Structure and Function*. Hinsdale, Ill.: Dryden Press, 1972.

Denes, Peter B., and Pinson, Elliot N. *The Speech Chain: The Physics and Biology of Spoken Language*. Murray Hill, N.J.: Bell Telephone Laboratories, 1963.

Dillard, J. L. *Black English*. New York: Vintage Books, 1973.

Dineen, Francis P. *An Introduction to General Linguistics*. New York: Holt, Rinehart and Winston, 1967.

Firth, John Rupert. *Papers in Linguistics, 1934-1951*. London: Oxford University Press, 1957.

Fishman, Joshua A. *Sociolinguistics*. Rowley, Mass.: Newburg House, 1970.

Greenberg, Joseph H., ed. *Universals of Language*. 2d ed. Cambridge, Mass.: M.I.T. Press, 1966.

Hall, Edward T. *The Silent Language*. Garden City, N.Y.: Doubleday, 1959.

Halliday, M. A. K.; McIntosh, Angus; and Strevens, Peter. *The Linguistic Sciences and Language Teaching*. Bloomington: Indiana University Press, 1965.

Heffner, R-M. S. *General Phonetics*. Madison: University of Wisconsin Press, 1949.

Hjelmslev, Louis. *Prolegomena to a Theory of Language*. Rev. ed. Translated by Francis J. Whitfield. Madison: The University of Wisconsin Press, 1969.

Hyman, Larry M. *Phonology: Theory and Analysis*. New York: Holt, Rinehart and Winston, 1975.

Jakobson, Roman. *Child Language, Aphasia and Phonological Universals*. Translated by Allan R. Keiler. The Hague: Mouton, 1968.

_____. *Studies on Child Language and Aphasia*. The Hague: Mouton, 1971.

Jespersen, Otto. *Mankind, Nation and Individual: From a Linguistic Point of View*. London: Allen and Unwin: 1946.

_____. *The Philosophy of Grammar*. London: Allen and Unwin, 1924.

Key, Mary Ritchie. *Male-Female Language*. Metuchen, N.J.: Scarecrow Press, 1975.

Kurath, Hans. *Handbook of the Linguistic Geography of New England*. Providence: Brown University Press, 1939.

Labov, William. *Language in the Inner City: Studies in the Black English Vernacular*. Philadelphia: University of Pennsylvania Press, 1972.

_____. *The Social Stratification of English in New York City*. Washington, D.C.: Center for Applied Linguistics, 1966.

Lehmann, Winfred P. *Historical Linguistics: An Introduction*. New York:

Holt, Rinehart and Winston, 1973.

_____. ed. *Language and Linguistics in the People's Republic of China*. Austin: University of Texas Press, 1975.

Li, Charles N., ed. *Subject and Topic*. New York: Academic Press, 1976.

_____. *Word Order and Word Order Change*. Austin: University of Texas Press, 1975.

Lyons, John, ed. *New Horizons in Linguistics*. Harmondsworth: Penguin, 1970.

McDavid, Raven I. Jr., and Duckert, Audrey R., eds. *Lexicography in English*. New York: New York Academy of Sciences, 1973.

Menyuk, Paula. *Sentences Children Use*. Cambridge, Mass.: M.I.T. Press, 1969.

Nida, Eugene A. *Componential Analysis of Meaning: An Introduction to Semantic Structures*. The Hague: Mouton, 1975.

_____, and Taber, Charles R. *The Theory and Practice of Translation*. Leiden: Brill, 1969.

Quirk, Randolph; Greenbaum, Sidney; Leech, Geoffrey; and Svartvik, Jan. *A Grammar of Contemporary English*. London: Longman, 1972.

Robins, R. H. *A Short History of Linguistics*. Bloomington: Indiana University Press, 1968.

Sapir, Edward. *Language*. New York: Harcourt Brace, 1921.

_____. *Selected Writings of Edward Sapir in Language, Culture, and Personality*. Edited by David G. Mandelbaum. Berkeley and Los Angeles: University of California Press, 1949.

Saussure, Ferdinand de. *Course in General Linguistics*. Translated by Wade Baskin. New York: McGraw-Hill, 1966.

Saville, Muriel R., and Troike, Rudolph C. *A Handbook of Bilingual Education*. Washington, D.C.: TESOL, 1971.

Scaglione, Aldo. *The Classical Theory of Composition: From Its Origins to the Present*. Chapel Hill: University of North Carolina Press, 1972.

Searle, John R. *Speech Acts: An Essay in the Philosophy of Language*. London: Cambridge University Press, 1969.

Stockwell, Robert P.; Schachter, Paul; and Partee, Barbara Hall. *The Major Syntactic Structures of English*. New York: Holt, Rinehart and Winston, 1973.

Trubetzkoy, N. S. *Principles of Phonology*. Translated by Christiane A. M. Baltaxe. Berkeley and Los Angeles: University of California Press, 1969.

Trudgill, Peter. *Sociolinguistics: An Introduction*. Harmondsworth: Penguin, 1974.

Ullmann, Stephen. *The Principles of Semantics: A Linguistic Approach to Meaning*. 2d ed. Glasgow: Jackson, 1957.

Vygotsky, Lev Semenovich. *Thought and Language*. Edited and translated by Eugenia Hanfman and Gertrude Vakar. Cambridge, Mass.: M.I.T. Press, 1962.

Whorf, Benjamin Lee. *Language, Thought and Reality: Selected Writings of Benjamin Lee Whorf*. Edited by John B. Carroll. New York: Wiley, 1956.

Wolfram, Walt. *Sociolinguistic Aspects of Assimilation: Puerto Rican English in New York City*. Washington, D.C.: Center for Applied Linguistics, 1974.

_____, and Fasold, Ralph W. *The Study of Social Dialects in American English*. Englewood Cliffs, N.J.: Prentice-Hall, 1974.

# INDEX

computational linguistics, 297–298
concord, 158
concrete noun, 209
conditioning, 129
congruence, 136, 158
conjoining, 156, 168, 190–192
conjugation, 126
conjunction, 163
conjunction reduction, 190–191
consonantal DF (CNS), 109
consonant chart, 65
consonants, English, 66, 80
constative, 235
constituent, 156
constraints, 280, 322–323
construction, 159
content, 39
content words, 158
context-free/sensitive rules, 114; phrase-structure grammars and, 178–181
context of situation, 227, 236
continuant DF (CNT), 109
contrastive grammar, 296
coordinate clauses, 167
coordinate compound, 143–144
coordination, 156, 190–192
coordinator, 163, 191
copula, 212
coronal DF (COR), 110
corpus, 22
correctness, 284
count noun, 137, 162
covert (class), 161–162
*Cratylus,* 316
creole, 277
cricoid cartilage, 58
CS (complex symbol), 212
curly brackets, use of, 179
cycle, 221
cycles per second (cps), 91
cyclic principle, 220–221

dative (D), 49
decibel, 91
declension, 127
deep structure, 19, 45
definite article, 162
deletion, 132
deletion transformation, 197
dental, 62
derivation, 25, 125, 141–147
descriptive adjective, 164–165
descriptive relative clause, 169, 194
Det (determiner), 181
determiner, 162, 164, 181
dialect, 7–8, 28, 276–282
dialect atlas, 276
dialect switching, 278–279
dictionary, 25
diglossia, 277
diphthong, 67–68
disability, language, 6–7

disambiguation, 229
discontinuous base, 128
discovery procedures, 38
dissimilation, 132
distinctive feature (DF), 96, 108–112, 320–321
dominance, 183
dominate, 183
dorsal articulation, 61
dorsum, 61
double bar juncture, 76, 86
double cross juncture, 76, 86
doublet, 246
Dravidian, 250
drift, 251
dual, 137
*dvandva,* 143
dyslexia, 8, 269

ejective, 70
elliptical sentence, 169
embedding, 156–157, 192–199
emphasis, 70, 131
emphatic (sentence), 167
endocentric, 157
English, phonemes of, 66–77; DF's of phonemes, 112; sentence types in, 159–160, 181–182; shifts in, 251; stages of, 244
epenthetic, 132
epiglottis, 60
EQUI, 194
ergative, 161
Esperanto, 286
ethnography of communication, 29, 282–283
etymology, 251
exercitive, 235–236
exocentric, 157
expansion of sentences, 163–166
expression, 39
external sandhi, 124, 131
extraposition, 205
extrinsically ordered rules, 117, 185

falling diphthong, 68
faucal, 61
favorite sentence type, 159–160
feature-changing rules, 114
field, semantic, 229–230
finite forms, 140
flap, 64
form, 37
formant, 93
formative, 124
frame, 22–23, 24
French, examples of, 61
frequency, 91
fricative, 62–63
frontal, 61
front of tongue, 61, 66
front vowel, 66
function word, 158

# ABOUT THE AUTHOR

WINFRED PHILIPP LEHMANN, Ashbel Smith Professor of Linguistics and Germanic Languages and Chairman of the Department of Linguistics at the University of Texas, received his B.A. from Northwestern College and his M.A. and Ph.D. from the University of Wisconsin. His area of current specialization is Indo-European linguistics. Professor Lehmann has done research in Norway as a Fulbright Fellow, and he served as Director of the Georgetown University English Language Program in Ankara, Turkey, for one year. He is the author of, among other books, *Proto-Indo-European Syntax*, *The Development of Germanic Verse Form*, *Historical Linguistics: An Introduction*, and *Language and Linguistics in the People's Republic of China*, which was the result of a visit to China as chairman of the American Linguistic Delegation to the People's Republic. Recently, Professor Lehmann became the first American to receive the Brothers Grimm Award, which is presented by Phillips University (Marburg) for distinguished academic achievement in the field of Germanic philology.